HISTORY OF THE
13TH/18TH ROYAL HUSSARS
(QUEEN MARY'S OWN)
1947 to 1992

Viret in Æturnum
§
Pro Rege, pro Lege, pro Patria conamur

by

Eric Hunt

To the Memory of my brother Donald
who introduced me to the Regiment

Copyright © Eric Hunt 1996

First published 1996 by
The Light Dragoons Charitable Trust

ISBN 0 9528335 0 6

Printed and bound by The Alden Press, Oxford

Contents

Foreword by Major General HSR Watson — vii
The Regimental Memorial — viii
Acknowledgements — ix
Preface — xi

The Link With The Past; 1715–1947 — 1

IN ARMOURED CARS 1947 to 1960

Introduction: Covering the Withdrawal from Empire — 6
1. North Africa and Egypt 1947–50 — 10
2. Malaya 1950–51 — 30
   Background to the Maria Hertogh Riots 1950 — 56
3. Hong Kong & Malaya 1951–53 — 58
4. Wolfenbüttel & Neumünster 1953–1958 — 86
5. B Squadron in Arabia 1957–58 — 111
6. Malaya 1958–60 — 126

ARMOURED REGIMENT 1961 to 1977

Introduction: A Professional Army — 144
7. Fallingbostel & Paderborn 1961–66 — 154
   Part 1 Operations & Training
8. Fallingbostel & Paderborn 1961–66 — 171
   Part 2 First Guidon & Other Events
9. Perham Down 1967 — 187
10. Münster 1968–72 — 199
11. RAC Centre Regiment 1972–74 — 221
12. Hohne 1974–77 — 232
13. Two Spells in Northern Ireland — 244
    Operation 'Banner' 1972 & 1975

ARMOURED RECONNAISSANCE 1977 to 1992

Introduction: Light Cavalry Role — 264
14. Omagh 1977–79 — 268
15. Wimbish 1979–82 — 293
16. Herford 1982–86 — 321
17. Tidworth 1986–91 — 340
18. Wolfenbüttel 1991–92 — 367

The Link With The Future; 1992 and Beyond — 376

A. Appointments — 378
B. Honours and Awards — 383
C. In Memoriam — 386
   Index — 388

Tables and Figures

1	Communist propaganda leaflet 1951	45
2	Definitions and Abbreviations (Anti Terrorist Operations in Malaya)	54
3	Casualties during the first four years of the Malayan Emergency	65
4	Second World War Battle Honours	108
5	Extracts from B Squadron Newsletters 1957–58	124
6	Extract from Lily Willy 1972	246
7	Extracts from War Diary January–May 1972	248
8	Extract from Town and Country 1976	254
9	Message from the Colonel-in-Chief 1992	375

MAPS

1	North Africa 1948–50	14
2	Egypt 1950	26
3	Deployment in Malaya August 1950 – June 1951	35
4	Operation Opportunity	49
5	Malaya (principal locations) 1950–53	57
6	Deployment in Malaya June 1951 – February 1952	61
7	Deployment in Malaya February 1952 – July 1953	71
8	Armoured Cars in Germany	101
9	Arabia 1957–58	112
10	Borders with Yemen	114
11	Muscat & Oman	119
12	Malaya 1958–61	130
13	Operation Jaya	133
14	Armoured Regiment in Germany	160
15	Aden 1967	193
16	Exercise Arbiter 1967	195
17	United Kingdom 1967, 1972–74	231
18	Suffield Training Area, Canada	235
19	Northern Ireland 1972 & 1975	250
20	Northern Ireland 1977–79	271
21	Cyprus	303
22	United Kingdom 1979–82, 1986–91	320
23	Germany 1982–86	331
24	Belize	350
25	Germany 1991–92	371

Illustrations

Frontispiece: The Guidon
Between pages 52 and 53:
1. & 2.   North Africa 1947–50
3.   Exercise in Egypt 1950
4. to 6.   Malaya 1950–1951
Between pages 84 and 85:
7. & 8.   Malaya 1953
9. to 11.   Ubiquitous scout cars – Germany, Arabia and Malaya
Between pages 180 and 181:
12.   Balaklava Centenary Ball 1954
13. & 14.   Malaya 1950–1953
15.   Guidon presentation 1961
16.   Admin Inspection in Fallingbostel 1962
Between pages 212 and 213:
17.   Replacing a Centurion engine
18.   Exercise in Malaya 1967
19.   FFR in Münster 1969
20.   Long Kesh 1972
Between pages 276 and 277:
21. & 22.   Barnsley 1969 & 1976
23.   Adventure training in Italy 1970
24.   Training in Canada 1976
25.   Guided weapon firing
Between pages 308 and 309:
26. to 28.   Omagh 1977–79
29.   Past and Present in Wimbish 1979
30.   Queen's Birthday Parade in Cyprus 1980
Between pages 340 and 341:
31.   The King of Jordan at the Families Weekend 1982
32.   Regimental Band in Hohne 1983
33.   Tidworth visit by HRH The Princess of Wales
34.   Exercising the Freedom of Barnsley 1989
Between pages 372 and 373:
35.   Norway 1987
36.   Exercise in England 1989
37.   Patrol in Cyprus 1991
38.   Last Parade

The author thanks the following for permission to reproduce the illustrations listed.
        Major PL Waddy 2, 4, 5, 6, 9, 11
        Soldier Magazine 35, 36, 37
        The Tank Museum 17, 29

FOREWORD

BY MAJOR GENERAL HSR WATSON CBE
COLONEL OF THE REGIMENT 1979–90

The History of The 13th/18th Royal Hussars (Queen Mary's Own) began with its formation in 1922 and from then until 1947 was chronicled by Major General Charles Miller.

This volume brings the story up to date and closes with the amalgamation in December 1992 of the The 13th/18th Royal Hussars with 15th/19th The King's Royal Hussars, to form The Light Dragoons. The book therefore concerns itself with what would usually be regarded as 'peacetime soldiering'. The events which it describes in Malaya and Singapore, Arabia, Northern Ireland and elsewhere could hardly be regarded as 'peacetime' in the usual sense of that word. They illustrate vividly the adaptability and versatility which a good Regiment must have and they emphasise the need for high standards of training and readiness to be maintained at all times. But alongside military professionalism, there is always scope for travel, sport and entertainment of all kinds, in which the Regiment and individual officers and soldiers and their families take part.

The story covers both the military and the extramural life of the Regiment and demonstrates that, whatever the challenges, it has always risen to the occasion and, whatever the opportunities, it has made the most of them. Above all, it is a story of comradeship and enjoyment, two of the principal benefits of regimental life.

Seventy years is but a short time in the history of the Army and its Regiments, but the 13th/18th Hussars have cause to be proud of the way in which they have carried on the fine traditions of their predecessors and of the splendid inheritance which they have handed on to their successors.

I commend this excellent – and enjoyable – book to everyone who has been associated with the Regiment throughout its life and especially since 1947.

1 January 1996

Stuart Watson

The Regimental Memorial

This book is to be published shortly before the dedication of the Memorial to all those who served in The 13th/18th Royal Hussars, between 1922 and 1992. The Memorial is sited in Normandy, some thirty kilometres inland from Caen, where one of the Regiment's principal battle honours was earned on 6 August 1944 – Mont Pinçon. The appeal for the funds needed was launched in 1995. A magnificent response came, not only from those who had actually served with the Regiment, including those on attachment from other regiments and corps, but from their relatives and friends. Heartwarming support also came from the inhabitants of the local *communes* of le Plessis Grimoult and St Jean-le-Blanc.

It is erected near the route which the two troops of tanks took in their dash uphill in 1944. It is signed from both Route D54 (Aunay-sur-Odon to le Plessis Grimoult) and Route D165 (le Mesnil-Auzouf to le Plessis Grimoult). From them visitors can approach by car and park near the gate leading to the Memorial. Plaques on the gate posts dedicate the area to the people of le Plessis Grimoult and St Jean-le-Blanc, in memory of those who suffered in the battles for the Liberation of France. A footpath through a copse (to be planted later in 1996) emerges to reveal the Memorial, a single block of Brittany granite, facing the panoramic view. Visitors can sit quietly on the steps beside it and pick out the roads and streams below the hill which were the scene of such bitter fighting in 1944.

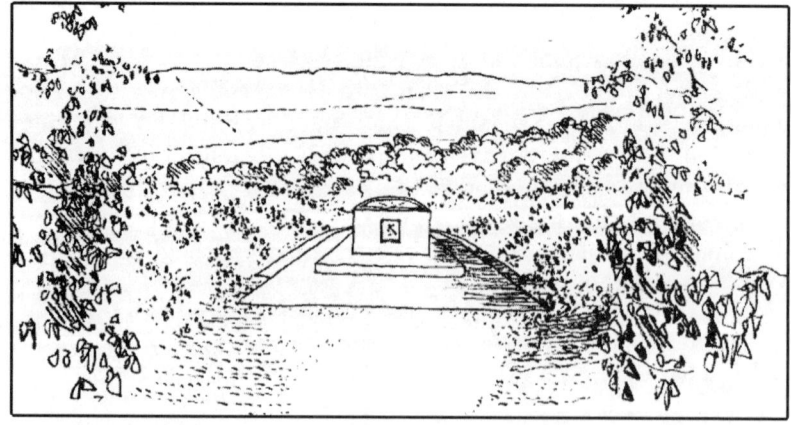

ACKNOWLEDGEMENTS

Having offered some four years ago to 'collate raw material' for a post-War History, I found myself 'writing' it. Much of the real writing comes from the contributions to the Regimental *Journal* and sundry *Newsletters* over the years, many of them anonymous. (Attribution of the majority of articles did not begin until the mid-1970s.) To those, traditionally reluctant, authors go my grateful thanks. They are coupled with a fervent hope that their successors in The Light Dragoons will bear in mind how much historians, especially of the amateur variety, depend on what they record.

I appealed to a number of those same contributors for help and the reaction from them and others has been most generous. As it has been spread over a long period, and three changes of address, I am afraid my record-keeping may have been indifferent, but the following is, I hope, a complete list of those who have commented, provided anecdotes and further details:

Col JCM Ansell
Capt MB Barty-King
Lt Col JW Bell
Lt Col JAC Blakiston
Col C Blount
Mr DWT Brough
Mr TE Christophers
Col GM Chirnside
Lt Col RT Cliff
Maj BJW Cobb
Lt Col DHE Coker
Maj Gen RA Cordy-Simpson
Maj DJ Delius
Sir Ralph Dodds, Bt
Mr J Durran
Brig DAG Edelsten
Col RJW ffrench Blake
Gen Sir Michael Gow
Maj MD Griffith-Jones
Lt Col CA Le Hardy
Col JRL Howard
Lt Col ER Jolley
Capt K M Local
Capt GE Locker
Col AL Mallinson
Mr NG Morris
Lt Col RCB Nutting
Maj NGA Payne
Maj WG Peto
Lt Col RNB Quicke
Lt Col PT Roberts
Lt Col JAMA Selfe
Lt Col NS Southward
Mr DM Steel
Col GMcL Stephen
Col AREdeC Stewart
the late Maj Gen PB Tillard
Maj HJ Tyacke
Maj PL Waddy
Maj J Wadmore
Maj Gen HSR Watson
Maj MJS Wilkins
Lt Col ERMcM Wright
Col EL Yorke

History of The 13th/18th Royal Hussars (Q.M.O.)

I also benefited from a practice, begun in the 1960s, of inviting commanding officers to provide a report for the Regimental archives on their time in command. I have drawn widely on the notes from those who complied.

The librarian at The Tank Museum, Mr David Fletcher, and his staff have been most helpful. Captain Gary Locker and his assistants from Home Headquarters, first of the 13th/18th Royal Hussars and then the Light Dragoons, have been a constant support. I have also been greatly assisted by Major Peter Waddy in compiling illustrations.

Mrs Auriol Griffith-Jones, early embroiled as a 'regimental wife' in the production of the Journal, and now a neighbour in Dorset, has provided a much-needed professional eye to the copy-editing. Her efforts have been supplemented by volunteer copy-editors in the persons of General Stuart Watson and my wife Gill, whose years as a civilian medical officer to the Regiment gives her, perhaps, a somewhat intimate insight.

Professional, and friendly, guidance also came from Mr Michael Whitlock of The Alden Press. It was a particular pleasure that The Alden Press could be involved. The Chairman, John Alden, and I were subalterns together in Malaya when he was undergoing ordeal by National Service. His son William, the Managing Director, also served in the Regiment. With their encouragement, the support of the Trustees of The Light Dragoons and the wonders of desktop publishing, it has been possible for the book to be published as a private venture by Home Headquarters.

Eric Hunt

Nags Head Farmhouse
Mappowder
June 1996

Preface

Regimental historians need to be aware of three potential pitfalls. They have to avoid trying to mention every possible associated name and action – otherwise they stand accused of writing indigestible regimental hagiography. At the same time they need to be scrupulously accurate in describing their Regiment's evolution, for a British regiment is in one sense an ever-growing living organism. And, thirdly they have to be extremely careful to avoid offending regimental susceptibilities while at the same time capturing that unique but often elusive item, the characteristic special ethos or charisma that distinguishes their regiment from all others, and goes to form one vital ingredient of its distinctive esprit de corps.

Book review by DG Chandler;
Journal of the Society for Army Historical Research Winter 1993

Regimental histories usually concentrate on the campaigns, battles, actions and incidents of active service. During the forty-five years covered by this record, the 13th/18th Royal Hussars, or one of its squadrons, deployed for only six years on active service, in Malaya and Arabia. Nearly three years in all were spent in policing the troubled province of Northern Ireland. Eleven were in England, where tasks varied from exercises in most of the continents to aid to the civil authority at home. Squadrons were detached to Cyprus several times, either in the British garrison of the Sovereign Base Areas, or as part of the United Nations Force. For most of the remaining years their stations were in Germany, where the British Army of the Rhine trained under sustained high pressure for global conflict.

The years in training may not have provided as much by way of historical anecdote as the operational years, but those who served during them played just as full a part in maintaining the Regiment's traditions and standards. Their pursuit of excellence in every activity ensured that when the passing opportunity for action came it was undertaken with skill, fortitude – and no little style. Comrades in arms were also members of a proud family who knew how to live and play together with good humour and who had that saving grace for the professional soldier – a keen sense of the ridiculous.

History of The 13th/18th Royal Hussars (Q.M.O.)

The Preface to The Memoirs of the 18th (Queen Mary's Own) Royal Hussars, 1906–1922 by Major General Burnett concluded:

> Regimental memoirs are no doubt dull reading for any but soldiers intimately concerned, and on that account an attempt has been made here and there in this narrative to introduce a human touch into a semi-official record of events, in the hope that a little of the dullness may thereby be enlightened.

In that respect at least, I have tried to follow the lead of my distinguished predecessor.

The Link With The Past* 1715–1947

(* The title used by Major General Miller for the opening chapter of his History.)

The 13th/18th Royal Hussars existed as a single regiment only from 1922 to 1992, but its history began in 1715 with the raising of the 13th Dragoons. By 1810 they were Light Dragoons and serving under Lord Wellington in the campaigns in Portugal, Spain and France until 1814, earning the battle honours: **Peninsula, Albuhera, Vittoria, Orthes** and **Toulouse**. They returned with Wellington to fight at **Waterloo** in 1815.

Over twenty years in India was followed by garrison duty in the United Kingdom and then action in the Crimean War. At **Balaklava** they were on the right of the front line in the famous Charge of the Light Brigade. They also took part in the battles of **Alma, Inkerman** and **Sevastopol**. Becoming Hussars in 1861, the Regiment was in continuous action in **South Africa 1899-1902** including taking part in the **Relief of Ladysmith**.

Having returned to India, they went to **France and Flanders** for the beginning of the First World War, but 1916 found them in **Mesopotamia** fighting against the Turks. There they gained distinction at **Kut al Amara 1917, Baghdad** and **Sharqat.**

The 18th Light Dragoons were formed in 1759. As Hussars they too served in the **Peninsula**, first under General Moore, covering his retreat to Corunna, later under Lord Wellington. Not long after taking part in the Battle of **Waterloo**, they were disbanded – victims of defence economies.

They were re-raised in 1858 and saw service in India before they also took part in **South Africa 1899-1902** and were amongst those in the **Defence of Ladysmith**. In 1903 they were created Princess of Wales's Own', becoming 'Queen Mary's Own' on the accession of HM King George V. After campaigning throughout **France and Flanders 1914–18**, they ended the War in the Army of Occupation in Germany. Their numerous

History of The 13th/18th Royal Hussars (Q.M.O.)

battle honours included: in 1914 **Mons, Marne, Aisne, Messines** and **Ypres**, in 1915 **Ypres**, in 1916 **Somme**, in 1917 **Cambrai**, in 1918 **Somme, Cambrai, Amiens** and **Hindenberg Line**.

In 1922 the 13th Hussars amalgamated with the 18th Hussars to form the 13th/18th Hussars, nicknamed 'the Lilywhites' from the white facings of uniforms inherited from the 13th Hussars. HM Queen Mary became Colonel-in-Chief of the new Regiment and the 13th/18th served for most of the years between the First and Second World Wars in India, stationed near the North West Frontier. Distinguished as the 13th/18th Royal Hussars (Queen Mary's Own) from 1935, they remained a horsed cavalry regiment until 1938.

After relinquishing their horses and returning to England it was only a few months before the 13th/18th crossed to France in 1939, as a 'mechanised divisional cavalry regiment'. In 1940 they covered with their light tanks the withdrawal of the British Expeditionary Force from Belgium, before being evacuated from Dunkirk.

When the expected German invasion of England did not take place, the Regiment began training for the Liberation of Occupied Europe. They had a very special role. On D Day in June 1944, equipped with Sherman 'DD' (duplex drive) tanks, which had been adapted for 'swimming', they launched into the sea from landing craft. They were amongst the first to land on on Sword Beach after a swim of some 5,000 yards in heavy seas. Once their tracks touched the shingle they dropped the canvas screens which had kept them buoyant and gave covering fire to the infantry advancing up the beach.

The 13th/18th played a full part in the battles to extend the Allied bridgehead and to capture Caen. By seizing the summit of Mont Pinçon, tanks of the Regiment then played a key role in enabling a general advance across the whole of the Allied front and the German Seventh Army began to crack. The way was open for the advance across France and Belgium to the Rhine and then into Germany. The Regiment took part in many more hard battles over the next nine months before they reached Bremen and VE Day was declared in 1945. For the next two years they were part of the Army of Occupation.

The Link With the Past

The full chronicle of the years until 1947 is told in the earlier histories:

HISTORY OF THE XIII HUSSARS (Two vols) by C.R.B. Barrett, 1911

THE THIRTEENTH HUSSARS IN THE GREAT WAR by Sir H. Mortimer Durand, 1921

THE HISTORICAL MEMOIRS OF THE XVIIIth (PRINCESS OF WALES'S OWN) HUSSARS by Colonel Harold Malet, 1907

THE MEMOIRS OF THE 18th (QUEEN MARY'S OWN) ROYAL HUSSARS, 1906–1922 by Major General Charles Burnett, 1926

HISTORY OF THE 13TH/18TH ROYAL HUSSARS (QUEEN MARY'S OWN) 1922–1947, by Major General Charles H. Miller 1949

and in:

LIGHT DRAGOONS by Colonel Allan Mallinson, 1993, which covers the story of all three Regiments together with that of 15th/19th The King's Royal Hussars (and their predecessors).

The Guidon presented by HRH The Princess of Wales in 1987. In the centre of each side is a wreath of mixed roses, thistles and shamrocks with a St Edwards Crown on the top. Inside the wreath is the Regiment's title and inside this again is the cypher 'Q.M.O.'. Below the wreath are the mottoes.

In the corners are small panels, two with the Royal badge of the white horse of Hanover, two with the Regiment's numerals on a white background. On each side are embroidered the Battle Honours, those awarded before 1914 on the obverse, those from the First and Second World Wars on the reverse.

Part 1

IN ARMOURED CARS

1947 to 1960

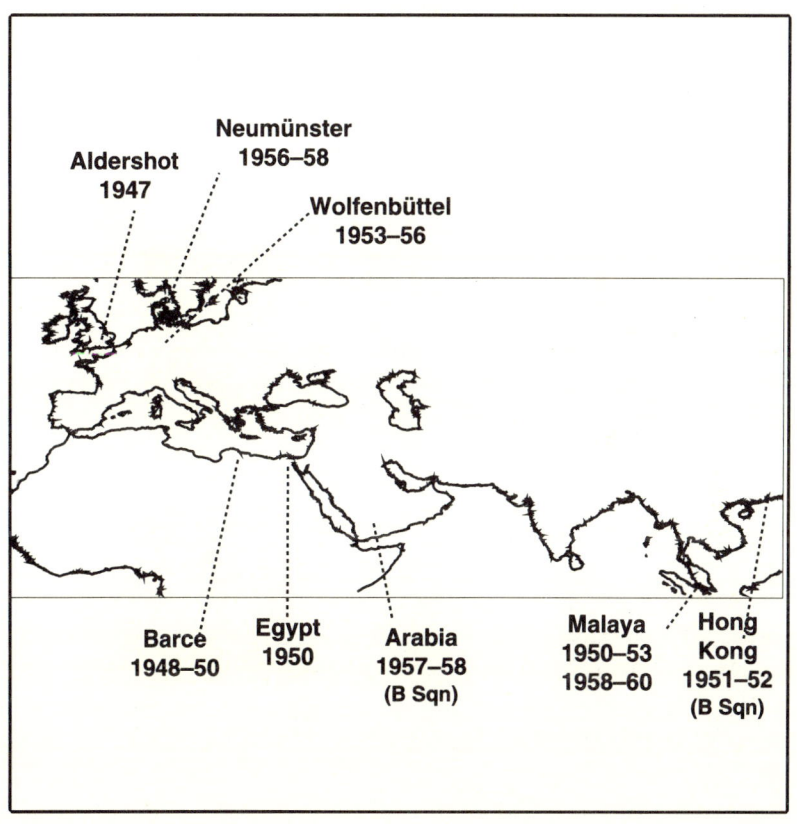

Introduction to Part 1

Covering the Withdrawal from Empire

In all the operations that covered the imperial retreat from the Far East, the Middle East and Africa after 1947, the British army displayed not only professional versatility, but its traditional qualities of cool-headedness and good humour. Its techniques of riot control avoided unnecessary shooting and bloodshed. Despite the provocation offered by the murder of comrades, sometimes in cold blood, the British soldier rarely went beyond roughness into the kind of persistent and systematic brutality to which other armies in similar situations resorted.

Britain and Her Army 1509–1970, Corelli Barnett.

Transition from War to Peace

Writing in *The Times* in 1993, about conditions at the end of the Second World War, Sir Robert Rhodes James said: 'Of all the European belligerents, we had not been invaded or occupied. Our armed forces had been victorious in every area of conflict. Our reputation was at its zenith'. Nevertheless, the war ended with Great Britain in poor shape; the costs of defeating the Axis powers had been enormous, in terms not only of financial and economic resources, but of human resilience. The civilian population was mentally and physically exhausted by the stresses and strains of over five years of rationing, aerial bombardment, contributing to the 'war effort' – and frequent reverses on the wideflung battlefronts before eventual victory. Food rationing was still in force and there were shortages of everything.

The war had postponed the response to demands for independence in Britain's world-wide empire, but had increased the pressure for change. Aspirations for a lasting peace and understanding between the wartime allies of the United

Introduction to Part 1

Nations were soon to show signs of strain. The immediate priority in Britain was speedily to demobilise the members of the armed forces enlisted for the war, but compulsory National Service had to be continued. There were substantial commitments to meet, both for maintaining an army of occupation in Germany and for continued imperial policing. Enforced military service was not to everybody's liking; it was one thing to call on the nation's youth to serve in time of war – peacetime conscription was a very different matter. For the armed forces, therefore, and particularly the Army, the transition from war to peace was traumatic – and the 13th/18th Royal Hussars were not immune to its effects.

Comings and Goings

In October 1945, as part of the Army of Occupation in Germany, the Regiment had reverted to the reconnaissance role in which it had begun the recent war. In place of the Mark VIB light tanks of 1940, there was a miscellany of vehicles including carriers and Chaffee light tanks. By 1948 the Daimler armoured cars were the principal equipment and the normal peace establishment of an armoured car squadron was of four troops. Each troop had an officer, sergeant and eight men manning two Daimler armoured cars, mounting 2-pounder guns, and two scout cars: Daimler or Humber. The 2-pounders' insignificant firepower was reinforced by a heavy troop of two AEC Matador armoured cars, and one scout car. The Matadors had 75mm guns, firing both HE and armour-piercing shells – and often served as ad hoc recovery vehicles. A support troop with twenty-four assault troopers was carried in wheeled GMC armoured personnel carriers. Daimler armoured cars were to remain with the Regiment for the next fifteen years, but the Daimler scout cars were replaced in the mid-1950s by Ferrets and the GMCs by six-wheeled Saracens. (The Regiment had converted to tanks before the Saladin armoured cars arrived.)

The end of the war in 1945 was followed by the departure to civilian life, not only of all those called up during the war years, but of the pre-war reservists – largely technicians – who had been recalled to the colours in 1939. Since 1945 there had therefore been many comings and goings, of both officers and other ranks. Conscription under the 1947 National Service Act

History of The 13th/18th Royal Hussars (Q.M.O.)

was initially for only one year and the shortage of men meant that A Squadron had to be temporarily disbanded for more than a year. Some of the new officers came from British regiments being disbanded, such as The Reconnaissance Corps, or reverting to the Territorial Army, like The Inns of Court. Others were posted from the Indian Army after the British withdrawal from the subcontinent. In 1948 the first Regular officers from the newly-formed Royal Military Academy at Sandhurst began to arrive.

Regular soldiers amongst the troopers and junior NCOs were soon in a minority; most of the soldiers were National Servicemen, the principal source of manpower during the Regiment's time in armoured cars. The machinery for proper recruitment of regular soldiers was not yet under way and with no traditional recruiting area on which to draw the quality of the intake was varied. (The involvement with South Yorkshire was not to come until 1958.) The problem was not the Regiment's alone and it was recognised in January 1952 by the setting up of the Boys' Squadron at Bovington.*

---

* In January 1952 'an experiment for the RAC' was launched with the establishment of the **Boys' Squadron** Royal Armoured Corps. 'Its object is to train senior non-commissioned officers and warrant officers for the Corps. . . . the age limits are 15 to 17½ years . . . One third of the boys' working time is devoted to general education. A strong effort has been made to obtain instructors of exceptional character and efficiency. High standards, morally as in technical skill, are of great importance to boys away from home. On completion of his training a youth should be ready to take his place immediately in a good tank crew and have all his technical as well as his general military training at his fingers' ends. From first to last special emphasis will be laid upon the development and encouragement of the spirit of leadership, so that the training shall bring with it enterprise and initiative as well as technical competence. . . . It is never possible to be certain how such organisations will develop, and this still is in an early phase of its existence. Those responsible for it have been pleasantly surprised by the speed with which it has got into its stride and the attraction which it has already exercised upon a good type of boy. . . . The Army today has no need more pressing than that of providing for the future a body of energetic, well educated senior non-commissioned and warrant officers.'

(From *The Times Weekly Review*, 27 March 1952)

The experiment was indeed a success and the Boys' Squadron developed, via 'Junior Leaders' Squadron' to 'Junior Leaders' Regiment'. The 13th/18th benefited both from its products and from its challenging appointments for officers and NCOs. The Regiment was another casualty of 'Options for Change' in 1992, but it is likely that one will be revived, for the Army as a whole.

Introduction to Part 1

From 1943 to 1945 there had been a remarkable degree of stability in the Regiment's principal appointments, with no changes amongst the Squadron Leaders, the Adjutant, Quartermaster or Regimental Sergeant Major. Since the end of the war, however, changes had been frequent. The departure in 1948 of Regimental Sergeant Major AL Hind was particularly keenly felt; he had held his post with great distinction for much of the war. He then speedily restored pre-war standards, despite the posting to the Regiment of a number of rebellious soldiery from disbanded regiments, whose only interest was in 'demob numbers'. Lieutenant Colonel RA Hermon had assumed command in 1947, but his tour was unfortunately to be cut short by illness. The Adjutant, Captain HSR Watson, provided much needed continuity. He had been Regimental Signals Officer throughout the campaign in North West Europe and his first spell as Adjutant was from June 1945 until August 1946. He returned for the second spell shortly before the Regiment sailed for North Africa. Captain F Sweeting, who had been Quartermaster since 1942, was also still in place.

To North Africa, Malaya, Germany and Arabia

With so much upheaval in the Army, the Regiment was fortunate to be posted to a station where it was to a large extent left to its own devices and could find its peacetime feet. At the time, however, there was some regret that they could not to be in England for the 1948 Olympics, for which the Regiment was to run the Military Pentathlon. After two pleasant years in North Africa the Regiment was to have four more stations as an armoured car regiment. Two tours in Malaya provided invaluable operational experience, as did a year on detachment in Arabia for B Squadron. In between the Regiment had five years of more orthodox soldiering with the British Army of the Rhine, first in Wolfenbüttel and then in Neumünster.

Chapter One

North Africa and Egypt 1948–50

In Transit through Aldershot

Major General Miller's *History* finishes with the Regiment in Wolfenbüttel and under orders to move to the Middle East, via Aldershot, in October 1947. Notice of the 'secret' move was not received until mid-September and it was some days before it could be published to the Regiment as a whole. The *Journal* asked: 'Why this rush? We assume because somebody had suddenly decided to remove most of the Army from Germany and had little idea of the difficulties involved.' The original plans were for a move to Palestine. However, the ending of the British Mandate in Palestine, on the creation of the new state of Israel, brought an early withdrawal from one imperial responsibility. It then seemed likely that there would be at least one summer in England; plans were made for drawing up vehicles and getting on with some training.

Like much of the travel and daily life in the late 1940s and early 1950s, the journey from Germany to England was made more difficult by what sometimes seemed simple bloody-mindedness, but perhaps was just a symptom of the general fatigue. For example there was a strike of porters at Harwich 'who, with that charity which is all too prevalent in our country today decided that they were unlikely to get good tips from soldiers' wives and therefore refused to work at unloading baggage.' As a result, the majority of the families were unable to get through Customs before the boat-train left.

Willems Barracks at Aldershot was an unconverted pre-war cavalry barracks, unused for several years and filthy dirty.

> The whole barracks, the pride of so many regiments before the war, appeared to have been deliberately sabotaged in a big way. It had, apparently, for a time been used as a transit camp for German prisoners of war. It caused no surprise when, from behind the old riding school, we flushed a very large dog fox. As some wag said, it was probably the only thing in the barracks which could be flushed.

North Africa and Egypt 1948–50

Another story had it that the previous occupants were Canadians immediately prior to D Day. It was also very cold – the first-floor barrack rooms were meant to be heated by the occupants of the stables on the ground floor. The acting Commanding Officer, Major JR Cordy-Simpson, managed to get some more fuel by telling Headquarters Aldershot District that otherwise he would send the whole Regiment on leave.

Withdrawal of the basic petrol ration made any sort of Regimental Reunion difficult, but the officers did give a dance at the Aldershot Club: 'the Band played, but had the buffet and the bar to compete with, and remembering Britain's general austerity, it was not surprising that dancing was the third choice for a large number.' *Journal* entries for the next few years were to show a frequent preoccupation with food.

Before Christmas leave was over another warning order arrived for a move – to an unspecified destination in the Middle East. Most of the time was occupied with re-organisation of the squadrons, including re-forming A Squadron, but some training was achieved with a few armoured cars. Meanwhile: 'We were unable to find out our destination. Barce, Benghazi, Tripoli, Fayed and Khartoum were constantly mentioned and with each change a new port of embarkation was detailed.' The advance parties were told, only twenty-four hours before they left Aldershot, that all except B Squadron would go to Tobruk. B was to go to Tripoli en route for Misurata. The main body left Farnborough for Liverpool 'in the very early hours of 7 February, in the usual bitterly cold and crowded troop train'. Despite the hour, the Colonel of the Regiment, Brigadier JN Lumley, was standing in the pouring rain at Liverpool to see them off.*

Sea Trooping

A feature of the post-war years until 1960–61 was the use of ships for troop movement. The many garrisons throughout the world needed a constant two-way flow of individual reinforcements, especially as National Servicemen were unlikely to be able to spend much more than a year at a station which was

---

* Joining the 13th Hussars in 1908, Brigadier Lumley was awarded the MC in the First World War and commanded the 13th/18th from 1929 to 1933. He was appointed Colonel in 1942.

any distance from the United Kingdom. Major units needed a great deal of space, especially if they took vehicles and equipment with them, as did the Regiment when it moved from Egypt to Malaya.

The journey to North Africa was in the coal-burning *Empire Test*, allegedly not intended for Atlantic conditions. There were severe storms for much of the way to Gibraltar and the majority of the Regiment were sea-sick. The *Journal* noted that Trooper Pearson's teeth: '. . . in the company of a lot of other things, disappeared beneath the waters of the Irish Sea'. At 10 am on the roughest day of the voyage the smallest of the band boys was reported missing. A long and increasingly worried search was started, which eventually resulted in his being found curled up in a small corner at the extreme stern of the ship. On being asked what was the matter, the reply, a masterpiece of understatement, was 'I feel unhappy'. Once through the Straits, however, the voyage took on more agreeable aspects.

Troop deck accommodation had changed little in the previous fifty years, with hammocks slung above the tables to which meals had to be fetched from the galley. Officers were much better off; though often crammed into cabins designed for far fewer people, they had more space above decks. Wives were normally separated from their husbands, presumably to allow for more intensive occupation of cabins, but it was reminiscent of Victorian workhouse rules. That was certainly the attitude of the OC Troops of the ship which moved the rest of the Regiment from Tobruk to Port Said. There were four majors in one cabin and the young bride of one of them on her own in a cabin for six. A request for her husband to join her was turned down with an abrupt: 'We don't allow that sort of thing on this ship'.

Converted corvettes, manned by the Merchant Navy, were used for moving small numbers of men between the various ports serving the many garrisons scattered around the Mediterranean. B Squadron travelled from Misurata, when rejoining the Regiment in Cyrenaica, in the LST (Landing Ship Tank), *Evan Gibb*, in which A Squadron later went to Egypt. The latter journey was memorable for two days of storms when the squadron cooks were all seasick, as were many others. The ship rolled, pitched and yawed, the vehicles following suit on their

North Africa and Egypt 1948–50

suspensions – at a different tempo.

Compared with air movement, sea trooping not only took an inordinate time (the journey from Egypt to Singapore in 1950 took over a fortnight), it could take the edge off military preparedness. Against that, the slow movement through time zones and climates meant that there was not the problem of acclimatisation and 'jet lag' experienced with air trooping. At its best it could be very pleasant; a small community, almost completely isolated from the rest of the world, making its leisurely way across the ocean with flying fish and dolphins to watch by day, and the occasional whale spouting, and phosphorescent waves at night under romantic skies. This was still a world in which much of the atlas was coloured pink and at all the ports of call there would be British garrisons and a welcoming Regimental band playing at the quayside. (There seemed also to be an inordinate number of Movement Control Officers.)

Cyrenaica

On arrival in North Africa the Regiment relieved the King's Dragoon Guards, who had moved from Palestine in 1947 when the British Mandate ended. Regimental Headquarters, HQ and C Squadrons were based in Barce, a pleasant station on a small plain amongst the craggy hills of Cyrenaica's Jebel Akhdar*. To begin with, A Squadron was sixty miles away in the port of Benghazi and, until mid-1948, B Squadron was in Misurata, Tripolitania, nearly six hundred miles from RHQ. C Squadron went to Apollonia on the coast for the winter months of 1948–49, and A Squadron was detached again from September 1949 to February 1950 at the harbour town of Derna.

Cyrenaica was an area redolent of much more than the desert battles of recent history. There had been Greek settlements along the North African coastal strip from around 680 BC. By Roman times piracy was a principal activity from the small harbours and in order to suppress it the Romans annexed Cyrene in 74 BC. Three hundred years later it was a strongly Christian area, but in 642 AD Arab forces advanced into Cyrenaica in the first phases of the westward expansion of

---

* Green mountains.

Islam which was to reach to the Pyrenees. A Berber empire in the twelfth and thirteenth centuries was eventually succeeded by the Ottoman Turks in the sixteenth. On the decay of the Ottoman Empire, Italy invaded Libya in 1911 and established an unenviable reputation for the cruelty of its colonial regime until its armies were evicted in 1943. In 1945 Britain was installed by the United Nations as the protecting power of the ex-Italian colonies of Cyrenaica and Tripolitania, pending international agreement as to their future.

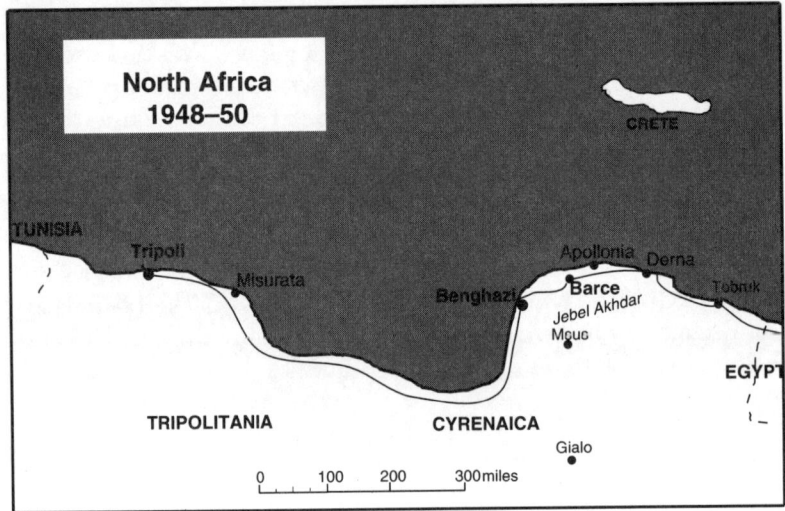

Taking Stock

At first the principal concern for the Regiment was simply how to administer its widely separated elements, often over extremely tenuous lines of communication. The supply route to Barce, for example, was over a very difficult road and the unreliable vehicles made every journey a hazardous business. B Squadron in Misurata was 132 miles from their District Headquarters in Tripoli and squadron vehicles had to make daily journeys of a hundred miles for rations and about fifty miles for water. Before drivers learned the art of avoiding 'blow outs', the Regiment went through tyres at an alarming rate. The vehicles were relics of the war years: South African, American and British in an unhappy hotch potch.

North Africa and Egypt 1948–50

Such was the state of armoured cars and scout cars that the REME workshops in Benghazi worked on nothing else until they were in a reasonable condition. There was a chronic shortage of spares and casualties of desert warfare often provided a more fruitful source of supply than the Ordnance Depot. Such was the dry atmosphere that vehicles which, some six or seven years before, had been knocked out or simply broken down, were in good enough condition to be cannibalised.

The lack of spares was particularly felt in Headquarters Squadron which had to maintain enough roadworthy transport vehicles to make the daily supply runs; any vehicle off the road awaiting spares was often stripped to keep others going. To compound the problems of administration, the King's Dragoon Guards had not been on peace-time accounting and entirely new ledgers had to be drawn up.

Life in North Africa

In many respects, Barce and the other stations were a great improvement on the drab conditions in post-war Britain. Having to rely largely on Regimental resources for sport and recreation was no bad thing. The Band had rejoined in Aldershot and was a considerable asset. Except for a short period when the Regiment was at Wickham Market and for three days at Goch* in 1945 they had been away since September 1939.

Despite Italy's appalling colonial record, their settlers had established many excellent small farms and it was sad to see the land reverting to camel scrub, grazed by the ubiquitous goats, while politicians wrangled over the country's future. The Barce plain itself was still being cultivated on the grand scale by the British Administration and wheat was harvested by up to twenty combines working in echelon.† Winter tended to be cold and wet and summer hot, but not so hot as Egypt. May

---

* At Goch they had had a narrow escape when a German shell landed among the chairs which had just been put out for a concert.

† 'One night as Orderly Officer I saw a long line of lights crossing the distant Jebel, and heard the unmistakable sound of tracked vehicles. I woke the Adjutant to warn that we were facing an imminent armoured assault. On his instructions (before he went back to sleep) I watched through the night some thirty vehicles approaching, then stopping while camp fires were lit. I must admit some disappointment when day dawned and I could see twenty combines.'
Colonel JRL Howard

brought the unpleasant, but fortunately short-lived, winds of the *ghibli* (the Egyptian *khamseen*).

Before leaving Aldershot, Regimental property in store since 1939 had been retrieved and the pictures and silver made a great deal of difference to the appearance of the Officers' and Sergeants' Messes, despite the efforts of the local Arabs employed as dockers at Tobruk. They smashed almost everything they handled. In several respects conditions must have been very similar to those in a small cantonment in pre-war India – and similarly it was often more agreeable for officers than for other ranks. There were few amenities and it was worthy of note when the camp cinema acquired a second projector and A Squadron bought themselves a wireless (which was never switched off 'unless the electricity fails which happens from time to time'). Barce itself had two major drawbacks for soldiers. Unlike Apollonia and Derna, it was not near the sea. The sand and dirt accumulated in the back of a 3-tonner, on such trips as were attempted, tended to outweigh any temporary relief found in the sea. The other main lack was of female company. Efforts to overcome this included squadron dances, which led off with a B Squadron 'Ball'. Tremendous care was taken in the preparations. The nurses and auxiliaries at Benghazi Military Hospital, after solemn assurances as to their welfare, had agreed to risk the long journey. A magnificent repast of hare and partridge had been prepared by the cooks; the Regimental Band was ready to play; the lovely ladies embussed and, half way in the middle of nowhere, the borrowed bus had a puncture – and no jack. After seven very cold hours on the road they did at last arrive at midnight, having gallantly decided to press on. The usual rules prevailed for the wives on station – they could have only one dance with their husbands in the course of the evening. Another treasured memory is of a visit by the District Commander accompanied by his daughter. Their departure was delayed while one sensitive subaltern dashed into the Officers' Mess and returned to present her with a geranium, plucked from its pot and wrapped in a month-old copy of *The Times* – airmail edition.

Concert parties were mounted and even amateur dramatics had a showing. There were two performances in Barce of a Ben

North Africa and Egypt 1948–50

Travers' farce, *Thark*, which was produced by Captain ER Jolley and the Medical Officer, Captain JD Brackenridge. They were followed by a performance in Benghazi, when a power cut meant that much of the second act was played by the light of candles and hurricane lamps, and one in Derna, where there was neither stage door nor dressing rooms. Nevertheless each presentation was much appreciated by the audiences.

A handful of families had been able to accompany the Regiment and they were joined by a few more over the next two years. The pioneers had little furniture; forewarned, one couple brought their double bed from England. Most had to cook on two burner paraffin stoves and 'they were fiendish contraptions liable to flare up without warning, scattering greasy black soot throughout the building'. 'Many of the most elementary necessities of life were lacking. An abundance of Elizabeth Arden did little to make up for these shortcomings' (Families Letter in the *Journal)*, but slowly things improved and 'even such luxuries as refrigerators' appeared. The few quarters were allocated on the points system, taking into account length of separation, service and seniority. C Squadron Leader, Major DHE Coker, recently married and therefore low on the list, managed to hire from the Custodian of Enemy Property a small Italian cottage near the Arab quarter. (Some Egyptian school teachers had refused to accept it because it was well below the standard they required.) Rations were meant to be supplied by the Army on repayment, but when C Squadron was in Apollonia, Major and Mrs Coker had to buy their meat in the local market. At first only goat was available, tough goat, and it took some months for a supply of more edible meat to be authorised for them.

A leave scheme by charter aircraft to the United Kingdom was particularly welcome both for single officers and men and unaccompanied husbands. The scheme was the brainchild of Captain PCA Bridgland, East Surrey, a staff officer at Cyrenaica District, who in 1958 was to become the Regiment's Paymaster. (In 1948, incidentally, there were no attached members of the Royal Army Pay Corps and pay was the responsibility of Squadron Seconds in Command. The task was made particularly arduous in North Africa when the Army changed the system of documentation and a massive overhaul of every individual's pay account had to be undertaken. Those who were subalterns at the time recall being hauled in to assist.

Individuals visited Mediterranean resorts such as Cyprus and the Lebanon, in both of which the various communities were then living peacefully together. *The Times of Malta* reported in September 1948 that the Band also got away:

> Bandsmen of the 13th/18th Royal Hussars drank iced beer at an open-air Valetta cafe after their Palace Square programme on Saturday and said 'Ah civilisation!' They had come from the wilder and woollier part of Cyrenaica, on the fringe of the desert, to play . . . for a Valletta crowd. It was their first real glimpse of 'real civilisation' since they left England in February this year . . . [the Band] has a full programme for its fortnight's stay in Malta before returning to Benghazi and thence to the wilderness.

Sport

All the usual team games were played though there was only a limited amount of competition from the few major units stationed in Cyrenaica. In the absence of other means of recreation, Regimental Headquarters ordained that exercise was to be taken by everybody, every afternoon. Basketball pitches sprang up everywhere and 'baseball' (really it was rounders) and six-a-side hockey were pursued with great vigour. (A start was made with digging a swimming pool, but despite many laborious hours it never saw water.)

After mechanisation in 1938 the only horses in the Regimental stables were usually owned privately or Regimentally, but in Cyrenaica some were still Government-owned. The Regiment took over from the King's Dragoon Guards an assorted collection ranging from 'a 17-hand ex-1 Division cavalry charger to a stocky little 14-hand Arab stallion'. Some of them had been brought from Palestine and others had apparently been 'liberated' during the Italian campaign. One bay Italian mare 'who plays polo and can jump' was reported to have been bought for a tin of spam after the battle on the Garigliano.

Major Sir Delaval Cotter and Major MWH Bell were successively the Masters of the Barce Vale Hunt. The pack, also inherited from The King's Dragoon Guards, were not all pure

North Africa and Egypt 1948-50

foxhound; some had been brought from Palestine, where a pack had been formed to hunt jackal. Drafts from various other sources included some from a pack in Baghdad, who may have been descendants of the Bobbery pack which the 13th Hussars had in Mesopotamia after the First World War. The Earl of Feversham, who had commanded the Regiment for a time in the North West Europe campaign, gave a stallion hound from his Sinnington pack and another dog came from the Crawley and Horsham. (One of the Orderly Officer's chores in the troopship *Empire Test* was to exercise, and clean up after, hound puppies who travelled out with the Regiment). The country round Barce was 'nothing like high Leicestershire. We have a plain of red earth ten miles long and four miles wide, which is as heavy as lead in the wet and scentless in the dry weather . . . arable land surrounded by *jebel* and scrub, the rocks on the south side rising very steeply for some 300 feet and making a horse-proof obstacle. The scrub is full of flowers in the winter so the hounds get a grand smell of everything except foxes.' One fox was killed when a horse trod on it, but that was the only victim in the first eighteen months.

Race meetings were held regularly at Benghazi, and one at Derna during A Squadron's time there. They included various special events such as camel races for the locals and on one occasion there was a Regimental race with mounts found from the ponies which normally drew the local *gharris*. This provided several exciting occasions in the paddock as there was one mare amongst eleven stallions. With more excitement at the start several jockeys dismounted involuntarily and when the flag at last fell about half the field refused to start.

The Regiment put on a Horse Show in the autumn of 1948. A varied programme included tent pegging, which was won by Squadron Sergeant Major Grimwood, a veteran of mounted days (when he was a 10th Hussar). There was also a dog race and a goat driving race. The final event was wholly traditional: a parade of the Barce Vale foxhounds who were trotted round the ring to the strains of 'John Peel'.

For those who shot, the opportunities were wonderful. Coveys of chukor, a red-legged Mediterranean partridge, could be spied from a jeep and then walked up through the rocks of the *jebel*.

History of The 13th/18th Royal Hussars (Q.M.O.)

The range of craggy hills also held hares and there were pigeon and doves in the cliffs and deep holes, while in the desert were bustard, golden plover and sand grouse. Not least, in the winter the marshes near the coast (and on the Barce plain itself when it flooded) were full of mallard, teal, pintail, garganey, shoveller and gadwall.

Operations
The Regiment came under Headquarters Cyrenaica District in Benghazi. The District was under operational control of GOC Malta, as was Tripolitania District under which B Squadron came while they were in Misurata. Wireless communications were a major preoccupation as links had to be maintained, not only with Benghazi and the detached squadrons, but with Headquarters 1 Division in Tripoli. It was also necessary to keep in touch with vehicles sent on the regular post-runs along the deserted coastal roads. By endless experiments with Heath Robinson aerials incredible ranges were achieved, helped by a massive US Army set which the King's Dragoon Guards had acquired. (The Royal Signals Troop were enthusiastic hams who kept touch with amateur radio enthusiasts throughout five continents, but that had to be stopped when it was discovered that one of the regular links was in the USSR.)

The ending of Britain's Mandate in Palestine brought the unpleasant task of escorting some 260 Jewish prisoners, convicted of terrorism in Palestine, who were being repatriated from camps in Kenya. They included men convicted of the King David Hotel bombing in 1946, when ninety-one people were killed. It was feared that the locals, if they knew of the operation, would attempt a mass slaughter and in July 1948 a composite squadron under Major JM Howson guarded the airfield at El Adem as six Lancaster bombers and twenty Dakota transports arrived with the party and their escort from Kenya. After the ex-prisoners' not inconsiderable baggage was off-loaded by the Regimental escort they then had to be taken in lorries to Tobruk, for embarkation to the newly created state of Israel. They took pleasure in taunting their guards at every opportunity and not a little restraint had to be exercised: 'only two, however, fell in the water whilst transferring to their ship'.

North Africa and Egypt 1948–50

In 1948 and in 1949 the Regiment was required to deter Tunisian volunteers from trying to get through Cyrenaica, on their way to Egypt. From there they hoped to take part in the Palestinian conflict. The operations involved close co-operation with the Cyrenaica Defence Force, CYDEF*, with whom the Regiment had excellent relations. In 1948 the *Journal* reported on the best turned-out horse and rider event at the Regimental Horse Show: 'It was a pleasure to see the first-class grooming, saddlery and turn-out of the CYDEF entries'.

The Regimental also provided Desert Rescue Patrols (principally from Reconnaissance and Transport Troops and the LAD†) who worked with the RAF and civil air lines to locate and rescue survivors from aircraft which crashed in the desert. Fortunately they were involved only in practising with the RAF, often traversing difficult country as well as wireless operating over long ranges.

Premature Change of Commanding Officers
Taken ill in August 1948, Lieutenant Colonel Hermon had to be invalided home in September, cutting short his time in command to the Regiment's dismay. He was replaced by Lieutenant Colonel EH Tinker who, apart from a brief spell as Second-in-Command in 1946, had been away from the Regiment since 1936. From his service with the Transjordan Frontier Force (later the Arab Legion) he was a fluent speaker of Arabic and placed particular emphasis on good relations with the local Arabs. They greatly appreciated his contacts with them even if his Jordan Arabic was barely comprehensible to them! This probably contributed to the almost total absence of civilian crime in the immediate neighbourhood.

Training in the Desert

Colonel Tinker had spent much of the war in the Middle East and his personal experience was valuable in training the Regiment in desert conditions. But the principal mentors in navigation by sun compass and the best ways to negotiate the

---

* CYDEF was a British-officered police force *cum* gendarmerie, which was to form the basis of the Senussi Royal Guard for the future King Idris. As such they were a principal target in Gaddafi's 1969 coup.

† Light Aid Detachment REME.

History of The 13th/18th Royal Hussars (Q.M.O.)

difficult terrain were Majors Howson and Meares, whose Indian Cavalry regiments had taken part in the wartime desert campaigns. Sometimes even ice was encountered on the Jebel in winter and mud near the coast after January rain.

Colonel Tinker was remembered for his innovatory training ideas. The short period which National Servicemen had to serve meant that there was a continuing need for training new arrivals, both to complete the limited RAC trade training received by recruits and to get new intakes up to Regimental standard generally. In the winter of 1948–49 this was undertaken by C Squadron. In a camp on the coast at Apollonia, the site of the ancient port for Cyrene which had been ruined in a great earthquake in early AD, they ran courses in driving and maintenance, wireless and gunnery. Lieutenant BJW Cobb, in charge of D&M, scoured the desert for abandoned scout cars to use as classroom models and Lieutenant JRL Howard organised rigorous training for assault troopers, including live overhead fire. (Assault troopers, as non-tradesmen, otherwise tended to feel second-class citizens.) In the following years each squadron was made responsible for one subject and they were kept particularly busy when large drafts (one of 140 men) arrived to take the place of those going on release. However, the Apollonia experiment was a useful precursor of the Training Wing which was to play a major part in the Regiment's first tour in Malaya.

In his *History,* General Miller commented that the value of new regulations in the 1920s, making a certificate of education a prerequisite of promotion, was not appreciated by many regimental officers. They thought that the time spent in the classroom '. . . could be better employed in other forms of military training', but, writing immediately after a war in which Army Education had amply demonstrated its value, he went on: 'There can be no one today who does not appreciate the need for an ever-increasing standard of intelligence and understanding on the part of the soldier in every rank.' Certainly that was now fully understood in the Regiment. Most of the new arrivals began with a four weeks' concentrated education course (instead of being taken away for two to three hours a week throughout the year), which enabled the maxi-

North Africa and Egypt 1948–50

mum number to obtain their third class certificates and so become eligible for promotion to junior NCO. The syllabus covered not only the usual academic subjects, but also instruction in a variety of sports, map reading, musical appreciation, regimental history, talks on Cyrenaica and the Arabs, and a weekend visit to the classical remains at Cyrene.

Potentially, the desert provided ideal training ground for armoured cars, but the state of the vehicles was such that an exercise of any size and scope was a prized rarity, preceded by months of hard preparation. Even then it relied on the genius of the squadrons' fitters to keep the vehicles going. It also meant that few members of the Regiment had enough practice properly to master the intricacies of the sun compass. That never seemed to worry Major MWH Bell, who could place his finger on a featureless map (which accurately portrayed the featureless terrain) and say 'We are there' . . . and 'we were'.

One exercise had as a target the oasis of Msus, at the crossroads of the wartime desert campaigns. Any satisfaction for B Squadron in finding it was more than a little diminished when, as the sun came up over the overnight close leaguer, a figure was sighted on the far horizon. It materialised into an elderly Bedouin who, after exchanging the time of day, contentedly plodded straight due south. He clearly knew exactly where he was. He must also have had a long walk as there was no water hole marked for some two hundred miles. On another occasion, in the same area, Sergeant PJ Davis of A Squadron 'had the dubious pleasure of seeing one of the wheels of his scout car dissolve into mist when it struck a mine'. Many of the vast number of mines laid during the Second World War had not been cleared and before venturing into a new area enquiries would be made on the likelihood of encountering them. The best source of information was usually the local Bedouin of whom there was the, doubtless mythical, story that they checked on the whereabouts of mines by sending their wives in front of their grazing livestock.

In his memoirs *Call to Arms,* General Sir Harold Pyman recalled that when he was Chief of Staff Middle East Land Forces:

History of The 13th/18th Royal Hussars (Q.M.O.)

> ... the C-in-C and myself took our American opposite numbers in the off-duty time of a conference to see the battlefield at Sidi Rezegh. This of course brought back many memories to me ... The old ET mines were as usual exploding in the early spring sunshine and I think the Americans believe to this day that this was all organised as local colour ... It all became more realistic to me when I realised that the young officer piloting us had driven us into the middle of a charted minefield. As there were a considerable number of VIPs in our company, it was with some relief that I deposited them back at base ... As for our young navigator who had led us astray, he went off back to his Headquarters at a great pace and found himself with a ticket to the UK next day.

The 'young navigator' was Lieutenant GM Chirnside; he had hastily changed the party's route when he realised that they were approaching a minefield, but the repercussions for him were not as General Pyman believed and he was certainly not returned to England.

Word had it that contractors had already made one or more fortunes from recovering desert debris, including untold miles of valuable signal cable. The harbours too had to be cleared and Lieutenant PL Waddy, sent with his troop to run the transit camp at Tobruk, came across Arabs dismantling mines in order to make home-made underwater explosive charges.

Superhuman efforts were required to have nearly all the vehicles on the road in May 1949 for a month's Regimental Camp at Ghemines, about thirty-five miles south of Benghazi. The Camp began inauspiciously with a particularly nasty *ghibli* which miraculously blew itself out, to be succeeded by four weeks of ideal weather – until the last night when, after the tents had all been packed, it poured with rain. The month concluded with a week long exercise, Gialo (named after an oasis), which provided a number of adventures long remembered by those involved.

Repeating a Regimental enterprise during wartime training, all the officers were taken off in September 1949 for a week's training at Maddelena, on the road from Barce to Derna where the Italians had built a Community Centre. A number of empty, and more or less weatherproof, buildings were taken over. In their spare time the officers shot a large amount of

North Africa and Egypt 1948–50

game – and it was that which provided the feast for the B Squadron Ball already mentioned. Meanwhile the Regimental Sergeant Major, Mr Greenslade, assumed command and took the rest of the Regiment out on a two-day dismounted exercise.

In September 1949 A Squadron was sent to Derna. A pretty little town, on the edge of the sea, it was reportedly destined to be one of Mussolini's holiday resorts. It was overlooked by a beetling escarpment up which the road to Tobruk made its way by a series of hairpin bends and had figured frequently in wartime newsreels as fortunes veered in the North African campaigns. The numerous *wadis* and gorges of the area provided ample scope for dismounted training at a Regimental Support School, including a battle course, run by A Squadron.

The Regiment and A Squadron suffered a severe blow in October 1949 when Sergeant AGD Loader, the Troop Sergeant of 4th Troop, was killed in a road accident near Tmimi, about sixty miles east of Derna. His party had been scouring the desert debris for spare parts. The son of Regimental Sergeant Major E Loader, he had served as a boy in the Band from 1938 and was then with C Squadron during the North West Europe campaign.

> He was a most excellent NCO, who never spared himself in the service of the Regiment in which he spent most of his life, and of which he was so proud.

Canal Zone

A Squadron had to move on again in January 1950, this time to Egypt where, after the war, all British forces had been concentrated in the vast depot and stores area of the Canal Zone. The rest of the Regiment was to follow in April, changing places with the 16th/5th Lancers. Those who had visited the Canal Zone were not expecting great things and Camp 53 at Fanara, near Fayed, had little to offer in the way of scenery. It was a mixed tented and hutted camp sited on an expanse of sand beside the Treaty Road and surrounded by barbed wire entanglements. Anglo-Egyptian relations had begun to deteriorate and were to worsen steadily over the next few years; movement was therefore very restricted. It seemed likely that the Regiment was to have a frustrating time.

History of The 13th/18th Royal Hussars (Q.M.O.)

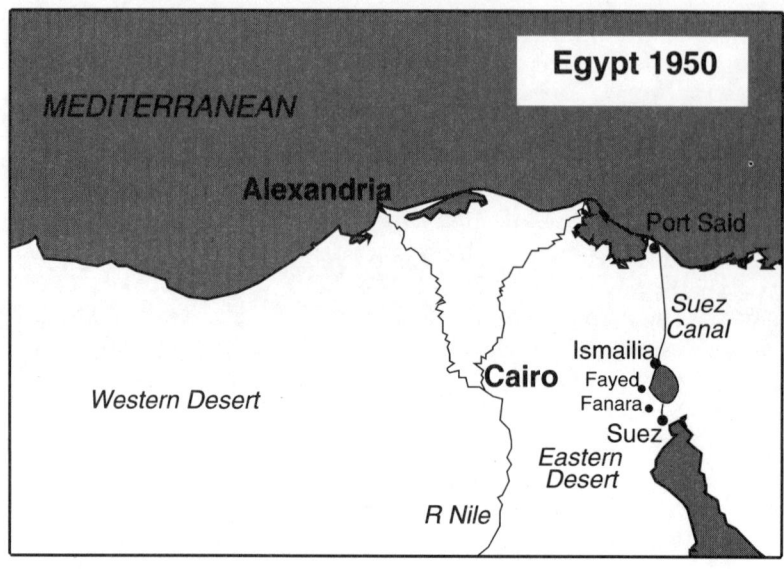

A Squadron arrived early in order to take part in a major Middle East Land Forces exercise, Groundnuts, named after the abortive and ruinously expensive Government project in East Africa. Beforehand they had to paint all their vehicles in sand colour. (In Cyrenaica they were, surprisingly, painted green.) Their armoured vehicles were further camouflaged with a layer of sand on the wet paint; an enterprise which was to be regretted. After the backwater of Cyrenaica it was a rude, if salutary, shock to be operating with other arms and the RAF during the ten-day exercise in the Eastern Desert, south east of Cairo. During it the Squadron acted as screen and provided reconnaissance for 3 Infantry Brigade Group.

By the time the rest of the Regiment arrived in Egypt, in late April, it was well known that another move was in the offing, to Malaya. However, it remained officially secret for several days in order, apparently, that there could be a single announcement in the Far East of the substantial reinforcements being brought in to combat Communist terrorism.

Gratifying testimony to the reputation which the Regiment had earned in Cyrenaica came in letters from the British Resident and the Assistant Commissioner of police:

North Africa and Egypt 1948–50

I have much pleasure in forwarding the attached letter from the Commissioner Cyrenaica Defence Force.

May I also take this opportunity of adding my own personal thanks to yourself and all ranks of your Regiment for the outstanding interest and goodwill shown towards both the Administration and the Cyrenaican population. Their co-operative attitude has done much to further British prestige and cement the good relations between Cyrenaica and Great Britain.

... I would be most grateful if, on behalf of this Force, official thanks could passed to the Commanding Officer of the 13th/18th Royal Hussars for the whole hearted co-operation with and assistance rendered to the police by this British Regiment during its stay in Cyrenaica.

The meticulous behaviour and bearing of all members of the Regiment and its very good relations with the police and civil population have, without doubt, done much to enhance British prestige and engender goodwill and respect. It is with genuine regret that we view the departure of the 13th/18th Royal Hussars from this territory.

Men, Vehicles and Ships

The orders for Malaya plunged the Orderly Room into a frenzy of activity, working out who was and who was not eligible for the move. The demands of operations in Korea and Malaya meant that the liability of National Servicemen was raised in stages from twelve months to two years, but those with less than six months to serve were barred from going to the Far East. Many regulars were also approaching being 'time expired'. A third of the Regiment proved to be ineligible and the sabre squadrons were therefore considerably depleted before reinforcements could arrive and be trained.

The families could move only when accommodation could be found for them; if that was not within three months they would have to return to England. Alternatively, they could go back to England and take a chance on being called forward from there to a quarter in Singapore or Malaya in due course. It was a difficult decision for families to make, as many had already suffered a year's separation before being able to get out to Cyrenaica. Some did elect to return home, but most chose to stay and were lucky enough to join their husbands quite soon.

History of The 13th/18th Royal Hussars (Q.M.O.)

To get to war establishment, needed for Malaya, new vehicles had to be drawn up from the depots in Tel el Kebir and they, of course, were painted in sand colour, not the green required in Malaya. (A Squadron still had actual sand on some armoured cars which, several layers of green paint later, would have to be laboriously stripped off whenever one was handed back to Ordnance.) Typical of the chaos was that many boxes, drawn up in a hurry from Ordnance, were found in Malaya to contain driftwood, scrap-iron and other assorted rubbish. Instead of the expected vehicle kit in one box for a 'new' armoured car were gardening tools. Thefts from Ordnance Depots were not the only threat; in one incident thieves winched a water truck out through the perimeter wire of the Regiment's guarded and brilliantly lit vehicle park, under the very eyes of the sentries.

The Move to Malaya

The move to Malaya was complicated to say the least, involving two aircraft and five ships. Some of the vehicles went in the SS *Glenorchy* and the remainder in the SS *Ben Macdhui* – together with a number of Regimental dogs, of which more below. B Squadron's advance party travelled in HMT *Devonshire*, some of its main party in HMT *Orduna* and the remainder in the *Empire Pride* with the rest of the Regiment.

In mid-June 1950 the *Empire Pride* made its way through a Red Sea which lived fully up to its reputation. A following wind and baking temperatures made conditions very unattractive. The only 'air conditioning' for the troop decks was what could be taken, already very hot, through canvas scoops rigged on the open decks. Once into the Indian Ocean there were storm warnings and there were very rough seas for four days. Keeping individual training going and persuading people to take some exercise required more than a little effort. However, at Port Said a large quantity of small arms ammunition had been taken on and, in calmer weather, firing practice took place from the stern at floating targets.

The Regimental Dogs

In Cyrenaica members of the Regiment had the usual mixture of pet dogs; some had come out with their owners, others had been acquired from a variety of sources. A limited number had

North Africa and Egypt 1948–50

been allowed to travel to Egypt, but getting them to Malaya was a different kettle of fish. The Advance Party in Singapore, commanded by Major MWH Bell, received a signal: 'Fourteen regimental dogs despatched in ship [*Ben Macdhui*]. Arrange safe transit to destinations.' Simple enough, but Singapore banned canine imports and, worse, the signal had leaked. When Captain PB Tillard arrived at the quayside he found a Customs officer at the bottom of the ship's gangplank, where one remained for the rest of the ship's stay, It became a conflict *à l'outrance*. Customs were damned if a dog were to land; the Advance Party was damned if all did not. Those Singaporeans in the know watched with interest.

The Master of the *Ben Macdhui* sympathised. But he had clearly been told that, if one single four-footed creature got off, his ship would not be able again to berth in Singapore. Nor could he heave to out at sea, because that would have to be entered in his log, which Customs would scrutinise on his next visit. However, he was persuaded that he might just slow the ship down a bit.

There followed a demonstration of how the Army could unite when faced by such a challenge (bearing in mind that all concerned were strangers to the Regiment). The RASC lent a landing craft, the 4th Hussars a 3-tonner, plus its inevitable armoured car escort. Some way up the east coast of Malaya, the ship slowed down opposite a secluded cove, the dogs were slung over the side in a net and the landing craft beached them on the sand. After the motley pack's frantic dash to the first trees they had seen for a long time, Lieutenant BJW Cobb and the 4th Hussars rounded them up and took them to their destinations. This was both kind and brave – brave, not just because of the risk of disciplinary fury, but because the dogs included one Peter belonging to Captain ER Jolley. He was a fearsome Kerry Blue whose sole aim in life was to cause death to all within his reach.

Back in Singapore, face was saved: by Customs who had prevented the dogs landing, by the Advance Party because they had nevertheless reached their destinations. The Regiment, when it docked later, passed through Customs in a friendly atmosphere of mutual respect.

Chapter Two

Malaya 1950–51

Strategic Target
Britain's involvement with Malaya began in 1782 when The East India Company acquired Penang as a naval station on the route to China. 260 years before, the Portuguese had arrived at Malacca, centre of their valuable spice trade, and that fell into Dutch hands in 1641. The Dutch East India Company dominated trade in South East Asia until the nineteenth century. After Stamford Raffles founded Singapore as a free trade port the Dutch handed over Malacca in return for British settlements in Sumatra. A series of treaties instituted protection over the nine Malay States, but only Malacca, Penang and Singapore were directly administered by Britain.

During the nineteenth century the Industrial Revolution created a world-wide demand for raw materials and for new markets. By 1900 Malaya was meeting nearly half the world's demands for tin and rubber was rapidly becoming a staple commodity. The opening of the Suez Canal and the construction of a Malayan railway contributed to the increase in trade and the western states of the peninsula became very prosperous. With the rest of South East Asia, Malaya and Singapore became attractive strategic targets for Japanese expansion.

When Japan invaded Malaya in 1942 the population was an ethnic and religious mix, only 48½ per cent of whom were Malay; 38 per cent were Chinese and 12 per cent Indian, aboriginal tribes in the interior and Europeans made up the remaining 1½ per cent. The Malays had been Muslim since the early sixteenth century and the other principal religions were Buddhism, Hinduism, and Christianity.

Communist Insurrection
Chinese immigrants had been largely responsible for the development of the tin industry; they were also small farmers and market gardeners who squatted in previously undeveloped

Malaya 1950–51

areas. (Indians, mostly from Southern India, worked on rubber estates and on public works such as roads.) The Japanese singled out the Chinese for particularly brutal treatment during their occupation and many fled into the jungle to join the Communist-led Malayan People's Anti-Japanese Army (MPAJA), which was actively supported by the British.

After the Japanese defeat in 1945 the British were generally welcomed back by the Malayan and Singaporean populations and, as wartime allies, the Malayan Communist Party overtly co-operated with the the returning administration. Meanwhile the MPAJA hid their British-supplied arms in jungle caches. The Party's aim was to take over government by covert political infiltration. However, despite the efforts of the Communists to wreck it, a Federation Agreement between the British and the leaders of each community was inaugurated in February 1948. Political means having failed, in June 1948 the arms caches were opened and a campaign of terrorism began, as part of the overall Communist struggle against 'Imperialists' throughout Asia. Despite reinforcements for the Army, including the 4th Hussars, the situation deteriorated rapidly and by 1949 much of Malaya's economy was being attacked by the renamed Malayan Races Liberation Army* (MRLA), particularly the isolated rubber estates and tin mines.

During 1949 and 1950 terrorists were operating in units of up to 200 men and were killing over 100 civilians a month. This was clearly not a temporary problem which could be fairly speedily solved; it was accepted that a protracted campaign was inevitable and that a programme was needed for resting and re-training the infantry battalions. Further reinforcements were needed to provide the necessary reliefs and strengthen the striking force, as well as provide a much-needed boost to civilian morale. As the only armoured unit, the 4th Hussars were soon over-stretched by the increasing demands for escorts and patrols, hence the call for the 13th/18th. The latter was to take over in the southern half of Malaya, allowing the 4th, less a detached squadron in Hong Kong, to concentrate on the north. (Singapore was largely unaffected by the Emergency.)

---

* Although there were a few members of the other races claimed by that title the great majority of the MRLA were Chinese.

History of The 13th/18th Royal Hussars (Q.M.O.)

Shortly before the Regiment arrived, General Sir Harold Briggs was appointed Director of Operations. He gave his name to the Plan which would eventually result in the total defeat of the Communists. A key element was to provide security for the rural population while removing the main source of MRLA food supplies, funds and recruitment. This would give momentum to the scheme by the High Commissioner, Sir Henry Gurney, for transporting half a million Chinese squatters from their isolated shacks and vegetable patches on the jungle fringes to protected sites. The latter were initially called 'Resettlement Areas' and later 'New Villages'. The military component of the Plan was a security framework throughout the country, superimposed on which were to be main striking forces. These were to destroy the terrorist gangs through a series of systematic clearance operations, starting in Johore and moving northwards until the MRLA remnants were driven over the Thai border. The Army's primary role was therefore to seek out and destroy terrorists in the jungle and on its fringes; its secondary role was that of supporting the Federal police in such tasks as enforcing food denial measures and curfews.

Special Establishment
The Regiment's various parties arrived in Singapore during June 1950 and moved to the transit barracks at Nee Soon. With depleted strengths and vehicles suffering from a sea voyage and the tender handling of dock labourers, it was a formidable task to man and equip even B Squadron, which was to go 'up country' first. To save military manpower, unloading of vehicles had to be left to Singapore Harbour Board contractors who then towed them to an Ordnance Park. (It was heartbreaking to see vehicles, already dirty, rusty and damaged from the sea journey, being further ruined by men with no knowledge of the Daimler fluid flywheel and pre-selector gearbox.) The barrack square at Nee Soon was littered with tool kits being checked and vehicles being prepared. A few people were sent to the valuable jungle warfare courses at the Kota Tinggi School, but the Regiment's principal mentors were the 4th Hussars. They lent NCOs to help with training and arranged attachments for officers and NCOs to their squadrons in Johore and Negri Sembilan.

Malaya 1950–51

It was a totally new environment, with narrow winding roads cut through jungle and rubber estates instead of the broad expanses of the desert. The Malayan peninsula is not only in the Tropics, it is influenced by both the north-western and north-eastern monsoons. The result is a climate which changes little throughout the year, with frequent heavy rain combining with the heat to produce a consistently high humidity. In the early part of the year it can rain particularly hard, as the Regiment was to find.

Infantry battalions tackled the principal, offensive, role of seeking out and destroying terrorists. The armoured car regiments' prime task was to keep the roads open and to protect legitimate travel. On its own that would have been a soul-destroying occupation for any self-respecting regiment, but the 4th Hussars had demonstrated that, given the necessary initiative, there was scope to carry out offensive operations – albeit on a limited scale. The 13th/18th had new tactics to learn and new drills to practise for the conduct of road patrols, for the escort of food convoys and VIPs, and for hunting communist terrorists (CTs) in the jungle. In Malaya each sabre troop needed its own 'infantry', able to dismount speedily in case of ambush or to react to the fleeting opportunities of fighting in close country with an ad hoc foot patrol. There was therefore a special establishment in which each squadron was supposed to have five identical troops, each with an officer, sergeant and twenty men.

All the troops had two Daimler armoured cars and two GMCs, specially modified for Malaya. The heavy troops were disbanded as their AEC armoured cars were too big and cumbersome for Malaya's tracks and bridges. There was no need for squadron headquarters to deploy tactically in vehicles, but a few scout cars were retained in each squadron for escort use. Some troops had to be led by sergeants and there was a permanent shortage of crewmen. The continuation of the Cold War in Europe and the outbreak of the Korean War meant that

---

* This 'mounted infantry' role was not new to the Regiment; the 18th Hussars, for example, had several notable dismounted successes against the French during the Corunna campaign and against the Germans during the opening months of the First World War.

History of The 13th/18th Royal Hussars (Q.M.O.)

Britain had few troops to spare for Malaya, though National Service was extended to two years in August 1950 (after being cut to eighteen months since its introduction in 1947). Regular soldiers were allowed to serve only three years overseas and there was a manpower crisis every time drafts left for England.

Initial Deployment
In mid-July 1950 B Squadron under Major ERMcM Wright moved to Kluang in central Johore, relieving C Squadron 4th Hussars and coming under command of 26 Gurkha Infantry Brigade. (Two troops from A Squadron and one from C had been needed to provide five troops.) First one, then two troops were detached at Jemaluang, near Mersing on the east coast. Their first incident came on 26 July, the night after taking over from the 4th Hussars. Two troops out in support of an infantry operation were fired on by 'bandits'. It was a taste of the swift encounter with a near-invisible opponent that was to be the Regiment's life for the next three years. Only four days later came first sight of an enemy, with the capture of a member of the Min Yuen, the CTs' civilian organisation which operated in the villages and provided food, money and information for the armed and uniformed units in their jungle camps (*see* p 54).

A month later Major MWH Bell took C Squadron into Negri Sembilan, further north, with their troop back from B Squadron. Based at Seremban under command of 63 Gurkha Infantry Brigade, their first troop detachments were at Kuala Lumpur and Tampin.

Later in August, Regimental Headquarters and A Squadron (still below strength) joined B Squadron in Kluang. The newly-constructed camp consisted of tents and huts, known as *bashas,* thatched with palm leaves (*attap*). In the general haste it had been erected with everything the wrong way round from the plans; the Officers' Mess was not only near the jungle edge, but was also the first place encountered on the approach road – whereas the Guard Room was almost the last. Officers therefore had to have their pistols with them the whole time. The *attap* thatch was surprisingly cool, but the whole camp site was damp, even for Malaya, with clouds of mosquitoes and other insects at night. Despite the climate and the general activity:

Malaya 1950–51

The main thing which newcomers to Malaya notice is the extra weight which all ranks seem to have accumulated during their short stay in the country. After England's miserable meat ration of eightpence a week it is good to see steaks again and to be back on an active service scale of feeding. There is no rationing and with Australia and New Zealand providing for us, we are in a good position. Fruit is plentiful . . . bananas and pineapples grow almost like weeds . . .

By November, A Squadron (Major J Meares) could move to Kuala Lumpur, the Federated States capital in Selangor, having taken one troop back from B Squadron. Under command of 18 Infantry Brigade, the Squadron had detached troops with the infantry battalions at Kajang and Kuala Kubu Bahru.

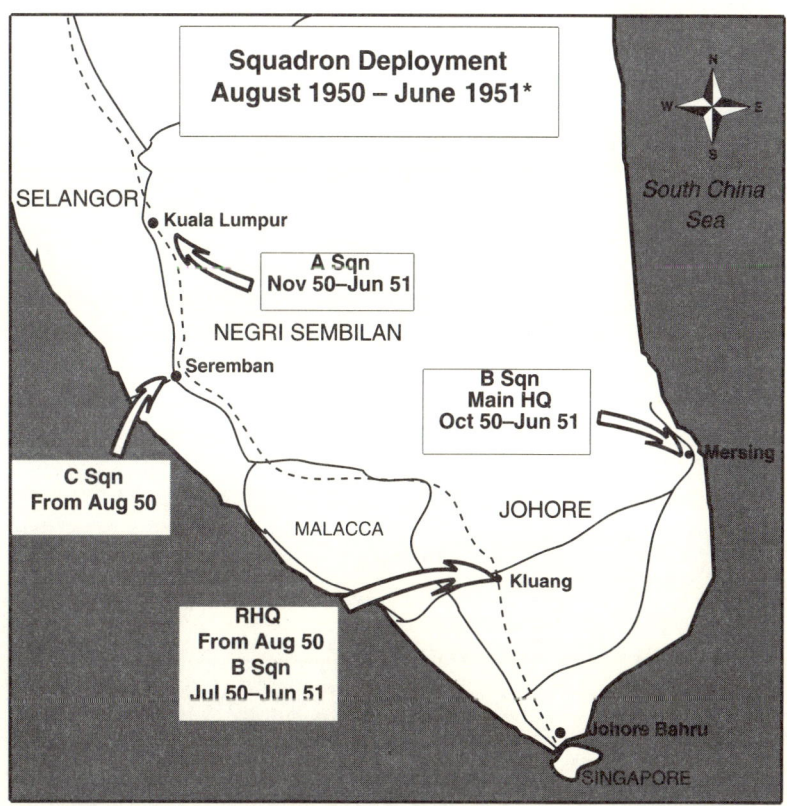

* *See* page 57 for a map showing the principal locations in Malaya 1950–53

History of The 13th/18th Royal Hussars (Q.M.O.)

This dispersion was to be the pattern for the rest of the tour in Malaya. Not only were squadrons at a distance from and largely independent of Regimental Headquarters, but troops were often some way from their squadron headquarters. Detached troops sometimes lived on their own; more often they were based on an infantry battalion or company camp. Some of these camps were very simple; others were more organised and Jemaluang, the longest continuously-occupied camp, became quite elaborate. By the end of the tour some twenty-three places would have housed detachments varying in size from one to four troops and for periods ranging from days to years. A troop normally spent one to three months on detachment before being replaced by another, but circumstances varied widely.

The effectiveness of the Regiment would depend on how many of the enlarged troops the sabre squadrons could deploy. The administration of squadrons also needed bolstering, in order to cope with being detached at such distances on a permanent basis. To make as many officers and men available as possible, Colonel Tinker made the bold decision in November 1950 to disband Headquarters Squadron, except for a small Regimental Headquarters and the Band. Each squadron became self-accounting and had two captains, one to deal with administrative and the other with technical matters, each being supported by an expert of the rank of Squadron Quartermaster Sergeant or higher. (In the middle of 1951 the Band had to return to England for a year's tour with a Training Regiment.) The REME workshops at Kuala Lumpur and Kluang could support A and B Squadrons respectively and the Regiment's main LAD moved to Seremban to back up C Squadron. As each squadron was under operational command of different brigades the role of Regimental Headquarters was limited at this stage largely to personnel matters.

Johore, July–December 1950 *(B Squadron)*
The wealthy state of Johore had been the scene for many of the earlier attacks, when the CTs had been in gangs of up to three hundred strong. By now that policy had been abandoned by the MRLA and much smaller groups were operating from jungle fringes wherever Min Yuen support was adequate, largely in

Malaya 1950–51

the central and east coast areas. The main road north went through Ayer Hitam, just to the west of Kluang. Through Kluang itself went the railway link between Singapore and the principal Malayan towns. The east coast road then reached no further north than Endau and along it went daily convoys between Mersing and Johore Bahru, taking fresh-caught fish one way and returning with a variety of supplies for the few coastal towns and villages. Much of the road was edged by jungle, as was the lateral road to Kluang, and there were any number of positions from which CTs could ambush vehicles.

In late October 1950 the demands of the food convoys and the frequency of terrorist attacks in the north-east of the State led B Squadron to move its 'main' headquarters and two troops from Kluang to Mersing. The Squadron's patrols and escorts were being ambushed about once a week, fire being opened at point blank range – normally some twenty to thirty yards. Even so, it was difficult for crews to stay awake in the humid heat and vehicle commanders were required to stand up at all times. It was still usually impossible to tell where the enemy were as they stayed well back in the thick cover. There were no casualties at first, though Corporal DM Steel had a narrow escape when a bullet fired from a high bank entered his armoured car and splattered around inside cutting him on the arms and face. On 22 September, however, a half troop escorting a convoy was fired on and Lance Corporal R Hudson was wounded and later died.

To counter any feeling that convoy escorts were little more than Aunt Sallies, Captain PB Tillard, again the acting B Squadron Leader, encouraged troops to return fire even if no enemy was to be seen. On one occasion he surreptitiously set out groups of red-painted man-sized targets in likely ambush positions, to be engaged as convoys passed by. This worked well until headlines appeared in the local press: 'Bandits' New Terror Technique – Red Replicas along Roads'. Prudence prevailed and the targets were quietly removed. 'How could the war be carried to the enemy – so far as convoy duties allowed?' The rattle of vehicles crossing the frequent wooden bridges could be heard far into the jungle, so surprise could seldom be achieved. One technique was to drop off a line of ambushes from moving vehicles. This looked as though it would have an early success when two CTs walked straight down an ambushed path – only to be missed at a few yards range when the bren gun misfired. To be fair, inflicting casualties on the terrorist was notoriously difficult, particularly for vehicle-mounted soldiers, but the score was opened soon afterwards. Near the road from Mersing to Jemaluang was a marshy area some three to four hundred yards wide, which it was thought the CTs used to skirt. A logging track ran across this into the jungle. Before dawn on 7 December 1950 a line of ten ambushes was laid along about 3,000 yards of the track by four of B Squadron's troops, acting as a stop line for a sweep of the jungle area by Gurkha infantry. The sabre troops had to return by noon, to resume convoy duties, and had begun heading back along the track. However, as the last ambush party (Sergeant M Dedman) was reached there was a burst of firing. The section had seen two armed CTs crawling up a stream and opened fire, as did the other ambushes when they arrived. Then the armoured cars, waiting with the other vehicles to take them back, joined in with enthusiasm. Some hundreds of rounds later, when peace had been restored, it was assumed that there were two riddled bodies to be recovered. Not a bit of it; both were still very much alive, one admittedly had a slight wound, the other made off so fast he twisted his knee and was captured. The Gurkha commanding officer subsequently came to offer his congratulations on this notable triumph; he also expressed the polite hope that his men might be warned the next time, as they would not wish to miss another Alamein!

Another 'enemy' was encountered at about this time. An urgent signal from Jemaluang arrived at Squadron Headquarters: 'Cookhouse evacuated. Occupied by tiger.' But by the time that Captain Tillard arrived the young, but certainly largish beast had been despatched and Lieutenant JS Mangles, the detachment commander, was contemplating some amateur skinning and curing. This encounter with local fauna prompted Captain Tillard and Mr Mangles to try snipe shooting in the surrounding swamp; the day after they went out, a flagpole flying the Communist flag appeared where they had been. It was first seen by the local police who sent out two unfortunate

Malaya 1950–51

constables to pull it down. Both were blown up; the flagpole had been booby-trapped.

Riots in Singapore, December 1950 *(B Squadron)*
Four days later B Squadron was to be on operations of a different kind. Its 'main' headquarters and four of its troops were in the Mersing/Jemaluang area, while 'rear' headquarters, two sabre troops and the Administrative Troop were in Kluang, some sixty miles away. The camp by the sea at Mersing had already been flooded in November and moved to another site. On the night of 11 December the sea flooded the new site 'to mattress height', but that was only an overture to what was to follow. At 2130 hours the telephone rang: 'There is trouble in Singapore and the complete Squadron is to be there by 0430 hours tomorrow morning'. In the Squadron's three camps feverish activity ensued, master-minded by Captain JW Bell, the Squadron Second Captain. In Kluang it had been pay day and he had to retrieve a number of soldiers from 'places of entertainment'. There then followed night drives of a hundred miles or so, which saw the complete Squadron in Johore Bahru by 4.30 am, ready to cross the Causeway to Singapore.

Meanwhile, Captain Tillard had arrived in Singapore in the small hours. He was immediately co-opted onto the ad hoc Emergency Committee by GOC South Malaya District, Major General Dunlop; it consisted only of senior officers from the Navy, Army, Air Force, police and Colonial Office – and one captain of Hussars. On returning to the Squadron, Captain Tillard's first task was to explain that the potential foe was not the mainly Chinese CTs they had been fighting in Johore, but rather the friendly and peaceful Malays whom they had been doing all they could to support. (In Singapore the Malays were in a minority; some 77 per cent of the total population were Chinese, 12 per cent Malay and 9 per cent Indian and Pakistani.) The trouble had begun with Malays demonstrating over the outcome of a court case concerning the betrothal of Maria Hertogh, a Dutch girl, to a Malay man. She had been left as a baby with her Malay *amah* (nursemaid) when her parents fled from Indonesia after the Japanese invasion. (See end of Chapter for a full account of the background.) The demonstrations had deteriorated into a day of rioting, burning and looting with little action being taken by the police; largely Malay themselves they were inclined to sympathise with the rioters. The Governor (and Commander-in-Chief) of Singapore had therefore called on the Army for help in restoring law and order, but not before seventeen people had been killed.

An immediate concern for General Dunlop's Committee was that men of a Malay unit based on the outskirts of Singapore might mutiny and join the rioters. As a first priority Lieutenant Mangles' troop therefore staged a breakdown at the end of the road leading to the barracks, with guns pointing towards the camp. Whether or not they had entertained other ideas the Malay soldiers stayed inside. It would obviously have been very nasty had they emerged and taken sides with the rioters.

At 6.30 am Squadron Headquarters and three of the troops went on a flag march through a town with 'burnt and burning cars in every street'. The remaining troops entered the centre of the city at 9.30 and the Squadron was directed to the Cathedral Square where a gang of about two hundred hooligans was rioting round the Cathedral and the Supreme Court. At first the situation appeared out of control, but action by 5 and 6 Troops (Lieutenants RS Beresford and PL Waddy) eventually cleared the crowds. The account in the *Journal* continues the story:

> This little lot was dispersed by charging round at full speed with three cars abreast while the rioters' bottles and stones were answered by our tear gas bombs. We were new to these bombs and at first they affected us as much as the mob. One was used against some rioters who had hidden in a culvert. To quote an ex-farmer – 'it made a ferret look slow'. The hooligans soon split up into small gangs and eventually dispersed. There were great moments such as when a certain officer chased a brick thrower to the roof of the Capitol Theatre and brought him back alive; or when a certain NCO [Corporal J Hodkinson] went to work armed with a fan belt and commented on the speed at which the crowd dispersed; when a Troop put in a spirited bayonet charge against a crowd that was hacking down the door of the Cathedral; and when another Troop managed to compress eleven prisoners into one GMC! [with the crew on top].

Malaya 1950–51

On another occasion the Squadron Leader's lone GMC came across a hundred or so rioters trying to break into a large Government building. They greeted it with a hail of stones and the crew dismounted and threw stones back. Cricketing expertise stood them in good stead. 'We threw better than they did and they dispersed quite happily'. By evening order had been more or less restored in the centre of the city and troops patrolled further afield dealing with various minor skirmishes. They were finally stood down at about midnight. After seventy-two hours without sleep most people were nearly asleep on their feet – and some managed to achieve it leaning against armoured car mudguards.

Meanwhile Lieutenant BJW Cobb with two troops of C Squadron moved hurriedly to Johore to take over the food convoy tasks. The gap which had been left by B Squadron was soon made all too clear. On the day that they tackled the rioters in Singapore, their remaining half troop in Mersing was ambushed while escorting the daily food convoy to Kota Tinggi; a civilian vehicle was blown up with a grenade which also wounded a passenger and a woman in a nearby hut.

Most of B Squadron remained in Singapore until January 1951. There they spent Christmas as the guests of the REME Workshops, who not only entertained the Squadron but also overhauled and re-painted their vehicles. However they went back to escorting duties in January 'with renewed enthusiasm. Singapore had become very boring and very expensive when there were no riots and most people were glad to get back to Johore.' As a final act, General Dunlop asked the Squadron to stage a mounted march past round the Cathedral Square, the scene of the first action. 'We stationed two armoured cars either side of the saluting dais, in front of the Supreme Court. When the parade was over they were supposed to move off after the VIP party. But one of them refused to start. With incredible presence of mind the other also stayed where it was until darkness fell and both could be retrieved, unnoticed, by our fitters. This drew praise from the General, who warmly congratulated the Squadron on the fitting climax provided by its thoughtful and impressive gesture, in mounting guard over the Supreme Court throughout the day. It would have been a shame to disillusion him!' (Major General PB Tillard). The people of Singapore also expressed their gratitude, in a tangible way: money flowed into a Squadron Private Account whose riches were to be the envy of PRIs for years to come. (The Army had been unpopular with some of the European population, many of whom had returned after the war to find their houses occupied by soldiers. The successful quelling of the riots and the protection offered to civilians changed that attitude overnight.)

In retrospect, any blood lust of the Muslim mobs had been largely sated by the killings of the first night, while the Squadron was moving down from Johore. But no-one knew this at the time and the temper of rioters is notoriously unpredictable. There is little doubt that the unexpected and dramatic presence of British armour patrolling the streets played a large part in preventing any resurgence.

B Squadron had to return to Singapore twice, in April and July 1951, in order to provide cover against possible further unrest during hearings of the appeal against the Maria Hertogh ruling. For the third hearing, in late August, an ad hoc D Squadron moved down to Singapore for a week.

Negri Sembilan, August 1950–July 1951 *(C Squadron)*
As B Squadron in Johore was re-deploying troops from Mersing to Jemaluang, the monsoon reached its height. Jemaluang was cut off by floods for a week and the troop escorting the food convoy to Kota Tinggi was marooned there with some Gurkha infantry. Both parties received their rations by air, including a particularly potent brand of rum in tins.

Further north in Negri Sembilan, C Squadron's detached troop at Ayer Kuning also suffered from the heavy rain, with their camp being flooded to a depth of three feet. At this stage C Squadron also had troops for much of the time at Pertang Estate and at Rompin. Squadron Headquarters and the two remaining troops were at Rasah Camp, about two miles from the centre of Seremban, on the road to Port Dickson. Bordered on the west by the sea and to the north, east and south by Selangor, Pahang and Malacca, Negri Sembilan was more heavily populated, and cultivated, than much of the B Squadron area. There were numerous rubber estates, some of them very large. Tin was dredged in several of the valleys and

Malaya 1950–51

even the smallest valleys were cultivated and dotted in rice growing areas with Malay kampongs. Elsewhere there were huts of market-gardening Chinese squatters. The main road and railway arteries of the peninsula passed through Seremban itself. By 1951 the Squadron area also took in the Settlement of Malacca through which went the coast road. That was in a 'white' area from the security point of view, where traffic could move on the roads without restriction or escort. As the various rivers had to be crossed by ferry, however, that was not a major advantage.

The principal task from Seremban itself was escort duty, augmented by dismounted patrols, while the detached troops were mainly occupied on road patrols, especially on the estate roads, as well as dismounted patrols when time and opportunity offered. C Squadron's opportunities to take offensive action were limited to what could not be tackled by one of the battalions in the area, but they had in any case a formidable task in trying to keep open the roads and tracks.

An example of the problem was the Ladang Geddes estate in the Rompin area. Owned by the Dunlop Rubber Company it extended over some 40,000 acres with many divisions and subdivisions and with its own complex road system. It was bounded to the north and east by the dense jungles of Pahang, from which CTs could infiltrate into overgrown areas of the estate. Through murder and intimidation they supplied themselves with food and money extorted from workers. They would also make forays against lorries carrying rubber latex and slash young rubber trees, all of which was aimed at wrecking the estate economy. Ladang Geddes alone could have fully absorbed the Rompin troop on routine daily patrols, but they had twenty other smaller estates in their area as well as the main roads to cover.

A measure of success for the many hours of patrol work would be a significant reduction in the number of buses and estate lorries burnt by CTs in a particular area. Patrol routes and timings, of course, had to be changed frequently in order to maintain surprise. That was not possible with food convoys, which had to be run at scheduled times for the benefit of potential users, who were not allowed to travel unescorted. On

History of The 13th/18th Royal Hussars (Q.M.O.)

15 May 1951 a half troop under Sergeant W Anderson, returning from food convoy escort duty, came upon a burning bus and were ambushed by about thirty CTs*. A GMC was hit four times, more accurate fire than usual. The dismounted section went in speedily, under covering fire from their armoured car, and a pair of shoes was found in the ambush position – still warm. The trail was lost in the very heavy jungle fringe, but the troop hoped that the bare-footed terrorist found it as difficult going as they did.

Propaganda Attack

In April 1951 Lieutenant JP Paige's troop undertook a new detachment, after the village of Titi had been threatened with attack. Any confidence that its 8,000 Chinese inhabitants might have had in the Security Forces had been set back severely when a platoon of 1st Malay Regiment was eliminated in two well-planned actions. There were then only twenty Malay police in the isolated village and there was no information coming in. Despite the known presence of several large terrorist gangs the troop had no direct encounters; vigorous patrolling ensured that there were no more incidents before they handed over to a company of 2nd/7th Gurkha Rifles. Before the troop left, however, a courier was killed on 2 July by a Gurkha ambush party on the Titi perimeter. On his body were found propaganda leaflets addressed to the 'British Soldiers'. 3rd Troop were the only British soldiers in the area at the time and they were presumably the targets. The leaflet is reproduced as printed; apart from a few typographical errors the English is remarkably good. Much was made of the continued rationing in Britain, but a gradual abolition had, in fact, begun. Chocolate and sweets were freed from restriction on 2 February and eggs on 26 March. Cheese, butter and margarine rationing did not end until 8 May 1954, while meat rationing continued until 3 July 1954.

---

* At this stage the enemy were actually still called 'bandits'; from early 1952 they were officially identified as 'Communist Terrorists' or 'CTs', but they remained 'bandits' in the Army's vernacular.

Malaya 1950–51

To the British Soldiers

BRITISH SOLDIERS!
Some days ago the British Government announced a further cut of 20% in the meat ration of the British people. Each person today is only entitled to purchase 8d of fresh meat (equivalent, according to the Associated Press, to a slice no larger than two match boxes) and 2d worth of the tinned meat a week. The present fresh meat ration amounts to only half of the lowest ration prevailing in wartime Britain! Reduced rations and soaring costs of living (with drastic cuts in the housing programme and other social services in the offing) - although they don't mean a thing to the moneybags - constitute the price the British people are made to pay for the expansion of the British imperialist War machine. Goering's slogan of "Guns instead of Butter" has been taken up with unprecedented Zeal by Churchill and Attlee.

BRITISH SOLDIERS! What does this mean for you? It means that while disease, mutilation and death await you in Malaya (and your comrades in Korea), increasing poverty and want are overtaking you, your families and friends in Britain. And all this because you, your families and friends are allowing your lives and fartunes to be moulded by the disastrous war policies of Britain's imperialist rulers.

The British Communist Party which upholds the finest traditions of the British people, has time and again denounced the colonial war in Malaya as an integral part of a diabolic plan to plunge the whole World into another war - an "atomic" war in which the very existence of the British nation wolud be placed at stake. The trials and tribulations of the British people during the last World War would almost be a picnic compared to these which they would have to endure in another.

Here is what a British woman said in an open letter to the people of Malaya in September last year; "I am a European woman who served in the army against Fascist aggresion; my husband was a pilot in the Air Force. During that period it was brought home to me that the ordinary people do not want war as it brings them misery and despair while to the few and anscruplaus business basiness men, who take care to keep out the danger, it brings increased profits. But we are numerous and they are few, so if we are united and resolute our desire for peace must prevail . . . ."

(This letter, Signed "Margaret Wright", was published in a Chinese Newspaper, the Nan Chian Jit Pao on 13th September, 1950. The hirelings of British imperialism in Singapore banned this paper on 21st September, 13 days after it had launched a campaign to collect Signatures for the Stockholm Peace Declaration).

BRITISH SOLDIERS! You can and must do your part in the momentous struggle to defend World Peace which is gaing on in every part of the World. You owe this at least to your families and your nation (not that tiny fraction of the population represented by Tweedle-dum Churchill and Tweedle-dee Attlee but the millions of honest industrious and peace-loving Working people of Britain). First and Foremost: Demand to be sent back home! Tell your families and friends at home to oppose actively the new disarmament programme and take part in collective actions for the defence of World Peace! Tell them to demand the immediate repatrition of all British Soldiers serving overseas!

BRITISH SOLDIERS! Adopt malingering and other Similar tactics! Promtly surrender when engaged in battle - We only want your arms not your lives!

Down with the War Mangers! Long Live World Peace! Down with British Imperialism! Long live the Friendship of the British and Malayan Peoples!

Issued by the Publicity Department Headquarters of the 2nd Regiment, National Liberation Army of Malaya.

History of The 13th/18th Royal Hussars (Q.M.O.)

There are two versions of an incident at the troop detachment at Ayer Kuning in April. The official account said that a sentry was fired at and that the round tore the flash eliminator from his rifle and ricocheted through the brim of his jungle hat. His rapid response with four rounds (unlikely to have been successful, bearing in mind the state of his rifle) turned the troop out. They saw two CTs haring through the rubber, but the follow up party lost the tracks once they reached the jungle. That story was treated elsewhere in C Squadron with some suspicion, albeit tinged with admiration for quickness of reaction. The alternative version was that a trooper discharged his rifle while cleaning it and to his relief saw that the round had only struck his neighbour's rifle. He was alleged then to have leapt to his feet, crying 'there they go' and blazed away into the jungle thereby destroying any evidence that his weapon had been discharged improperly. (An example for the historian of the caution with which 'eye witness accounts' should be treated!) Later in April a Tamil CT surrendered to 2nd Lieutenant DDA Harris's troop at Ayer Kuning and led a patrol to where his comrades had been. They had wisely decamped, but the patrol recovered his hidden rifle and ammunition.

A few days later the troop arrested three food suppliers identified by the defector.

By August 1951 C Squadron felt that:

> ... with four bandits wounded and a share in ten other kills ... we have at last officially opened our score. [But] It is regretted that Peter, the Squadron's Kerry Blue Terrier, has failed to live up to our operational prowess and has not recorded an officially recognised 'kill' since April, though the bodies of several *pi*-dogs have been found near the Squadron lines in a condition not normally associated with natural demise. His only properly witnessed score during the period has been a Sapper-owned Alsatian which had to be given iced-water baths to revive it after a two-minute engagement. For this we claim an official 'wound', and hope that our new reinforcement, in the shape of Captain Elliot's dachshund Rhona, will give us clear superiority in this field in the future.

The fighting spirit of Peter matched his owner's, Major ER Jolley. First as Second-in-Command and then as Squadron Leader, Major Jolley ensured that every opportunity for

Malaya 1950-51

aggressive action against the terrorists was seized by C Squadron. He spent a lot of time himself on foot with the 7th Gurkha Rifles and his close relationship with them enabled Squadron officers and men to take part in a number of dismounted operations, first with the Gurkhas and later with the Royal West Kents and the Fijians.

Selangor, November 1950–July 1951 (*A Squadron*)
Kuala Lumpur, in the state of Selangor, was the Federation capital. In 1950 it was a sleepy, provincial place compared with the bustle of cosmopolitan Singapore, but terrorists had been active on the outskirts from an early stage, particularly in the Ampang area where there were a number of Chinese squatters. From the city two major roads ran north and north west; one towards Perak and Kedah, and also to Fraser's Hill, one of Malaya's two hill stations. The other went through Pahang towards Kelantan and Trengganu. Both ran through hilly country and the many twists and bends were notorious for ambushes, particularly on the stretch towards Bentong.

A Squadron did not have so many food convoys to protect as the other squadrons and the emphasis was more on direct mounted support for the infantry battalions of 18 Infantry Brigade, together with dismounted operations such as jungle patrols and ambushes, cordons during searches of villages, and assistance with resettlement of isolated squatters. (Major Meares, like Major Jolley, was an enthusiastic proponent of aggressive foot patrolling.) As part of the campaign to deny food to CTs, one task involved spending the night in villages and searching the inhabitants when they left at first light to work in fields or rubber estates. At Kuala Kubu Bahru, on the road north, a troop was permanently in support of, firstly, the 2nd Scots Guards and then 1st Royal West Kent, while at Kajang*, to the south west, another troop operated with the very successful 1st Suffolk.

The A Squadron base in Kuala Lumpur was a requisitioned sports ground, Coronation Park, shared with the Brigade

---

* It was at Kajang, in the early months of the Emergency, that the Communists had made one of three unsuccessful attempts to establish 'liberated areas' which they hoped to claim as governed by the people.

History of The 13th/18th Royal Hussars (Q.M.O.)

Signal Squadron. The pavilion served as Squadron office. (To begin with, any officers in station slept in the changing room, though they ate in the Brigade Headquarters Officers Mess.)

For a time in December 1950 it was thought that the rioting in Singapore might spread to Kuala Lumpur; A Squadron practised a plan to counter this, together with several flag marches through the city with all their available armoured cars. Later in the month they were able to revert to normal operations and on the 22nd opened their score with two contacts in the Bukit Mandei area when four troops mounted a number of ambushes in the jungle. Although two CTs both escaped when fired on by a section, one is known to have died later from his wounds. Later the same day another party killed a second terrorist.

Escorts for VIPs were already a heavy commitment, coupled with the need to protect the movement of money from Kuala Lumpur to Kuala Lipis in Pahang, and gold from the mine at Raub to Kuala Lumpur. In all, half a million pounds worth of bullion was escorted without loss and the Squadron was presented with a silver rose bowl by the Hong Kong & Shanghai Bank in recognition of their services.

In February 1951 Sergeant H Whiteley added another terrorist to A Squadron's tally when, searching for possible ambush positions while on road patrol, his party found a newly used track. Following this up, they came on a terrorist camp. The sentry guarding the camp was shot and in the fight which followed another is known to have been killed. An action such as this was some compensation for many hundreds of road patrols with no successful contact.

Operation Opportunity
In 1951 A Squadron took to the water for the Regiment's first seaborne landing since 1945, albeit on a slightly smaller scale than in Normandy. For some twelve months there had been little or no terrorist activity in the area of Selangor near the west coast and there had been no military units stationed there. Early in 1951, however, terrorist gangs were being harried to such an extent inland that some were moving west, and the local Min Yuen started to increase their activities in the Klang and Port Swettenham areas. Lorries transporting

Malaya 1950–51

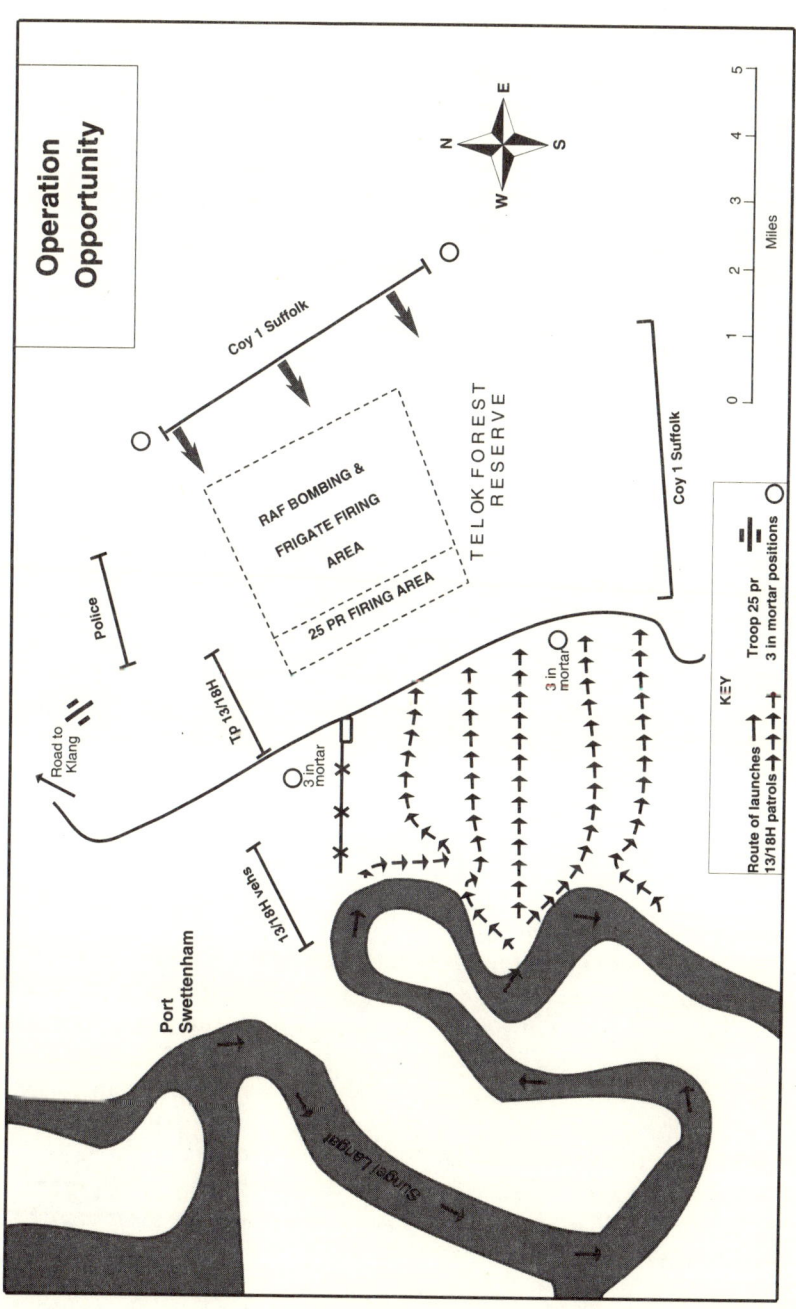

latex from the rubber estates were being burnt and there were a number of murders. A foot search was carried out by A Squadron to see if the Telok Forest Reserve, a large area of jungle south of Klang, was being used by CTs. A terrorist camp was found at the northern end of the Reserve, but the occupants escaped on the approach of a patrol. Intelligence reports said Min Yuen leaders living on the approaches to the Reserve gave warning of the approach of military or police patrols.

In an ambitious combined operation, devised by Major J Meares and commanded by 1st Suffolk, the outlying areas of the forest were to be screened by a landing from the Sungei Langat estuary to the west and operations in the north and south, with the object of forcing CTs into the forest and using it as a killing area. In Phase One a company of 1st Suffolk moved into the southern end of the forest. Phase Two was the sea landing, for which four landing parties were found by troops of A Squadron. With police guides they embarked at 3.30 am on 25 April in police launches and sailed up the estuary to unknown destinations. (As in June 1944 the landing sites were not known until sealed orders were opened after sailing.)

After the dawn landing each patrol moved inland, sometimes wading through mangrove swamps. They went through an area which had previously regarded itself as inaccessible to authority – even during the Japanese occupation. Surrendered CTs guided patrols to known houses where recognised suspects were collected from their beds. By 1115 am the patrols reached the road bordering the forest reserve; screening was complete and some twenty suspects had been detained, sixteen of whom were wanted men. Twelve were subsequently charged for serious offences under the Security Regulations.

Now a fire plan, formidable for Malaya in 1951, was put into action. For thirty minutes RAF Sunderland flying boats bombed and machine gunned the Telok Forest, supported by four-gun salvos from the 4-inch guns of a Royal Navy frigate, anchored off Port Swettenham. The armoured cars of A Squadron had picked up the remainder of their crews from the foot patrols and were able to follow the naval and air strikes with prophylactic firing with their 2-pounders and machine guns on the western edge of the Forest, together with a troop of 25-

Malaya 1950–51

pounders from 25th Field Regiment RA. That was followed by mortar fire on the northern and southern ends of the forest, while a sweep through the area from east to west was carried out by another company of the Suffolks. The dismounted patrols of A Squadron searched up to 500 yards in from the west, to lying-up positions waiting for the Suffolk patrols to come out. The morning's activity had been more rewarding, as all that was flushed out by the bombardment were hordes of wild pig. They galloped through the Chinese squatter area in the north, much to the inhabitants' annoyance; they could not shoot them for fear of being mistaken for CTs. The real CTs were assumed to have laid low and hoped for the best.

If nothing else it was a virtuoso display of the versatility of armoured car troops.

Johore, January–July 1951 *(B & A Squadrons)*

The pattern of incidents in Johore during the first six months of operations continued into 1951. Convoy escorts were fired on fairly frequently by gangs of a dozen or so. Bren guns, rifles and sten guns might be used together with the occasional grenade.

On 28 May a convoy escort saw a Communist flag beside the road; the armoured car fired into the jungle to announce its presence and CTs retaliated by firing on the escort's APC. On another occasion an armoured car, during an ambush, fired off half its ammunition and then had to stop when a tree, cut by the HE, fell across the turret.

The most spectacular ambush took place a month later on the Mersing–Endau road, when the leading GMC of a convoy escort, under 2nd Lieutenant GW Scott, was fired on by CTs with two rifles and a sten gun. The GMC moved on with the crew returning fire, but the armoured car was unable to fire immediately because one vehicle in the convoy had halted. However a Royal Australian Air Force Lincoln bomber was overhead, returning from a bombing raid. Seeing the action below, they promptly joined in by strafing the terrorists' position and their line of retreat. As B Squadron had been entertaining some of the RAAF aircrew in their messes only a week before this seemed a most generous return for their hospitality. For their part the air crew said how pleased they were to have a break from bombing miles and miles of jungle.

A general reshuffle of the Far East armoured car regiments began in July 1951. The 4th Hussars were to return home in October after relief by the 12th Lancers, except for their squadron in Hong Kong, which was to be relieved by B Squadron, 13th/18th. Meanwhile the 4th had to send two troops to Selangor, when A Squadron moved to Johore in July. The plans for that move were complicated by the need to provide troops in Singapore for the second hearing of the Maria Hertogh appeal. A Squadron began to move troops south in early July, in time to allow B Squadron to move to Singapore on 23 July, but after a few days there was a further postponement of the hearing. While four of its sabre troops returned temporarily to Johore, B Squadron Headquarters was wrestling with the many complications of its move. As they were taking over 4th Hussars' vehicles in Hong Kong, all theirs had to be handed in. So far as men were concerned, those with less than four months to serve could not go to Hong Kong and had to exchange with others from A and C Squadrons.

Before the handover from B Squadron was complete, A Squadron had an early taste of Johore's terrorist activity. A stand-by troop was maintained at Jemaluang whose task was to turn out at three minutes' notice to investigate any suspected incident, or go out to help anyone in trouble. The task was never easy as it was standard terrorist practice to stage a small incident as a decoy for much bigger one. The commander of the stand-by force, therefore, always had to temper speed with caution, and to check back on the source of any information about a suspected incident. 2nd Lieutenant D Howard-Allen's troop was ordered out on 14 July to a suspected ambush on a light railway near a sawmill. When they arrived, one Chinese seemed a little too ready to give information; a trap was suspected and the troop refused to go with him. Next day Sergeant JC Thomas's troop investigated and found that the railway had been wired for electric mines and the jungle beside it sown with panjis (sharp-pointed bamboo stakes stuck in the ground). A week later two wooden bridges on the food convoy route to Kota Tinggi were found to have been sawn through and another bridge to have been blown up.

1. Guard of Honour for the Emir of Cyrenaica; L to R – Maj Wright, Brig Audland, Commissioner of Police, 2 Lt Orr.

North Africa and Egypt 1947–50

2. Daimler armoured cars of 2nd Troop B Squadron (2 Lt Sellick) training in the Western Desert.

3. AEC heavy armoured car in the Eastern Desert, on A Squadron reconnaissance for Exercise Ground Nuts.

4. Patrol from 6th Troop B Squadron (Sgt Oakley) finds PWD lorry after bandit attack on the Kluang–Mersing road.

Malaya 1950–51

5. Changing an armoured car wheel at Jemaluang.

6. SHQ Troop A Squadron (2 Lt Hunt) on the Bentong road.

Malaya 1950–51

Training
The Regiment had learned a great deal in the first year of operations; they knew, for example, that there had to be a clear distinction between the roles of a mounted road patrol and an escort, whether of VIPs or food convoy. In road patrols, action was deliberately sought so that CTs might be flushed out. In escorts the reverse was the case; the greater the vigilance by the escort, especially if this was obvious to the onlooker, the less chance of an ambush. Any relaxation by the escort could lead to terrorist attack and to unnecessary casualties. The strain of constant vigilance over long periods without any apparent terrorist activity could be wearing in the extreme. It became clear that the sabre troops were beginning to get tired as a result of months of intense activity, yet there could be no opportunity for the whole Regiment to be withdrawn for rest and re-training, as was the practice for infantry battalions.

For most of the first year RAC crewman training in the Regiment had in any case been deliberately neglected in the effort to get the maximum number of men on operations. Standards suffered as a result. It was also necessary to train reinforcements. As well as the frequent departure of National Servicemen, three years had passed since leaving Aldershot and any regulars then with the Regiment had come to the end of their permitted overseas tour and had to be replaced. Lieutenant Colonel JR Cordy-Simpson, who took over from Lieutenant Colonel Tinker in February 1951, therefore decided to withdraw sabre troops from operations two at a time and to re-train them together, on a three-week refresher course. In May the Training Wing was set up and did excellent service for the rest of the tour. It had a staff of one, sometimes two, officers and a sergeant instructor in each of the four main subjects: wireless, gunnery, driving and maintenance and assault trooping.

The Wing ran induction courses for reinforcements on their arrival, as well as concentrated refresher courses for complete sabre troops. Apart from anything else the courses enabled individuals to be upgraded in their trades – and earn some more pay. It also provided opportunities for them to meet people from other squadrons. Later on, after Regimental

History of The 13th/18th Royal Hussars (Q.M.O.)

DEFINITIONS AND ABBREVIATIONS

From *The Conduct of Anti Terrorist Operations in Malaya* Third Edition. 1958

CT [Communist Terrorist]
Those who in any way actively further the subversive Communist campaign for the purpose of overthrowing the Government of the Federation [of Malaya] by resorting to or instigating violence and who:

    a. By the use of any firearms, explosive or ammunition act in a manner prejudicial to the public safety or to the maintenance of public order.
    b. Incite to violence or counsel disobedience to the law or to any lawful order by the use of any firearm, explosive or ammunition.
    c. Carry or have in their possession or under their control any firearm without lawful authority therefor.
    d. Carry or have in their possession or under their control any ammunition or explosive without authority therefor.
    e. Adhere to the CT gangs as couriers or camp followers.

Min Yuen
The term 'Min Yuen is short for 'Min Chong Yuen Tong' meaning The People Movement. It covers all activities by the Masses, and the Masses' leaders, in aid of the Party. It follows therefore that a Min Yuen worker can be a Party sympathizer living in the jungle but engaged in controlling the Min Yuen organisation. The term Min Yuen is adjectival and not a noun.

Vegetation
Principal divisions into Rubber, Primary Jungle, Secondary Jungle and Swamp. Interspersed with these is open ground covered in belukar (low scrub and bushes), lallang (long grass) or cultivated land and padi [rice fields].

<u>Rubber</u>
Visibility is often good up to several hundred yards. Trees are often planted on a fixed pattern and at a fixed density. Except where an estate has been neglected there is very little, if any, undergrowth.

<u>Primary Jungle</u>
This is very thick and contains trees 150 ft or more in height with comparatively little undergrowth on the jungle floor. Tracking is easier in primary jungle as signs left by CT in parting a way through the undergrowth are visible.

<u>Secondary Jungle</u>
Where for any reason primary jungle has been removed a secondary growth of every kind of bush, creeper or bamboo takes command quickly and soon forms a dense mass that is difficult to move through. The density and height of growth varies in accordance with the time that has elapsed since the cutting of the original forest.

<u>Swamp</u>
On low lying ground in coastal regions swamp extends over considerable areas. The swamp consists of water and mud into which a man may sink knee deep and frequently deeper. The whole area is covered with trees and thick undergrowth which reduces visibility to a few yards.

Malaya 1950–51

Headquarters had moved to Seremban, tactical training was carried out in an area near Kongkoi. This had been placed out of bounds to civilians, following a series of ambushes in which the Malay Regiment had suffered a number of casualties. Live ammunition could therefore be fired without undue regard for safety precautions and the site of the worst ambush provided an excellent place to practise anti-ambush drills.

For much of the time, after a spell as troop leader in C Squadron, Lieutenant JRL Howard was in charge of the Wing and his energy and enthusiasm contributed largely to its success. That success was not confined to training officers and men of the Regiment. In June 1952 the Wing undertook the training of the first fifty instructors for a newly created Home Guard. They ran three courses lasting two weeks each for 'a remarkably intelligent and friendly bunch.' (Colonel JRL Howard) 'I suspect few survived as each was placed on his own in a New Village with half a dozen shotguns and told to form their own "Neighbourhood Watch".' The Wing's Home Guard Training pamphlet was adopted for use by Home Guard throughout Malaya by their Commander, General de Fontblanque. (Later in the same year the Wing was charged with a much bigger task.)

Under Orders for Hong Kong

In August 1951, while B Squadron was preparing for their move to Hong Kong, warning arrived that the rest of the Regiment was to move there in May 1952. They were to take over from 3rd Royal Tank Regiment, as an armoured regiment equipped with Comet tanks – and form the first reserve for operations in Korea. This meant that conversion training had to begin, without any relief from the operational commitment. HQ Squadron was also to be reformed, in anticipation of the return to a normal establishment. B Squadron was to pave the way in Hong Kong as advance party.

History of The 13th/18th Royal Hussars (Q.M.O.)

The Maria Hertogh Riots, Singapore 1950

(I am indebted to Mr Nigel Morris CMG LVO QPM for his account of the events leading up to, and his own involvement in, the Maria Hertogh affair. At the time Mr Morris was Acting Deputy Commissioner of Police in charge of the CID and Special Branch. EEH)

A baby girl was born to Dutch parents in the Dutch East Indies, just before the Japanese invasion in December 1941. The girl's proper name was Maria Hertogh, but her parents, who had other children, decided that her best chance of survival was to hand her over to their Malay *amah* in whom they had complete trust. They gave her money and she agreed to take the baby back to her *kampong* in north-east Malaya. The Hertoghs succeeded in escaping from Indonesia with their other children and the *amah* brought up the little baby as her own. The girl knew nothing of her antecedents, never learned to speak any language other than Malay and was brought up as a Muslim in the *kampong* which was her home. In 1949, eight years after they had fled and four years after the end of the War, her father and mother succeeded in tracing their former *amah* and started the long legal process of regaining custody of their long-lost baby. Neither she nor her adopted mother wanted her to be handed over to the 'foreign' parents, whom they considered had abandoned her soon after birth. The final case was heard in the Singapore Supreme Court where the father won and the Judge ordered her to be handed over to the nuns of a Roman Catholic Convent into whose care the Government had, unwisely, put her. This fuelled the anger and fury of the Malay population.

Just before the girl went to the convent, the Muslims had quickly had her 'married' to a Malay school teacher to try to put her out of the reach of her parents. Unbelievably, the High Court in Singapore still found in favour of Mr Hertogh and I had the unpleasant task of dragging her away from the nuns and then organising her escape from the Supreme Court and getting her through a back door of the Court House. Meanwhile a Woman Police Officer was dressed up in Maria's clothes in order to draw the attention of a rioting crowd of about 6,000 Malays at the main entrance. That enabled me, with great reluctance, to get her into a car at the back door and drive her to the airport where I had an aeroplane waiting to fly her (with her father) to Holland. The rioting continued for about a week.

Maria (Hertogh) married a Dutchman and in 1994 they were living outside Amsterdam. The Hertogh Riots turned out well for Mr Morris. The then Commissioner of Police was on home leave in England at the time and had just been chosen to take over as Deputy Inspector General

Malaya 1950–51

of HM Overseas Police Forces. The Acting Commissioner had two Deputy Commissioners, one in charge of the Uniform Branch, and one, Mr Morris, in charge of CID and Special Branch. As a result of the riots, the Commissioner lost his prospective appointment and the Acting Commissioner and the other Deputy Commissioner were made to resign. As a result, Mr Morris gained early promotion in 1951 to Commissioner of Police. After six years as Commissioner (during which there were serious, Communist-inspired, riots) he was himself appointed Deputy Inspector General at the Colonial Office, before becoming the Inspector General.

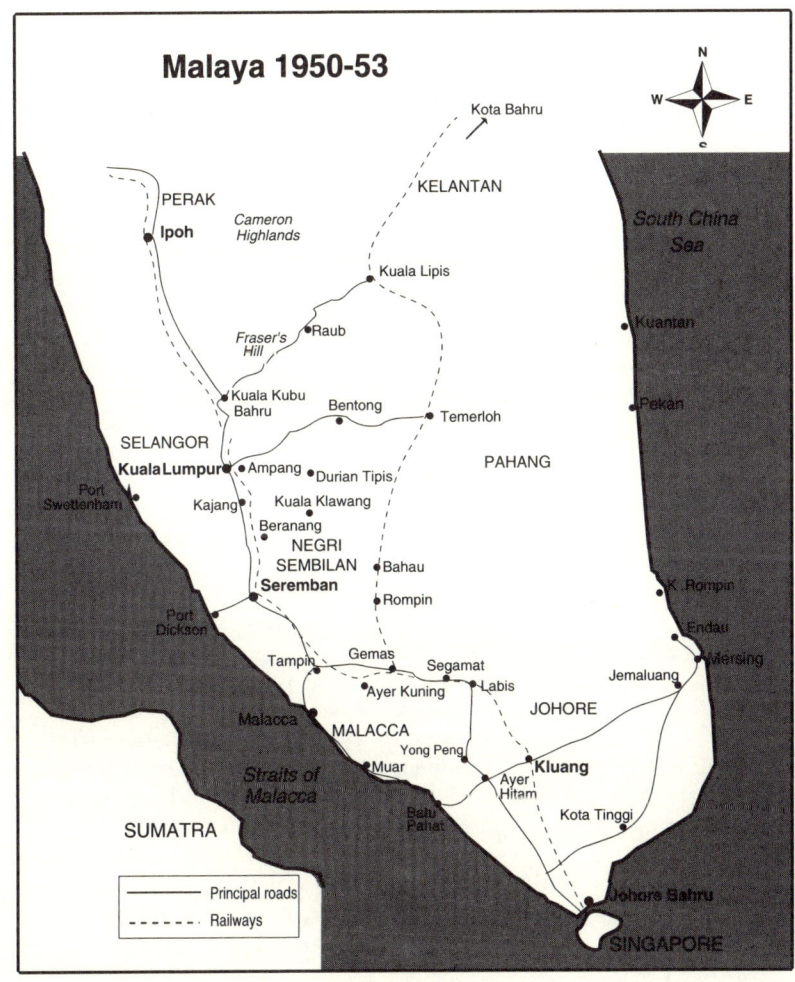

Chapter Three

Hong Kong and Malaya 1951–53

Hong Kong Interlude
Once B Squadron reached Hong Kong they occupied Tai Lam Camp, a collection of Nissen huts, but '. . . quite one of the nicest camps that this much-travelled Squadron has ever lived in. Tai Lam is by the sea, on the west coast of the New Territories, which provides excellent bathing and sailing . . .'. By comparison with Malaya the climate was very pleasant, even cold in winter, and there was plenty of sport.

Captain JW Bell, the Squadron Second Captain, recorded impressions of Hong Kong in 1952 in the *Journal* :

> This is a land of contrast. It is possible to step out of an air-conditioned super cinema, walk for five minutes and enter a walled village such as has been a feature of Chinese life for a thousand years. Model factories, with housing for workers and welfare schemes, are set up by modern Chinese employers next to places where the ancient family craftsmen of China, working by hand, seem unaware of the march of progress. . . . Although the constant threat of Red China on the doorstep tends to make trade unstable and long term credit practically non-existent, there is a vitality of effect in the air that a visitor to Hong Kong cannot help noticing at once. This has been caused by factories in Shanghai closing down through political pressure from Red China and starting up in the Colony. These new industries are giving employment to many inhabitants of Hong Kong and changing it from a trading port into an industrial centre. . . . The industry of the Chinese is a feature of Hong Kong. One is amazed by the rapidity of building – new homes seem to grow overnight. This attitude is most refreshing and is a tonic to those who feel that the term 'a good day's work' is a thing of the past. The cheerfulness, cleanliness and good manners of the Chinese population and the fact that on the slightest excuse, celebration is in order, gives the Colony a festive air.

The official arrival and engagement of the civil labour by Captain Bell was reported by someone else as:

Hong Kong and Malaya 1951–53

. . . a tremendous pantomime. He swept in, followed by some thirty Chinese with their grandmothers, grandfathers, strong sons, comely daughters and babies in arms waving letters, passes and chits, all proclaiming with strong voices at the same time their ability and sole ambition to work for the Squadron. The 'great employer' having divested himself of his bush shirt and seated himself and his prickly heat under the fan bellowed for silence, and with the help of the Squadron police commenced to get some semblance of order. In this he was assisted by a Chinese interpreter (stolen from Brigade) and a Gaelic interpreter (SSM Jepson). Thus, after many explosions of wrath, 'velly many smiles and bows', the civilian staff for the Squadron was engaged.*

The Squadron's families lived chiefly in Kowloon with its blocks of modern flats and shops full of bargains. It also provided entertainment for the soldiers though much of that was expensive and most not very desirable.

As part of Land Forces Hong Kong, the Squadron's main operational task was to patrol the border between the New Territories and Communist China during which 'we gaze upon Comrade Mao's boys on the other side. They look like bandits to us.' The Squadron also took on the manning for short periods of one of the permanent Observation Posts on the frontier. This entailed an officer and ten other ranks living with the police in an advanced position, with a telephone and wireless set, 'watching for the Communists over the border to make any move that will give us cause for concern'. Anti-smuggling patrols with the police were subsidiary tasks which were 'amusing if nothing else, and provide good training for the would-be rugger players. . . . [They] entail lying up for a night near the river frontier until the smugglers come along with their spoils. When the police challenge they usually drop their goods and bolt, and then the chase begins.' (An echo of the eighteenth and nineteenth centuries when the Regiment's forebears had to help the Revenue in their unpopular pursuit of smugglers into England.)

---

* Fifteen years later Lieutenant Colonel Bell returned to command the Hong Kong Regiment.

History of The 13th/18th Royal Hussars (Q.M.O.)

Negri Sembilan, August 1951–February 1952 *(C Squadron)*
Meanwhile, in Malaya, August 1951 had seen the worst single ambush that the Regiment experienced. Fifty terrorists ambushed a half troop of C Squadron (2nd Lieutenant Harris) in a cutting some twenty feet deep, on the Rompin–Bahau road in Negri Sembilan, the banks on both sides of which were covered in jungle. The driver of the GMC in the lead was hit in the hand and lost control of the steering wheel, whereupon the vehicle overturned in the ditch and the crew were thrown out. The armoured car then entered the cutting and engaged the CTs with Besa machine gun fire, while the GMC crew, all of whom had been wounded, took up positions behind their wrecked vehicle. When the armoured car opened up with its 2-pounder the CTs withdrew and the wounded could be extricated, but the injuries to the troop's Junior Civilian Liaison Officer, Teh Hock Kong, proved fatal. 'Teh' was approaching fifty and and the father of five grown up children, but 'he was well worth his place in the Troop, was popular with his comrades, and always took his share in the day's patrols and the night's guards, as well as in any other operation undertaken on foot'. A follow-up by the 1st/6th Gurkha Rifles showed that four terrorists had been wounded from fire from the armoured car and a fifth surrendered to the follow-up party.

On the night of 6 September a newly-joined National Service officer was killed accidentally. A patrol of three sections from C Squadron, under command of Major ER Jolley, had moved to an ambush position in the Seremban area, guided by several captured and surrendered terrorists. Unfortunately, before reaching the proposed ambush position, the patrol encountered two terrorists. Fire was opened, which warned other terrorists in the area, and in the course of a short fight, one section killed a terrorist and almost certainly wounded another. The commander, 2nd Lieutenant J Harden, went back to report, leaving instructions that the section was to fire again should there be any movement to their front. A little later movement was heard and the section fired, killing Mr Harden. In the confusing surroundings of the jungle and on a very dark night, he must have mistaken his path when returning and approached his own ambush from the wrong side.

Hong Kong and Malaya 1951–53

Two other incidents showed how much chance or mischance entered into operations against the terrorists. Three vehicles of a C Squadron troop, under Lieutenant JRL Howard, went to the aid of a police post which was being attacked by some thirty CTs just after midnight. When things quietened down, two of the vehicles went noisily away with their lights blazing, leaving behind Lieutenant Howard in the remaining armoured car. At 5 am the terrorists attacked again and were undoubtedly surprised by their warm reception. Later in the same month, September 1951, two armoured cars in support of Gurkha foot operations, were firing blind into the jungle to deter the terrorists from using or moving through that particular area. In spite of there being no particular targets for the guns to be aimed at, intelligence reports later showed that two terrorists had been wounded by the firing.

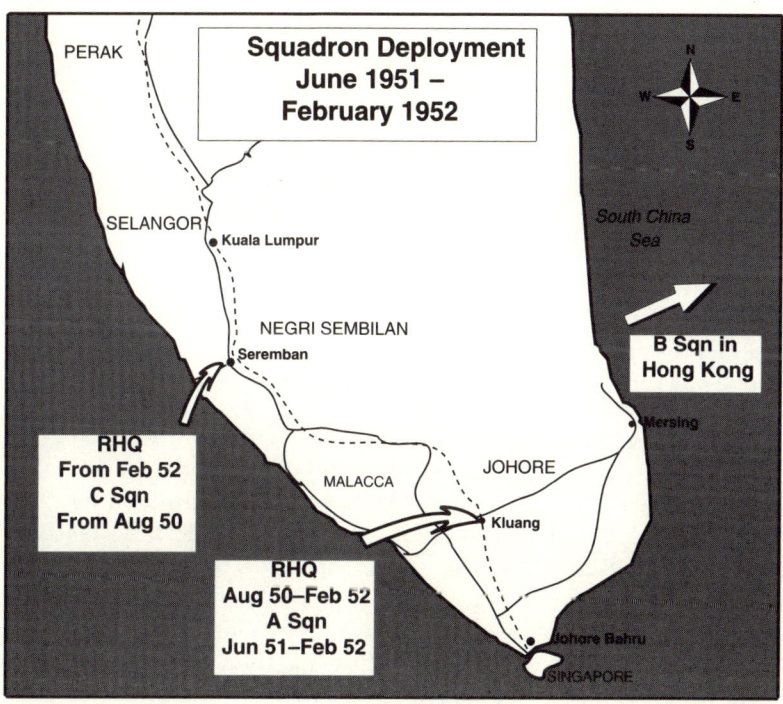

History of The 13th/18th Royal Hussars (Q.M.O.)

During October and November 1951 CTs terrorised rubber estate workers in Negri Sembilan and some other states into striking. Although only a small number of CTs was involved, for a time they were completely successful and the supply of latex was greatly reduced. The coaxing of reluctant tappers back to work was achieved with the help of continuous armoured car escorts. This was an additional strain on the sabre troops, who had still to meet their normal commitments after getting the tappers to work 'at a very non-union hour in the grey light of dawn'. However, in a short time the demoralised workers were confidently back to their normal routine.

Throughout the tour all the Squadrons owed a great deal to the support from 3-tonner drivers, storemen, REME fitters and recovery crews, and Royal Signals mechanics. They not infrequently found themselves under fire. On 27 February 1952 Trooper A Robbins, returning to Seremban from Rompin with the ration truck, was engaged by shotgun fire in the cutting where 3rd Troop C Squadron had been ambushed the previous August. The escorting scout car had halted to make some minor adjustment, unnoticed by those in the ration truck. However, Robbins 'who is a prominent scatter-gun sportsman at home when the gamekeepers are away, was heard nonchalantly to remark as the pellets crashed about his ears: "I'm no flaming pheasant" and drove on, though at rather an increased speed.'

Johore, August 1951–February 1952 *(A Squadron)*

> From the operational aspect the last four months have been quiet and the Squadron has been tied down to a timetable routine of convoys on the east coast of Johore enlivened by small bandit ambushes of three or four men firing a few rounds fairly regularly four times a month. (A Squadron *Journal* notes, January 1952)

On 18 August 1951 Corporal D Fraser was commanding the armoured car at the rear of a food convoy escort in the Mersing area when he heard firing from behind. The armoured car turned back to find a party of 3rd Malay Regiment being ambushed. They opened fire with the 2-pounder and the terrorists withdrew, bloodstains showing that at least two had been wounded. The ambush must have been intended for the food convoy, but something had prevented – or deterred – the terrorists from springing it.

Hong Kong and Malaya 1951–53

Later in the year, in mid-November, an A Squadron foot patrol under Sergeant JC Thomas was returning to Jemaluang in a GMC, when they came upon a party of some twenty armed CTs about to burn a bus on the Endau–Mersing Road. One was holding up the passengers with a sten gun. The GMC came under heavy bren gun fire as it slithered to a halt. Sergeant Thomas ordered bayonets to be fixed and the crew charged up the bank, firing as they went. At this the CTs quickly retreated. They could not be caught in the follow-up, but a careful search then, and again the next day, showed that two had been wounded. They had left behind some of their packs, containing useful documents, as well as the bus conductor's money bag, which was duly returned to the bus company. For his gallantry and leadership on this occasion and on 6 July, Sergeant Thomas was subsequently awarded the Military Medal.

The East Johore Bus Company was often in difficulty as it was easy for the terrorists to attack single buses and extort money from the passengers, or indeed from the company in the form of 'protection'. Earlier in the year B Squadron had tried a variety of counter measures including soldiers concealed on buses with radios linking them to follow up parties. 'It was amusing to notice the reactions of the passengers to the arrival of eight heavily armed civilian-type soldiers on their laps. It certainly spurred the drivers to fresh efforts and the sections emerged more frightened of them than any number of bandits' – but nothing was fully effective until the terrorists had been driven away from the roads and into the deep jungle.

On 1 January 1952 A Squadron:

> . . . experienced a rare bit of bandit cunning. A foreign sounding voice came on the telephone and said that a convoy commander wanted the Scammel at once to recover a GMC named Agombi, which had broken down.

Fortunately the informant's timing was wrong; the convoy which he reported to have reached Kota Tinggi could not possibly have done so by then. No action was taken, therefore, and when the convoy commander reached Kota Tinggi he reported that all his vehicles were in good order and that he knew nothing of the call. 'One wonders what sort of reception the bandits had prepared for the Scammel as it chugged slowly down the road.'

History of The 13th/18th Royal Hussars (Q.M.O.)

The small-scale ambushes could still inflict casualties. On 16 January 1952, when the GMC at the rear of the Kota Tinggi convoy was fired on with bren and sten guns, Troopers SE Edge and JH Anderson were wounded, Edge seriously – though he made a full recovery.

Floods had come again to East Johore at the beginning of January. This time A Squadron borrowed a 'very ramshackle' DUKW (amphibious truck) from the police, with which they returned stranded planters to their homes and delivered food and ammunition to Gurkhas who had been cut off. Unfortunately one journey was all that the DUKW could manage and its place was taken by a Royal Engineers' assault boat.

The detachment camp at Jemaluang now boasted a new cookhouse and 'dining hall', fitters shop, hard standing for vehicles, a football field, 'quite a good garden' – and a flourishing pig farm run by the fitters. Charlie, the Chinese kitchen hand, was very impressed by the new cookhouse; he said it was bigger and better than the home of the headman of his village.

Death of the High Commissioner

Another phase of the Briggs Plan had been launched in June 1951 when strict food control checks were imposed on shopkeepers and workers going to the rubber estates and tin mines, in order to prevent food being smuggled to the terrorists. However, the outlook in the summer of 1951 seemed bleak – for both sides in the conflict. The majority of the Malayan Chinese did not join the Communists but nor did they increase their support for the authorities, despite great efforts made by the Malayan Chinese Association. Even though there was a steep rise in terrorist losses, as a result of the major operations in southern Malaya and the 'framework' operations throughout the country, the flow of recruits to their ranks did not dry up. The original strength of the MRLA's active gangs, some 3,000, had more than doubled. The casualty figures speak for themselves (*see* Table).

In October 1951 the High Commissioner of Malaya, Sir Henry Gurney was killed in an ambush on his way to Fraser's Hill. Sir Harold Briggs retired in December and died soon afterwards. This was at a time when Britain appeared nearest

Casualties during the first four years of the Malayan Emergency				
	1948	1949	1950	1951
Civilians killed and missing	401	494	752	668
Police and soldiers killed	149 (60)	229 (65)	393 (70)	504 (124)
Total	**550**	**723**	**1,145**	**1,172**
(Military killed shown in brackets)				
CTs eliminated *	693	1,207	942	1,401
(*killed, captured or surrendered)				

(Table from *Withdrawal From Empire* by General Sir William Jackson)

to being defeated in its efforts to protect Malaya from Communist domination, while preparing to hand over power to a democratic government. In fact in that same October the Communists themselves decided that they could not achieve a military victory; they would concentrate in future as much on the political struggle to win wider support, as on military operations. The latter were to be kept at platoon level with an emphasis on ambushes.

Two months later both A and C Squadrons were required at short notice to escort Mr Oliver Lyttelton, Colonial Secretary in the new Churchill administration, on a tour of inspection. After the assassination of Sir Henry Gurney, this was not surprisingly treated as a major operation and the Commander-in-Chief received a signal from London as to his welfare.

Mr Lyttelton knew Malaya well and 2nd Lieutenant TE Christophers took him on several visits to old cronies, in an armoured car with a wooden '2-pounder'. He was told: 'You need to be careful of me, young man, the Prime Minister has issued the order "Let Lyttelton live" '. (Another version has it that the signal was: 'Lyttelton *will* live' which certainly sounds more Churchillian.) After an evening visit to an Australian tin miner the troop had a problem getting their charge back into the turret and an even greater problem getting him to stay in it with his head down. On the return journey he was determined to look out and get some fresh air; inevitably his hat blew off in one of the most dangerous places and Mr Christophers had to stop, climb out and retrieve the hat while the Secretary of State, head well out of the turret, yelled at him to hurry up.

The Regiment was not aware then of the significance of the visit. Mr Lyttelton:

Mr Lyttelton – a contemporary cartoon by Lt JRL Howard

> . . . carried out an exhaustive and exhausting three week familiarisation tour . . . with instructions from Churchill to revitalize the political and military campaigns. He was appalled by what he found. In his view the malaise stemmed from constitutional and administrative muddle, lack of clarity in the division of responsibility, and the enervating effects of the climate on government officers. . . . In his report to the British Cabinet he put his finger on the three key appointments of High Commissioner, Director of Operations and the Commissioner of Police. He recommended that one man should combine the first two to end the split personality of the Federal Government . . . (*Withdrawal From Empire,* General Sir William Jackson)

Malaya under Templer

In February 1952 the dynamic General Sir Gerald Templer was appointed as both High Commissioner and Director of Operations. Given extensive powers by the British Government, he re-invigorated the flagging Briggs Plan and saw to it that there was much greater liaison and co-operation between both the different levels of civil administration and the Security Forces. Civilian morale was raised by emphasising the British intention to grant independence as soon as the security situation permitted. Chinese resettled in the New Villages were encouraged to take responsibility for their own affairs and in September 1952 full citizenship was granted to all aliens born in Malaya. Templer hoped that that this would contribute towards forging a united Malayan nation – and remove a main element in the Communist appeal to the Chinese settlers. The Regiment, particularly B Squadron, was to see a great deal of him.

Hong Kong and Malaya 1951–53

Far from reducing strengths, it was necessary to reinforce the Security Forces. The Regiment's move to Hong Kong was cancelled and B Squadron was to return to Malaya. The opportunity was taken to shift Regimental Headquarters in February 1952 to Seremban where they and C Squadron moved into Paroi Camp. The tactical deployment of the Regiment was improved, with Regimental Headquarters in the same town as its formation headquarters, South Malaya District, rather than 150 miles from it. The wholly hutted Paroi Camp was also a great deal better than the low-lying, damp and mosquito-ridden camp at Kluang. At the same time A Squadron's base was moved to Johore Bahru, alongside Headquarters 26 Gurkha Infantry Brigade. Fresh training problems were created by the change of plan as several drafts of reinforcements had all been tank-trained in anticipation of the Regiment's move.

Selangor, March–December 1952 *(B Squadron)*

When A Squadron moved south in 1951 their place in Selangor had been taken by two troops of the 4th Hussars. It became a squadron station again when the 12th Lancers relieved the 4th. On 5 March 1952 B Squadron, still led by Major ERMcM Wright, took over from the squadron of the 12th in Kuala Lumpur, moving into what had been a transit camp. They speedily had the name changed to Lajj Camp* as they were constantly referred to as the 'Transit' Camp and received such requests as 'beds for two and sixty' or 'three in close with escort'. Since A Squadron's departure to Johore, eight months before, VIP escorts had become the primary role in Selangor. The other major tasks were road patrols and food convoy escorts, but B Squadron, like the other squadrons, took every opportunity that came their way to take offensive action. They could deploy on foot into the Kuala Lumpur rural outskirts, without being too far distant should escorts be required at short notice – as they often were.

In April 1952 B Squadron seized with relish the task of standing in for a company of infantry for six weeks, although normal commitments had still to be met. They took under command a platoon of 1st Suffolk and two Iban trackers for the

---

* Named after the 13th Hussars' First World War charge against the Turks.

period.* Despite all their efforts no casualties were inflicted or prisoners taken, but there was one near miss which at least provided some variety to the Squadron menu. A patrol under Captain G Stocker went into the jungle west of the Bentong road, some eleven miles from Kuala Lumpur, in the hope of finding a party of CTs reported in the area. Resting at the top of a hill 1,700 feet high the patrol heard someone making his way slowly towards them. He turned off before reaching them and dropped down the hill. Captain Stocker with one NCO and the Iban tracker set off to try to stalk him. Despite the very thick jungle the CT's track was picked up and they were closing with him when he was alarmed by a noise. There was the noise of a mad rush and then silence. The stalkers continued to crawl and after some minutes the Iban whispered 'Tuan' and excitedly pointed to movement in the undergrowth. Captain Stocker saw what appeared to be a crawling figure some 30 yards ahead, half hidden by trees. He fired, the CT flew to the right, his dog flew to the left, and in the centre 'a poor innocent boar lay dead at the foot of a tree'; a charge down the hill failed to flush their quarry. At least the pig made good eating, though one of the carriers commented 'a blank bandit would have been a blank sight lighter than this blank pig'.

The permanent troop detachment at Kuala Kubu Bahru was withdrawn in mid-1952, but was reinstated not long afterwards to support the West Kents on Operation Sickle, while another troop at Klang was helping the Suffolks on Operation Hammer. These two operations were comprehensive assaults on the terrorists' food supplies, during which all surplus food in distribution centres in the two areas was withdrawn and the movement of all food was rigidly controlled. That meant that all food to lonely mines and estates had to be escorted, usually by the armoured car troops. The idea was that the CTs would be forced to approach the villages and mines more boldly to fetch food, or else surrender. It was rated a success, with an above average number of kills, captures and surrenders.

The Bentong road continued to have the highest priority for daily patrols, trying to ensure that vehicles travelling across

---

* Ibans, of head-hunting stock from Borneo, were amongst the great variety of people who served in the Security Forces during the Malayan Emergency.

the hills to the east coast were not molested and above all, that no food lorries were ambushed. In August 1952 a patrol was shot at by about six CTs armed with rifles and at least one bren, but by the end of 1952 the Squadron could record that there had been a clear period for some months.

Negri Sembilan, March–December 1952 *(C Squadron)*
The railway from Singapore to Kuala Lumpur and Ipoh was a principal terrorist target. In 1950 and early 1951 the civilian night mail trains between Singapore and Kuala Lumpur were so frequently derailed that a military train was substituted for them. It averaged less than twenty miles an hour, and usually ran two or more hours late. The advantage of more comfortable travel than by road had to be weighed against the risk of being marooned between two derailments or other blocks on the line.

Much of the East Coast line had to be relaid after the Japanese had taken away the rails for the Siam 'death' railway. That too was a CT target and in March 1952 C Squadron's troop at Rompin was called out when the daily train was blown up three miles from their camp. A large amount of HE was detonated under a bridge as the centre of the train crossed it. The CTs opened fire, but were driven off by the few troops and police on board in a twenty-minute engagement, though many of them were wounded and stunned. Pursuit of the CTs was impracticable, but 2nd Lieutenant CB Jacques's troop did sterling work recovering the dead and wounded; .

In the same month, 2nd Lieutenant GV Goodey's troop was engaged on a week's operation with 2nd/6th Gurkhas against sixty terrorists in the Jeram Padang area; for 48 hours the troop carried out practically non-stop road patrols in the area, pausing only to bring down fire in support of the Gurkhas. Although the bulk of the CTs broke up into small groups and managed to escape, one was killed and another captured.

Like B Squadron, C Squadron had opportunities from time to time for more sustained dismounted operations, when there were gaps between infantry battalion reliefs. Two and a half troops under Lieutenant ACP Pitcairn took over a company base at Durian Tipus, 'a small village on the Pahang border with little to commend it'. With never more than forty men they could not achieve as much as the normal hundred or more of an infantry company, but they patrolled actively, finding a number of CT camps of varying age. Ambushes lasting up to a week were unsuccessful, but on two occasions arms and ammunition caches were found.

By January 1953 C Squadron notes in the *Journal* could say:

> In the last few months the situation in Malaya has taken a decided turn for the better and Negri Sembilan is no exception. Nevertheless our patrols, convoys and escorts throughout the State have continued unabated. During the period we have had troops on detachment in a number of places including Glendale Estate, Kuala Klawang and Rompin. The last we gave up in December 1952, after two years' occupation, and our troops are now stationed at Jeram Padang nearby.

Federation Armoured Car Squadron

A major task for a specially augmented Training Wing came in September 1952 with the formation of an embryo Federation Armoured Corps. Previously all the local units had been trained as infantry, but now it was decided to raise an armoured car squadron as well. The Regiment seconded the key staff for the new unit, including the Squadron Leader designate (Captain AW Gage), Squadron Sergeant Major (Sergeant JC Thomas) and Squadron Quartermaster Sergeant (Sergeant J Hipkiss). The soldiers came from the Malay Regiment and the Malay Signals Regiment and, as would be the case in most armies, the parent units often seized the opportunity to dispose of their least desirable members. Colonel JRL Howard recalled: 'We were allocated no interpreters at first and, with the arrogance of youth, thought we could cope without until the first day in Kongkoi (very much bandit country) with fifty assault troopers with whom I had no communication!' The Training Wing instructors, drawn from the best NCOs in the Regiment, performed wonders and by 1 October the Squadron was operational, six weeks after being formed. (Two of those weeks were spent at the Regiment's jungle training area at Kongkoi.) On 1 November they began taking over from A Squadron responsibility for the north-west corner of Johore.

It was with some pride that the Regiment watched the new Squadron go into action and the close connection led to an affiliation in 1953 with The Federation of Malaya Armoured

Hong Kong and Malaya 1951–53

Car Regiment, which in 1960 became the 2nd Federation Reconnaissance Regiment of Malaysia.*

Johore, March–December 1952 (*A Squadron*)
When A Squadron moved to Johore Bahru, on 4 February 1952, a troop (2nd Lieutenant HJ Tyacke) was detached to Segamat in the north of Johore, where there was a great deal of CT activity. Throughout March the troop was involved in a big operation in support of infantry, taking to their feet on several occasions when the roads on one rubber estate gave way under their vehicles. At one point the troop had the cooks and pipers of 1st Cameronians under command for a patrol, during which two CTs were sighted running into swampy scrub, but could not

---

* In 1959 the Malaya Armoured Car Regiment was composed of 40 per cent each Malays and Chinese; the remainder were Indians and 'Malayans'.

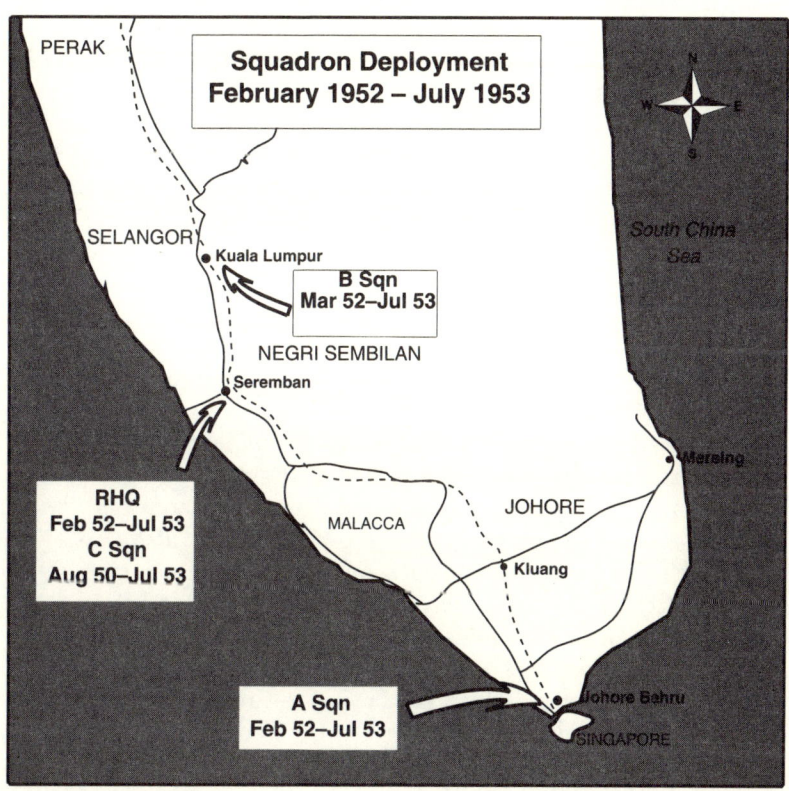

be tracked down. Their next greatest excitement came when rubber tappers reported 'a new bandit camp'; it turned out to be one just vacated by a Cameronians platoon.

That detachment ended in June and the troop was moved across to Jemaluang, making the detachment there up to three troops – nearly half the effective strength of the Squadron. But six weeks later another troop from Johore Bahru had to be found for Kluang, following the renewal of CT attacks on food lorries between Yong Peng and Labis. The troop escorted both north- and south-bound lorries, but the strain on their vehicles from the long daily sessions was relieved in October when a troop from C Squadron was added to the detachment. Yong Peng in particular was notorious at this stage for its support of CT activity. (The wholly Chinese village was reputed to have been settled many years before by immigrants making their way up the waterways from the west coast. Its existence was not discovered until the road was built some time later.)

The Kluang detachment was soon meeting other commitments, including VIP escorts and other patrols and operations laid on by 26 Gurkha Infantry Brigade. (Their Headquarters had moved to Kluang in September 1952, being replaced in Johore Bahru by 99 Gurkha Infantry Brigade.) The detachment lived in the lines of 2nd/6th Gurkha Rifles and, during their *Dushera* festivities, several of them were invited to the Battalion's *Kalahatri Nautch* and Headcutting Ceremony. Both were marathons of endurance, but well worth attending.

During this period the 2nd/6th suffered an unusual number of casualties from CT ambushes and 1st Fiji Infantry Regiment was stationed in Yong Peng itself in order to dominate the area. The Fijians had not been in Malaya long (the battalion had only been raised in 1951), but a number of their officers and other ranks had seen wartime service against the Japanese. They speedily made their presence felt and killed a number of terrorists. (They were little less terrifying on the rugger field where, playing in bare feet, they notched up cricket scores against most of their opponents including the Regiment.)

At the beginning of December 1952 2nd Lieutenant JCM Ansell's troop from C Squadron could return to Seremban as the newly formed A Squadron of the Federation Armoured

Corps had arrived in Kluang. Lieutenant EE Hunt's troop remained until Christmas to act as 'nursemaids' to the newcomers and to introduce them to the area.

Jemaluang was no less active than before with the detachment providing eight food convoy escorts a week and two or more daily road patrols, as well as helping the police and Federal Jungle Companies in night ambushes and foot patrols. During one of the latter, on 12 July 1952, a patrol under 2nd Lieutenant JF Alden, operating with the police encountered fifteen CTs leaving the village of Jemaluang with food and medicine. First contact was made by the police who wounded four terrorists as they fled. Following up, Sergeant F Harrison found one of the wounded lying in a ditch, fumbling with his clothes in a suspicious manner. As a major of Gurkhas had, that week, been killed by a wounded terrorist, Sergeant Harrison gave him the *coup de grâce*. A large quantity of food and medicine was recovered and not long after that contact the village was 'resettled' behind a more easily defended perimeter. There was then much less CT activity in and around the village.

In early September the armoured car at the rear of a food convoy on the Kluang road received a burst of fire at the driver's visor, one bullet going in through the open slit. The driver, Trooper J Hull, with great presence of mind pulled the armoured car across the road and halted pointing directly at the ambush position, saving the gun having to be traversed before it could be fired. Those CTs got away unhurt, but a week later there was a successful encounter. A police informer said that three terrorists would be meeting him on 11 September, between 8 and 9 am, at a point on the Kluang road. In the small hours a patrol under 2nd Lieutenant DA Newby laid an ambush at the rendezvous. At 9.05 the informer passed and said that the terrorists were coming in ten minutes; fifteen minutes later he returned and said that they were five minutes behind him. At 9.30 two armed CTs walked right into the ambush position and one was killed. Although the other was wounded in the leg he managed to get away despite the patrol's careful search.

The Commanding Officer subsequently received a congratulatory message from the High Commissioner which included: 'It is not often that the Regiment gets such a chance and I am glad that you did not fail to make the most of it'. A Squadron notes recorded: 'With more information of this sort coming in and the growing confidence of the villagers of Jemaluang, we should soon be able to chalk up a few more successes in that area'.

From Johore Bahru itself, where there was usually no more than a sabre troop and the scout car troop, a full day convoy escort had to be undertaken four times a month, as well as road patrols. The convoy took food to a large number of estates and 'the welcome the Squadron receives from the managers has to be seen to be believed – the pineapple estates are particularly popular'.

VIP Escorts

Sir Henry Gurney had been killed in 1951 when his car had been ambushed after going ahead of the police escort. From then on most, if not all, VIP escorts became the responsibility of the two armoured car regiments. The task was one with an inevitably high profile.

The most important single escort was undertaken in separate stages by B and C Squadrons for the four-day visit of the Duchess of Kent with her son, the young Duke of Kent, in October 1952. For the journey from Malacca airfield to Seremban via Tampin C Squadron were lucky, the weather was fine and everything went smoothly. B Squadron, on the other hand, who took over the escort for the journey to Kuala Lumpur, had to endure torrential rain for more than twenty-four hours of their leg, as well as a change of plan while they were on the road. On the return trip the rain stopped, the sky cleared – and two RAF Hornets providing air cover 'made up for what they had missed by nearly knocking our aerials off'.

Looking after the High Commissioner in his frequent travels throughout the country was a particular challenge. B Squadron, based in Kuala Lumpur from March 1952, found many of General Templer's escorts, which would consist of not less than a warning vehicle, a close escort and a tactical follow-up party. An armoured car was converted for the General's personal use and his armoured Humber saloon was often driven

Hong Kong and Malaya 1951–53

by Sergeant A Clegg of B Squadron. There had always to be guaranteed radio contact from the escort to its base and thence by telephone to Kuala Lumpur and Singapore. That was no easy task with high frequency wirelesses.

On one occasion:

> ... we escorted General and Lady Templer to the North-West corner of Selangor. Once again two troops were needed, commanded by Lieutenant Dodds and 2nd Lieutenant Gregory. Mr Gregory had to transfer his entire troop to Land Rovers and Jeeps in order to compete with the country road. It was a dusty and bumpy journey, but as usual made entertaining by the High Commissioner's remarks and observations.

En route a Chinese bus struck one of the vehicles, knocking it off the road (and taking away the side of the bus). An hour or more was spent waiting for a recovery vehicle and, bearing in mind General Templer's notoriously short temper, an outburst was expected. Not a bit of it; the hold up was accepted with complete equanimity – and the Templers shared in the tasting of some locally bought durian fruit.

Apart from protection against ambush while travelling, it was also the escort's job to protect the VIPs at any stops en route. There were no terrorist attacks on any Regimental escort during the three years in Malaya and it was also a matter of Regimental pride that men and vehicles should be immaculate in their turn-out. (That tended to contrast sharply with the appearance of those on jungle patrols, particularly after they had been out for a few days.)

B Squadron also provided the guard and staff on the special train which the High Commissioner used for two of his tours of Malaya. The first was from Kuala Lumpur to Singapore, on the line which the CTs had been trying unsuccessfully to block since 1949. The second was from Kuala Lipis to Kota Bahru over the new stretch of the East Coast railway. About forty men were needed, with Major ERMcM Wright as OC Train and Captain RJ Dodds the Escort Commander. They lived on the train for over a week on each occasion, much enjoying the fine fare provided by Malayan Railways – payment for which the Squadron somehow manage to evade.

Great emphasis was placed on keeping secret all VIP movement but on one occasion, when the High Commissioner was due to visit Mersing, there was known to have been a leak. A decoy staff car with an A Squadron subaltern, bedecked with brass hat, travelled with its own escort a short distance in front of the escort proper with the General in his armoured car. The subaltern, 2nd Lieutenant DWT Brough, was on the point of leaving for the United Kingdom on completion of his National Service: 'The glamour of wearing the brass hat was much reduced by the fact that it was so large, not only covering my ears, but almost my nose as well!' More run-of-the-mill escorts, varying from one or two scout cars to a full troop, were provided by all three Squadrons on almost a daily basis.

The Last Six Months
Christmas 1952 was the first in Malaya when most of the Regiment could be withdrawn from operations and could celebrate in peace. Even so, in Seremban the peace was shattered on Christmas Eve when an Auster aircraft taking off from the airstrip at Paroi Camp failed to leave the ground and crashed into the Sergeants' Mess lavatory. There were some who claimed that this was further proof of the Warrant Officers' and Sergeants' sins, because on Easter Day earlier that year a freak storm had hit Paroi and demolished most of their Mess, with several other buildings. (The damage in both cases was easily mended and the buildings went up again almost as quickly as they went down.)

Shortly after Christmas a visitor to the Regiment provided a fascinating link with the past when the Earl of Drogheda went to see B Squadron during a visit to the Far East. The Earl's ancestor raised the 18th Light Dragoons in 1759, and was their Colonel for sixty-six years. He planted trees in his park at Moore Abbey, Kildare to represent the two original squadrons as they stood on their first parade. Most of the trees were still standing when a detachment of the 18th Hussars marched through the area in 1881 and the Earl told B Squadron that many were still there in 1953.

But operations continued in 1953 and on 21 January an important terrorist, a member of the local Communist committee, surrendered to the A Squadron detachment at Jemaluang. He was starving, welcome proof that food convoys in the area over the previous two and half years had not been in vain. A fortnight later A Squadron wounded another CT in an ambush on the outskirts of Jemaluang village. Yet terrorist contacts were becoming increasingly scarce:

> The main North–South road running up the centre of the peninsula was practically closed by terrorist activity in 1950, 1951 and 1952 and civilian traffic took the slower coast road through Malacca which crossed two ferries. Some military vehicles still used the centre road, but these had to be accompanied by an escort. In 1953 the centre road was graded as a safe road for single vehicles, and is now used freely by lorries, buses and private traffic. (Major MWH Bell, the Second-in-Command, writing in the *Journal* on 'Malaya in Retrospect')

'Hearts and Minds'
The Regiment was frequently involved with the often distressing relocation of people and their belongings to New Villages. (Once established, however, the villagers appreciated the great improvement in their living conditions. Such benefits as house and land ownership, piped water, clinics, schools and social amenities all contributed to a more attractive life.) Initially, New Villages remained potential sources of supply and information to the enemy, despite being wired in and guarded by Malay police or Home Guard.

But there was remarkable success from anti-terrorist questionnaires. For these operations a village would be surrounded and the people confined to their homes. Each head of household was then given a questionnaire about terrorist activities in the area, to complete in private and place in a sealed box. Members of Village councils were taken with the boxes direct to the High Commissioner himself, to see him opening them. One such council was from Jemaluang and Lieutenant EE Hunt, the detachment commander, went with the village elders to a Singapore airfield and from there to Kuala Lumpur and Government House. For people who had seldom been further afield than nearby Mersing it was an awesome experience; coming face to face with General Templer was almost too much, though the interpreter probably spared them the more colourful elements of his conversational style.

As roads became safer and the terrorists were driven deeper into the jungle, the emphasis in Malaya gradually turned from

History of The 13th/18th Royal Hussars (Q.M.O.)

direct action against the terrorists to winning over the civilian population to the side of the Government. On the one hand this took the form of impressing the civilians by displays of fire power, parades and such events as the searchlight tattoo held at Seremban in November 1952. On the other, it tried to establish greater contact between civilians and Security Forces through sport and social gatherings, band concerts and the like. The Regiment became involved in all these activities (the Band had rejoined in April 1952) and, as ever, the natural friendliness of the British soldier paid dividends. Squadrons adopted one or two villages and soldiers spent quite a lot of time in them, and villagers made several visits to Regimental camps.

Death of the Colonel-in-Chief

In March 1953 HM Queen Mary died. She had been Colonel-in-Chief since the amalgamation in 1922 and before that Colonel-in-Chief of the 18th Hussars since 1914. She was first linked to the 18th in 1903 when King Edward VII approved their designation of 'Princess of Wales's'. She showed close personal interest in 'my Regiment of Hussars' throughout nearly fifty years.* Major General CH Miller, who had succeeded Brigadier Lumley as Colonel in April 1952, represented the Regiment as a pall bearer at her funeral.† The Regiment also provided a detachment of three officers and eighteen other ranks in the funeral procession. Led by Lieutenant Colonel Sir Delaval Cotter, with Majors JM Howson and DHE Coker, they marched immediately behind the official mourners, heading the parties from Queen Mary's other Regiments.

---

* She was reported to have been most displeased when the Regiment passed through Aldershot in 1947 without informing her that they were in England. The barracks, indeed a number of the soldiers themselves, were not thought to be fit for the Royal visit which would probably have been demanded.

† Major General Miller had joined the 18th Hussars just after the start of the Second World War. He commanded the 13th/18th from 1936 to 1939 and in the Second World War became Major General Administration of 18 and 15 Army Groups under General Alexander. He also served as Chief of Staff to the Duke of Gloucester when HRH was Governor General of Australia. His *History* of the Regiment from 1922 to 1947 was published in 1949.

Hong Kong and Malaya 1951-53

Coronation Celebrations
Not long afterwards, the Coronation of Queen Mary's granddaughter, HM Queen Elizabeth II took place. As well as providing a representative detachment in London under Captain JHW Marr, the Regiment contributed to the various ceremonies throughout southern Malaya from its greatly dispersed detachments, although anti-terrorist operations had to suffer as little interruption as possible. In Kuala Lumpur, where the most important parade was held, the Regimental Sergeant Major, WO1 HR Parnaby, was the Parade Sergeant Major and a small detachment from B Squadron took part, resplendent in the new No 3 Dress (tropical white equivalent of blue No 1 Dress). From C Squadron another small detachment paraded at Malacca, while in Seremban the Band and both a mounted and a dismounted party from C and HQ Squadrons took part. Further south, A Squadron paraded at Johore Bahru and even the detachment at Jemaluang was represented at a ceremony on the small *padang* at Mersing, with the local Gurkha battalion and the police.

Observance of Balaklava Day
In 1950 most of the Regiment was still based on Kluang and the Sergeants' Mess *Journal* Notes could record that 'The usual Balaklava celebrations were held . . . ', including a Ball which was 'a great success; the local population were full of praise for the efforts made for their entertainment'. In subsequent years arrangements were often made with neighbouring units to take over duties so that there could be a day's holiday for the detachment concerned. (In return they would take over on similar occasions such as the Gurkha festival of *Dushera*.) In 1951, for example, the local brigade commander allowed the 3rd Malay Regiment to take over the daily convoy for two days. That left A Squadron's Jemaluang garrison free – up to a point; they still had to keep the stand-by troop at readiness. 'Reveille was sounded in the usual manner, but instead of Bandmaster Geggie and the Band, Craftsman Barnes REME and his musicians performed. A certain amount of brass was in evidence and a lot of wind . . . Privates Trott and Ellis ACC provided a first class dinner which was followed later by an inter-troop football competition on the Mersing *padang*. . . .'.

History of The 13th/18th Royal Hussars (Q.M.O.)

For C Squadron the day 'was remarkable for the fact that for the first time in fifteen months the Squadron was able to get together as a whole'. B Squadron were in Hong Kong at the time and, without operational commitments, were able to have a very full day together, including a Balaklava Dinner at which the Band of 1st Wiltshire played.

Similar arrangements were made in 1952 by which time B Squadron was in Kuala Lumpur where:

> Reveille Tea was taken round by the Sergeants to the tune of the Regimental March. The music was put over on the new 20-speaker radio which runs round the tent lines using the gramophone record made by the Band [during their time in England].

Meanwhile, in October 1952 in Paris, Major JM Howson was representing the Regiment at an Old Comrades Reunion of the 4ème Chasseurs d'Afrique. Since 1854 there had been a close liaison between the 4th Chasseurs and the 13th Light Dragoons (and its successor Regiment). When the remnants of the Light Brigade were trying to reform after the Charge, the fate of the party seemed sealed, their horses were tired out and they had lost much of their cohesion. The Chasseurs, who were recent arrivals from Algeria, saw their desperate straits and, without waiting for orders, attacked the Russian batteries which were harassing the flank of the Light Brigade. In a brilliant charge they overran the infantry outposts which forced the Russian guns to limber up and retire with their escort of two battalions. The Chasseurs' gallant action was largely instrumental in helping the Light Brigade survivors to effect a successful withdrawal. Major Howson gave an account of the Reunion:

> The parade started forming up on the Champs Elysées at 6pm . . . there were some 1,000 old comrades from both the Spahis (who were also celebrating the Day) as well as from all twelve regiments of the Chasseurs . . . as well as serving soldiers from both the Chasseurs and the Spahis, the latter looking very 'Beau Geste' in their long sand coloured cloaks and carrying long sabres. . . . The French marching pace is both considerably shorter and faster than ours, and the march up the incline towards the Arc de Triomphe at light infantry speed was both remarkably difficult and tiring. Fortunately, stationed as I was almost immediately behind the Band, keeping in step presented no great problem. . . . at the Arc de Triomphe the parade fell in around the tomb of the Unknown Warrior. At the head of the

Hong Kong and Malaya 1951–53

Stone there is a large bronze bowl in which burns a perpetual flame. On our arrival this flame was only about six inches high. The Colonel Commandant of the 4ème Chasseurs, a trooper of the same Regiment and I were placed opposite the bowl . . . We were then handed a large bronze sword and given some rapid (and to one of us anyway, completely unintelligible) instructions. Before the desperate feeling of mental paralysis had cleared, the trumpeters sounded the Last Post. Colonel de Vitrac and the soldier then guided the sword into a key-way within the bowl of the flame. The whole bowl was given a slight turn which caused the flame to spring into renewed brilliance, making a most effective and dramatic scene. The Band then played both National Anthems and finally, as a most pleasant compliment, broke into the Regimental Quick March 'Balaklava'. . . we dispersed to reassemble for Dinner . . .

What took the gilt off the gingerbread was the intimation, which I received shortly before dinner, that I would be required to make a speech. . . . At length emboldened by Dutch courage, I got to my feet and in the most deplorable French apologised for the 'wounds which I was about to inflict upon the French language'. This only too obvious statement of fact turned an extremely friendly audience into an actively helpful one . . . having drunk toasts to France and to the Chasseurs, I sat down, feeling that on that day anyway I had earned the Queen's Shilling. There followed a most unexpected turn. An NCO rose to his feet saying 'Now for the Cavalry Charge for the Major of the English Hussars'. The whole room thereupon started beating time on the tables; at first at the normal speed of a horse's walk. On the command 'Trot', the tempo of the beating was quickened to the appropriate speed; leading through the Canter to the Charge, when, coupled with the usual vocal encouragement, the rhythm reached its climax. The noise was astonishing, with the wine glasses leaving the table a good six inches at each stride. . .

Sport and Recreation

Sport at Regimental level inevitably took a back seat during the period in Malaya, despite strenuous attempts by Lieutenant Colonel Cordy-Simpson to persuade squadron leaders that cricketers should be available for matches. Yet a great deal of sport was played at squadron and troop level including even rugby football which, despite the climate, was a popular game. There were inter-squadron competitions in association football, cricket, athletics and boxing. Some ingenuity was needed to ensure adequate representation, as for example when a patrol from Kluang to Seremban was composed largely of hockey players. Much to their credit, however, a Regimental soccer team (based largely on an excellent C Squadron team) reached the Malayan Final of of the Far East Land Forces Cup and in 1953 won the the Far East Land Forces Cup itself.

A number of individuals were also in the State teams of their respective squadrons' areas, in football, rugby, cricket and athletics. In athletics, however, the arrival of the Fijians and units from West Africa meant that competitors of quite a different class appeared on the scene. Three members of the Regiment performed at Malaya national level (both civilian and military): Trooper J Hird in soccer and 2nd Lieutenants AA Gregory and DG Mee in cricket. Dinghy sailing could be enjoyed from both Port Dickson and Singapore and the Commanding Officer with 2nd Lieutenant JCM Ansell won every cup at Port Dickson. They even managed second place in an unfamiliar boat in the Far East Regatta held at Singapore. Polo was being played again in Singapore and Kuala Lumpur, but it was possible for only one or two people to take occasional advantage of it and turn out for an amateurish chukker or two.

Local Leave

Leave entitlement during the tour was mostly accumulated for return to the United Kingdom, but some local leave was taken and the opportunity was sometimes seized to send a complete troop on a short break to Singapore – to coincide, for example, with attendance at one of the Christian Leadership courses run by the Chaplain's Department. (The latter had to compete during daylight hours with students who had been making the most of their evenings sampling Singapore's nightlife.)

The travel restrictions meant that leave in Malaya, apart from the fleshpots of Singapore, was usually not easy though some got to the island of Penang and Lieutenant JP Paige, a keen naturalist, enjoyed himself hugely in the King George V National Park in the north of the country. A number of individual expeditions were made to areas as yet unexploited by the tourist industry, including Australia, Borneo, Ceylon, Japan and Tahiti.

Hong Kong and Malaya 1951–53

Often no less enjoyable were exchanges, both official and unofficial, with other services and nations. During the war in Korea and in view of the plans for the Regiment to be equipped with tanks, Major ERMcM Wright went on attachment there to the 8th Hussars and later Lieutenant JS Mangles got himself a spell with the 5th Inniskilling Dragoon Guards and Major KR Foster sailed in Korean waters with a Royal Navy frigate. A French officer stayed with the Regiment in exchange for Major WG Denney's attachment in Indo China. Closer to home, Sergeant A Evans and four troopers went for a cruise in Malayan waters with a Royal Naval frigate, as did Lieutenant EE Hunt with the minesweeper flotilla. (This sort of hospitality was often returned, when the visitors would be subjected if possible to a 'jungle bash'.)

Retrospect on the Campaign

In July 1953 operational commitments were handed over to the 11th Hussars. The Regiment's primary task since July 1950 had been on the roads where over 4,000 food convoys were escorted and over 400 VIP escorts provided without loss of life, food or vehicles. The sabre troops had covered 3.5 million 'vehicle miles' and been involved in 146 'incidents'. The Regiment had also seized what opportunities it could for aggressive patrolling on foot and killed four Communist terrorists, wounded and captured three and wounded fourteen more. Those figures do not, of course, bear comparison with the achievements of the infantry battalions. During roughly the same period 1st Suffolk, the most successful British battalion, accounted for 195 CTs. (At the end of the Emergency it was calculated that, on average, it took 1,000 patrol hours to effect a capture and 1,600 for a kill.) The Regiment's own casualties were six dead: a lance corporal and trooper killed by enemy fire, an officer by our own fire and an officer and two troopers in accidents during operations. One trooper was seriously wounded and a corporal and seven troopers were slightly wounded.

> In considering the effect on the Regiment of three years in Malaya, it must be admitted that the employment of armoured cars in that theatre is the worst possible training for operations in Europe or the desert. Map reading is unnecessary except when

moving on foot through the jungle because there are few roads, and these are so well marked with milestones that Army and police alike have developed the habit of describing a spot as the '– th mile, So-and-so Road'. There has been no occasion to practise the use of field glasses owing to the general absence of distant prospects, and although wireless communication has been maintained over surprising distances, there has been no chance of using a normal squadron net of thirty-odd stations. Squadrons have not operated as squadrons, and RHQ has had no chance to become mobile: nor has it been possible to practise the supply echelons in their normal role. Against this, all officers and senior NCOs have gained a much wider knowledge of administration than is usually considered necessary and, because troops have had to live and operate very much on their own, junior leaders have gained self-confidence, initiative and self-reliance. Lastly, the very fact of having fought against a live, if not very formidable, enemy should be of benefit to all ranks in the early stages of a future war...

Perhaps the most notable changes in the country at large have been in the attitude of the civilian population. In 1950 and 1951 troops motoring through villages, especially in Johore, received hostile looks from the Chinese population and no co-operation. Nowhere was this more noticeable than in Jemaluang, yet, when the A Squadron detachment left the village, there was a farewell ceremony, presents were exchanged and much good will was displayed on both sides. (Major MWH Bell in the *Journal*)

It was perhaps not unexpected that a presentation (a Malayan *kris*) should be made to A Squadron by the predominantly Malay town of Mersing. What was remarkable was the gifts of a cigarette box and an embroidered Chinese good luck banner from the 'grateful people of Jemaluang' to the 'Champions of the People'. A Squadron was also given a miniature *parang* by the Government Workers Union, Mersing and a *kukri* from 99 Gurkha Infantry Brigade. C Squadron received a silver cup from the village of Ulu Beranang.

Discipline
Since even the best of soldiers are not saints, detachments had to waste escort hours on ferrying offenders to and from formal hearings of anything more than the most trivial offence – and possibly losing the services of potentially good soldiers. Ways round were found, bearing in mind that this

7. Coronation Parade in Kuala Lumpur –
B Sqn contingent (Lt Helyar) in the new No 3 dress.

Malay 1953

8. Farewell party from the villagers of Jemaluang
for the A Squadron detachment.

Ubiquitous scout cars

9. 1954: RHQ Daimler ('dingo') on wintry exercise in Germany with the IO (Lt Hargrove).

10. 1958: B Squadron Ferret crossing a wadi in Arabia.

11. 1959: A Squadron Ferret leaving a ferry in Malaya.

was active service. Those whose offence would have merited a spell in the cells might be asked, escort and witnesses having been marched out, whether they might prefer to donate an appropriate sum to the Squadron Private Account (a welfare fund used for the squadron as a whole). They invariably would. One troop was sited, miles from anywhere, by an attractive stream; the troop leader (Lieutenant BJW Cobb) is reputed to have invited his minor offenders to walk blindfolded along an overhanging branch, until they fell into the stream. Their sins were then regarded as purged.

Officially therefore, there was scarcely any crime. Whether such a simple, sensible and popular approach would be feasible in these days of intensive media scrutiny is another matter.

Farewells

The Regiment had made many friends over the past three years and there was something more than the customary farewells on their departure. In each of the squadron areas the various detachments, such as Jemaluang, were sped on their way in a most hospitable manner.

> We began to realise, from the spontaneous acts of local civilians and others, how much our work had been appreciated and that, though often routine and tedious, it had not gone unnoticed.

After a handover to the 11th Hussars in July 1953, spread over a week in order to avoid any interruption to convoys and escorts, A and C Squadrons held farewell parades for their respective brigade commanders. B Squadron:

> ... left Kuala Lumpur by the night train and our tremendous send-off was in the nature of a farewell for the Regiment since we were its only representatives stationed in Kuala Lumpur. General and Lady Templer headed the list of well-wishers, who included the British Adviser, the Chief of Police, the Chief of Staff and the whole of 18 Brigade staff.

The Regiment was concentrated for a week at Selarang Barracks, Singapore, the first time that they had been together as a whole, even briefly, since 1950. There they held a ceremonial parade for the Commander-in-Chief, Far East Land Forces, General Sir Charles Keightley, who thanked the Regiment for their hard work in the campaign against Communist terrorists.

Chapter Four

Wolfenbüttel and Neumünster, 1953–58

Return to Europe
On 23 July 1953 the Regiment boarded the *Empire Trooper* in Singapore and 'after a comfortable and uneventful voyage reached Southampton on 26 August', having been overseas for five and a half years. Thirty-three days was well over the time which the newer troopships were taking for the journey; the *Empire Trooper*'s engines were not operating to best advantage and in heavy seas she gave the distinct impression of going backwards.*

Another feature of the days of troopships was that a large amount of home leave was usually accumulated, before it was practicable for people to be sent back to the United Kingdom. Major units therefore had to stage through transit camps in England on the way to Germany, or vice versa, to allow for a mass exodus on embarkation or disembarkation leave plus any accumulated leave. Inevitably the barracks were of lower standard than those in permanent use and Quorn, an ex-prisoner of war camp between Loughborough and Leicester was a particularly bad example. Little had been done to it since it housed German prisoners of war.

> The weeds, before the Advance Party arrived, had progressed so well that the long, low, asbestos sheeting huts were almost obscured. Heating ... was provided by two small coke-burning stoves. This would have been tolerable if there had been sufficient fuel, but the ration was about two buckets a day. The weather was very cold in October ....

Just to demonstrate that the Regiment was back in the Home Country of the 1950s, there was a strike of petrol tanker

---
* It compared favourably, of course, with sail power in the days before the Suez Canal was built. In 1840 the 13th Light Dragoons embarked at Madras in February and did not reach Gravesend until June – after a tour in India of twenty- one years and three months.

drivers in London in October and a party of two officers and fifty men had to rush to London to help. Much to their regret, after making three deliveries:

> ... the threat of the Regiment's intervention was enough to bring the strike to an end almost at once. Fifty-two disappointed Lilywhites returned to Quorn, all hopes of driving petrol tankers, or even double-decker buses, through London dashed.

On 4 November the Colonel, Major General Miller, inspected the Regiment and attended a memorial service for those who had lost their lives while serving. Shortly afterwards Lieutenant Colonel JR Cordy-Simpson completed his tour in command and handed over to Lieutenant Colonel Sir Delaval Cotter, Bt.

Germany in 1953

The onward journey to Germany was of a piece with the rest of the transit period. The special train left Quorn station on 25 November: 'During the long journey to Harwich the train broke in two on several occasions, and we became used to frequent stops, followed by the most shattering jolts as the engine came back to find us. We arrived in Harwich to find the the ship unable to sail due to fog. . . . We drew into Wolfenbüttel station in the early dawn of 27 November.'

Since the Regiment was last there, in 1947, conditions in West Germany had improved considerably, but there was still considerable unemployment which had been aggravated by the large numbers of refugees. In 1949 the Federal Republic of Germany and the German Democratic Republic (DDR) had established the division between West and East and by 1950 over 16 per cent of the population came from the 'lost territories' and another 3 per cent from the DDR. As well as the unemployed and refugees there were over one and half million war-disabled. This could have been the scenario for political extremism, but a combination of factors contributed instead to the beginnings of the German 'Economic Miracle': the Western Allies had not exacted punitive reparations as they had after the First World War, instead Germany had been a major beneficiary of the Marshall Aid programme; the rate of unemployment was to remain higher than in Britain until 1960 and this kept down wage demands; above all the German 'work ethic' motivated people at all levels. (It would have been hard then to believe that, thirty years later, when the Regiment was in Germany for the last time before amalgamation, the German Economics minister would produce a report prescribing what must be done to overcome an international image of the country as work-shy and over-regulated. In 1993 the Chancellor, Helmut Kohl, described Germany as having 'the oldest students, the youngest pensioners and the most idle machines'.)

The wartime ally against Germany was now the potential enemy and 1949 also saw the signing of the North Atlantic Treaty between the United States, Canada and ten European countries. Over the next forty years this military alliance against the Russian threat was to dominate Britain's defence policy, and often determine how the Regiment itself was employed. When the Russian empire disintegrated the rush to reduce defence spending was to lead to another amalgamation.

Second Tour at Wolfenbüttel

In Wolfenbüttel the Regiment replaced the Life Guards as the armoured car regiment of 11 Armoured Division. That meant a return to Northampton Barracks, close to the boundary between the British and Russian occupation zones. A largely amicable handover had a mildly fraught moment in the closing stages when the Quartermaster of the Life Guards invited Major HSR Watson, commanding the advance party, to consider buying 'their' Officers' Mess table. Major Watson said that it would have been an interesting possibility had it not been that the 13th/18th had left the same table behind, when last in Northampton Barracks in 1947.

By 1953 relations with Russia had worsened considerably. Operational plans assumed that a Russian attack would mean a withdrawal to the Rhine, before reinforcements could be brought in for any counter-offensive. The Regiment's operational role was initially to act as the right half of 1 (BR) Corps screen in the planned withdrawal, then to revert to being under command of 11 Armoured Division. 1st The Royal Dragoons covered the left flank. The move back was over largely unmarked minor roads and tracks from the borders with East Germany to the Rhine. The maps then being used were indifferent and route finding was a challenge in itself. The Regimental centre line went via Hildesheim, across the river

Wolfenbüttel and Neumünster 1953-58

Weser at Holzminden, through the Eggegebirge via Höxter and Bad Driburg. The route remained surprisingly rural as far as Wuppertal; there the scenery changed dramatically and the overhead urban railway dominated the road. The Regiment finally crossed the Rhine by the Neuss bridge, where wireless contact had to be made with Headquarters 11 Armoured Division in the teeth of very bad interference from local power lines and the like. Once in the Ruhr:

> ... crew commanders soon realised that a great deal of skill plus a modicum of luck and the ability to read signposts was necessary if they were to follow the correct route ... this part of the country is virtually a continuous built up area and is represented on the map by a large black smudge with a few major roads winding through it.

The Regiment was still 'on active service' and probably the most 'active' aspect was patrolling the inter-zonal border, checking on any incursions from the Eastern Zone and gathering information and intelligence on Russian and East German forces stationed the other side of the border. These patrols were normally at troop strength and were usually accompanied by an officer of the British Frontier Service. Although mostly without incident there was occasional confrontation with the East Germans who liked to move the boundary markers westward.

Amongst the handings- and takings-over were several changes in Regimental appointments as well as that of Commanding Officer. For the first time since 1942 there was a new Quartermaster, Major JJ Reynolds. The outgoing Quartermaster, Major 'Busty' Sweeting, had served continuously with the Regiment since enlisting in 1926. As Regimental Quartermaster Sergeant from 1939 and as Quartermaster since 1942, he had been 'the stand-by of all the Commanding Officers under whom he had served'. The Second-in-Command, Major Rugge-Price, returned to the job he had last held in 1946 as the self-styled 'oldest rear link in the world'. There was also a new Adjutant and a new Regimental Sergeant Major and the squadrons had a number of changes. C Squadron noted that they had 'three Squadron Leaders – three Seconds-in-Command; only one Troop Leader remaining; two Squadron Sergeant Majors; four Squadron Clerks all in one year'.

History of The 13th/18th Royal Hussars (Q.M.O.)

Almost for the first time since last in Wolfenbüttel in 1947, the Regiment was complete with no detachments. But after working up to a high degree of expertise in the special conditions of Malaya, the requirements of more conventional soldiering had to be re-discovered in the demanding annual cycle of Rhine Army training, exercises and administration. It was made the more difficult, after the years of North African and tropical heat, to be subjected to a particularly cold winter. Two soldiers were brought back unconscious suffering from exposure after their vehicle broke down, though the other side of that coin was that a number of people were able to take up skiing for the first time in the nearby Harz mountains. Not everybody could make the adjustment from active service in and around the jungle and some young NCOs who had been outstanding in Malaya proved less reliable in the very different environment of Rhine Army. Some changes had to be made in the Corporals' Mess.

Sabre squadrons reverted to the normal establishment for an armoured car regiment, with two armoured cars and two scout cars in each reconnaissance troop, a heavy troop and a support troop. Regimental and squadron headquarters were equipped with command vehicles based on half-track chassis:

> Those who are not acquainted with this machine might realize its comforts by imagining a journey at 20 to 30 mph along cobbled roads in a boxed-in farmer's cart, with no springs, some two dozen tin cans banging about inside, and above the din Lance Corporal Sparkes [actual name] shouting into the microphone of the 52 Set in a heart-rending effort (usually successful) to get in touch with RHQ. It is usually about the fourth day that tempers reach breaking point.

At that stage in Regimental Headquarters Lieutenant EE Hunt, the Signals Officer, sometimes found himself being 'put under arrest' by a frustrated Commanding Officer – until the next *konditorei* came into view and tempers could be restored over coffee and sticky cakes. Sheer fatigue was a problem, as a future Commanding Officer, Lieutenant JCM Ansell, found when the far side of the Rhine had been reached on one exercise. After three days and nights without sleep, he was half awake in the passenger seat of a 3-tonner, filled with petrol. The driver, one of the Regiment's nine Trooper Smiths, nodded

Wolfenbüttel and Neumünster 1953-58

off while they waited at a level crossing and the vehicle inexplicably rolled forward into the path of a German train. They were carried some way down the line and Smith was seriously injured and had to be invalided out of the Army. (He made a good recovery.) Mr Ansell miraculously escaped with nothing more than a bruised back.

Headquarters Squadron, which had existed only on a skeleton basis since being reformed in 1951, had to grapple, not only with the strict centralised administrative standards demanded in BAOR, but with the requirements in the field to replenish the sabre squadrons at night, over considerable distances.

Royal Parade and Battle Royal

After a fine spring, the weather in the summer of 1954 was atrocious and a divisional exercise which should have taken place in August was first postponed and then cancelled; 'It had been so bad that the harvest had been seriously delayed, and it was clear that an armoured division motoring about the country would do it no good, and would not be fair to the farmers'. The weather had already played havoc in July with a visit to BAOR by HRH The Princess Margaret. B and C Squadrons, each with troops of A Squadron attached, took part in her inspection of 33 Armoured Brigade Group at Sennelager, followed by an impressive march past in vehicles of the complete Brigade Group. The parade was a great success although, 'Needless to say, it rained, not only on the day itself – so much that HRH was forced to turn back in her helicopter and to complete her journey by road – but all the rehearsals were wet too'. Amongst the Massed Bands for the occasion were the Regimental musicians; they thought that they 'probably produced more bubbles than music'.

What was left to be harvested was in by the time of Exercise Battle Royal in the autumn. Notable amongst the events of the next few years, these were Army manoeuvres which involved the several corps, British, Belgian and Dutch, of Northern Army Group. It was probably the last exercise to be held on such a scale, paid for as it was from German 'Support Funds'. It was reminiscent of the 1944-45 campaign in Northern Europe except that 'nuclears' had now to be taken into account. 11

History of The 13th/18th Royal Hussars (Q.M.O.)

Armoured Division, responsible for providing the umpires and for exercise administration, gave the Regiment a variety of jobs. The principal one was to man and control an Umpire 'Phantom' organisation, inspired by the work of Phantom regiments during the war. The task was to provide the Chief Umpire, Major General HE Pyman, with instant reports on the entire exercise area. Troop leaders, mounted in scout cars, reported by wireless direct to Regimental Headquarters on the activities of the formation headquarters which they were monitoring. Regimental Headquarters, sited next to Umpire Headquarters, was then able to provide information often thirty minutes ahead of reports making their way through the normal nets. The subalterns were then called in for late night debriefing in the 'Big Top', a huge marquee. At one session 2nd Lieutenant B Worthington received applause from the multi-starred national and international visitors, and a commendation from the CIGS, for his scathing critique when invited to comment on one divisional commander's conduct of the day's battle.

The other Battle Royal commitments were to provide atomic umpire teams and to run the Control HQ camp. The latter housed some 300 officers and 1,200 soldiers (including Women's Services) of all nationalities and services. On the final inspection of the site it was under water. The Divisional CRE, lately an instructor at the Staff College, was heard to say that, if a student at the Staff College had suggested that a squadron of an armoured car regiment would be a suitable unit to run a camp for 1,500 soldiers, ranging from a 'seven star' general to a woman private, in the middle of a field under water, he would not only have been sent down, but would probably have been invited to consult an alienist. In the event a drier site was found and a very successful camp was run for ten days.

> On the peak day of the exercise, we were housing or feeding one 'Seven Star' Marshal of France, two Field Marshals, and General Gruenther, the Supreme Allied Commander, Europe, in addition to the senior commanders from HQ Northern Army Group.

Crimean Centenaries

1954 was also the Centenary of the Battle of Balaklava. The Regiment celebrated its principal battle honour with a weekend of celebrations which included a ceremonial parade, sport, a

Wolfenbüttel and Neumünster 1953–58

fête and an all-ranks dance. The Parade, at which the salute was taken by the Colonel of the Regiment, Major General CH Miller, included a dismounted march past led by the Commanding Officer mounted on a grey and carrying the Balaklava Sword*. That was followed by a drive past of some seventy to eighty vehicles. The spectators included the Divisional Commander, Major General Pyman, and representatives of Belgian and United States units in the area as well as a number of German guests. The report in the *Wolfenbütteler Zeitung*, whose Editor was invited, shows that the opportunity was taken to enhance good relations with the neighbours.

> As the 13th/18th Royal Hussars celebrated one of the most important days of honour of their Regiment in the barracks, and did not make a military demonstration out of it, one can see what they take Balaklava Day to be – a family fête of the Regiment. As they did not only invite English guests but also Germans to this family fête, and as they showed such an affectionate hospitality to them all, we wish to say that we think this is a gesture of a thoroughly successful contribution to unite all honest Europeans in one great family. . . All the visitors were witnesses of a military occasion, which was not a demonstration of force, but of excellent military discipline.

Later in the day, the Band:

> . . . made an entirely new departure for a cavalry band by beating 'Retreat'. This was an impressive ceremony, excellently carried out – perhaps even those diehards who had opposed it will now be willing to see it become part of 'traditional' ceremonial.

The Officers of the Light Brigade's successors held a Balaklava Ball in London attended by HM The Queen and at that year's Rhine Army Horse Show the Light Brigade Regiments managed to mount a full dress musical ride. The Regiment's contingent was Lieutenant MC Lloyd and three soldiers.

The following year 'The Committee of the Centenary of the Cavalry of the Crimea' invited attendance at 'the Ceremony of the Flame, a Banquet and a large Military Mass in Paris'. The Adjutant, Captain JRL Howard, and 2nd Lieutenant DJStJ Loftus on 8 October found themselves:

> . . . being organised in rows with two hundred old French

---

* Reputed to have been carried at The Charge of The Light Brigade.

History of The 13th/18th Royal Hussars (Q.M.O.)

> Comrades ready to march up the Champs Elysées . . . an American colonel appeared from nowhere to ask 'Might I march behind? I just can't resist a band'. Accompanied by a dashing Italian cavalry officer, heavily medalled, we set off wondering whether it was more tactful to be in step with the band or the generals all around us. We halted beneath the Arc de Triomphe, the evening sky a dark background to the bright colours of the Tricolor regimental banners, lit by the flickering flame which is kept burning in memory of those who have died for France. A voice hissed in my ear *'La Marche Balaklava'* and the band struck up our Regimental march.

At the Banquet:

> I noticed how remarkably similar to our own old comrades the guests looked. There was Colonel This of the 13th, sipping his wine, or old General That of the 18th adjusting his monocle, and only an occasional shrug of a very French shoulder betrayed a Cuirassier or a Spahi Algerien. . . . As we returned to our hotel, absorbing the wonderful atmosphere of Paris . . . a drawl passed in the darkness 'but dahling I'll swear they're Warwickshire Yeomanry'.

The Military Mass in the Madeleine the following day was 'a magnificent and a very moving service'; during the address specific mention was made of the comradeship of the 4ème Chasseurs d'Afrique and the 13th Light Dragoons and as the Mass continued it was interspersed with the trumpet calls of each of the French cavalry regiments played in echoing harmony from a balcony high in the domed roof.

Life in the British Army of the Rhine

From an early stage after post-war demobilisation, military activities in Rhine Army were conducted at a vigorous tempo. For the majority, the annual cycle began with winter largely devoted to individual training, although occasional exercises provided experience of operating in the rigorous conditions of the North German Plain. In the spring, troop and squadron training prepared for the major exercises of the year in the summer and autumn. Throughout the winter and spring Regimental and squadron headquarters were also turned out on two or three-day signals exercises (later termed 'command post exercises' [CPXs] as US terminology was increasingly adopted by NATO forces). Many exercises followed the routes

Wolfenbüttel and Neumünster 1953–58

expected to be followed by the Regiment in its operational role. Keeping in touch, between troops, squadrons, Regimental Headquarters and the higher formations, was obviously critical and the distances involved were well beyond the alleged capacity of the elderly 19 and 52 wireless sets still in use. Contact was maintained only by considerable skill – and the selection of specific positions, despite the poor security which that entailed.

The large training areas and gunnery ranges previously used by the German Army had been requisitioned, but while the Regiment was in armoured cars, a great deal of training could take place over the country generally, as could large scale manoeuvres like Battle Royal. The payment for any damage was borne by the Germans as an element of post-war reparations.

There were also a number of other benefits paid for from German reparations. Large numbers of German civilians augmented the staffing of offices, messes and workshops. Domestic servants were provided for officers' families and senior other ranks, and all ranks could obtain duty free drink, petrol and tobacco. Until a programme of building quarters began, families lived in requisitioned houses.

Ample facilities and the large number of major units meant that there was also a very full sports programme, both in team games and in a variety of other activities including winter sports, sailing and shooting. Wolfenbüttel, however, as a 'border' garrison, was often a long way from many of the venues and successful teams found themselves travelling considerable distances. However, local facilities were good (the *Stadtbad Wolfenbüttel* was used for Regimental swimming, and the Stadium for athletics) and the isolation from other units provided an incentive to obtain fixtures with German teams.

On 5 May 1955 came the ending of 'Occupied' status for West Germany. The Federal Republic regained its sovereignty and was admitted to NATO, for which it was to raise a force of 500,000. The main significance for the British Army was that BAOR ceased to be an 'Active Service' station. A progressive curtailment also began of the various benefits, such as domestic staff, for which the Germans had paid.

History of The 13th/18th Royal Hussars (Q.M.O.)

The *Journal* thought that the German population was more 'consistently friendly'. 'In fact their reaction now is more usually connected with our immediate behaviour than with what has happened in the past.' Relations with people in Wolfenbüttel had been distinctly chilly in 1953. This was partly as a hangover from the early days of the Occupation and partly because of an unfortunate incident, when the Life Guards had arrested and put into their Guardroom the Headmaster of a school near the barracks whose boys had persistently disobeyed orders to stay off the sports fields. As the earlier quotation from the local newspaper shows, attitudes had now changed considerably. Their new status also meant that German police were able to exercise direct authority over British troops and families. However, when the Adjutant, Captain JRL Howard, visited the Wolfenbüttel police chief in May 1955 to ask how he wished to implement the change in relationship, he responded: 'Let's leave it as it is – it seems to work rather well.' Close links were established with local families. Indeed there were a number of local marriages – and many more over the years ahead, during the Regiment's successive tours in different towns. By 1955 the number of families with the Regiment had risen to seventy.

Berlin Detachments

In 1946 the Regiment had had to provide a squadron in Berlin, to act as the mobile reserve of the British brigade 'in case of any insurrection amongst the population of the British sector'. With the onset of the Cold War, the Berlin Brigade, with their American and French counterparts, demonstrated the continuation of the Western Occupying Powers' rights, which continued after West Germany regained sovereignty. From time to time in the years ahead the Regiment therefore found itself again sending a squadron on detachment to Berlin, but now it was to relieve the permanent squadron so that they could complete annual range firing at Hohne. In June 1955 when A Squadron made the journey through Helmstedt and over the River Elbe, the vehicle party:

> . . . caused no small stir at the border posts. . . The AECs in particular could not have attracted more interest from the Russian guards if they had been atomic cannon.

Wolfenbüttel and Neumünster 1953-58

The Squadron stood in for 1st Independent Squadron Royal Tank Regiment for three enjoyable weeks in a barracks at Spandau, next to the prison where 'certain Nazis still languish'.

Fraternal Contact

> Appearing as suddenly as Cinderella's Fairy Godmother, Colonel Plummer, US Army, landed on the football pitch in his small personal aircraft having flown 200 miles from Bad Hersfeld. 'I couldn't get through on the 'phone . . . ', he explained.

The visit, one day in 1955, was to invite the Regiment to take part in an International Day being staged by the 3rd Battalion, 14th Armored Cavalry. It took the form of a tattoo in which French and Belgian armoured units also took part. Over a hundred members of the Regiment, including the Adjutant and Lieutenant Ansell, stayed as guests of the Americans for three days.

> We brought our own cooks, who were quickly seized by the Cook Sergeant and converted to the US way of life; dressed in American cooks' white clothing, with American badges of rank, they became, except for an occasional careless word in 'limey' indistinguishable from their hosts.

The Regimental band played between the demonstrations of each contingent: silent drill by the Americans 'with their nine inch arm swing very strange to our eyes', a French mass motor cycle display 'performed soberly to a whistle', the Belgians with tanks, jeeps and 'murderous unarmed combat'.

The Regiment's contribution was three minutes of foot drill in quick time, followed by eight motor cyclists in bright blue helmets, white shirts and dark blue breeches who gave a brisk musical ride, carrying lances with pennants flying. The drill squad returned in slow time and 'were given a tremendous reception by a crowd of over 2,000 who had never seen this type of drill before' and the performance was rounded off by the motor cyclists who 'burst onto the area at full throttle, through paper hoops, and into a wildly skidding figure of eight' before a series of individual performances culminating in the team going through the traditional flaming hoops. (The foot drill had benefited from the kindly attentions of Squadron Sergeant Major E Garbutt, shortly to depart for a tour at Mons Officer Cadet School.)

History of The 13th/18th Royal Hussars (Q.M.O.)

Then 'our tug of war team successfully pulled ten sturdy Americans, but were well beaten by the serious French who were not only vast but skilful'. Apparently they had been trounced the year before and admitted that this time they had drawn their team from their whole division.

> In the evening dancing, drinking and celebrating followed till the early hours – how well we were looked after! ... every American soldier put himself out to be a friend and host. One British and one American cook were seen after a splendid evening's entente feeling their way doggedly along the perimeter wall muttering 'there mush be a gate shomewhere'.

Sport in Wolfenbüttel

After their achievements in Malaya, much had been expected from the Regimental soccer team, but the loss of six players who finished their service meant that initial success in the 1953/54 Army Cup was not followed through. It was to be a number of years before there were any major successes. In sport generally, the best results at Wolfenbüttel were achieved by individuals, although the Tug-of-War team won both the Brigade and Divisional competitions.

A notable exception was in skiing, where the Regimental team, led by Lieutenant KC Maule, came second in the BAOR Championship in 1955. From amongst them Lieutenant Maule and 2nd Lieutenant WJ Whiteley were chosen for the BAOR team. Mr Maule was summoned to Norway the following October, to join the party training for the Olympic langlauf team; sadly for him, but fortunately for the Regiment, he was not selected. He therefore returned in time to prepare the Regimental team for the Brigade and BAOR championships. Despite blizzards and sub-zero temperatures, in which several of the competitors and officials suffered from frostbite, the Brigade shield was won by a handsome margin. That augured well for the Rhine Army meeting and first the langlauf and then the downhill and slalom teams were so well placed that, at the start of the twenty kilometre Patrol race the Regiment was leading overall. The team came sixth which was good enough to win the Championship.

Other BAOR selections in 1955 were 2nd Lieutenant M Holmes for tennis and 2nd Lieutenant GD Roynon for both

Wolfenbüttel and Neumünster 1953–58

cricket and squash. At fencing Captain EE Hunt won the BAOR sabre and epée competitions. Major CG Dorman captained the Army Team in the 1955 National Gliding Championship.

It was probably easier for the Army to keep horses in Germany than in any other station. There were ten 'elderly ex-German horses who are most useful in teaching young officers to ride' whose combined ages totalled 150 years, but they were succeeded by new young stock as well as some privately-owned mounts. Wolfenbüttel was too far away from where polo was being played, but show jumping and hunter trials provided plenty of challenge, while some individuals went out with local German *Hubertus* hunts, following a rider over prepared jumps. 2nd Lieutenant DJStJ Loftus on one occasion organised a return match, hosted by the Regiment, complete with Band, schnapps and a tea party to follow. His course was somewhat more severe than the German equivalent and a number of those who took part, hosts included, came off several times.

The Commanding Officer and Major Howson shared a three-year-old filly who had some success on the local race courses. (Major Howson managed to arrange, for at least one season, that the grass in the barracks was left to grow so that he could get a crop of hay from it, despite the distinctly unmilitary impression it created.)

The Schleswig Holstein Peninsula

In March 1956 the Regiment again relieved the King's Dragoon Guards, this time in Neumünster, Schleswig Holstein. The KDG had built up good relations with the town and that obviously contributed to the welcome received by the 13th/18th.

Initially the Regiment had a dual operational role as Corps Armoured Car Regiment of 1 (BR) Corps and as Armoured Car Regiment of Allied Land Forces (ALF) Schleswig Holstein. (The Corps commitment ended in August 1957, as part of a BAOR reorganisation.) Although for operational purposes the Regiment was detached from the rest of Rhine Army, wireless communications had to be maintained with HQ 1 (BR) Corps at Bielefeld. In the ALF Schleswig Holstein role they came under the Danish Brigade stationed at Rendsburg, further north on the Schleswig Holstein peninsula.

History of The 13th/18th Royal Hussars (Q.M.O.)

The Danish Brigade* was part of the force defending the left flank of NATO's Central Sector, running along the East/West German border where it met the Baltic at Lübeck. In the event of hostilities the Regiment would form the covering screen on the line Lübeck–Hamburg, with a defensive line on the Kiel Canal. Subsequent withdrawal would have involved crossing the Danish border into Jutland. This was the Regiment's first experience of operating with an allied Army and despite communication difficulties, which included wireless procedures as well as the language problem, the arrangement worked well. Continuous interference from the signal traffic of ships in the North Sea and the Baltic, and those on passage through the Kiel Canal, meant that keeping in touch by wireless was the most intractable problem.

Frequent exercises were held with the Danish Brigade, when the Royal Dragoons (based at Wesendorf) often figured as enemy. Other contacts with the Danes included such exchanges as an A Squadron composite troop with a platoon of a Danish infantry company. 'Many oaths of "friendship unto death" were made at a social evening held during the visit.'

The Schleswig Holstein Peninsula varies from fifty to seventy miles in width, but because of terrain and communication problems it was not an easy front to cover. Lieutenant Colonel AAK Rugge-Price, who took over from Lieutenant Colonel Cotter in November 1956, commented: 'the Regiment had to re-learn the rule that it is a cardinal sin to motor out of contact with your immediate superior'. All officers above the rank of Captain had seen service during the Second World War and tactical doctrine in Rhine Army was inevitably based on that experience. The nuclear threat was now added, but that had little effect on basic tactical doctrine other than to underline the importance of rapid concentration and deployment of forces in order to avoid offering nuclear targets to the enemy. The requirement for information about enemy dispositions was similarly enhanced and to further this the armoured car regiments later became the first to incorporate helicopters into their establishment.

---

* Denmark's interest in the area was of long standing; they had exercised sovereignty over the two duchies of Schleswig and Holstein from the sixteenth century, until invaded by Prussia and Austria in 1864.

Wolfenbüttel and Neumünster 1953–58

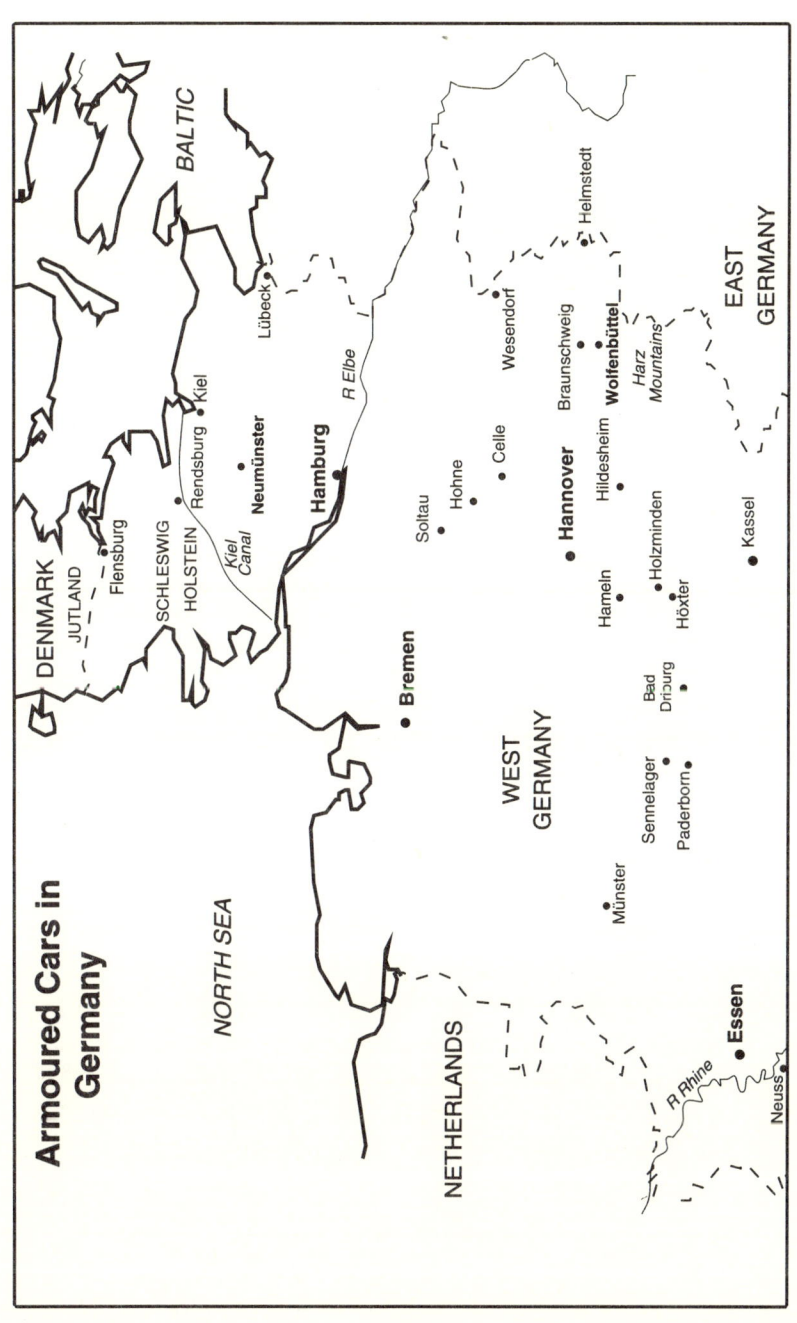

History of The 13th/18th Royal Hussars (Q.M.O.)

The risk of fatal accidents is a sad feature of all military exercises and in one month, August 1957, there were two deaths during Regimental exercises: Trooper E Wells of A Squadron and Lieutenant M Clogg of the Royals.

Neumünster

Neumünster was even more out on a limb than Wolfenbüttel. This had the usual advantage, of not being too close to superior Headquarters, and disadvantage, of being a long way from military sporting and social contacts. McLeod Barracks, on the outskirts of the town, had been built during the Nazi regime and had accommodation, garages and workshops of a standard hitherto unknown to the British Army. The whole complex was built round a large parade ground and was completely self-contained with its own offices, stores, gymnasium and church. As had been the case at Wolfenbüttel, however, there was no officers' mess; Wehrmacht officers had invariably lived out. As Neumünster had no large houses, the officers were housed in requisitioned villas and dined in a house whose only merit was a room just large enough to hold the Mess table. On guest nights even this proved inadequate and the overflow enjoyed a subsidised meal at a restaurant in the town.

The *Journal* commented in October 1957:

> The changes during the past year have been far too many to enumerate. Every officer appointment, with the exception of three troop leaders, has changed and we hope that they now have settled down for a few months at least. [However] . . . It is of considerable interest that the Sergeants' Mess has become stabilised and most of the sergeants are now on a 22-year engagement.

One change, at the beginning of the year, was a welcome innovation. A new post was created of Technical Quartermaster, in place of a Technical Adjutant. Lieutenant PJ Davis was the first incumbent, on promotion from Regimental Quartermaster Sergeant. This ensured that the increasingly complex accounting and administrative demands of the Regiment's holdings of vehicles and their equipment could be undertaken on a more stable and consistent basis. The holders of the appointment would not only have had considerable prior experience of 'Q' matters, but would be able to stay in their

Wolfenbüttel and Neumünster 1953–58

appointments longer than those appointed as Technical Adjutants. It also provided a valuable addition to the number of appointments into which deserving warrant officers could be promoted.

Sport in Neumünster

Despite moving away from the Harz mountains, the Regimental Skiing Team won the BAOR Championship for the second time running in 1957. Bad weather and lack of snow at Gastein meant that the Army Downhill had to be cancelled. Instead there was a Giant Slalom in which the Regiment was placed fifth, improving to fourth in the ordinary Slalom. The team then came sixth in the Army and BAOR Langlauf at Winterberg. The hot favourites for the final event, the Army and BAOR Patrol race, were 44 HAA Regiment, winners for the previous four years, but they were pipped at the post by the Regiment's four representatives, led again by Lieutenant Maule. Corporal D Holmes went on to ski for the Army in the International Patrol Races at Andermatt – in his second year on skis. In 1958 the langlauf team did well in the Divisional Championships and went to Winterberg with high expectations. Spring weather and a complete absence of snow sharply lowered morale, but eventually the meeting began and the Regiment was away to a good start, winning the Army and BAOR Relay Race. In the Army Patrol, there were difficult snow conditions over a very trying 20 kilometre course. A loose rifle on one of the packs slowed the team down considerably and Trooper Seton very gamely finished the last few kilometres only semi-conscious. However, they still came second. By the time of the Individual Langlauf Corporal Holmes, by now a stalwart of the team, had been lost on release from the Army, but Lieutenant Maule achieved third place and the others were all in the first sixteen of a field of 154 starters. Sadly that was to be Lieutenant Maule's last appearance for the Regiment before resigning his commission.

The Regiment's Cricket eleven won the BAOR Championship in 1956, during a season in which they were beaten only once, by a Royal Navy team – HMS *Defender* and HMS *Delight* – in a game when the full strength could not be mustered. Their captain, 2nd Lieutenant GD Roynon, also played regularly for

History of The 13th/18th Royal Hussars (Q.M.O.)

BAOR and was joined by Trooper R Wintle in the 7 Armoured Division team. (Wintle scored 130 against 4 Infantry Division.)

From the individual prowess available great things were expected of the Athletics team in 1956, but the team failed to get beyond the 7 Armoured Division's Support Group Championship. At an International meeting in Neumünster, which provided top class competition, the Regiment won the 4 x 200 and 4 x 400 metres relays and 2nd Lieutenant CJW Haines (a British 'A' Team member) came first in the 400 metres. He went on to win the 7 Armoured Division and Rhine Army individual 400 metres and the Army and Inter Services 440 yards. Another notable performer was Sergeant M Howden who won the 1500 metres at the Divisional meeting.

In other major sports the best that could be said of the soccer and rugger teams was that they were 'young teams and it is hoped that with more experience they will attain more successful results in the Army and Cavalry Cups'. But B Squadron:

> ... had the curious distinction, as a result of beating the Jutland Dragoons' squadron at football, of achieving quite a blurb in the Danish press. We think it probably the first time, in the long history of the Regiment, that the activities of one of its sub-units have been recorded in Danish.

In squash and tennis there was better fortune (Lieutenant Colonel Sir Delaval Cotter was a member of both teams during his time in command). The Regiment was represented in the BAOR, Army and Danish Squash Championships and the team were runners-up in the 1956 BAOR inter-unit competition. 2nd Lieutenant GD Roynon played for Rhine Army regularly and 2nd Lieutenants MM Orr and M Holmes occasionally. Mr Holmes was the leading light at tennis, playing for BAOR and becoming the Neumünster champion for 1956. He and Mrs DHE Coker also won the BAOR mixed doubles that year and the Regimental team won the Divisional competition. In 1957 Lieutenant Holmes was BAOR singles champion and a partner in the Doubles Championship.

Sailing was now justifying its own coverage in the *Journal* with Korsar, a 30 square metre, chartered for the season at the British Kiel Yacht Club. Although she was used for cruising rather than racing, first and second places were won at the first regatta of the 1956 season. In that year's RAC regatta, crewed

Wolfenbüttel and Neumünster 1953–58

by Captains Waddy, Delamain and Pearce (the Regiment's EME), she won both legs of the race. Sailing was not confined to Korsar; there was also plenty of activity in dinghies as well as a number of trips in 50 and 100 square metre boats.

The Regiment, much to its surprise, also did well in fencing in 1957, coming second in the BAOR competition and fourth in the Army Championship. This was a notable achievement for a largely inexperienced team, of whom three were National Service junior ranks. Captain EE Hunt had won the Rhine Army Individual sabre competition again in 1956, but in 1957 could manage only second in the sabre and third in the epée; at the Army championship he came fifth in epée.

Holstein has a charming agricultural countryside and the inhabitants were for the large part friendly farmers, all of whom kept horses for show-jumping as a sideline. The King's Dragoon Guards had been instrumental in putting show jumping back on its feet in the area and had run local competitions for the benefit of the Germans. The winter show, held in Neumünster's excellent indoor arena, involved some four hundred entries and it was with considerable relief that the Regiment learned that the locals were now prepared to take full responsibility for its organisation. Neumünster had far more varied rides to offer than Wolfenbüttel and a hunter trial course was built on the local training area. All horses were now to be privately owned, advantage being taken of what was on offer from living in the centre of the Holsteiner country.

In 1956 individual successes at both hunter trials and the Hohne military show included Captain GM Chirnside winning the Trial at Bad Segeberg. No prizes were won in the individual events of the Army Hunter Trials at Dorfmark, but the Regiment won the Desert Rat Team event and gained fourth place in the Captains and Subalterns. In 1957 Dorfmark provided better fortune, with Captain Mangles on Granit coming sixth in the Rhine Army One Day Event and Major JJ Selwyn sixth on Jenko in the Novice Individual Hunter Trial. The team could only manage seventh place in the Desert Rat Team event, but as they had been unable to practise together before that was quite creditable. Good relations with the Neumünster Riding Club produced invitations to several drag hunts which culminated in a big meet on St Hubert's Day, 'enlivened with much horn-blowing, and a dance afterwards at an adjacent *gasthaus*, at which riders had to attend in full hunting dress'.

Annual Inspections

The Regiment earned good reports on its administration during their time in Germany in the 1950s, but Major General Pyman, the Commander of 11 Armoured Division, had doubts about technical know-how. He even expressed some scepticism, during earlier training from Wolfenbüttel, as to their having changed their approach from the days as horsed cavalry in India, when he had been there in a Royal Tank Corps armoured car company. (He conveniently forgot the Regiment's capture of Mont Pinçon with their tanks in Normandy, when he was BGS under General Horrocks, Commander 30 Corps.)

In March 1954 he reserved judgement :

> This unit has recently joined the Division from Malaya. The Regiment has got an alert air about it, is settling well in its new environment, and making great efforts to become administratively well found. I hope and expect that this keenness will be reflected in their tactical and field administrative work in the summer months. The regiment is obviously accustomed to administering itself very well, and should soon fit itself to BAOR conditions.

But after the Inspection in December 1954 he said:

> The standard of drill was first class as was the men's bearing on parade. The sword drill of the Officers was outstandingly good. Generally, the standard of administration revealed on the inspection was sound and in keeping with the high traditions of the Regiment. I consider that the knowledge displayed by the young officers is not up to the standard required by officers of the Royal Armoured Corps with regard to the performance and characteristics of their vehicles.

However, his comments, in private and public, on the performance of the Regiment's young officers as Phantom umpires on Exercise Battle Royal could not have been more laudatory.

The parade for the Inspection the following October was 'one of the colder ones. Most of the officers could not feel their swords and one man, recently returned from Malaya, succumbed to the cold . . . '. However, the new Divisional Commander, Major General JDA Anderson, was able to report:

Wolfenbüttel and Neumünster 1953–58

... I am glad to say that the points noted on last year's inspection show great improvement and the professional knowledge of junior officers appears to me now to be satisfactory. Morale throughout the Regiment is excellent and in general I consider this a sound, serviceable and efficient unit without ostentation. A pleasant happy spirit pervades the barracks.

In December 1956 Brigadier Block wrote: 'The general administration of the Regiment is thoroughly sound and well directed ... general air of well-being throughout Regiment and great esprit de corps is evident'. The following year his successor as Commander Royal Artillery 7 Armoured Division, Brigadier Baker: '... A very good parade. Although the standard of the Regiment at last year's Administrative Inspection was high an improvement has been made this year ... particularly noteworthy that no grading below GOOD ... in any of the ancillary inspections. Morale and esprit de corps throughout the Regiment is obviously very high ...'.

Recreation and Local Contacts

The considerable body of German nobility living in the neighbourhood of Neumünster were hospitable towards the Regiment, although they did not mix with the townspeople nor take part in political activities. Many owned large estates and shooting invitations were numerous. These varied from the *Kesselring* hare drive to beating the forest for pig, but all concluded with 'the inevitable dinner which one sat down to at the conclusion of hostilities and which frequently continued to the early hours of the morning'. At least one landowner, Graf Thun Hohenstein, was trying to re-establish partridges and pheasants and Prinz Moritz of Hesse and his agent were working on similar lines. For the shooters, however, pride of place went to the wild fowling for which this part of Germany is justly famous. The Regimental game book records the incessant pursuit of geese and duck, 'even if as time went on it appeared that half Germany was shooting the same marsh'. Another family who deserve mention for their hospitality to the Regiment were the von Bethmann Hollwegs whose nephew Alec did his National Service with the Regiment. (His troop were not a little tickled by the salutations he received from estate workers when driving through the neighbourhood.)

History of The 13th/18th Royal Hussars (Q.M.O.)

Sport apart, Hamburg, Lübeck and Kiel all offered good food and entertainment within easy reach, while at Travemünde there was a fully fledged casino. Sailing at Kiel and holidays in nearby Denmark completed an agreeable picture.

New Battle Honours
In 1957, twelve years after the ending of the Second World War, the Regiment was awarded seventeen Battle Honours. Nine were selected to be emblazoned on a Guidon which was also approved for the Regiment to carry – in place of the Drum Banners on which Battle Honours had been emblazoned as horsed cavalry. Shortly afterwards the Queen approved a change in colour of the Regimental Facings, from white to buff. Plans began to be made for a Guidon to be presented, but it was several years before that was possible. Indeed, the Regiment did not know until later in the year whether it would survive the massive cuts which were to be made in order to implement the Sandys' Defence White Paper of April 1957.

Second World War Battle Honours*

North West Europe 1940
Dyle	Withdrawal to Escaut

Ypres-Comines Canal

North West Europe 1944–45
Normandy Landing
Bréville	Caen
Bourgébus Ridge	Mont Pinçon
St Pierre la Vielle	Geilenkirchen
Roer	**Rhineland**
Waal Flats	**Goch**
Rhine	Bremen

* Honours in heavy type to be borne on the Guidon

Arrival of the Bundeswehr
Towards the end of the Regiment's stay a battalion of the newly re-formed German Army, the *Bundeswehr,* was sent to Neumünster. The *Bundeswehr* eventually took over the barracks and assumed the operational role previously carried out by British forces.

Wolfenbüttel and Neumünster 1953–58

These troops, obsessed by the desire to escape from the old Wehrmacht image and appear truly democratic, proved harder to co-operate with, due to the difficulty of finding anybody prepared to make a decision without reference to higher authority. As might be expected, they were punctiliously correct and always anxious to help. Unfortunately they were viewed with deep suspicion by the local civilians whose memories of the pre-war Wehrmacht had been far from happy.

By January 1958 the Regiment was taking part in a NATO winter exercise in which they acted as enemy opposing a German division and part of the Danish Brigade. This was the first full-scale exercise by the new German Army in Schleswig Holstein and it was given great publicity from newsreel and television photographers as well as the press. One Regimental exploit was recorded in the next edition of the Bundeswehr magazine under the heading of 'Umpiring during NATO Exercise House Warming':

Danish Tank commander – 'Stop! My six 24-ton Chaffee tanks are far superior to your three British armoured patrol cars.'

British Corporal – 'But you would not have hit at our speed.'

Danish – 'You are surrounded. Surrender!'

British – 'Quite impossible! I carry out only an order given by my own commander.'

Danish – 'You surrender.'

British – 'A 13th Hussar never capitulates! You will not get our armoured cars.'

Danish – 'I insist.'

British – 'I was in Korea.* Unwounded and a prisoner of war? Impossible for a 13th Hussar. I will fight till the very last moment!'

German Umpire – 'The umpire speaking – my decision is final.'

British – 'Not in everything.'

German – 'If you don't obey, I must report to the Commander.'

British – 'All right then.'

German – 'I decide. The six superior tanks of the Jutland

---

* The magazine presumably confused the Malayan campaign with Korea.

History of The 13th/18th Royal Hussars (Q.M.O.)

Dragoons have put out of combat and destroyed the few British armoured cars. The British patrol cars, however, do not surrender. They show break-through flags, proceed to Bad Bramstedt where they reinforce as new troops their 13th/18th Hussars Regiment.'

Danish – 'Thanks for your assistance.'

British – 'That is correct, Sergeant. You understand our attitude.'

Amongst the German visitors to the Regiment in December 1957 was Vice Admiral B Rogge, Commander of *Wehrbereichts Kommando 1*, and famous as a 'Q Ship' captain during the Second World War when he was noted for his humane treatment of captured Allied seamen.

Leaving Neumünster

In May 1957 B Squadron had left for a year's detachment in Arabia, an account of which follows. The rest of the Regiment stayed in Germany until April 1958:

> The last weeks in Neumünster saw a series of farewells, the most touching of which must surely have taken place at the railway sidings! Many will look back on Neumünster with happy memories. The barracks were first class. A number of people learnt some German, a tribute to the friendly relations which existed between ourselves and the inhabitants of the town. The Regiment will always remember their kindness . . . It was particularly fascinating to witness the birth of the new German Army at first hand, and the close co-operation with our friends the Danes will always be remembered with great pleasure.

Chapter Five

B Squadron in Arabia 1957–58

Problems in the Middle East

Seven years after the Regiment's tour in Libya and Egypt the scene in the Middle East had changed considerably. Arab nationalism, personified by the Egyptian ruler Colonel Nasser, was strongly influencing all Arab regimes and British interests in the region were under increasing threat. In May 1957, five months after the abortive Suez operation, the Regiment was warned off to relieve a 15th/19th Hussars squadron in Arabia and in August B Squadron, led by Major ER Jolley, left Neumünster on their way to Aden for a year's operations.

They first had two months in England for leave, hurried driver training on the Ferret scout car, which was to be the principal equipment, some field firing and elementary Morse instruction. By the time the main body left on the *Empire Orwell* from Southampton they were all suffering from 'Asian' 'flu – with which they infected the rest of the ship. Fortunately they had recovered by the time the *Orwell* reached Aden, where they disembarked on 25 October, Balaklava Day.

Distances in Arabia are vast. The south eastern corner of the Arabian Peninsula, where the Squadron was to be deployed, is roughly equivalent in extent to India, south of a line joining Bombay and Calcutta. From the Colony of Aden itself to the frontier stations on the Yemen border was only between one and two hundred miles, but the East Aden Protectorate was almost as large as France, while the distance from Aden to central Oman, via the air route then used through Bahrain, is roughly equivalent to that between London and Moscow.

B Squadron was responsible for the support of infantry units operating on the Aden–Yemeni border. In the West Aden Protectorate and Lahej they were to undertake convoy protection and escort duties. In the East Aden Protectorate they were to assist the Hadraumi Bedouin Legion with maintenance of

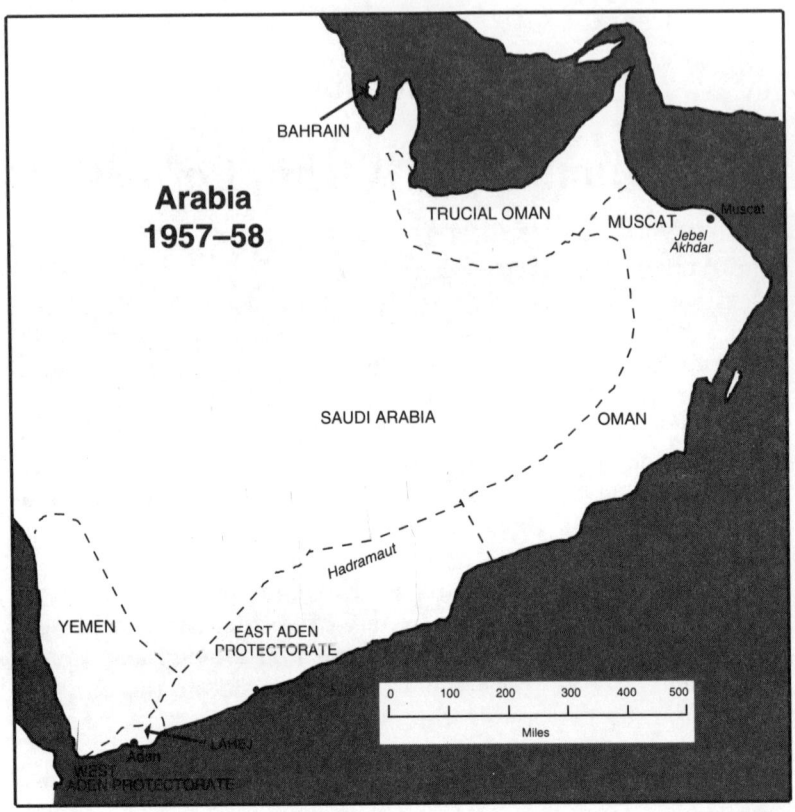

law and order. Finally, in Oman they were to support the Sultan's Armed Forces and carry out convoy protection and escorts. To begin with there were only four sabre troops for this mammoth task, three of which were detached: at Dhala in the West Aden Protectorate, at Riyan in the East Aden Protectorate and at Nizwa in Oman. They were reinforced early in January 1958 by two troops from A Squadron and in mid-April half the Life Guards air portable squadron came under command.

No less awesome than the operational commitments was the supply problem. The detached troops were largely dependent on air supply and the only source of arms, ammunition and technical stores was the base at Aden. These had to be drawn,

B Squadron in Arabia 1957–58

packed and consigned by the small Squadron HQ under the full rigours of peacetime accounting – which embraced even the replacement of vehicles damaged by mines in Oman.

West Aden Protectorate and the Aden–Yemeni Border
A leading article in *The Times* of the period said:
> The Aden–Yemeni frontier is one of the grimmest fighting areas in the world. Bare, inaccessible and sun-baked mountains carry it from the sea to the interior; interspersed are flat expanses of gleaming sand, pitted with close shuttered, mud-walled villages and stone peel-towers in which the border barons keep watch and ward. There is no movement save that of the camel herds, shepherded by small boys, or the sudden pillar of dust raised by a roving scout car. Those who fight this war are men either bred to it since birth or attracted there by temperament. It has gone on for centuries . . . and the federation of the Yemen with the United Arab Republic [of Egypt and Syria] (UAR) had led to fiercer fighting. In the spring of 1958 heavier weapons, brought in from Iron Curtain countries, were reported. A temporary penetration was made into the Western Protectorate. The Sultan of Lahej defected to the Yemen and the British Chargé d'Affaires was virtually expelled from the Yemeni capital. By all reckonings the prospect looked bleak.

Dhala
The detachment at Dhala was initially of only one troop under 2nd Lieutenant MB Barty-King; they were to see a great deal of action. Their duties included escorting convoys half way to Aden, patrolling the Yemen border in the Dhala plateau and carrying out patrols and escorts on the plateau itself. They worked closely with infantry of the Aden Protectorate Levies (APL) and looked to them, for example, to picquet the passes most vulnerable to ambush on the convoy route.

Officially no state of war existed with the Yemen, but as the unmarked frontier ran across a featureless plain it was easy to cross it by accident and so draw Yemeni fire. 'Rules of engagement' permitted returning fire at Yemeni positions, sited in stone sangars about 1,000 yards across the plain. Patrols were also likely to be fired on by dissident tribesmen operating inside the Protectorate but under Yemeni direction. In one encounter in January 1958, Government Guard forces supported by the

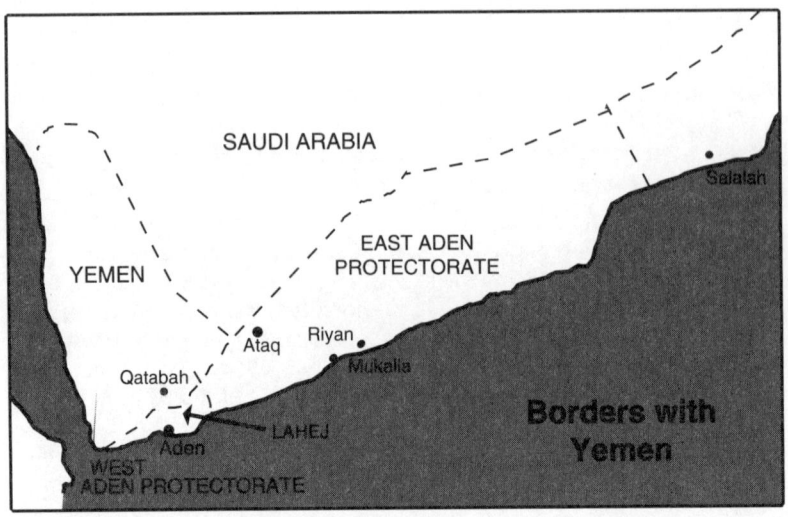

troop were engaged and one Guard and five dissidents were killed, two of the latter by the troop's fire; they included the sheikh known to be the local leader.

Engagements from across the border included field artillery fire (probably 75 mm) which was 'surprisingly accurate, shells falling within 25 yards'. In January the sabre troops twice 'trailed their coats' in the Sanaa Fort area in order to draw Yemeni fire and enable their artillery and machine gun positions to be pinpointed for air strikes by RAF Venoms. During a fortnight's visit to the Squadron by the Commanding Officer, Lieutenant Colonel Rugge-Price.

> . . . we managed to bribe the Yemeni to shoot him up while he visited Sanaa Fort . . . ; at least, the latter took place, the former being the construction which the CO was disbelieving enough to place on the incident.

The detachment at Dhala occupied a tented rock-walled camp 5,500 feet up in the frontier mountains. For supply, they were occasionally visited from Aden by ad hoc convoys, which took twenty-four hours to traverse eighty-five miles of sand, *wadi* beds and tracks. Otherwise they relied on twice-weekly flights of Pembroke aircraft to their strip, 5,000 feet up. After 10.30 in the morning taking off was unwise because of the high winds. Like the other Squadron detachments the troop received by air 'turkeys, Christmas puddings and all the rest of the Christmas

B Squadron in Arabia 1957-58

paraphernalia . . . on schedule . . .'. But they also had a visit on Christmas Day – by the Emir of Dhala:

> The time was that convivial hour preceding Christmas lunch. The occasion was the Emir's unexpected visit to 2nd Troop's detachment canteen which Corporal B____l runs. It must be admitted that, on that particular morning, 'mine host' had already sampled his own wares. The Emir was accompanied by his brother and a retinue of thirty hawk-eyed warriors. An uneasy hush followed their unexpected entrance. The establishment of cordial relations was obviously up to the NCO in charge. Corporal B____l was aware of the honour done to his canteen by the visit but was unaware of the identity of Emir. With commendable initiative he advanced to the nearest table, placing one arm around the Emir's shoulders and the other around those of his brother, he bestowed on each a winning smile and enquired with great charm 'Which of you two f____s is the Emir?'.

In late April 1958 there was a major Yemeni incursion into the Jebel Jihaf together with local dissidents. The Yemenis besieged Fort As Sariz where the Political Officer Mr Roy Somerset had taken refuge. The B Squadron *Newsletter* reported that on 28 April 'SHQ operated tactically for the first [and only] time since coming to Arabia and with a full Squadron as escort (4th Troop, two troops LG and one troop APL Armoured Car Squadron) set out to escort the Infantry relief column [1st King's Shropshire Light Infantry and APL] from Aden to Dhala.' All this attracted a great deal of publicity in the British national press, and Major Jolley wrote that 'Enough has already been written of this daring move and of the eighty miles "running fight" it entailed. In point of fact seven shots were fired at us in all throughout the relief.'

> At Dhala, however, the infantry was faced with a real task in establishing itself on the *Jebel Jihaf* on which, by 30 April, considerable numbers of dissident tribesmen plus Yemeni regulars had gathered.

No 3 Company Aden Protectorate Levies finally stormed the Jebel after an engagement lasting fourteen hours and and the fort was at last relieved. 2nd Lieutenant Barty-King's troop had a lively time, in which they were joined later by another troop (Lieutenant AH Blount) which had come up with an infantry relief column for which B Squadron provided the escort.

During the infantry attack on 1 May both 2nd and 4th Troops were in continuous action in support of 1 KSLI on the easier going at the north side of the Jebel . . . throughout the engagement the troops buzzed like bees at the bottom of the escarpment, ever ready to give covering fire, but bitterly frustrated that their Ferrets couldn't make their way up the 2,000 feet ascent which was strictly on-foot only. The single exit at the top was only three feet wide. . . [but] They had quite a spirited day and succeeded in drawing off a considerable number of enemy from the infantry's attack on the precipitous south face.

Over the next fortnight the B Squadron group escorted three further convoys from Aden to Dhala and were ambushed on three occasions. One 3-tonner, driven by Trooper J Clunie, 'collected seven more bullet holes, bringing the total for that vehicle to ten in all'.

On 5 May 2nd and 4th Troops re-enacted our January 'coat trail' in front of Sanaa Fort. Both troops were extremely active there on 7 and 8 May, driving right up to the enemy sangars on Cameron Ridge and doing a lot of shooting.

Both 75mm gunfire and 12.7mm HMG fire were used against them and, largely as a result of their efforts, the guns and HMGs in the Qatabah area were pinpointed and written off in RAF bombing sorties. 2nd Lieutenant MB Barty-King was awarded the Military Cross:

For courage under fire, determination and leadership whilst commanding a troop of his regiment over a period of many months. On one occasion by skilful tactics he forced Yemeni tribesmen occupying sangars in Aden Protectorate to evacuate their positions and thereby imposed on them heavy casualties.

Lahej

The defection to the Yemen by the Sultan of Lahej in early 1958 was followed by the the Tribal Guards abandoning their posts in central Lahej and on the Lahej/Yemen border. The Squadron was therefore faced with two hundred odd miles of unguarded frontier with the possibility of the Sultan sweeping over it with a 'liberating' army backed by the UAR. The frontier area consisted of hard packed gravel plains – perfect tank going – and the situation was judged to be sufficiently serious to warrant the deployment of an element of the Strategic Reserve

B Squadron in Arabia 1957–58

from the UK. This included a half squadron of the Life Guards which remained under command B Squadron until the end of the Squadron's tour. But 'unceasing' patrolling in the Lahej region provided little by way of action to report, so that the Squadron *Newsletter* was reduced to recording such excitements as the sighting of a Yemeni water truck filling from a well on Protectorate territory and its being chased back across the frontier. On another occasion one of the Life Guards' troops stumbled into an inter-tribal cattle war and was shot at by both sides without being able to retaliate, because of the Political Officer's veto.

Abayan

2nd Lieutenant MAC Stocker's troop initially moaned bitterly at being based at Aden in a reserve role, but they soon found that they were likely to have their hands full. Most of the early operations, principally convoy protection lasting several days, were in potentially dangerous country. Arms from the Yemen had been coming into the Western Protectorate. In mid-December the troop moved to Abayan, forty miles to the East along the coast, with a company of the Aden Protectorate Levies (APL) where they were to be for a month. There was a generally anti-Government, pro-Yemeni attitude in the Abayan area. A slowly deteriorating situation had come to a head, after several inter-tribal murders, when the son of the local sheikh took to the hills at Yemeni direction. He took with him 140 riflemen of the Government-maintained Tribal Guard and 10,000 Maria Theresa dollars from the State Treasury.

After that the troop was airlifted at short notice to Ataq, on the borders of the two Aden Protectorates. From there they moved overland to Al Kabr in Wahadi territory to relieve the Hadraumi Bedouin Legion garrison of a fort besieged by dissidents. The troop reached its objective after two days of appalling going, taking one day to cover twenty five miles. The route lay in a *wadi* bed carpeted with boulders so large that jacks had frequently to be used to get the Ferrets over them. Their 3-tonner was kept going only by an airdrop from Squadron Headquarters of essential spares. On arrival they found all quiet, but on the return journey the troop was ambushed twice while moving through a narrow gorge with sheer walls some 600 feet high and Trooper S Wheeler was wounded. He was evacuated by helicopter, 'the pilot putting in some startling flying by descending into a *wadi* to get below very low cloud and thereafter flying between the walls of the *wadi* to reach the landing zone'.

Riyan

Most of the country then forming Eastern Aden Protectorate (EAP) is 5,000 to 7,000 feet up and the going was incredibly rough. Initially the detachment at Riyan (Lieutenant AH Blount and 2nd Lieutenant DBE Pike) was occupied practising infantry co-operation with troops of the Hadraumi Bedouin Legion and Mukalla Regular Army. They were subjected to nothing worse than occasional stonings by small boys to an accompaniment of shrieks of 'Nasser! Nasser!'. The detachment shared a camp with an RAF airstrip on the edge of the sea and enjoyed some of the best underwater fishing in that part of the world. To approach Riyan by land, over the 430 miles from Aden, was possible only at certain times of year, when the tides allowed motoring on the beaches. Then it took five to six days. Rations and canteen stores were supplied when a six-monthly ship called at Mukalla to be off-loaded by lighter. All other items came in by twice-weekly flights of RAF Valetta aircraft. As EAP remained quiet, Riyan was evacuated in August 1958, by which time the detachment had trained the Hadraumi Bedouin Legion in gunnery, driving and maintenance so that they could use Ferrets supplied through the Colonial Office.

Oman

At the eastern end of the Arabian Peninsula fighting broke out in Muscat and Oman in July 1957, when factions hostile to the Sultan, aided and abetted by Saudi Arabia and Egypt, inflicted heavy casualties on the Oman Regiment of the Sultan's forces. An appeal from to Britain for help brought in British infantry from Bahrain, Trucial Oman Scouts and a troop of 15th/19th Hussars (B Squadron's predecessors). A speedy and successful operation, supported by cannon and rocket fire from RAF Venoms, against their strongholds in Firq and Nizwa drove out the rebels who retreated to a plateau in the *Jebel Akhdar*.

B Squadron in Arabia 1957–58

About twenty miles by ten, the plateau is between 6,000 and 10,000 feet high and some 400 miles round the base. The rainfall is enough for peaches and pomegranates to flourish and men have lived there for centuries, confident in its legendary impregnability. (The last assault had been attempted by the Persians in the tenth century with, it is said, the loss of nine tenths of their 10,000 troops.) Its villages and irrigation systems made it self-contained for food and water and it was approachable by paths so steep that a few determined and well camouflaged snipers could offer opposition out of all proportion to their strength. The rebels had plenty of arms, including both heavy and light American anti-tank mines, mortars and heavy machine guns. From this mountain fortress the rebels made occasional forays to occupy villages commanding the main tracks and to mine, ambush and burn vehicles of the British Oil Company drilling in Oman.

The Sultan's Armed Forces (SAF) had not been notably successful in dealing with the rebels. The troop at Nizwa was

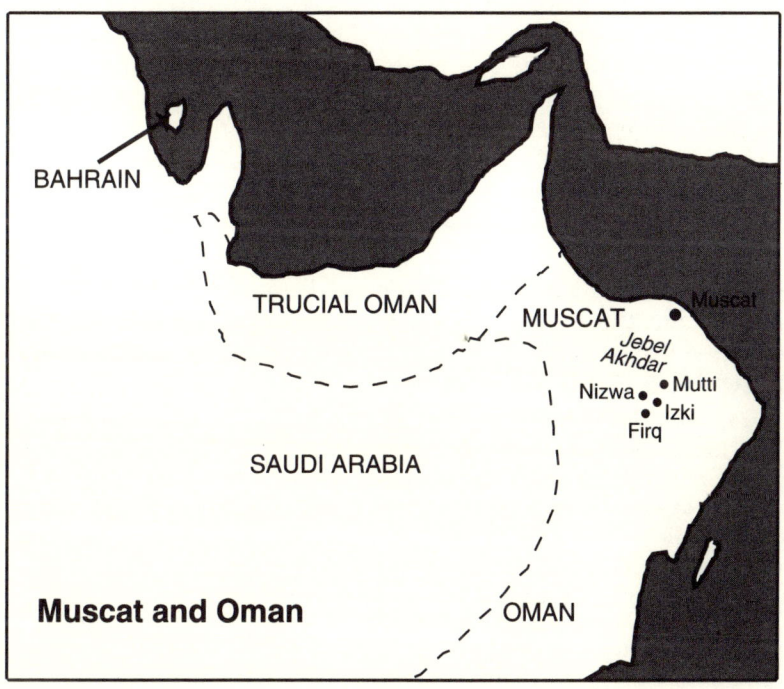

Muscat and Oman

part of a British contingent provided to expand and reorganise them which:

> ... consisted of a few British regular officers seconded to SAF, a handful of Marine Commandos, Royal Corps of Signals and some medical personnel. A troop of armoured cars from the 13th/18th Hussars and a few RAF pilots made up a total of under fifty British servicemen of all ranks, something less than the army of 10–20,000 that Radio Cairo claimed was deployed in the Oman. (*Brush Fire Wars,* M Dewar).

The troop (Lieutenant M Holmes) was there primarily as an emergency reserve to bolster SAF morale and to seal off the rebels in the Jebel Akhdar. It also undertook bi-weekly convoy escorts, other escorts as required and supported the SAF in offensive operations. Later it was joined by a troop from A Squadron (2nd Lieutenant AF Ramsay) which operated on the seaward side of the Jebel at Iski, in support of the Trucial Oman Scouts (TOS). The troops occupied dug-out emplacements covered by tents and protected by sangars.

Nizwa was entirely dependent on air supply through an airstrip at Firq three miles from the detachment's camp. HQ Land Forces Persian Gulf initially provided from Bahrain their rations, canteen stores and mail, which came in once a week by Pembroke aircraft. (Commander Land Forces was Brigadier EH Tinker who commanded the Regiment 1948–50.) Later on the detachment was able to draw fresh rations from the local oil company base. A troop NCO was permanently based in Bahrain to organise these arrangements.

On 30 March 1958 two Ferrets of 5th Troop, under Sergeant DM Steel, were escorting a column of TOS into the Wadi Mutti area, some three miles from the Troop base at Iski. As the column passed the outskirts of Mutti village it came under heavy fire from the Jebel Akhdar, overlooking the village.

> Sergeant Steel immediately attacked, directing his scout cars' fire against the tribesman ambushers and effecting a successful diversion to cover the deployment of the Trucial Oman Scouts. The open barren country offered little protection from the ambushers' fire and Sergeant Steel's immediate action saved many casualties. During the initial attack one British officer was shot and fell. Sergeant Steel manoeuvred his scout car to shield him. Then, dismounting, he went to his aid, but found that he had been fatally wounded.

B Squadron in Arabia 1957–58

. . . returning to his scout car he saw an Arab soldier lying wounded in the open and ran to his assistance. After helping to bandage his wounds he returned to his vehicle to find the Trucial Oman Scouts were preparing to launch an attack on the tribesmen's positions. Deploying his cars he directed covering fire while the Scouts moved into position across the open terrain for the main assault, but the enemy withdrew. Sergeant Steel again moved in to support the re-deployment of of the Scouts from the *wadi* area. Withdrawing from the *wadi*, firing began again and Sergeant Steel returned to the *wadi* in an attempt to draw the dissidents' fire and locate their positions for the mortars . . .

Later in the afternoon an attack was launched and Sergeant Steel again moved his scout cars in to support the ground troops and cut off reinforcements trying to reach the enemy tribesmen. As the attack progressed, a plan to blow up their main water supply line was made. The demolition party with their charges moved forward in a Land Rover and prepared the charges against the supply line. Before these could be exploded the party came under fire and were pinned down. Their vehicle was damaged and made unserviceable.

Sergeant Steel again moved forward and directed covering fire and a diversion to cover the withdrawal of the demolition party. Later, providing a shield with his scout cars, the demolition party went in under cover of the guns and successfully demolished the water line.

In the early hours of the following day, Sergeant Steel re-entered the area with three scout cars to recover the damaged Land Rover. Under cover of two scout cars Sergeant Steel took over the damaged vehicle and was towed out of the *wadi* by the third scout car.

That account was published later in the year, in the *Times of Malaya and Straits Echo,* after Sergeant Steel was awarded the Military Medal:

For determination and leadership when commanding a troop of scout cars in support of a patrol ambushed in a bare and precipitous *wadi*. On four occasions he dismounted, in the open and under fire, to assist the wounded and recover equipment. During some thirteen hours of almost continuous action he displayed inspiring courage.

The Squadron *Newsletter* recorded that during the latter part of the tour both the weather and operations hotted up considerably in Oman. The rebels received reinforcements from Saudi Arabia, not only of money, but of weapons and trained men. Mining increased and in the second half of July 1958 five Ferrets were lost, making thirteen in all during the Squadron's tour.

> Throughout 1958 an average of twenty military vehicles a month were destroyed by mines on the road between Muscat and Nizwa. Later in the year between August and December when a squadron of the Life Guards had succeeded the Hussars, the new squadron managed to lose 80 per cent of their Ferret scout cars. (*Brush Fire Wars*).

Vehicle casualties had to be evacuated by tank landing craft from Axaiba (near Muscat) to Aden and replacements brought in by the same means. That meant towing the wrecks over a hundred miles or so of mined track.

Retrospect

For the first six months B Squadron's strength never exceeded 137. They were then augmented by a half squadron of the Life Guards. Of its eventual eight sabre troops, not less than seven were detached from Squadron Headquarters and a small detachment headquarters administered the two isolated troops operating in the interior of Oman. The only source of arms, ammunition and technical stores was the Base in Aden. Squadron Headquarters had to draw, pack and despatch what was needed by air – and keep full peacetime accounts. Their Ferret scout cars served them well:

> ... taking *wadi* boulders, lava flow, rock, dune sand, gravel and even quicksand in their stride with great aplomb. They are unquestionably very good little vehicles. [but] Our B vehicles, which do not appear to have been intended to stand up the sort of punishment they got out here, are a constant headache. ... they just cannot take the going when it becomes really rough, for any length of time. Engine mounting brackets break, steering arm bolts shear off from their mountings, front axle check straps snap, body and chassis bolts work loose, springs and shock absorbers break, radiators split, transfer case mounting bolts shear off, while the amount of backlash in rear axles becomes frightening. All in all they keep our fitters busy. (B Squadron *Newsletter*)

B Squadron in Arabia 1957–58

The only way that Major Jolley could keep in touch with his Squadron was by air and before they left Aden he had covered some 57,000 air miles.

It is the custom amongst Arab tribesmen for the dead to be removed whenever possible when retreating from a skirmish. In operations against them it was therefore impossible to make any accurate assessment of their casualties. However, intelligence reports and information from informers indicated that B Squadron troops might have been responsible for as many as fifty enemy casualties in their thirty-three separate engagements. It also went on record that the containment of the Oman rebels to the Jebel Akhdar was largely due to the operations of the two troops stationed there between October 1957 and March 1958.

The Squadron had a total of sixty-nine hospital admissions during the year, mainly through heat exhaustion, but that compared favourably with those of:

> ... every British infantry battalion serving in the Theatre at the time; the worst sufferer being a battalion which had previously been based in England as part of the Strategic Reserve. . . . Nevertheless the Squadron was in much poorer condition on relief than when it had first been deployed, the loss in weight being an average of twenty pounds per man and from fifty-six to eighty-four pounds in extreme cases.
>
> The tour provided ample proof that the British soldier is at his best in adverse conditions. . . . In Arabia it was found necessary to sentence only one soldier to detention during a period of almost a year. This may have been accounted for by the fact many soldiers voluntarily forswore alcohol while on detachment: one of them at least, a hardened imbiber in Germany, carrying on with his task until he dropped in his tracks from heat exhaustion. . . . For officer, NCO and trooper alike Arabia had its lessons. In particular, every young Troop Leader, fully occupied by the tactical problems of his command, learned early on how valuable it was to be able to trust his Troop Sergeant with the unending details of detachment administration. It is not too much to say that B Squadron owed to the quality of its Sergeants no small measure of its success in Arabia.

As ever much was also owed to the attached personnel.

> There is little that is glamorous in catering for jaded appetites on a field cooker in 135° F, nor is it comfortable to work for hours on

History of The 13th/18th Royal Hussars (Q.M.O.)

end in similar temperatures at the repair of a mined scout car or a faulty wireless set; all at the end of an L of C* up to 2,000 miles in length and dependent to a large extent on one's own skill and resource. Our attached personnel were, however, almost entirely first-class, our REME fitters in particular performing miracles of improvisation; often commanding or driving scout cars at times of need in addition to their other tasks.

When eventually relieved it was by the Life Guards, less a squadron – a tacit acknowledgement that B Squadron had been absurdly over-stretched.

* L of C = Lines of Communication

Extracts from B Squadron *Newsletters*

1957

Date	Place	Event
11 Nov	Dhala	2 Tp with APL inf coy on patrol on plateau, ambushed by 6–10 riflemen; two APL wounded before column able move on under covering fire from Ferrets.
2 Dec	Dhala	CO (Lt Col Rugge-Price) shot at while inspecting frontier fort Sanaa.
4 Dec	Oman	1 Tp during patrol to Tanouf captured three rebels from Jebel Akhdar.
9 Dec	Dhala	2 Tp ambushed between Dhala & Thumier; 3 ton shot up.
19 Dec	Dhala	2 Tp ambushed on patrol between Sanaa & Lakmat and Duki; all tp vehs hit.
30 Dec	Dhala	2 Tp ambushed on patrol between Sanaa & Lakmat and Duki.
31 Dec	Nizwa	1 Tp camp fired on.

1958

Date	Place	Event
4 Jan	Dhala	2 Tp Sanaa/Lakmat Ad Duki area, supporting patrol Govt Gd, fired on by some 15 dissidents; Gdsmn killed & five dissidents – two by 2 Lt Barty-King.
7 Jan	Dhala	2 Tp ambushed during escort Govt Gd convoy; one gdsmn killed.
14 Jan	Dhala	2 Tp in support APL inf colm and sec 75mm guns fired on from two sangars; Tp engaged at short range, under cover 75mm and mors.
19 Jan	Al Kabr	3 Tp reached Al Kabr, after airlift 17 Janto Ataq, in order relieve besieged Hadraumi Bedouin Legion garrison of fort.
20 Jan	Dhala	2 Tp in support similar colm 14 Jan fired on by 75mm & heavy MG.
21 Jan	Ataq	3 Tp ambushed in gorge on return journey; in two hour action Tpr Wheeler wounded. Tp withdrew.

B Squadron in Arabia 1957–58

Extracts from B Squadron *Newsletters* (cont)

1958

Date	Location	Event
22 Jan	Ataq	3 Tp again ambushed in gorge; running action until reached open country.
30 Jan	Dhala	2 & 3 Tps with tp APL Armd C Sqn in support APL bn, sec arty 'trailed coat' in Sanaa fort area. On Yemeni reaction Venom aircraft strike called down.
16 Feb	Firq	1 Tp 3 ton blown up on mine near Firq
26 Feb	Dhala	2 Tp assisted clearing ambush of Govt Gd patrol; one enemy killed.
3 Mar	Nizwa	1 Tp ambushed while escorting Muscat Armed Forces column.
30 Mar	Nizwa	Trucial Oman Scouts patrol ambushed near Iski, losing offr & OR; extricated by 5 Tp.
31 Mar	Nizwa	3 Tp fired on & Ferret mined while escorting MAF one rebel killed.
9 Apr	Nizwa	3 Tp escorting 5.5 in guns ambushed in Kamah area.
23 Apr	Nizwa	3 Tp Ferret mined in Kamah area.
24 Apr	Nizwa	Land Rover mined Nizwa.
28 Apr	Dhala	SHQ with 4 Tp, two tps LG, tp APL Armd C Sqn escorted inf relief column.
1 May	Dhala	Inf attack Jebel Jihaf with 2 & 4 Tps in support.
5 May	Dhala	Over four days 2 & 4 Tps operated in Sanaa area, bringing down 75mm and heavy MG fire from enemy sangars and enabling air strikes to destroy pin-pointed positions.
7 May	Dhala	Three more convoys escorted to Dhala, with three ambushes.
16 May	Dhala	2 Tp on patrol with Govt Gds cleared rd block, assisted by 4 Troop.
19 May	Firq	5 Tp Ferret mined.
17 Jun	Nizwa	3 Tp, reduced to two vehs through heat exhaustion & jaundice, broke up Wadi Muti ambush in which RM colour sgt killed.
21 Jun	Oman	2 Tp on 800 mile escort of Comd SAF round Jebel.
27 Jun	Kharad	5 Tp patrol from Kharad engaged from across border.
8 Jul	Dhala	LG Tp fired on near Lakmat-ash-Sub.
14 Jul	Nizwa	4 Tp shoot against attempted ambush Wadi Tanouf killing one.
19 Jul	Iski	2 Tp Ferret mined.
29 Jul	Nizwa	4 Tp Ferret mined.
30 Jul	Nizwa	4 Tp Ferret mined.
30 Jul	Dhala	3 Tp engaged briefly while on convoy.
31 Jul	Iski	2 Tp under sporadic mortar & SAA fire to 6 Aug.
2 Aug	Iski	2 & 4 Tps each lost Ferret from mines.
4 Aug	Dhala	3 Tp fired on from sangar; charged & captured kit left by fleeing Yemeni.

Chapter Six

Malaya 1958–60

Interlude in Dorset
The Regiment, less B Squadron, left Neumünster in April 1958 for a staging camp at Piddlehinton in Dorset. Some individual training was followed at the end of July by another round of packing and then embarkation leave. It was much more agreeable than had been the stay at Quorn in 1953:

> The normally peaceful Dorset countryside has echoed and reverberated with the noise of vehicles on their training runs, but the risks which the local inhabitants have had to run when driving their cars on the narrow country roads near the camp has in no way affected their friendliness and hospitality towards the Regiment. We could not have spent our English summer in a more attractive or more welcoming part of England.

Return to Malaya
That interlude preceded the Regiment's embarkation at Southampton in HMT *Oxfordshire* on 26 August for a second tour in Malaya. They found the *Oxfordshire* to be a far cry from the *Empire Pride* and the *Empire Trooper*, in which they had previously travelled to and fro. It was 'equipped with every mod. con. except air conditioning, as was especially noticeable in the Red Sea. . . . The passage of the Suez Canal was interesting and was very smoothly organised under the new management.' *

B Squadron was picked up at Aden, on 7 September, and the Regiment arrived in Singapore on 17 September, a journey of twenty-two days. This too was a marked improvement on the previous voyage from Singapore, which had taken thirty-three days.

> Singapore showed signs of much new building . . . but Nee Soon was much the same, the transit accommodation now being corrugated iron 'godolphins' instead of tents.

---

* The Egyptian Government, following the 1956 Anglo-French invasion.

Malaya 1958–61

Yet again the King's Dragoon Guards were to be relieved, but this was for the last time. They were victims of the 1957 Sandys' Defence Review, and were returning home for amalgamation with the Queen's Bays.* Although it was little more than five years since the Regiment's earlier tour, the comings and goings of National Service meant that only a handful of the junior NCOs and troopers had previous Malayan experience. However, in the Officers' Mess all the field officers and several captains were old hands, as were all the warrant officers and sergeants.

Final Stages of the Emergency

By July 1957, 60 per cent of Malaya had been declared 'White Areas' (where there were no curfew or other Emergency restrictions) and the following month the country had achieved full independence from Britain, but stayed in the Commonwealth. Singapore's independence followed in 1959. (It was not until 1963 that 'Malaysia' was created.) From 1957, operations against the terrorists by British forces were therefore conducted under an Anglo-Malayan Defence Agreement. Continuing successes by the security forces against the MRLA, including mass surrenders in Perak and Johore early in 1958, The military commitment could continue to be scaled down and normality returned for the civilian population.

There was already only one British armoured car regiment in Malaya, as the King's Dragoon Guards had taken over both regiments' tasks when the 15th/19th Hussars completed their tour in May 1957. When the Regiment relieved them they were based on Ipoh, in the north of the country, less a squadron in Johore. Ipoh, which is capital of the state of Perak and the second largest town in Malaya, is also the centre of one of the main tin-producing areas.

As in 1950–53, the Regiment's operational duties were to include road patrols, VIP and food convoy escorts, curfew-breaking patrols and assistance to the police in identity card checks and searching of villages. Some dismounted patrols and ambushes were also mounted in cultivated areas and on the jungle fringes. Sabre troops were again made up of two

---

* To become 1st The Queen's Dragoons Guards.

armoured cars and two armoured personnel carriers. The armoured car was still the Daimler, but the scout cars were Ferrets and six-wheeled Saracen APCs had taken the place of the GMCs. HQ Squadron remained intact, as the Regiment was neither as dispersed as before, nor was there the pressing need for as many people as possible to be deployed 'at the sharp end'. In sharp contrast to their previous stay in Malaya the Regiment was not fired on once throughout the tour, nor did they suffer any casualties from enemy action.

Ipoh
On 6 October 1957 the Regiment, less C Squadron, moved into Ramillies Camp, C Squadron having already moved in late September to Johore Bahru. Ramillies Camp was 'something of a hotchpotch with various other small units in different corners of the camp and nothing approaching a tidy layout. The *bashas* were of various ages . . .'. After the Regiment had been there for some weeks it was decided that the Camp might be occupied for a matter of years, rather than months, and improvements put in hand included a new sewage system, a better cookhouse and NAAFI canteen, and several basketball and badminton pitches. Neighbours included the command post of Headquarters 28 Commonwealth Brigade Group, 1st Loyals and 2nd/6th Gurkha Rifles. 28 Brigade Group's main headquarters were in Taiping about fifty miles to the north.

An early visitor to the Regiment was the Under Secretary of State for War, Mr Julian Amery, accompanied by the Commander-in-Chief, General Sir Richard Hull, and the Military Secretary, General Sir Hugh Stockwell*. The Minister had had to spend ten days in hospital in Singapore on first arrival and had been advised to drink only Lucozade during his tour. The Mess Secretary therefore obtained a bottle of 'at least Lucozade type', and this was placed on ice. 'Mr Amery's Private Secretary was taken to be shown this attractive item, but as the door of the refrigerator was flung open to reveal it, there was a sickening crash and it lay shattered on the floor.' Luckily the Private Secretary had brought a supply with him.

---

* GOC Malaya during the Regiment's previous tour.

Malaya 1958–61

South Johore, 1958–59 *(C Squadron)*

C Squadron, led by Major BJW Cobb, was just in time to take part in the final stages of Operation Tiger, in which the remaining twenty terrorists were being cleared from South Johore. From 23 September they had a troop detached at Tampoi, under 2nd Lieutenant MC Whitaker. Shortly afterwards the rest of the Squadron moved out from Johore Bahru to a palm oil estate four miles along the Kluang–Mersing road.

> After a few false alarms and seeing an interesting selection of snakes, the Squadron returned to barracks for a few days, having gained a lot of experience in a short time.

The next Squadron turn-out was to Simpang Rengam where limited ambushes and dismounted patrols were carried out. The nearest approach to an incident was the discovery of a food dump and the sighting of five CTs who escaped into the jungle. During this period the Squadron also provided escorts for the Under Secretary of State for War and the Chief of Staff of the Nepalese Army. A short time later two troops maintained patrols for twenty-four hours a day on a very isolated stretch of road fifty miles from Johore Bahru on the Kota Tinggi road. They were based on 'No 4 Lee' and 'saw a lot of wild life if nothing else ... '.

This proved to be the last troop detachment in the south of Malaya as the successful conclusion of Operation Tiger enabled South Johore to be declared 'White'. It also freed the Squadron for a move. In early January 1959, they went back across the Causeway to Nee Soon in Singapore, but not before they had dismantled the camp at Tampoi and moved all the shelters to Nee Soon for use as improvised garages.

Perak, 1958–60

Meanwhile A Squadron, led by Major HSR Watson, had come under operational command of 28 Brigade Group for the continuing operations in Perak. The Brigade Group, commanded by Brigadier J Mogg ('a great soldier's soldier'), was successor to the famous Commonwealth Division which had been formed for the Korean war. It included Australian, British, Gurkha and New Zealand battalions, an Australian battery and a Commonwealth squadron of sappers. Most of the activity to begin with was in an area north and south of Kuala

History of The 13th/18th Royal Hussars (Q.M.O.)

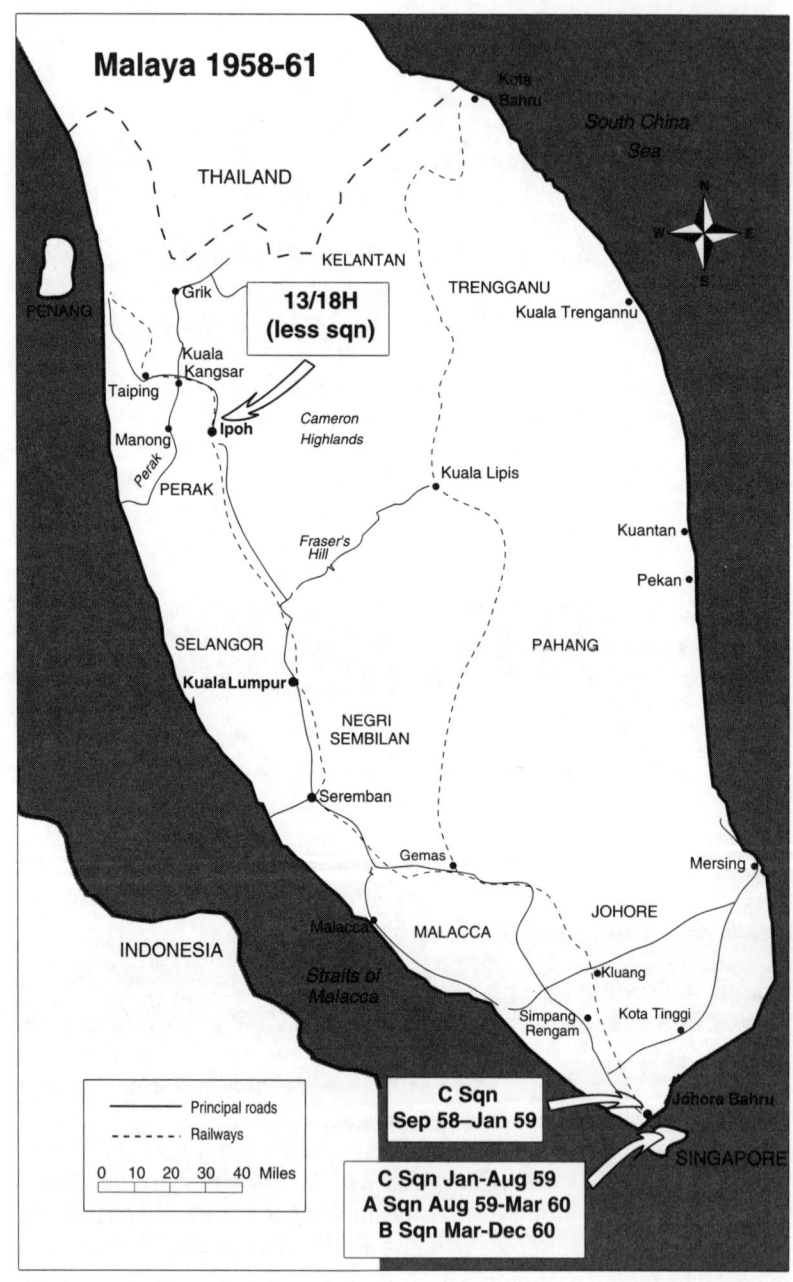

Malaya 1958–61

Kangsar on Operation Jaya, whose aim was to clear CTs from Northern Perak. It involved the Squadron in foot patrols in the jungle, usually for five days at a time, but one was out for ten days. Led by Lieutenant B Barrett on loan from the Royal Australian Armoured Corps, it went into 'what seemed to be solid *attap* growing on vertical slopes'. They found a track on which a week or two later the 2nd/6th Gurkhas ambushed and killed a terrorist, 'graciously attributing half the credit for the kill to the efforts of our patrol'. Road patrols were carried out throughout the operational area, identity cards checked, curfews and other Emergency restrictions enforced as well as general 'showing the flag'. Early in 1959 the Squadron was transferred for a while to Operation Ginger in the immediate area of Ipoh, where almost all the work was in vehicles, before returning to the Jaya commitments. Interspersed with operations were two expeditions with Regimental Headquarters to Singapore, nearly 400 miles away, for practice in the Internal Security role and a number of VIP escorts. On escort duty 'the main impression . . . as on our last visit to Malaya, was of the great speed at which Daimlers and Saracens are expected to go, often on wet and slippery roads . . .'.

B Squadron was kept in reserve while they recuperated and re-trained after their exertions in Arabia. They also needed reinforcements to replace their considerably depleted strength, as men completed overseas tours or left on National Service release. Led by Major G Stocker who had taken over from Major Jolley, the Squadron embarked on two Exercises named Bughunt. The first involved a move to the Thai border and the second an expedition into Central Malaya. Both had as a subsidiary aim the collection of rare insects and the British and Liverpool museums did well from the scheme. In May the Squadron was ready for operations again and they took over on Jaya from A Squadron. They soon had three troops on detachment, one each with 3rd Royal Australian Regiment and 1st New Zealand Regiment and one on its own. By November the work load had increased considerably, as the emphasis changed to convoying food in the restricted areas covered by the operation. It then involved six troops for every day of the week which meant that every sabre troop and a composite troop from

Squadron Headquarters was on duty every day for some three months, during which the monthly distance covered leaped to well over 40,000 miles. To reduce unnecessary mileage they moved nearer to the operational area and set up camp on part of a rubber estate called Gapis. This was 'an almost ideal squadron camp, with a dilapidated house for offices, stores and messes, "Gurkharized" tents, a good cookhouse and showers, and electric light'.

C Squadron replaced B Squadron in February 1960, for the last stages of Operation Jaya. Major PB Tillard was now C Squadron Leader, after an interregnum under Major Watson when Major Cobb had succumbed to a particularly virulent attack of sprue. Initially they continued with escorting food convoys. That was coupled with daily surprise checks on curfew enforcement, with the police platoon which was attached to the Squadron and lived in the same camp. Operation Jaya's principal target was a group of six 'hard-core' CTs living in the Bubu forest; the main CT force was now based out of reach over the border in Thailand. Those remaining in Malaya were:

> ... very experienced in existing and, unco-operatively, have strict orders not to contact the Security Forces at all and only to meet their remaining civilian chums when absolutely essential. Their aim is only to survive and, by surviving, to hope to retain in being some skeleton Communist organisation. ... The convoys were fun if arduous, especially in the north to Grik which involved a round trip of 150 miles, the track near the border being very rough indeed. Our new drivers quickly either conquered or crashed and, considering we were averaging 40,000 miles a month, the latter were fortunately few.

The worst of them was on the Grik track when Sergeant E Davies's Ferret plunged down a near-vertical cliff into the rocky, fast-flowing river beneath. He broke both legs and several other bones, but managed to hang on to a tree over the river. Trooper R Beasley, the driver, was trapped in the upside-down Ferret with all hatches banged shut and his head in a tiny air space under the wireless. Both were undoubtedly saved by the coolness of the JCLO [Junior Civilian Liaison Officer], who himself had been flung thirty feet down the bank. Despite the isolated spot, Sergeant Davies was evacuated by helicopter to Taiping in only a few hours and then back to England.

Malaya 1958–61

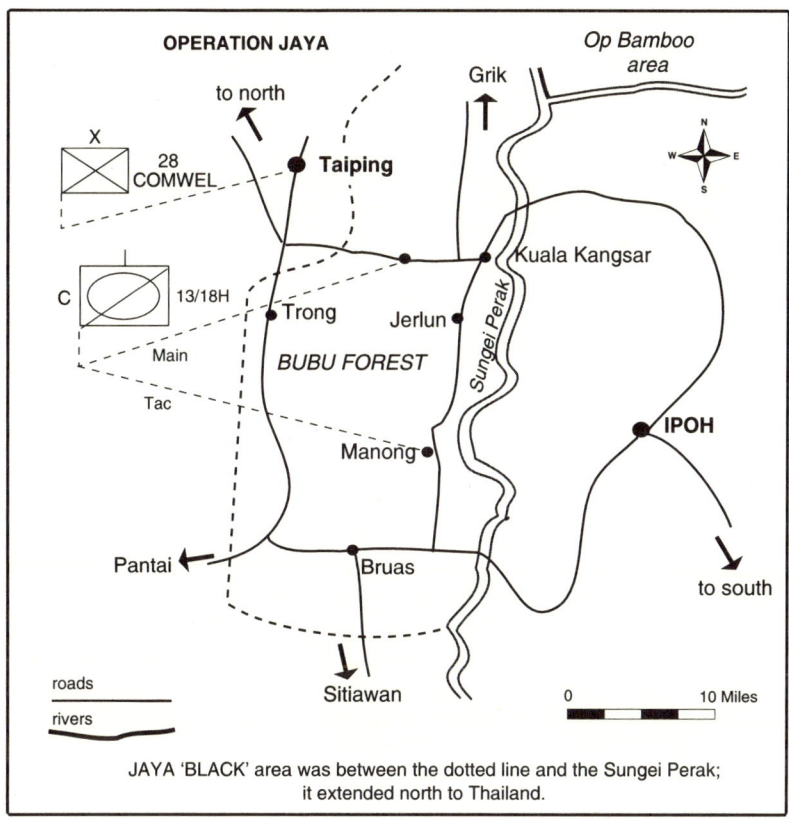

JAYA 'BLACK' area was between the dotted line and the Sungei Perak; it extended north to Thailand.

Our other enemy was the local fauna . . . 4 Troop repulsed the attack of a 15 foot cobra which reared up level with the driver's hatch . . . SHQ Troop almost lost a Ferret to a mechanically minded reptile knocked off a bough by their aerial into the turret . . . the crew bailed out, leaving the snake in command. Luckily it could not drive and a determined counter attack with wireless aerials restored the situation.

Frustrated with the lack of contact with the real enemy, Major Tillard and the head of Kuala Kangsar's Special Investigation Branch hatched a phony incident in the hope of attracting any CTs who might possibly be operating nearby. A half troop 'drove furiously' up a logging track to the edge of the jungle and there opened heavy fire. Meanwhile a Chinese detective, suitably disguised and slightly 'bloodstained', emerged from his hiding place on the floor of the Saracen and was later seen by many loggers and tappers seeking the aid of his Communist comrades. His 'escape' was also prominently announced in the local papers. Unfortunately:

> ... this honey pot did not attract the right bees although, since we only told the Brigade Commander at his next weekly O Group, it did attract various comments from our antipodean colleagues – made in the nicest possible way of course.

On 25 March the overall stability of the whole country persuaded the Government to lift the food restrictions. But:

> ... just as thoughts of leave, training, et cetera were beginning to rear their restful heads, seven smart, well-uniformed CTs were seen in the Squadron's usual area between Jerlun and Manong. They were not locals and had probably been sent down from Thailand to bring words of good Communist cheer.

Immediately six companies of Anglians, New Zealanders, and Gurkhas were rushed into the jungle with a view to surrounding them. Equally quickly, 'Tilforce' was formed, of about battalion strength, consisting of C Squadron, three platoons of police, one platoon from the Royal Australian Regiment and one troop from the Australian Field Battery. Their task was to block the exits east from the jungle.

> Whilst Squadron Tactical HQ risked their heads, by setting up in a relatively shady coconut grove, the ambushes were sheer hell for the troops. As darkness fell, the din of the mosquito arose, but mosquito repellent was banned since terrorists could smell it a mile off . . . Eventually it was accepted that the terrorists had retired north into Thailand rather than south and the operation was called off . . .

Although two troops were subsequently lent to the Australians in Grik to help them patrol the Thai border, this was the Regiment's last anti-terrorist operation in Malaya.

Hussar Admirals

In December 1959 2nd Lieutenant GE Turle was detached for a month as Officer IC Boats, Grik. He was the first of several to fill this unusual appointment for cavalry officers. Known unofficially as 'The Admiral', the lucky incumbent held sway over sixteen boats under contract to the Army. They were about sixty feet long and were usually powered with 40 hp outboard motors. The 'driver' and the 'conductor' in the two-man crew were Malays, and the boats could carry either seven fully equipped men or a thousand pounds of stores. The fleet operated over some hundred miles of the Perak and Temengor rivers. In an area where there were no roads they were the only practical means of re-supply or reinforcement for the units operating in the jungle north and west of Grik, apart from very limited air-drop and helicopter supply.

The rivers have numerous rapids which in several places extend more or less continuously for several miles. Wild life abounded, but the thickness of the jungle cover meant that there were only occasional sightings of the resident elephants, tigers and other game. Assisted by a Malay Civil Liaison Officer the 'Admiral' was responsible for such matters as the maintenance of the craft's motors, briefing of crews, liaison with units and Brigade Headquarters, supervision of loading and despatch and payment of contractors.

End of The Malayan Emergency
In 1959 there had been only twelve terrorist incidents and twenty-seven contacts by the Security Forces and more and more areas were declared 'White'. On 31 July 1960 restrictions ended everywhere except in some zones along the border with Thailand, on the other side of which a hard core of survivors of the MRLA had taken sanctuary. That enabled the State of Emergency to be formally ended and a Victory Parade to be held in Kuala Lumpur on 1 August. The Regiment provided the leading contingent (mainly A Squadron) in the Commonwealth mounted section of the parade, with Major JW Bell commanding vehicle column as a whole. The salute was taken by the Paramount Ruler, HM The Yang Di-Pertuan Agong. It was an impressive affair, with the marching and vehicle columns taking over one and a half hours to pass the saluting base.

> Most rehearsals had to start at 4 am to avoid morning traffic. This meant little normal sleep for nearly a week. When the Squadron officers passed two elephants at 3 am on the main street of Kuala Lumpur it had a decidedly sobering effect. It was half a mile later when a voice was heard: 'Did you by any chance see two elephants?' The relief in the voices of those that replied was patently obvious.

Later in the year, the Commanding Officer, Lieutenant Colonel DHE Coker, was received by the Deputy Prime Minister of Malaya (the Prime Minister was at the United Nations General Assembly). On behalf of the People of Malaya, Tun Abdul Razak presented a ceremonial *kris* in appreciation of the Regiment's efforts in the battle to rid the country of Communist terrorists. The following year, when the Regiment was back in Rhine Army, a silver cigarette box arrived from the Federation of Malaya Police, in recognition of the assistance given to them during the Emergency.

Internal Security in Singapore
C Squadron's role in Singapore was Internal Security as there continued to be threats of unrest for which the police might need support. In 1955 and 1956 there had been serious rioting and in October 1956 a squadron of King's Dragoon Guards had spent five days patrolling and enforcing the curfew.

> IS training became our main preoccupation . . . one would often meet someone carrying a notice saying 'Disperse or We Fire'.

The squadron also provided the opposition for inter-battalion internal security competitions, in which each battalion, with its allotted police squad, had to deal with situations such as dispersal of a crowd. The troopers took with some relish to the freedom 'to fight with and taunt the police with impunity' and 'considerable zest was put into the task'. A Squadron replaced C in August 1959 and found itself undertaking such contrasting tasks as mounting the Commander-in-Chief's guard as well as providing the 'motley crowd' for riot drill practice. For the final changeover B Squadron relieved A Squadron in March 1960.

Operational plans also called for the reinforcement of the Singapore-based squadron by Regimental Headquarters and another sabre squadron. This was practised on a number of occasions and was demanding while it lasted, involving as it did some 1,000 miles on Malayan roads and seventy-two hours without sleep. 'The drivers and crew commanders have a right to feel slightly smug' said one squadron report, after receiving a congratulatory message from GOC Singapore District on the speed and efficiency of the practice, including an accident and breakdown-free move.

Malaya 1958–61

Training and Other Matters Military
With manning still dependent on National Service the arrival of new drafts was again very disruptive during the second tour in Malaya. However, training, both individual and collective, was much less difficult than during the previous tour, even if it lacked the realism which the Regiment's own jungle warfare area had then provided. When squadrons were not actively deployed on operations a number of exercises were undertaken. A Squadron in 1960 had an exercise 'to test endurance'. This achieved such a result that an early morning attack to capture gold bullion from an Ipoh bank on the last morning of the exercise (with profits for all), had troop leaders trying to offer their shares in exchange for sleep. Also from Ipoh, C Squadron reported on an exercise which was a

> ... walk up through the jungles of the Cameron Highlands ... It was for most of the Squadron their first experience of the jungle and it was interesting to find out who knew where we were.

Preparation for the conversion to tanks on return to Europe began towards the end of the tour and B Squadron undertook from Singapore some preliminary training in armoured tactics which included an exercise around Gemas on the mainland. A troop also twice acted as enemy in Brigade exercises on the Kluang–Jemaluang road 'so well known to us from some ten years before'. Whenever possible exercise routes took the participants to the coast and so provided the opportunity for 'Rest and Recuperation' (R & R – another phrase from US Army usage) on sandy beaches.

Colonel of the Regiment
In September 1960 the Queen approved the appointment of Colonel VAB Dunkerly* to be Colonel of the Regiment in place of Major General Miller. He contrived a visit to the Regiment soon after appointment which included travelling the length of Malaya to see the squadrons in Singapore and the operational area in the north, a Regimental parade at Ipoh, visits to a rubber estate and a tin mine, as well as sundry social events. There was 'a thought that such a tour in Malayan heat would

---
* Commanded the Regiment from June 1944 until invalided home in October, handing over to Lord Feversham. He resumed command in June 1945 finally handing over to Lieutenant Colonel Hermon in 1947.

be too much of a good thing for someone straight from England. However, such was Colonel Dunkerly's energy that he thrived while we old Malayan hands wilted in our efforts to keep pace with him.'

Administrative Inspection
According to the records the Regiment was subjected to only one Administrative Inspection during the tour. That was by Major General JAR Robertson, GOC 17 Gurkha Division at Ipoh, while Brigadier WC Walker, Commander 99 Gurkha Infantry Brigade Group checked on A Squadron in Singapore. Both went well and General Robertson reported:

> I was entirely satisfied with my inspection and the unit. Administratively the unit is sound, the parade was first class, and the men of the Regiment I met were of high quality.

But his overheard comment to certain senior infantry officers that, 'the best drill parade I have seen in the Far East was given by a cavalry regiment' was not appreciated everywhere.

A week beforehand C Squadron had been warned that they would be required to parade in an air-portable role.

> This was a new thought for the Far East, but after an immense struggle with bumf, and great co-operation from the rest of the Regiment, the Squadron eventually stood firm on parade. The difficulty was to get off. The square was small and the vehicles many. However, ornithology came to the rescue and we drove away rapidly like the 'Oozalum Bird' – very rapidly in ever-decreasing circles until . . . We were much helped by the Band who finished with a spirited rendering of 'Gone Away'.

Commonwealth Alliances
After the Second World War the *Journal* continued to show as Allied regiments one from Australia, the 18th/23rd Light Horse (Adelaide Lancers), and two from Canada, 17th Duke of York's Royal Canadian Hussars and The Manitoba Mounted Rifles. All were victims of post-War amalgamations or disbandments, news of which which came through somewhat slowly. In 1948 the Regiment heard that, having been 'linked' in 1930 the 18th Light Horse and the 23rd Light Horse were 'unlinked' in 1936. In the War the 18th had been part of 2 Armoured Division and when that was disbanded in 1944 so were its units.

Malaya 1958–61

It took until 1958 to hear (with apologies) from the Canadian Defence Department that the Manitoba Mounted Rifles had changed its role to anti-aircraft artillery in 1937 and had been disbanded in 1945. Also in 1958, The 6th Duke of Connaught's Royal Canadian Hussars amalgamated with the 17th Hussars to form The Royal Canadian Hussars; the 13th/18th alliance continued with the new Regiment, but sadly there was no new alliance with an Australian regiment.

Sport

More attention could be given to sport than was possible during the first tour and full advantage was taken of what was on offer in Malaya, where there is great enthusiasm for all forms of sport. The dispersion of squadrons on detachment meant that it was still difficult to field successful teams at Regimental level. However, the Regimental Eleven did well, winning many of its matches and losing the Army Cup to a Royal Anglian team which included at least two Tottenham Hotspur players. Of soccer the *Journal* noted:

> Playing football in temperatures well into the eighties, on bone hard pitches, for an hour and a half, against Chinese, Indian and Malay teams, who not only play continental football, but are also about three yards faster than us, has been an experience that few of our players have encountered before.

There were no major successes, but the groundwork was being laid for a team which was to be much improved in Germany.

The Regiment's arrival coincided with the beginning of the rugger season and they were able to field two complete teams after the efforts in Germany to get a core of long-service players. The Regimental team reached the Malayan Inter-Unit semi-finals and had a number of games against local teams. In 1960 the pending departure meant that they could not pursue the Army Cup, but they won half the fourteen games played.

In hockey the Regiment also reached the semi-final of the Inter-Unit competition in 1959 and a number of members were included in the Perak Armed Forces (Imperial) Team, playing in a competition where the standards were very high. The following year there was just time to complete all their matches in the Brigade hockey league and secure second place. The overall result was nine games won out of thirteen.

History of The 13th/18th Royal Hussars (Q.M.O.)

In cross-country running, too, the competition was intense, especially from the extremely fit Gurkha battalions. They took the first five places in the Divisional event, but the Regiment's team finished a creditable sixth.

Cricket flourished, according to the 1959 *Journal*, and in the first half of that year's season the Regimental team was undefeated in fifteen of twenty-two matches. They were finalists in the Northern Zone of the Army Cup and expected to win the Final. (Something went amiss, however, with recording their achievements for the rest of the tour; there were no cricket notes in 1960.) Several Regimental players turned out regularly for the Perak State team and at least two, Troopers J Isles and J Wassung, played for the Army in Malaya.

In athletics there were creditable performances in 1960, with the track event team either winning or coming second in every event in the Brigade Group competition, but weaknesses in the field events brought the overall place down to second. Against much stronger competition in the Divisional Championships 'there was an obvious need for more coaching and training' and the Regiment finished third. The star performer was 2nd Lieutenant NL Karmel who won the 400 metres and came second in the 200 metres. (The following year, a civilian again, he was selected for the Great Britain team which toured the Near East.)

Polo was now being played fairly widely in the principal towns of Malaya as well as Singapore. It was greatly aided by an arrangement for ponies to be moved at the Malayan Amateur Racing Association's expense for periodic Race Meetings at the different courses round the peninsula. Polo tournaments were fixed for the week before the race meeting, at which the versatile ponies would be taken on to the race track to run over distances varying between a two furlong scurry and one mile. In this encouraging environment the first Regimental Polo Team to play since 1939 took the field at the December 1958 Ipoh Tournament. Individuals were able to get quite a lot of experience playing for other teams and Major ERMcM Wright's enthusiasm and skilful coaching meant that, here too, useful groundwork was laid for the future. (Although it was to be several years after leaving Malaya before the Regiment was

Malaya 1958–61

again reasonably near a polo centre.) At the race meetings there were a number of successes on Regimental ponies; the jockeys in the Ladies' Races included Mrs Coker, the Commanding Officer's wife, and Mrs Tillard, C Squadron Leader's wife.

After the successful revival of fencing in Neumünster all the fencers except Lieutenant PJ Davis had left the Regiment on other postings or release. It was not until 1960 that, through the efforts of Mr Davis, a team was raised again. Despite all but one of their number having no previous experience they won the Divisional Team Championship and represented Malaya in the FARELF Championship in Hong Kong.

Farewell to the Armoured Car

The days with armoured cars were now fast coming to an end and the Regiment received notice that it was to move back to Germany and convert to tanks early in 1961. On 31 August 1960, the Commander-in-Chief, Far East Land Forces, General Sir Richard Hull (himself a cavalryman) was Inspecting Officer at the Regiment's Farewell Parade to the Armoured Car. The *Journal* records:

> A particularly dashing parade on Ipoh Airport had been arranged including a musical ride by the whole Regiment mounted in vehicles. Unfortunately, HM The Yang Di-Pertuan Agong, Paramount Ruler of Malaya, was on his deathbed, therefore a large public parade was not possible. A brief parade 'Crews Front' on the Regimental parade ground was substituted at very short notice. The CinC, in a short speech, complimented the Regiment on the work carried out in Malaya and the high standard of turnout of crews and vehicles. He regretted that the proper parade could not take place but felt sure that all our vehicles would have started!

An unusual compliment was paid to the Regiment in November when The Sultan of Perak invited the Officers and their wives to dinner at his *Istana*.* 'His Highness showed a particular interest in the Regiment throughout our tour in Malaya and we had had the pleasure of meeting him both socially and officially on many occasions.'

---

* *Istana* = palace

History of The 13th/18th Royal Hussars (Q.M.O.)

After handing over to The Royals in mid-December, the Regiment returned to England in the *Nevasa*, B Squadron from Singapore and the remainder from Penang.

> By comparison with life on the old troopships, travelling on HMT *Nevasa* was luxury indeed . . . Our pleasure was increased too by several old friends in the crew from *Empire Trooper* days, not least Commodore Bond who can always be guaranteed to produce a happy voyage . . . the Band, as always, got no rest at all. Entertainment featured large over Christmas and the New Year and recollections of the voyage now seem to centre on mammoth meals and a continuous round of enjoyment. In particular the children must surely remember Father Christmas's appearance in a lifeboat . . . It seemed very soon after leaving Malaya that we were in Southampton Water and there on the quayside through the cold gloom of a winter evening we could see the banner of the Regimental Association waved by that stalwart Old Comrade Mr Abbott . . . The following morning [5 January] the Regiment disembarked and dispersed straight on leave. This time, though, there was a difference for we were all to rejoin the Regiment in its new home in Germany. . . [rather than have a period in a transit camp]

It was to be the Regiment's last journey by troopship. The economies of air travel were all too obvious: at 1957 prices, a passage to Singapore cost £120 against £45 for contract air trooping. A three-week journey had to be set against a two-day flight.

Part 2

ARMOURED REGIMENT

1961 to 1977

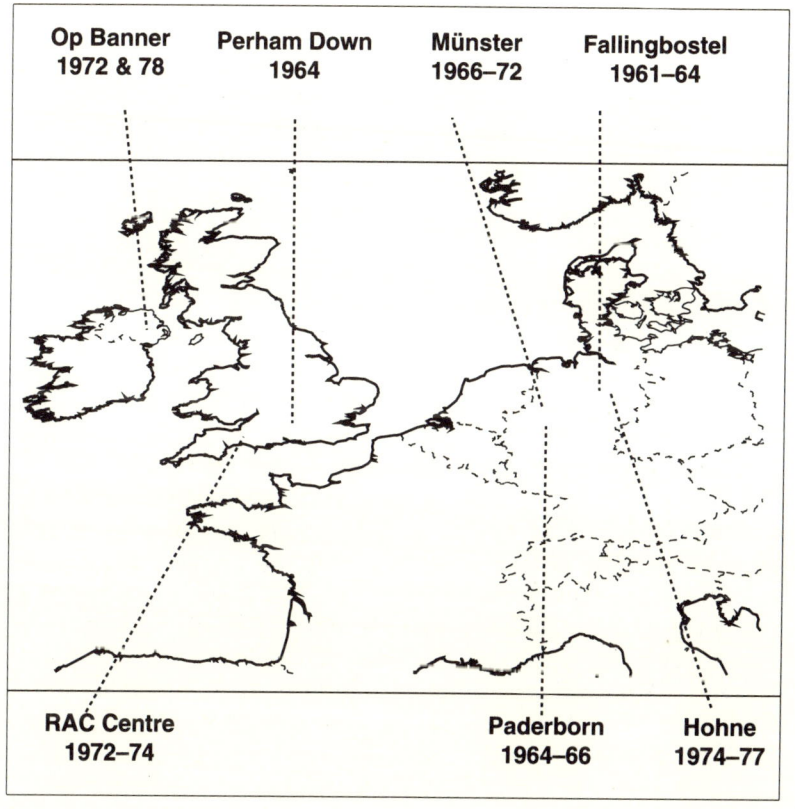

Introduction to Part 2

A PROFESSIONAL ARMY

Once more a small, professional, all-volunteer Army of about the same strength was in being, but not deployed all over the world. It was still in the Far East, in the Middle East, in the Caribbean; there were still troops in Cyprus, in Gibraltar, in Malta, even in Libya; there was a garrison in Hong Kong, there were soldiers in Aden, the strategic reserve stationed at home would, with the help of the Royal Air Force, mount exercises in many parts of the Commonwealth; there was above all a powerful, well-equipped and highly trained British Army of the Rhine, where some 55,000 soldiers lived, worked, married, exercised and fulfilled Britain's treaty obligations.
Gentlemen in Khaki by Major General John Strawson

A Major Change of Role for the Regiment
The desert campaigns apart, the 1939–45 War had provided only limited scope for armoured cars. They came into their own in the post-war years when the British Army was continuously deployed on campaigns against various forms of guerrilla. Armoured car troops were often ideally suited for the sort of operations demanded during the withdrawal from imperial responsibilities. This meant that their regiments were much more likely to be posted to stations outside Europe, often with tasks at troop level. Junior officers and NCOs therefore had the maximum scope for developing personal initiative.

Armoured regiments, on the other hand, had little opportunity for employment outside Rhine Army. Their only employment on actual operations was for the Korean war and the 1956 expedition to Port Said. In 1961 a squadron of tanks was also with the force sent to Kuwait, to counter an Iraqi threat of invasion.

Introduction to Part 2

Only eight of the twenty-six regiments of the Royal Armoured Corps were equipped with armoured cars; many of the remainder had been stationed in Germany for protracted periods. Some rotation of roles was thought desirable and, in 1961, the 13th/18th Hussars were the guinea pigs for a time-consuming and expensive conversion process. It involved extensive re-training of most tradesmen and a considerable shift in tactical training – and attitudes. Medium reconnaissance calls for high standards of map reading and, in the days of the No 19 wireless set, of signalling. Junior commanders have to be able to sum up and report speedily on what they find, which in turn demands a good general knowledge of a potential enemy's organisation and tactics. Essential qualities are an independent mind and a capacity to improvise and adapt to a variety of situations. By contrast, the armoured regiment's role calls for close co-operation with other arms, particularly artillery and infantry. Their essential skills are gunnery, in which the whole crew of a tank is involved, and tactical movement with other arms. A tank crew must bring the main armament to bear effectively and speedily. At troop and squadron level the aim is to direct the maximum firepower on enemy targets, particularly armour.

Defence Policies and Economies

During some sixteen years, when the Regiment was equipped with 'main battle tanks', there was almost continuous modification to British defence policies. As well as the financial difficulties which influenced defence policy, events on the world stage would affect the Regiment directly or indirectly.

There had been political pressure since 1945 both for the reduction of the British Empire and for greater emphasis on Britain's role in Europe. There was also substantial economic pressure for more 'cost-effective' armed forces. In their mid-1950s review of Britain's defence policy, the Eden Government had to take into account the build-up of nuclear weapon strengths by the major powers and to accept that the United Kingdom was trying to do too much, in too many spheres of defence. The 1956 Suez débâcle made it clear that the days were past for Britain to go it alone. The radical changes in the 1957 Defence White Paper by Mr Duncan Sandys were therefore intended to lead to a reduction in overseas garrisons and to a smaller, all-regular Army geared primarily to nuclear war in Europe. A Strategic Reserve based in Britain would be deployed by air if operations outside Europe were required.

Events in the Middle East over the next few years showed that dependence on air mobility was not enough, on its own, to justify reduced overseas garrisons. The need for troops to be acclimatised on arrival in different climatic zones reduced the effect of speedy movement from Britain; the limitations of 1950s aircraft meant that heavy equipment had to be stockpiled in or near an operational theatre. In 1962 a new Minister of Defence, Mr Harold Watkinson, with Lord Mountbatten as Chief of Defence Staff, announced modifications to the Sandys policy. With the remaining larger colonies progressing to independence, account had still to be taken of threats to remaining British interests east of Suez. Two 'assault ships', *Fearless* and *Intrepid*, together with the commando carriers *Albion* and *Bulwark*, significantly improved the capability for combined operations. Major bases were to be kept in Aden and Singapore.

Two years later Mr Healey became Defence Secretary under Mr Wilson. In February 1966 his first Defence Review set out three principles: Britain would not undertake major military operations without allies; military obligations would not be accepted unless the country concerned provided the base facilities, and no attempt would be made to maintain bases in an independent country against its wishes. The Aden base was to be given up when South Arabia became independent in 1968.

The state of an already fragile British economy was made much worse in 1966–67 by the combined effects of seamen's and dockers' strikes, the closure of the Suez Canal because of the Arab/Israeli Six Day War and the accompanying Arab oil embargo. Yet again, Defence had to find the bulk of the savings needed. A Supplementary Defence Statement in July 1967 announced the halving of the forces in South East Asia by 1970–71 and total evacuation by the mid–1970s. A brigade group was to be brought back from Germany and the overall loss to the Army would be seventeen more major units. A year later the timetable was brought forward again:

Introduction to Part 2

> Britain's defence effort will in future be concentrated mainly in Europe and the North Atlantic area. We shall accelerate the withdrawal of our forces from Malaysia and Singapore and complete it by the end of 1971. We shall also withdraw from the Persian Gulf at the same time.

By 1971 the military withdrawal from Empire was over; the political transition to a multi-racial Commonwealth was almost complete and the third attempt to join the European Economic Community was successful. Britain seemed likely to be better able to avoid involvement in 'other people's wars'. By then, however, there were again 'Troubles' in Northern Ireland. They were to play a significant part in commitments for the Army as a whole and the Regiment itself. Nevertheless 1974–75 brought further Defence cuts under another Labour administration.

Not such a Dull Life
In the event, the Regiment had more variety over the next sixteen years than might have been expected when they relinquished armoured cars. From 1962 to 1964, based at Fallingbostel, they were one of the three armoured regiments of 7 Armoured Brigade Group. The next two years were spent in Paderborn as the armoured regiment of 4 Guards Brigade. That meant a change in tactical emphasis, with each sabre squadron supporting one of the Brigade's three battalions. 1967 was a year of great variety in England, with expeditions to Aden and Singapore. Next year they were back in Germany, again in 4 Guards Brigade, but this time in Münster and with another change in tactical grouping and another conversion, to Chieftain tanks. Soon afterwards came communal rioting and then terrorism in Northern Ireland. Armoured and artillery units in Rhine Army were called on for tours of duty as infantry and the Regiment's first spell on Operation Banner was in 1972. That was followed by two years in England when they manned the Royal Armoured Corps Centre in Dorset and provided the Demonstration Squadron at Warminster. The years as an armoured regiment were completed with three years back with 7 Armoured Brigade at Hohne, during which there was another four month spell in Northern Ireland.

History of The 13th/18th Royal Hussars (Q.M.O.)

At Home in Yorkshire

Until 1958 most cavalry regiments did not have a particular part of the country from which they recruited, nor did they have a permanent 'home' in Britain, as did the infantry. In 1947 one territorial link was created when the Regiment was formally affiliated to the Warwickshire Yeomanry,* one of the oldest yeomanry regiments. The 13th/18th provided the Yeomanry's permanent staff, usually the commanding officer or second-in-command, the adjutant and some twenty warrant officers, NCOs and troopers as instructors and drivers, storemen etc.

Part of the National Serviceman's commitment was a period with a Territorial Army unit, after full time service, during which a minimum number of 'drills' had to be completed. The Royal Armoured Corps element of the TA therefore had little difficulty in being up to strength for their mobilisation role of reinforcing the regular armoured divisions, Nevertheless, their effectiveness on mobilisation would have been severely limited, as 80 per cent of Yeomanry were National Servicemen whose annual training was nowhere near enough to keep them proficient. The 1957 Defence Review pointed out that in global war it would, in any case, be impossible to transport more than a small part overseas and the TA armoured formations were to be done away with. In the resulting cuts the Warwickshire Yeomanry amalgamated to form the Queen's Own Warwickshire and Worcestershire Yeomanry, with whom the Regiment continued for a short time to be affiliated.

In 1958, however, each regular regiment was allocated a recruiting area. For the 13th/18th Hussars their home was now to be South Yorkshire and the East Riding. The bulk of the men coming into the Regiment would in future hail from Barnsley, Doncaster, Rotherham, Sheffield and the surrounding areas. That also meant a change in Yeomanry affiliation, to the Queen's Own Yorkshire Yeomanry.†

---

* Troops of volunteer cavalry in Warwickshire, raised in 1794 against the threat of French invasion, were formed into a regiment in 1797.

† The 1957 amalgamation of three Yorkshire Yeomanry regiments. Until 1960 the affiliation was shared with the 9th Lancers.

Introduction to Part 2

The involvement in Yorkshire was consolidated in 1962 by the creation of a Home Headquarters. Until then the Regimental Association was run by volunteers and for all other purposes the Regiment operated from wherever it was stationed. Home Headquarters opened at York on 1 July 1962 with a staff of two, Lieutenant Colonel JR Palmer, a retired Regimental officer, and a clerk. It was soon clear that theirs was an indispensable, and economic, operation and it was difficult to imagine how it had been possible to operate without a Home HQ for so many years. Equally it was hard to remember what life had been like without the territorial link with a particularly vibrant and idiosyncratic part of England.

But in 1967, with the other reductions in the Services made by the beleaguered Wilson administration, came the swingeing cutback of the Reserve Forces. There was no longer to be a Territorial Army composed principally of local units and the Queen's Own Yorkshire Yeomanry was disbanded in 1969. A small cadre of officers and NCOs remained in office to carry on the name of the Regiment and retain the property and funds. All that remained of the British yeoman cavalry was to be one regiment – the Royal Yeomanry – with squadrons of armoured cars in different parts of the country. This latest retrenchment in the face of economic crisis was justified by an assumption that limited war was unlikely and that the nuclear missile exchanges of global war would prohibit any mass movement of reinforcements. However, in 1971, another twist of fortune's wheel enabled the Queen's Own Yorkshire Yeomanry cadre to be disbanded in favour of A Squadron (Yorkshire Yeomanry) The Queen's Own Yeomanry, with other squadrons based on Chester, Ayr and Tynemouth. The Regiment resumed its affiliation with the Yorkshire Squadron and provided the permanent staff for the Squadron.

The End of National Service

One consequence of the reduced commitments assumed in the Sandys Defence Review was that there was no further call-up for National Service after 1960. Shortly after the Regiment's farewell to the armoured car, therefore, came the farewell to the National Serviceman. Since the passing of the National Service Act in 1947, conscription had enabled the Services, especially the Army, to achieve something approaching viability. Even so, manpower shortages had been a continual worry, particularly in stations such as Malaya, where lengthy voyages reduced even further the effective time that the National Serviceman could be with the Regiment. (Ironically the replacement of movement by troopship with air-trooping came just as National Service was ending.)

The call to the colours came at the age of eighteen, unless deferment was obtained in order, for example, to go to university. Initial training for the Royal Armoured Corps was carried out by Training Regiments. Each man received from twelve to sixteen weeks instruction according to the trade for which he was selected, but by the time he joined the Regiment he had only a rudimentary knowledge of his job. He had to have further instruction before he could qualify as a tradesman and properly take his place in an armoured vehicle. Although the Regiment managed, just, to be up to strength numerically, it tended to be short of high-grade NCO tradesmen, and at any one time as many as a third of crewmen were unqualified. Luckily the armoured car regiments tended to get recruits with higher than average intelligence, but even so, the part of their service when they could be regarded as fully effective was all too short.

The burden on the Regular soldiers was considerable, particularly on the squadron leaders. The heavy demand for staff and other 'extra regimental' appointments meant that the rapid turnover in junior ranks was matched by an equally rapid turnover of their seniors. The beginning of each collective training season in Germany would see a squadron taking the field with a team which seldom had less than 50 per cent new faces. The most damaging effect of this constant flow was not so much on the standard of training, but on the near impossibility of getting to know one's men and their capabilities.

One view of National Service is that it offered an excellent opportunity for a young man to broaden his outlook before starting his civilian career, which should have been retained as a form of post educational training for the country's youth. The young men themselves tended to think of it as an organised waste of time, although the majority when they left the

Introduction to Part 2

Regiment agreed that they had both enjoyed and would benefit from their military service – as much as anything because they felt that they were doing something for the community. (That attitude was more evident when the Regiment was engaged on active service, rather than training for it.) Militarily speaking, the cost of National Service in terms of the manpower that had to be diverted to training was out of all proportion to the benefits of an up-to-strength Army. Against that, together with the Territorial Army, it did provide a valuable link between the Services and the civilian population.

Writing in the mid-1990s, the prestige of the Army in peacetime has seldom been higher, which derives, at least in part, from the perceived professionalism of all ranks. That reputation has been gained by a Regular Army which, despite successive cuts in Defence budgets, has been able to develop soldiers' skills and attitudes to an extent which was often not feasible in the 1950s and early 1960s.

A sidelight on National Service, so far as the 13th/18th was concerned, was that armoured car regiments were a popular option for intelligent young men, who thought that the operational role was likely to provide a more entertaining way than most, of meeting their National Service commitment. Some had private means and not all could, or even wished, to become officers. Free from such burdens as officers' mess subscriptions they could indulge in ways that young officers could ill afford. At a time when there were few other private cars in barracks there would be an exodus of troopers and junior NCOs in their cars from Neumünster, bound for the fleshpots of Hamburg. To be fair, the 'failed potential officers' also provided a valuable resource in staffing Regimental and Squadron Headquarters, and the PRI Shop.

The *Journal* recorded the passing of an era:

> On 28 November 1961, the last National Serviceman wearing our cap badge will leave the Regiment. It is doubtful if any of those who watched the militiamen arrive at Shorncliffe on 15 July 1939 foresaw that it would be over twenty-two years before the Regiment returned to an all Regular basis. There is little doubt that the Regiment has received excellent service, both in peace and war, from these 'reluctant heroes'. Many of the key jobs could not have been filled without their help. Happily, the traffic has

History of The 13th/18th Royal Hussars (Q.M.O.)

not been all one way. They gained, unwittingly at the time, a sense of duty, comradeship and tradition from our long Regimental heritage. We formally record our gratitude to all National Servicemen who have served with us and wish them well, where ever they may be.

A remark made by a troop sergeant in Malaya, about his corporal in command of a section in a GMC armoured personnel carrier, shows the value placed on them by their regular comrades:

> He's a National Serviceman; he's got a wife and family; he hasn't got much time to do; and yet – he's always the first one out of the vehicle every time we run into an ambush.

The Regiment never placed any distinction between its Regular and National Service members, of whatever rank. A contributor ('K.H.O.') to the April 1951 edition of the *Journal* made the point in his account of a typical day on convoy duty in Malaya, 'Eight Men':

> The road is hard, hot and dusty. For an hour they have sat there, some on the hard floor, the lucky ones on a cushion or groundsheet, absorbing the bumps, the heat and the drowsy monotony of the jungle streaming by on either side. Tall trees, creepers, bushes, ferns, grass and swamps. Eight men in a GMC, eight individuals united as a crew, training, working and enduring as one. They are taking a convoy to a village up the road, sixty miles of dangerous road, there might be a terrorist on every corner.
>
> The driver, a National Serviceman, who never dreamt he should come to see and do the things he does now. The Crew Commander, a Regular NCO of several years service, still thinking of when he soldiered in the comparative luxury of Germany or the Middle East. The operator, another National Serviceman, whose time is nearly up, still doing his job as well as the rest. The Bren Gunner, by the rear door and his Number Two are Regulars. The Bren Gunner can remember Barce, but the other has only just arrived. Throughout the crew a mixture of Regulars and National Servicemen – mixed like an alloy that is stronger than its components. None have ever been in action before and they wait for the sound of bullets cracking by and the sight of wrecked and burning vehicles. Mile after mile, every man looking, waiting. The Commander gives an order, the driver changes gear and the convoy speeds up. Now a cool breeze is blowing but with it come the first unwelcome spots of rain. Soon

Introduction to Part 2

it falls like hail, stinging and blinding the driver and commander, soaking everything and everybody. Water runs down the barrels of their guns and trickles out of the breech, the grenades lie in puddles on the floor. Then, as quickly as it started, the rain stops and once more the way is hot and hard.

Now the most welcome time of all. A halt to rest and have a smoke. 'Halt', 'Dismount', 'Sentries Out'. Oh! what a relief to stretch one's legs, to be able to relax for a minute or two. 'Start Up', 'Advance' and on the convoy goes again. Another score of sleepy miles pass by. Now! This is the dangerous part. The crew watch closely, every bush and every dip may hide a terrorist - waiting.

Crack! Crack! There it is. The hurried message over the wireless 'Ambush Right. Rifle fire and bren'.

The driver speeds up to get clear, smoke rises from a smoke grenade thrown to mark the spot. There is still firing but now it is our own. The Bren Gunner sprays the bank, each rifleman picks a spot and fires. The Commander fires, watching the lorry behind to see that it is still all right. And then another burst of shots on the road in front of them.

The driver speeds up still more, cursing the hot empty cases bouncing down his back. Then quiet once more. The convoy halts, the sentries are posted. Check-up, no casualties, a few bullet holes in the cab of a lorry. Report to control. On again! the terrorists want the food in our lorries and the convoy must get through. A patrol will soon be out to search the area.

No more incidents and soon the convoy rolls into the village and halts. The crew unloads, dismounts and smokes. Another escort finished, another job done.

A New Source of Officers

The Regiment benefited greatly from the introduction of a scheme for commissioning more warrant officers than those needed for the two Quartermaster appointments. (The first Technical Quartermaster had been appointed in 1957.) First to arrive, in November 1963, was Lieutenant HJ Gwilliam who became Mechanical Transport Officer (MTO). In the days before the REME took responsibility for first line repair he had been the Regiment's 'Mechanist Quartermaster Sergeant'. (Sadly he was killed in a car accident in 1967.)

Chapter Seven

Fallingbostel & Paderborn 1961–66

Part 1 Operations & training

Lower Saxony

On 12 February 1961 the Regiment joined 7 Armoured Brigade Group of 1 Division. The new home was at Fallingbostel, a small town in Niedersachsen on the edge of the vast *Lüneburger Heide*. (Other garrison units included 5th Royal Tank Regiment, 21st Regiment RA and 7 Armoured Workshops REME.) The barracks lay conveniently by the newly-built autobahn between Hamburg and Hannover. They were on the opposite side of the tank ranges from Bergen–Hohne (near the site of the infamous Belsen concentration camp), where most of the other units of 7 Armoured Brigade Group were stationed. The Regiment was therefore much more part of the British military community than it had been in the outposts of Wolfenbüttel and Neumünster.

Wessex Barracks was said to have been used by the Wehrmacht as a 'summer' station; it certainly had little provision against the harsh winters of the North German plain. The cold was much in evidence in February 1961 for a Regiment newly arrived from the tropics. The exceptionally severe winter of 1962–63 followed, when coal barges were frozen up on the canals and no fuel deliveries could be made. That meant that the barrack-room stoves had an increasingly meagre ration of coke (there was no central heating). Supplementary supplies of wood were sought, often from illicit sources. Fortunately the thaw came before barrack-room doors began to disappear, but it was a near thing. (There was a doubtless uncharitable rumour that the better stoves had been removed by 8th Royal Tank Regiment on their departure for amalgamation with the 5th.)

Fallingbostel & Paderborn 1961–66 Part 1

Since the early 1950s there had been several changes in NATO strategy. The defence of continental Europe was then still based on fallback positions behind the Rhine.

> By 1959 the main defensive zone crept forward to the line of the Weser, the Fulda and the Lech, and then in the second half of 1963 NATO made up its mind to hold West Germany all the way up to the borders with East Germany and Czechoslovakia.
>
> (*Confrontation, the Strategic Geography of NATO and the Warsaw Pact* Hugh Faringdon 1986)

Reliance on overwhelming nuclear superiority had given way to the 'shield' concept. That envisaged mobile divisions holding up a conventional Warsaw Pact attack for long enough to allow talks to take place. For 7 Armoured Brigade this meant that its regiments had to be able to deploy speedily to its operational area east of the River Weser, there to undertake a defence in depth. 'Tactical' nuclear weapons were relied on to counter the overwhelming numerical superiority of the 'Fantasian forces', as Warsaw Pact troops were then called in exercise vocabulary.

Metamorphosis

In 1961 the Berlin Wall was built and the possibility of Cold War becoming armed conflict was as real as at any other time. The Regiment was therefore not allowed long in which to complete conversion. They were expected to perform on their remounts within three months of arrival from Malaya. But it was some eighteen months before the conversion back to tanks could be considered complete. 'We can now admit that we too were surprised at our success. We handled our new tanks like our old armoured cars, finding them similar, but harder to ditch: however we soon mastered even this technique.'

The principal equipment was the Centurion, which had proved its worth in the Korean War, initially Marks V and VII, armed with 20-pounder guns, later the Mark X with 105mm guns. Peace establishment allowed only three sabre troops to a squadron, each with three tanks. One of the three troops was equipped with the heavy Conqueror tank, with 120mm gun, designed to defeat the armour of the Russian JS 3. They were, however, victims to several basic design faults which had them more often 'off' than 'on' the road, although the troop leaders concerned would not hear a word said against them.

History of The 13th/18th Royal Hussars (Q.M.O.)

There were also new radios; a VHF range (C42, B47 and A41) had been introduced in 1960, and fitted to the Saracen APCs and Ferret scout cars in Malaya (the Daimler armoured cars had continued with No. 19 wireless sets.) Squadron headquarters had two 'command' tanks, with additional radios, and a third tank fitted with dozer blade. Regimental Headquarters had its own troop of 'control' tanks. (It was more convenient for them to use the Saracen command vehicles, but Regimental Headquarters was to be seen in tanks, both during tactical training and on the ranges.) A Reconnaissance Troop (led initially by Captain RT Cliff, with Sergeant J Hickey as Troop Sergeant) was mounted in Ferret scout cars; twelve were on the establishment, but there were only enough crews to man eight.

As a new trade structure was being introduced, every soldier had to be re-trained, not only onto strange vehicles, guns and radios, but also to a higher standard in order to retain his pay. A somewhat smug note in the 1962 *Journal*:

> We have now completed the full cycle of tests in our new role. The Annual Gunnery Practices have been fired and approved; we have acquitted ourselves boldly and victoriously on exercises, and were awarded the highest grading possible on our vehicle inspection, for which we received the congratulations of the C-in-C.

However, gunnery was not yet rated as important as it should have been. In order to have as many tanks as possible for tactical training, for a time tanks were taken out with only three crew members: commander, driver and signaller, but no gunner. The gun was often left in internal or external crutch because crews had not properly mastered the stabiliser system.

During that first eighteen months the Regiment also had to contend with an acute manpower shortage. After National Service had ended, the recruitment of a wholly Regular Army was inevitably slow and in January 1962 a squadron parade state often showed only two troopers available for duty; any others would be on individual courses.

Recognition of Skilled Tradesmen

The importance to the Regiment of skilled tradesmen was emphasised in 1963. As an additional recognition of those who classified as B1 Tradesmen, they were to wear the silver QMO monogram on their sleeve, previously the privilege of those

Fallingbostel & Paderborn 1961–66 Part 1

selected three times on Guard Mounting as Commanding Officer's Stick Orderly.

The Rhine Army Year

After a preliminary canter in April 1961, three exercises in June and July provided a first taste of training with tanks. Now able to go across country which armoured cars could not negotiate, they did not have the armoured cars' freedom to travel wherever there were reasonable roads and tracks. Allocations of space and time on the restricted training areas were strictly rationed and British units had to take their turn with other NATO forces, now including the Bundeswehr. Only in the autumn, after the harvest was in, was it possible to get 'exercise rights' outside the training areas. That year there were two exercises in September before the major Corps exercise, Spearpoint,* which lasted some ten days.

Spearpoint was the first exposure to large scale manoeuvres in tanks and the Regiment was, perhaps deliberately, kept on a tight rein. A Squadron had plenty of practice at hiding in woods, but 'our enemy was too chicken to give us much action' and C Squadron crew commanders all had:

> . . . excellent training in the art of manipulating fifty maps on a dark and windy night, but unfortunately the enemy was exceedingly shy and the only proof we had of his existence was that we were 'atomised' on numerous occasions. This somewhat boring occupation does have the saving grace that the best way to pretend to be dead is to be asleep.

On the few occasions that B Squadron was unleashed 'the umpires saw to it that we were soon stopped by fictitious blown bridges, nuclear explosions, or when imagination ran dry: "Halt here for two hours" '. However, B Squadron did find itself in the public eye when its 2nd Troop, 'deaf to every warning':

> . . . boldly plunged all three tanks up to their turrets in the infamous *Grosses Moor*. After over a week's hard work by soldiers from each of the squadrons and hordes of Germans, Sappers and the personal advice of BEME, CREME and several very distinguished generals they were removed over a specially built road.

---

* The name reflected the Corps sign of a javelin's head.

History of The 13th/18th Royal Hussars (Q.M.O.)

'Commanding Officers' Year'

In June of the following year, Lieutenant Colonel HSR Watson took over from Lieutenant Colonel Coker as Commanding Officer. He was told at the end of the 1962 training season, during which there had been the full cycle of exercises, that 1963 was to be a 'Commanding Officers' year'. No exercises with troops would be above regimental group level. What that meant for the Regiment over the next twelve months is a typical example of the relentless treadmill of the BAOR training and administrative cycle.

First came some twenty 'ancillary' inspections before the Administrative Inspection proper. 'The inspections were again a great success and reflect great credit on all ranks; a great deal of hard work was required, some of it under very unpleasant conditions in unheated hangars . . . .' Then came individual training. During the previous winter the emphasis had to be on basic Class III trade training; now it could be on Class I training and by the end there was a reasonable balance of the new RAC trades throughout the Regiment. As a break at the end of January 1963:

> . . . we skidded forth on Exercise Long John for 48 hours of Arctic warfare on a Soltau Training Area transformed by the very large quantities of snow strewn about it. Its beauties were perhaps not appreciated as much as they deserved, but our barrack home took on an entirely new appeal.

The journey out from barracks included a long hill and not all the Centurions made it to the top at the first attempt. For those following it was disconcerting, to say the least, to see a preceding tank gradually gaining momentum as as it slithered backwards; remarkably there were no accidents. (Such was the cold that crews augmenting their 'compo' rations with eggs found them frozen solid.)

Soltau was next visited in March, for five days troop and squadron training, and in August 1963 A Squadron spent a fortnight with 1st Royal Irish Fusiliers and 93rd (Le Cateau) Battery on the small Belgian training area at Bourg Leopold.*
As a 'motor' battalion, the Irish were mounted in wheeled

---

* Bourg Leopold was the town which B Squadron of the Regiment had liberated in a dashing encounter in September 1944.

Fallingbostel & Paderborn 1961–66 Part 1

Saracen APCs, whereas battalions in infantry formations had still to be moved in 3 ton TCVs (troop-carrying vehicles). Unusually, the battalion group was accompanied to the training area by the Regiment's Band and the Band and Drums of the Irish Fusiliers.* Despite the mud and the cramped conditions, the two bands managed to turn out immaculately for a performance before civic dignitaries and the British Ambassador in the *Grand Place* in Brussels, as well as playing in Ostend and Bruges.

A series of exercises came in September and October. Exercise Desert Rat gave:

> ... the tanks (and us) quite a hammering as Brigadier Leakey flung 5 RTR after the Regiment in a pursuit which moved us conveniently from the Hildesheim area to a position south of Paderborn, ready for the Divisional Commander's test exercise.

The final attack by 5th Royal Tank Regiment in Desert Rat was timed for the benefit of the visiting Defence Minister. As A Squadron was motoring hard across country for a counter-attack the Squadron Leader's knee 'disagreed with the main armament', but Major EE Hunt received little interest in his plight, until the VIP party were clear of the exercise area. (He then found himself being treated by his wife, the Regiment's 'civilian medical practitioner'. Dr Hunt had come out, appropriately gum-booted, to hold a sick parade between exercises.)

In October 1963 B Squadron made what was remembered from previous visits as an agreeable expedition to Berlin, to allow the Independent Squadron RTR to train at Soltau and Hohne. On arrival in the city there was nothing to indicate that it would not be a normal stay, although the Wall had been erected in 1961. Then the reverberations throughout the world of the assassination of President Kennedy seemed to focus on Berlin. Memories of the 1948-49 Berlin Airlift were revived as news came of convoy hold-ups; the Army was: 'continually on the alert and ready to turn out at very short notice. A sense of urgency and purpose prevailed everywhere ....' But there was apparently still time for the Squadron to take part in a full programme of sport – and nightlife.

---

* Bandmaster A Kershaw, 13th/18th, a warrant officer of long service, confessed that never before had he slept under canvas.

History of The 13th/18th Royal Hussars (Q.M.O.)

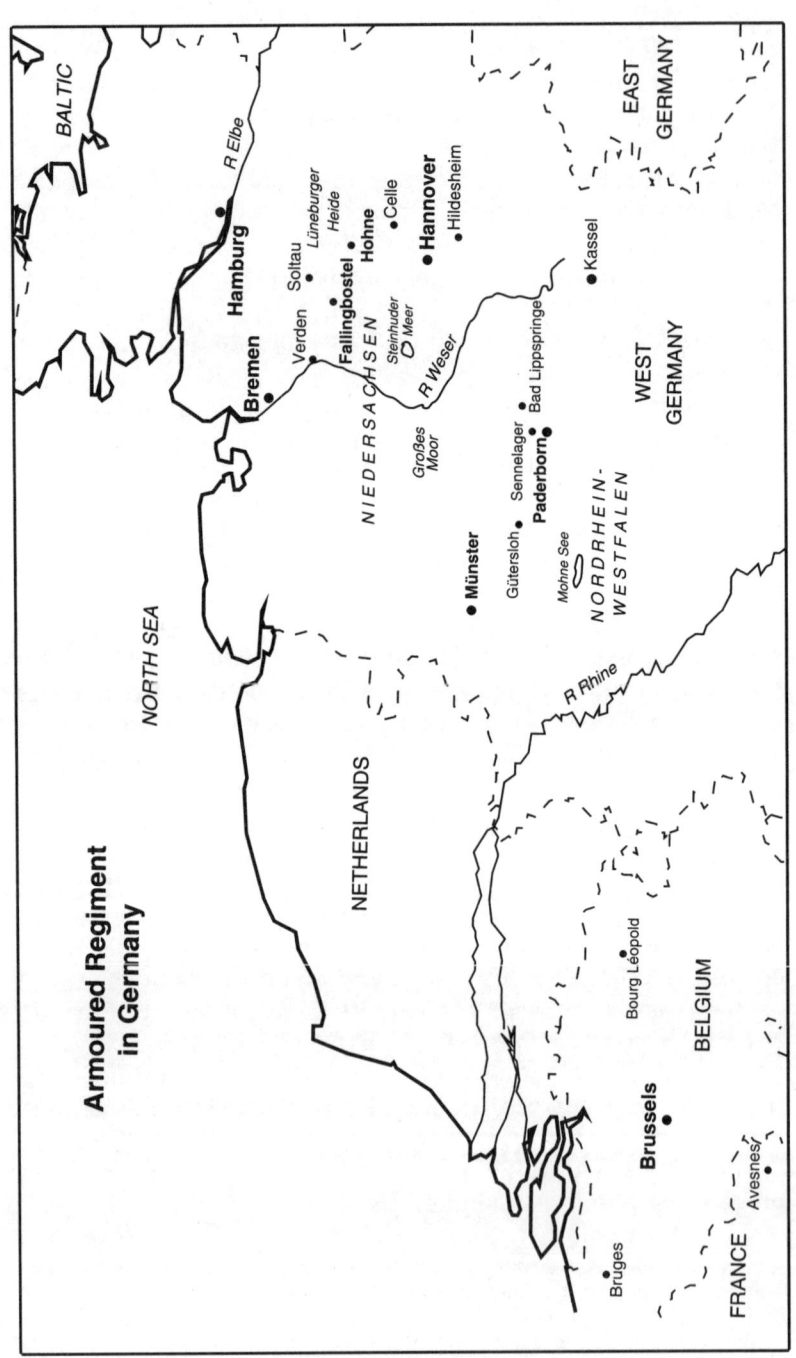

Fallingbostel & Paderborn 1961–66 Part 1

To North Rhine Westphalia

The next move was to Paderborn in February 1964, after handing over to the Royal Scots Greys. This was probably the least happy of the handings-over of the post-war years. Despite the first-class reports on the tanks from recent inspections and the efforts of crews to prepare them, the advance party of the Scots Greys frequently refused to take over vehicles without further cleaning.*

On a happier note, when the last contingent left for Paderborn by train on 14 February, a large party from all the neighbouring units came to see them off, including the Band, Pipes and Drums of the the Royal Irish Fusiliers.

> This was a charming gesture from Soltau Garrison which we very much appreciated. It was also mildly embarrassing as most of the Regiment had already departed. The self-importance of the rump of Headquarters Squadron was flattered by the send-off we had from Fallingbostel Station . . . The Main Party we were called – all twenty-five of us. We thought we would have to jump into the carriages, dash round the other side, jump in again, dash round, to make it look impressive. Real Charlies we felt, but we're versatile if nothing else.

Paderborn, in Nordrhein-Westfalen, had been the centre of one of the many ecclesiastical principalities which were independent until the beginning of the nineteenth century, a reminder of how recent was the concept of a unified Germany. In Barker Barracks, the Regiment was near the Infantry Training Centre and Training Area of Sennelager. This was not inappropriate, as it was now the armoured regiment of 4 Guards Brigade. For the first few months at Paderborn all troops were equipped with Centurions as Conquerors were held only by the armoured regiments of the 'forward' divisions. It was then decided that their fire power should be concentrated further back and the Regiment was issued with them again.

Squadrons of the Regiment were assigned for training to the battalions which they would support in operations. The line-up to begin with was: A Squadron with 1st Grenadier Guards, B Squadron with 1st Coldstream and C Squadron with 1st Royal

---

* On the face of it this was also an unnecessary move as the Scots Greys could have gone to Paderborn, but it may have been thought that three years at Fallingbostel was enough? EEH

Highland Fusiliers. By now the infantry battalions in Rhine Army had all been equipped with FV432 – tracked APCs. This transformed their battlefield mobility and infantry/tank communication.

D Squadron was formed for a while, as an off-shoot of Headquarters Squadron, consisting of MT, Reconnaissance and Royal Signals Troops and the wheeled element of Regimental Headquarters. The idea was to reduce the load on Headquarters Squadron, with nearly half the Regimental strength on its books, and to give the troops concerned a better opportunity to develop their own 'personalities'. The experiment was abandoned in 1965 but re-surfaced, first in the late 1960s when a Reconnaissance Wing was created and then in 1971 when Command and Support Squadron was formed.

Manoeuvring from Paderborn

Shortly after the move to Paderborn Lieutenant Colonel Watson handed over to Lieutenant Colonel PB Tillard. Another new appointment was of Captain RE Wagner, US Army, seconded to the Regiment for nearly two years. After a short spell as second-in-command to Major GM Chirnside, he took over from him as Squadron Leader of B Squadron. It must have provided the monitors beyond the Iron Curtain with plenty to puzzle over as, under his influence, the Squadron speedily acquired enough US Army jargon for their radio net to sound as if there had been a major change in NATO troop distribution. With B Squadron led by a Captain, C Squadron restored the titular balance under Brevet Lieutenant Colonel RS Beresford.

> In spite of the vexatious restrictions on tank training [principally track mileage] which we now endure, we have managed to have a full and useful season of training with our tanks.

Brigade and Divisional exercises produced 'some singular successes'. These included in September 1964 a charge by all three squadrons on to the 17th/21st Lancers' position in Exercise Noble Mob, in support of a 'nuclear counter-attack'. This 'may not have been war-like, but was great fun'. For C Squadron it was an exhilarating experience which nearly ended in disaster when 'we met B Squadron coming on to the objective from the opposite direction'. (Lieutenant Colonel Cockburn, the 17th/21st commanding officer, was not amused by C Squadron's

Fallingbostel & Paderborn 1961–66 Part 1

exuberance, and sought the Squadron Leader, Lieutenant Colonel Beresford, apparently with a view to putting him under arrest. This was thwarted until he had had time to cool down, by C Squadron Leader and his Second-in-Command, Captain RT Cliff, literally keeping their heads down, below closed tank hatches.) A Squadron, with strict instructions as to their route, went through the fences of a stud farm, but fortunately the damage control teams were close on their heels, before any miscegenation could get under way. B Squadron Headquarters and 3rd Troop bypassed:

> ... a large enemy force on a track built for nothing more sophisticated than a goat cart. This maneuver [sic] reclassified two bridges and one level crossing but resulted in the annihilation of one enemy squadron and most of an infantry company ...

Another memorable event came on a foggy night in October 1964. On Exercise Open Glove, a 4 Guards Brigade attack on 20 Armoured Brigade (including once more the Regiment's 'peacetime' friends and neighbours the 17th/21st Lancers) was to begin with a night assault across the Weser north of Kassel. Shortly before, a soldier from another unit had drowned in the river and strict orders were issued that no-one was to attempt a crossing unless all had life-jackets and safety boats were in place. The usually reliable Royal Engineers had mislaid the life-jackets and were behind with the bridge which they were building upstream. There was no prospect of anyone crossing until first light and the umpires sensibly departed for bed.

Thirty years later Major General Tillard recalled:

> It was a pitch-dark night, we weren't of course using lights and I was walking somewhat disconsolately along the river bank. Suddenly the Conqueror Troop under John Blakiston appeared, down a farm track. I said something on the lines of: 'Since presumably you're lost, you wouldn't like to get a little bit more lost and drive ten yards further on into the river? I'll try and carry the can at our court-martial. But you are not to lose anybody. Make sure the rest of the crew is out of the tank and that two of them have a firm grip of the driver's cross-straps. If it starts sinking – abandon it.' John bravely volunteered, the troop crossed and so did all the Regiment's tanks, once collected by the Adjutant [Captain DAG Edelsten] – itself no mean task.

History of The 13th/18th Royal Hussars (Q.M.O.)

Once across there was another stroke of luck. The Queen's Company 1st Grenadiers had waded the river elsewhere and were also across. With a little persuasion they were mounted on the backs of C Squadron tanks; unless we had fallen into some devilish trap it seemed we had achieved complete surprise and were already behind the enemy. My plan was therefore to leave the wooded hills overlooking the Weser, where the 'enemy' was likely to be concentrated, in order to outflank him. C Squadron was to make a wide and independent swing as fast as possible, close against the exercise boundary where no enemy was likely to be encountered. Meanwhile A and B Squadrons were to leapfrog up the edge of the hills as strong shield.

So, after first light, by the time the umpires found us, we were already half-way through the exercise plan. All kinds of entirely mythical hell were then – quite naturally – invoked to stop us!

Sundry Training Areas

Annual Troop Tests in the form of a competition had been a feature of training programmes for some time. In May 1965 the five tests were: advance and contact drill, withdrawal with the bridgelayer, a battle-worthiness check, night map reading and a dry battle run. The emphasis on work with the bridgelayer tank stemmed both from its value to the Regiment in negotiating streams and the problems involved in its movement and concealment. (The Centurion Bridgelayer carried a Class 80 single span bridge which could be launched across gaps up to 45 feet across. Swung through a 180 degree arc to be laid in position, the bridge took two minutes to lay, when it could immediately be crossed by tanks, and four minutes to recover.)

To provide some variety from the German training areas, periodic forays were made by individual squadrons to a camp at Larzac, in the south of France. This was surrounded by a training area and ranges on the Causse de Larzac, south of the tourist centre of Millau. The Causse is a desolate rocky plateau some 2,000 feet above the surrounding country, which supports nothing but a few sheep. It is an area of extremes, scorching hot in summer and bitterly cold in winter. The wind blows strongly or not at all. It had no great value for serious tank training but was rated a worthwhile place to go to for a pleasant change, despite the primitive living accommodation and the four-day

Fallingbostel & Paderborn 1961–66 Part 1

rail journey.* (The circuitous route from Germany avoided narrow tunnels which the flats with tanks could not negotiate.)

If a squadron was with its affiliated infantry battalion, much of the time at Larzac would be spent in company/troop and company/squadron training, as well as in getting through 'PE' tests and small arms classification. During one C Squadron visit a battalion/squadron exercise was staged which included a French infantry company and was supposed to include an air strike by the French Air Force.

> The Frenchmen had never worked with tanks before, but after a quick briefing they gave a most creditable performance . . . The only confusion was on the objective where there were more VIPs than enemy, and it was difficult to sort out t'other from which . . . The air strike arrived after we had returned to camp.

It was usually possible to get a day or two by the sea and C Squadron found that their allotted beach was adjacent to a nudist colony. 'Several cunning soldiers got themselves enrolled as honorary members but others did not seem to have the knack.' French hospitality was greatly appreciated; the visitors were always welcomed in a cheery way and their wine and fruit went down very well.

Another training area was at Vogelsang, in Southern Germany, which included the small village of Berescheid. The village was to give its name to one of the B Squadron tanks after an incident during their visit in 1965. Sergeant G Oliver's troop of Conqueror tanks was under command of a company of the Coldstream when they were ordered into Berescheid, which was outside the area for tanks. Sergeant Oliver, his not to reason why, descended on the sleepy village where the inhabitants were understandably alarmed and 'shouted some easily understood words at our well-behaved soldiers'; they 'with commendable restraint ignored all insults and drove on.' After an abortive attempt by the Burgermeister to stop the advance with his car – he realised belatedly that to turn three tanks round in the narrow street would create more damage – he telephoned 'every newspaper and TV company he could think

---

* Better accommodation was provided at Larzac for visiting French generals and Lieutenant Colonel Tillard was put up in the bungalow normally used by them. It included an attractive bedroom next door to his, with an adjoining door: 'Ah, but the General always brings such a pretty driver!'

of. So fantastic was his tale of vast damage and British insolence that the press and TV flocked to Berescheid next day like vultures round a corpse . . . '. The Squadron Leader, Captain Wagner, arrived to find he had a full scale press conference on his hands. 'He assured the masses that Sergeant Oliver's boys had not brandished pistols at the Burgermeister and forced him back over "a mile of road" (the village street was about 200 yards long).' After a few nice words in apology Captain Wagner departed the best of friends with all. That evening he appeared on TV all over Germany as the gallant American making up for the misdeeds of the beastly British.

Reconnaissance Troop and 'elements of most other troops in Headquarters Squadron' had the trip of the year in an exercise in Libya with 1st Coldstream Guards. In February 1965 some thirty men, led by Lieutenant CAGB Robinson and Squadron Sergeant Major F Harrison, made their way by air to El Adem, near Tobruk. For live firing with Browning machine guns:

> Mr Robinson took great precautions when laying down the arcs of fire, on the left a wadi, on the right a sandy crest dotted with bushes. Suddenly an excited bundle of rags, an Arab, emerged from the wadi and vigorously indicated that his wife and herds were down there. A pause while they all exit left. At the first burst of fire the 'bushes' galloped away.

Lance Corporal J Overend, from the Orderly Room, wrote in the *Journal*:

> Halcyon days were spent in the sea and on the various glorious beaches . . . We went on expeditions to the Tobruk battlefields, Cyrene, Apollonia and at one stage mixed with King Idris' royal cavalcade. We had a two day stay at Benghazi as guests of the 14th/20th Hussars and a three day stay at Derna.*

The return journey was by sea to Bari in Italy, on board the LST *Charles McLeod* with a party from the Coldstream.

> At Bari we were met by an impressive reception committee and our large escort of Carabiniere who were to escort us to the Franco–Italian border, then across the Apennines, including a breath-taking dash through Naples, the sirens of our escort wailing, and stops at Monte Cassino and the summer villa of the English College, Rome – where we were soundly thrashed at soccer by the student priests.

---

* Squadron Sergeant Major Harrison had been a Trooper in A Squadron at Derna in 1949–50.

Fallingbostel & Paderborn 1961–66 Part 1

In 1964 a few members of the Regiment took part in a forerunner of the regular training sessions for BAOR units in Canada. Lieutenant JAC Blakiston led a troop in a composite squadron for Exercise Pond Jump in the Wainwright Training Area. With Sergeant G Mallows as Troop Sergeant, Mr Blakiston had one 13th/18th crew and one each from the 11th Hussars and 5th Royal Tank Regiment. Whatever the military merits of the Exercise, those taking part thought that being guests at the Calgary Stampede had much to commend it.

Canadian Army Trophy Winners

In 1966 a Regimental team won the Canadian Army Trophy (CAT) for tank gunnery in a competition open to all the nations in the Central European region of NATO.

> This result, demonstrating the high professional skill now achieved by the Regiment, proved a fitting climax to our tour in BAOR. It was the culmination of two and a half years of hard work after we first put gunnery as our Regimental top priority.

The *Journal* attributed much of the success to the 'galvanizing energy' of Captain RE Wagner* who, as B Squadron Leader, was responsible for Gunnery Training. Annual Firing in 1965 was extremely successful, achieving the highest standards of any BAOR regiment, and a B Squadron troop led by Sergeant Oliver won the RAC Miniature Range Match.

On that performance the Regiment was invited to compete in the Canadian Army Trophy:

> After much head-scratching we decided to go ahead, although we realised that in doing so we would have to upset a great deal of the training for 1966 and cause considerable upheaval throughout the Regiment.

Winning CAT was set as No 1 priority and, as heartening pipe-opener, Regimental crews took first three places and the fifth place in the 1966 RAC Miniature Range Match, in which all armoured regiments then had to compete. From each squadron the crews most likely to be selected were then instructed on the CAT competition during May and June.

---

* Captain Wagner left the Regiment, on promotion, for a tour in Vietnam where his gallantry and leadership were rewarded with two Bronze Stars and a Silver Star – the equivalent of MC and Bar and DSO. He subsequently became a Major General.

History of The 13th/18th Royal Hussars (Q.M.O.)

Lieutenant Colonel RS Beresford took over command of the Regiment in early July and picked up the challenge with enthusiasm. After Annual Firing, the twelve crews selected for CAT training proper were formed into a composite squadron under Major JOG Paton. They began a seven-week training programme during which the FMR and CIM* were in daily use: 'the loaders were sweating their hearts out under SSI Gardner in the Gymnasium and there were regular spells of "flipping and puffing" with thunderflashes and canvas targets at Goldgrund', the local training area. This was relieved by a week at Hohne, firing with 20-pounders because of the shortage of 105 mm ammunition.

> By the end of the 20-pounder shooting we were full of confidence. We were getting scores which compared very favourably with the best obtained last year . . . we kept on for a further three weeks with dry training and preparing our tanks. Nothing was left to chance. Any component on a CAT tank which was the least suspect was changed and the Fire Control Equipment on each tank was adjusted to suit the individual requirements of that particular gunner . . . The magic word CAT opened all doors and we obtained help and advice from any and every unit and organisation that we approached.

By the end of training there was little to choose between any of the nine remaining crews, from whom the judges picked five crews to compete by ballot, plus one reserve. Crews and ammunition parties moved up to Hohne for a week in which all the competing nations, Canada, Germany, Belgium, the Netherlands and the United Kingdom, could practise. The Canadians were reported to be the main rivals, 'very fast and apparently accurate'. At the end of the second day of the competition, the Regiment's team was well in front, after a sparkling performance by Corporal M Howlett and his crew. Then all went awry and over the next two days the Belgians went into the lead. However, Staff Sergeant Hatton's crew were the first to fire on the final day and it seemed to the spectators that they had an excellent shoot.

The final totals had the Regiment 760 points ahead of Belgium, with Germany another 2,390 behind them. Highest scorers in the competition were Corporal Howlett's crew. They

---

* FMR = Field Miniature Range; CIM = Classroom Instructional Model.

Fallingbostel & Paderborn 1961–66 Part 1

received special plaques at the prize-giving, after the trophy proper had been presented to the Team Captain (and Regimental Gunnery Officer), 2nd Lieutenant RA Cordy-Simpson and Trooper P Rutherford, the gunner in Staff Sergeant Hatton's crew.

> This success set the seal on our tour in BAOR and will provide an example to the Regiment in future years of what can be achieved by hard work, application and single-mindedness of purpose.

The opposite side of that coin is the extent to which the concentration on a single, short-term aim detracted from all-round regimental efficiency. Instead of being a competition for 'real' tank crews the Trophy had already become a gladiatorial contest of national prestige, but at least in the 1960s it was still 'real shooting'. Later it achieved such prestige that:

> ... national industrial reputations came to be at stake and the atmosphere in which it was conducted became little short of frenzied. Fortunately for everyone, in 1985 the 'authorities' remembered that the defeat of the potential enemy, the Warsaw Pact, was of more importance than the defeat of fellow NATO regiments in tank gunnery, and the competition was suspended. By that time it had in any case become a contest between fire-control programmers ... (*The Light Dragoons,* Colonel Mallinson)

Adventure Training

In the 1963 *Journal* appears the first mention of 'Adventure Training' which was thought to be:

> ... well worthwhile, but it does take an inordinate amount of preparation, principally in the forecasting of details, months ahead, for the benefit of financial and diplomatic clearances ... A lot of people have got a great deal of enjoyment and useful experience out of this year's adventure training; next year we can hope for more expeditions with perhaps a little less fuss.

It was intended as a substitute for the varied experiences often provided by Imperial Policing and in particular, to create opportunities for the development of leadership skills amongst young officers and NCOs. In that first year the various Squadron Notes in the *Journal* refer to canoeing in France, camping in Denmark and Outward Bound courses in Norway.

By 1964 each Squadron was sending at least two expeditions in the summer, with soldiers getting to France, Sweden,

Norway, the Baltic Coast and the Mediterranean. Sailing, canoeing, mountaineering, bicycling, trekking and skiing were included in the fare and they all 'achieved the limited aim of providing a broadening experience and the opportunity to live dangerously'. One of the B Squadron parties canoed in the large River Schlei inlet, near the Danish border; two troopers had to be rescued by a police launch after they 'somehow went out to sea trying to find the others'.

The new D Squadron's expedition in 1965 was to the Corps Outward Bound Training Centre at Isefjaer in Norway, where Captain DJ Delius was Senior Instructor. 'Our smiles of greeting faded somewhat when we were ordered into the icy fiord for a "short" seventy yard swim.' After a hard day's session of canoeing practice they set out with their full Bergen packs on a trek to see if, against all the odds, they could find an Allied bomber which had eluded four previous expeditions.

There was a local story that it had been shot down during the Second World War, about 100 miles north of the camp. As no trace of it had been found, hopes of discovering it now – if it ever existed – were slight. The party, led by 2nd Lieutenant NPHR Chamberlin, had three days of hard trekking in a steady downpour of rain across 'marshy plains, mountainous plateaux, steep mountain sides and white water rivers' before they reached the search area. Each member of the party was given a sector to search and 'miles of hills, plain, bog, trees, and valleys were examined, but no aeroplane'. Mr Chamberlin, 'on a whim', finally set off to look at an area which seemed thoroughly unlikely and, remarkably enough, from the summit of a forested mountain he caught a glint of metal – and about two hundred yards away were five or six fire-blackened trees. Beneath the trees lay a Flying Fortress, remarkably well preserved – and invisible from fifty yards away. The party returned in triumph to a heroes' welcome at Isefjaer after getting in four days canoeing in warm sunshine.

Chapter Eight

Fallingbostel & Paderborn 1961–66

Part 2 First Guidon & Other Events

Presentation of the First Guidon

Six months after arrival in Fallingbostel the Regiment was presented in July 1961 with its first Guidon. 'First', that is, for the 13th/18th. The 13th Light Dragoons had carried Guidons until 1832, when all Light Dragoon Regiments gave them up, as their purpose as a rallying point in battle was inappropriate for light cavalry.* (The 18th had relinquished their Guidons on becoming Hussars in 1805.) In place of guidons, the kettle drums of the mounted bands carried cloths embroidered with the battle honours and the drum horse took centre place at ceremonial occasions. When Second World War battle honours were awarded, in 1957, the 'light cavalry' regiments were authorised to revert to the earlier practice.

It was no small feat, in the middle of conversion training, to mount such a major enterprise as the Presentation and an associated Guidon Weekend. The maestro for the occasion was Major JW Bell, as 'Guidon Officer' and the Regimental Sergeant Major, Mr EJS Garbutt, obviously played a prominent part on the parade ground. On 22 July the Regiment, drawn up in four Guards, received HRH The Duke of Gloucester with a Royal Salute. After his inspection the old Drum Banners were marched on. They were carried by Farouk, a BAOR 'patrol horse' more used to distinguishing himself in the show jumping arena and the cross country course, The Banners were then marched off for the last time to *Auld Lang Syne*. The Chaplain General (the Venerable ID Neill) consecrated the new Guidon and the Duke of Gloucester presented it to the Regiment, on behalf of The Queen. In his address, the Duke recalled his own

---

* There had been three, sometimes four, Guidons in each Regiment, the King's Guidon, of crimson silk and the remainder of silk in the colour of the Regiment's facings, light green in the case of the 13th and white for the 18th.

time when, as a subaltern in the 10th Hussars, he had been attached to the 13th Hussars some forty years before. The Guidon, carried by TQMS J Gwilliam, was then trooped through the ranks escorted by No 1 Guard, in a ceremony which borrowed heavily from the presentation of infantry colours.

> Despite the dullness of the day, there was a festive air to mark the occasion. The spectators' stands were draped with the Regimental colours. The children's tent, on a flank, had gay pennants reminiscent of a jousting tent. The background to the parading troops was gay with squadron, regimental and national flags, interspersed with pennanted scout cars . . . .

Some 1,200 spectators watched the ceremony including 800 guests who were entertained to lunch afterwards, 500 by the Officers' Mess and 300 by the Warrant Officers' and Sergeants' Mess. Amongst them was a large party from the Regimental Association, who stayed for the Guidon Weekend and :

> . . . made the weekend so much the more worthwhile as we could share it with many who helped to make the history emblazoned on the Guidon . . .

> Unless one has taken part in the preparation for such an event it is difficult to realise the effort put in by All Ranks to achieve the standard displayed on the Parade. In particular, the unsung heroes off parade, such as the Mess Staffs, the attached REME, Royal Signals and ACC who bore the brunt of much labour. To them, as well as to the parading troops, full credit is due.

'Attached Personnel'

That last quotation is a reminder of the extent to which the Regiment was always more than those who wore its cap badge. Both in numbers and in quality of their contribution to Regimental life the 'attached personnel' were a part of the whole. None demonstrated this better than Mr J Woodfield, the Artificer Sergeant Major of the LAD REME from 1950 to 1961, who saw continuous service through two tours in Malaya as well as in Wolfenbüttel, Neumünster and Fallingbostel. (He left on being commissioned, later reaching the rank of Lieutenant Colonel.)

Fallingbostel & Paderborn 1961–66 Part 2

It was not often that the cooks received any bouquets for their efforts, but in 1962 a team from the Cooks' Troop won the Divisional Cookery Competition and, as the *Journal* said:

> It was appropriate that our team . . . should consist of one Regular, Lance Corporal Coldham, one National Serviceman, Private Ward, and one Regimental Cook, Trooper Whitworth; this combination has provided what is undoubtedly the best food in the cookhouse that we can recall. . . . We never cease to be amazed at the number of choices we are offered, and can sympathise with that select group of subalterns who arrange to do extra Orderly Officer duties, just to get a square meal.

Another member of the Cooks' Troop, Private Turner ACC, was the very last of the nation's National Servicemen and so, briefly, was the hero of press and television.

Sundry Visitors

A feature of every year's Regimental records was a lengthy list of visitors; in 1963 for example, thirty-two visits were recorded including:

> An officer and seventeen cadets from Brighton College CCF.
>
> Eight officers from that year's Joint Services Staff College course.
>
> Members of the ship's crew of HMS *Irchin*.
>
> General Sir William Stirling, Commander-in-Chief Northern Army Group.
>
> Rt Hon Peter Thorneycroft, Minister of Defence.

The amount of preparation and effort required for each visit obviously varied enormously, but the Regiment always took pride in ensuring that, whoever came they should feel welcome and, depending on who they were, should be impressed, interested and entertained in appropriate proportions.

Recruiting Campaign

The manpower shortage made it all too clear how important recruiting was to be to the all-Regular Army, and the newly-formed Home Headquarters was soon to play a major part in helping the Regiment's recruiters. In July 1962 the Regiment organised its first major campaign in its new area. A team went to the West Riding of Yorkshire and over a three-week stay they visited Sheffield, Barnsley, Cudworth, Doncaster and

History of The 13th/18th Royal Hussars (Q.M.O.)

Mexborough. The Band played a leading part and in Barnsley faced 'its most critical (and appreciative) audience which included the expert representatives of five local brass bands.' The two most successful evenings were the two 'Hussar Nights' at the Sheffield Locarno Ballroom where the Band played for the peak hour of each session to large audiences. At the second of them a 'Miss Hussar' was selected by three members of the Recruiting team.

The friendly interest shown by soldiers' families, during the 1962 recruiting tour, prompted a plan for some of them to visit Fallingbostel. A specially chartered Vickers Viscount brought out a party via Manchester; with them and some who came by rail or road, there were nearly seventy friends and relations assembled for a Whitsun Weekend in 1963. It proved a great success – and was the forerunner of many such visits. The press showed interest and one paper, hearing that wives and girl friends might be allotted seats on a higher priority than mums and dads, produced an article headed: 'Mums Take Back Seat in Love Airlift'. (In fact the demand for seats almost exactly matched capacity.)

Sport

In Fallingbostel

The Regimental soccer team had begun to show promise by the 1961–62 season, when they lost only eight of the thirty-one games played. Unfortunately the losses included the Cavalry Cup semi-final, but in the local league they were convincing winners. After a good start to the next season the foul weather halted all football for three months and, when it was possible to play again, the obviously exasperated contributor to the *Journal* wrote: 'the team seemed to have lost all incentive to win'. However, in the 1963–64 season the Regiment won the 1 Division and BAOR Cups and were runners up in the Army Cup. The matches involved meant a great deal of travelling, not only for the players, but for their many supporters, who must have covered hundreds of miles making sure that 'Lilywhites!' was the dominant cry at successive grounds. The final of the Army Cup was against 16 Para RAOC/REME and was only decided after a replay the following day.

Fallingbostel & Paderborn 1961–66 Part 2

Hockey, too, produced some good results in 1961–62 which led to the final of the Divisional competition, where the Regiment's opponents scored the only goal in the last second of the game. But from then until 1965 the amount played did not even warrant an entry in the *Journal*. The biggest surprise in 1962 was in swimming, in which the Regimental team's victory in the Divisional Championships was 'a great tribute to their enthusiasm, and the determination of Bandsman Taylor who founded the team without anyone noticing what they were up to'. Sadly, that achievement was not followed up in the next few years.

Despite the heavy investment in manpower from Yorkshire, cricket results were patchy in 1962 and, when the 'very rewarding and enjoyable' season in 1963 came along, thanks were due in large part to the arrival of recruits from Barbados. One, Trooper F Batson, was credited with 'probably being one of the fastest and more deadly bowlers in BAOR'; he and the two brothers Barton played a large part in getting the team to the final of the Divisional Major Units Knockout Competition.

The Barbadians also featured in other sports, notably athletics, where the Regiment came first at the Brigade and third in the Divisional meetings. Trooper G Barton was a very good sprinter and his performance in the BAOR individual competition earned him a place in the BAOR team.

Amongst the star performers in several sports was a future commanding officer, Captain DJStJ Loftus. A notable athlete, he led the cross country team which won the Divisional Meeting in 1962 and at mounted sports had a particularly rewarding year with his horse The Fiddler. They won prizes in both cross country and show jumping events as did Farouk, who had been employed as Drum Horse for the Guidon Parade. In a German triathlon at Verden, Captain Loftus defeated three of the four members of the German pentathlon team training for the next Olympics. The rest of the stables were showing promise and a great deal of enjoyment was had with both the *Niedersachsen Meute* and The Wessex Drag*. Like the other outdoor sports equitation suffered badly in the winter of

---

* Run by the 14th/20th Hussars and then by the 11th Hussars.

History of The 13th/18th Royal Hussars (Q.M.O.)

1962–63. 'However, boring as the riding school may have become, there is no doubt that much was learnt and taught by both riders and horses.' Before the weather set in Lance Corporal A Thompsett and Captain JE Hok performed usefully in the Rhine Army Hunter Trials. By April it was possible to get out again and in a hunter trial run by the 11th Hussars, second place in the pairs event was taken by Major GM Chirnside on Finella and 2nd Lieutenant WJD Walter on Farouk. In 1963 the EME, Captain CK ffrench-Nobbs, came third in a local *Gelenderitt* (cross country race), despite being 'dismounted twice'. At that year's Münster Show fourth place was taken by Captain Loftus and Lieutenant JAC Blakiston, over a 'very large' Hunter Trial course, where many horses came to grief. Captain Loftus went on to win the BAOR One Day Event on Farouk, against stiff opposition, and come third in the Open Hunter Trial.

A racehorse appeared in the stables, owned by Captain AH Blount. Talbot Green lost no time in asserting his authority and grooms:

> ... were seen to be nursing bruises and a certain reluctance to enter his stall was detectable. He rejected out of hand the hay offered him, merely using it for bedding until better was produced.

Sailing was now featuring regularly. Regimental crews were experiencing the varied delights of the Baltic in 30 square metres and of the *Steinhuder Meer* in dinghies. In 1963 both a 6 metre and a 30 metre boat were chartered for short periods and four people were sent on helmsman's courses. The enthusiasm and effort paid off with a creditable third place in the Divisional Passage Race – after the crew had to gybe round from the leading position when their chart blew overboard.

The efforts of Captain CK ffrench-Nobbs and Staff Sergeant Instructor R Wills APTC, combined with the official encouragement of Adventure Training, also meant that canoeing began to be reported in the *Journal*. In one issue there was an account of an adventure by two officers who:

> ... decided to have a 'cabby'. After ten minutes travelling, they there did espy a fair pretty fräulein sitting on the bank in her 'Itsi bitsy, teeny, weeny polka dot bikini'. All eyes on her and concentration on the boat, nil. 'Whoosh' they were no longer looking at

Fallingbostel & Paderborn 1961–66 Part 2

this fair damsel, but were feeling the wet, cold, dirty substance around their manly torsos. As our two instructors were present, they proceeded without undue haste to give these two bodies a lesson in the art of how to right an upturned canoe. A lesson which proved invaluable to them.

The winter of 1964–65 saw the first serious attempt by the Regiment at competitive Alpine events since 1957. It was a fair start with the team being placed third at the Quadrant (Divisional) Ski Meeting and tenth, out of nineteen teams, in the Alpine Unit competition at the Army and BAOR Championship. 'As far as it is possible it is very important to keep the same together for a few years, otherwise top results will never be achieved.' pleaded the Skiing Notes in the *Journal* – with a sardonic Editorial Note: 'Perhaps this is the sort of propaganda which got the author a posting to Scotland'. At langlauf the Regimental team secured third and fourth places in the Divisional Relay and Patrol competitions, but could manage only thirteenth at Army and BAOR level.

1961 was an outstanding season for the wildfowlers, who were active not only on the north German coast but round the barracks. The total bag on the coast was two geese and 190 duck, of which one goose and 103 duck were obtained by five guns over three days. A further thirty-two were 'lost': 'We only had one dog then and, if you wanted to eat the duck yourself, you had to race him to it.' Plenty of 'happy pottering' round the camp was secured by a lot of hard talking and this produced forty-three duck, sixty-one partridge and three pheasants. But that was the last year for pottering rights, before the area round Fallingbostel went back to German control. The guns then all seem to have been posted elsewhere as the game book showed nothing for 1962 and 1963.

In Paderborn

The soccer team continued its successes in 1964-65; they lost only two of the fifteen games played in the Southern Section of the Westphalian League, but were knocked out of the Army Cup in the 3rd Round. This time, however, they fought their way to the final of the Cavalry Cup which they won convincingly – and for the first time since the amalgamation of the 13th and 18th. Even if the ultimate trophies eluded the team,

History of The 13th/18th Royal Hussars (Q.M.O.)

1965-66 was another successful season in which they reached the finals of the Army Cup and the BAOR zone of the Cavalry Cup as well as winning the 4 Division local league.* (One of the two brothers Kenyon, who had been stalwarts of the team for several seasons, was now the captain.)

With cricketing enthusiast Lieutenant Colonel Tillard in command, the Regimental XI reached the semi-final of the BAOR Cup in 1965 and the final the following year.

In downhill skiing some respectable, but not outstanding, results were obtained in the Alpine Championships at St Moritz. The langlauf team made much of the altogether rougher conditions under which they operated – including their accommodation in:

> ... a typical Bavarian farmhouse, best described perhaps as a cowshed-cum-barn with a few small rooms added on ... Austrian farmers believe in washing only on special occasions such as Christmas and after muck-spreading, so we relied on the German Army for showers ...

In equitation, Finella and Farouk continued to provide worthy performances. Mounted on them at the 7 Armoured Brigade Trials Captains DAG Edelsten and CK ffrench Nobbs came first equal in the Pairs Cross Country and Captain Nobbs and Farouk won the Heavyweight Race. Farouk was a major regimental asset and well-known BAOR character.† He won four open events in 1966 and an article in *Horse and Hound* on 'Hunter Trials in BAOR' included:

> ... even the very experienced horses hit timber and Farouk of the 13th/18th Hussars ridden by Major Chirnside won. Farouk is an enormous seventeen year old Army horse who has been galloping round Rhine Army courses for many years, but has had few such successful seasons as this one.

The principal polo grounds in Germany were at Bad Lippspringe, only a short distance away, so an effort was made to get polo underway again. By 1965 a Regimental team felt that

---

* The 18th Hussars won the Cavalry Cup in 1913.

† Acquired as a potential high class jumper, Farouk had been transferred to army ration strength some years before as a 'patrol horse' and then passed on from regiment to regiment. Originally for inter-zonal border patrolling places on establishment for these highly cherished animals was then justified as looking for blinds on ranges.

Fallingbostel & Paderborn 1961–66 Part 2

they had not disgraced themselves by winning the final of the Losers' plate in the Lippspringe tournament – with only two in the side who had ever played before. By the following year the greater part of riding activities was being devoted to polo and although there was little to show by way of results the ground was being laid for the future. Captain PC Beaver (also a leading light in langlauf) was team captain and the most successful player; he was selected to play in the Berlin Tournament. Two racehorses were in the stables for a while, when Tattoo owned by 2nd Lieutenant AR Esler joined Talbot Green. The latter showed distinct form, having been placed in eleven consecutive races, including two wins. Tattoo was also in the money in two races, gaining a second and third. But the vagaries of Army life took their owners from Germany and both horses had to be sold.

A number of people enjoyed both dinghy and Baltic sailing and racing and there were enough crews to run an inter-squadron sailing match on a very gusty day on the *Mohne See*: 'In all it was a memorable day with all plaudits being given to Captain Beaver and Mr Wilkins for the way they managed to finish each race last, disqualified, capsized or refused.' At the 4 Division Regatta in 1966 a Regimental crew skippered by Corporal S Hutton finished second overall.

The Regiment was tempted into entering the BAOR Canoe Race on the Weser in mid July 1964. The principal exponents were the LAD and the Assistant EME, Lieutenant M Cowan, having arrived with the Regiment only two weeks before, found himself in charge of the two teams. Using the heavy boats provided for adventure training, the first team did well to come tenth overall against competitors who were using the lightweight fibre glass variety. The following year six canoes were entered in a confident mood, which waned somewhat when the crews encountered a River Weser in full flood and running faster than it had ever done for a BAOR race. However, four of the teams were placed in a 'very strenuous race'.

Wildfowling resumed after a gap of two years. If the summary of successes in 1961 seemed 'unattractively to stress the slain, the same could never be true of 1964. Here, as far as the game book is concerned, the duck clearly won a complete victory.' Over seventy-three 'gun/days' a mere sixty-three wildfowl were knocked down on the coast 'and only those who have experienced a wild-fowler's bleak, black, icy vigil know quite how long it is – except, of course, for the duck who must have laughed like anything'. It was nevertheless rated a 'howlingly successful' season, despite the appearance on the coast of young German 'marsh cowboys'. More members of the Regiment went out shooting, compared with the preceding years, although most were no great threat to the duck. Another plus was the great friendliness of 'all the Germans we met whether shoot- or pub-owners'. Thanks to 'the admirable *Oberforstmeister*' it was also possible to shoot round Paderborn.

There was increasing enthusiasm for shooting in the Warrant Officers' and Sergeants' Mess and on Balaklava Day 1966 they took on the Officers' Mess with a team of ten at clay pigeons – losing by only one point. It was to become a regular event.

Local Relations
While in Fallingbostel the Regiment's officers were treated very hospitably by members of the *Gelbe Kreis*, an association of German ex-cavalry officers and their families. As many of the pre-war cavalry had hailed from Prussian families, they sought not only to come together as an 'old comrades' association, but to provide what aid they could to those who had been impoverished by the Communist takeover of estates in Eastern Germany and Poland. They were also anxious that the 'cavalry spirit' should be preserved in the panzer regiments of the new *Bundeswehr*. In January 1964 they held at Celle one of their: *Winter Ball des Gelben Kreises*, to which British guests came from all the armoured and artillery regiments of 7 Armoured Brigade, French from the 11ème Chasseurs à Cheval stationed at Vesoul, and American from the 14th U.S. Cavalry, at Fulda. But the hospitality was not only formal; *Gelbe Kreis* members in the Hannover area also entertained families from the Regiment in their homes. The Adjutant, Captain DJStJ Loftus, married Fräulein Almut Zirkler, the daughter of a *Gelbe Kreis* member, and other contacts made then continue to this day.

Help with the harvest, by soldiers from the Regiment, was well received by farms in the Paderborn area. In September 1964 a group of twenty from A Squadron helped the village of

London 1954

12. Balaklava Centenary Ball – HM The Queen Mother inspecting the Light Brigade Guard of Honour with HRH The Duke of Edinburgh and Major General Miller.

13. 3rd Troop C Squadron and local fauna.

Malaya 1958–60

14. Victory celebrations in Kuala Lumpur – Commonwealth mounted parade led by the Regimental contingent.

15. 1961 Guidon Presentation – Farewell to the Drum Banners.

Fallingbostel 1961–64

16. 1962 A Squadron crews front for Administrative Inspection: Cpl Caine and 2 Lt Payne with R to L, Cpl Moore, Tpr Mountain, L Cpl Newbery, Tprs Colgate, Williams, Barton, Dowdall.

Fallingbostel & Paderborn 1961–66 Part 2

Etteln repair the ravages of floods. Two troopers, J Howarth and M McGuire, distinguished themselves by being reported in the local papers as 'hard workers, no work was too heavy or dirty for them!'. As a gesture of thanks the village people gave a large dance in their village hall to which they invited all the families and soldiers. That led to a continuing association and in 1965 the Squadron gave a Christmas party to the village's children. 'Father Christmas distributed presents to the children who were soon inundated with streamers, whistles, paper and layers of sticky sweets. The noise in one of our attic rooms had to be heard to be believed.'

It has always been difficult, however, for a regiment to become very closely involved with the community in or near where they live. Even if the regiment itself stays in one place for a protracted period (which the 13th/18th never did), the individual members seldom stay longer than two to three years. While they are there they naturally come together more readily with each other than with the local community – who will not usually have particular cause to make social contact. Nevertheless, there was sufficient contact for many members of the Regiment to marry German girls – and that obviously assisted greatly with future contacts. It was a far cry from the 1945 fraternisation ban.*

Lilywhites in Avesnes

The Regiment was invited in 1962 to send the Band and a football team to take part in Remembrance Day celebrations in Avesnes, a small French country town near the Belgian border. It was a memorable, and demanding, visit for those who took part. Captain CJG Delamain was in charge and his French was given plenty of practice replying to toasts, making speeches – and introducing musical items. An overwhelming welcome in the town square was followed by a reception in the Town Hall where the champagne flowed freely. The next day there was a tour of five neighbouring villages and towns, at each of which there were similar ceremonies: a march from the outskirts, band performance and wreath laying at the war memorials.

---

* Fraternisation with German civilians by the invading Allies was strictly forbidden, but the ban did not survive for long after VE Day.

Champagne was always on offer, but 'regretfully we had to ration ourselves to one glass per reception'. The dance band played at a Gala Ball which went on into the small hours, but they and the rest of the party formed up at 9am next day for the Remembrance Day parade.

The Regimental Band led, followed by the town band, the *Pompiers* (fire brigade) with their band, ex-servicemen and notables. 'This huge procession marched around the the town stopping at the Gendarmerie, for a flag-raising ceremony, at two War Memorials, one French and one British, for wreath-laying ceremonies and at the military cemetery.' Here a Regimental trumpeter played Last Post and Reveille before the procession continued to the church for a Mass, at which the Band accompanied the choir. After a marching display outside by the Band 'the town campanologist played The Queen and Tipperary on the church bells in our honour'.

In the afternoon the football team managed to draw one-all with the town's amateur team, champions of the second division of their local league. 'The result, of course, could not have been better for the *Entente Cordiale* and this was even further reinforced by the twenty-four bottles of champagne which the two teams shared afterwards.' After all that there was an evening concert by the Band, another dance at which 'the Football team gave a mass demonstration of the Twist and had no shortage of partners thereafter', and a visit the following day to Maubeuge. Here they helped with a visit of British ex-servicemen to the various memorials and cemeteries of the town. The exhausted touring party eventually returned to Fallingbostel with an enduring memory of 'the splendid hospitality at every hand, which left us in no doubt that the British Army has some real friends in this part of the world'.

Anniversaries in 1965

Two anniversaries were celebrated in 1965: the Battle of Waterloo in 1815 and the raising of the 13th Dragoons one hundred years earlier. The Guidon and a party of seventeen under Major PL Waddy went to Brussels to take part in the Waterloo celebrations and the Band performed at the massed bands display. In London, Colonel VAB Dunkerly, the Colonel of the Regiment, with Major EE Hunt, represented the Regi-

Fallingbostel & Paderborn 1961–66 Part 2

ment at the Army Board's Dinner for HM The Queen. After dinner there followed a display on Horse Guards Parade in which the Guidon Party also took part, with the Colour, Standard and Guidon parties of all the other Waterloo Regiments. With the escort to the Guidon was Lance Corporal Wellington, one of the Regiment's acquisitions from the West Indies; he was inevitably named 'The Dook' by the press.

The 250th Anniversary of the formation of the 13th was marked by a substantial four-day programme at Paderborn – an enlarged and expanded version of the successful families' weekend held at Fallingbostel. The emphasis throughout was on a family gathering and the guests included some 230 families and friends of serving soldiers and members of the Regimental Association.

The highlight was a mounted parade, watched by over 800 spectators. The Commander-in-Chief Rhine Army was General Sir William Stirling, an old friend of the Regiment from pre-war days in Sialkot. With the Colonel of the Regiment he took the salute on the local Goldgrund training area where 'the whole Regiment, almost to a man, was on parade'.

After a trumpet fanfare the spectators heard the roar of tank engines as thirty-six Centurions and Conquerors took up hull-down positions in an arc with all guns bearing on the saluting base. The Guidon, the Commanding Officer and the escort of tanks and Ferret Scout Cars advanced to the centre and a general salute was fired from the right of the line. Pillars of coloured smoke then rose in front of each tank, from grenades thrown by the crew, so that each Squadron advanced to the review line through its own colour. From there, they advanced twenty yards 'in review order' to the inspection line, with their Browning machine guns firing. After an inspection from the Commanding Officer's tank, 'Balaklava', the Guidon and its tank escort led the Squadrons past the saluting base with the Regiment's B vehicles managing to keep station in the rear, despite the dusty and bumpy going. Finally the bridgelayer tank lumbered past. 'It had been a memorable parade, the weather was kind and nothing broke down.'

The impetus was maintained with the Anniversary Ball at which some 750 guests were entertained in a huge *Schutzenfest* tent alongside the dining hall, transformed into a mediaeval castle, complete with drawbridge and portcullis. Here the guests were greeted by two mounted Knights clad in 'chain mail' knitted (on very large needles) by Mrs Waddy, wife of Major PL Waddy, who had himself undertaken much of the construction. On the Sunday a Memorial Service was attended by over 700 people and, after lunch, there was a funfair. And so it went on, with evening entertainment provided by the Corporals' Mess, a display of equipment, visits to Paderborn and a final Band Concert and squadron club parties, before the guests departed on Tuesday morning.

This was also an early example of the invaluable part which Home Headquarters could play in Regimental life. Lieutenant Colonel Palmer and his one clerical assistant made all the travel arrangements for the families and friends wanting to get out to Paderborn.

'Married Pads'

By 1961 the number of officers and men accompanied by wives and families had grown to some 130, but there were never enough quarters on station to accommodate the increasing numbers of 'married pads'. A complicated 'points' system was administered by a Garrison committee who allocated vacant houses as fairly as possible, but there was often a protracted wait for individual families. At one stage some twenty lived forty miles away from Fallingbostel, in Hannover, and a few more were at Bergen–Hohne. Some lived in houses or flats approved as 'hirings', but such was the shortage that 'mobile homes' were brought into use for particularly hard cases. The 'caravanners' suffered more than most from the rigours of the winter of 1962–63 and Hannover residents had hair-raising journeys commuting along the autobahn. In Paderborn there were more quarters, nearer at hand, and by 1966 there were 109 families living there, with another sixty-six at Sennelager.

The Regimental Wives' Club provided a valuable means both of social gathering and support. Like everybody else they were heavily involved in the Guidon Weekend and over sixty wives entertained the Duchess of Gloucester to tea. However, their next Notes in the *Journal* expressed gratitude that they could now 'converse with their husbands on subjects other than

Fallingbostel & Paderborn 1961–66 Part 2

Weather, Drill and "Best Blues" '. At Paderborn they rejoiced in a club room of their own, where they sometimes admitted husbands – and sought to dispel the popular image of 'a circle of women who sit busily knitting while reputations fall like the heads into the basket of the guillotine'. Their part in the 250th Anniversary was to run 'The Olde Wives Club General Store' and a crèche at the fête.

Renewing of Old Friendships

In June 1964, HM The Queen and the President of the Republic of India approved a formal alliance between the Regiment and Skinner's Horse.* The two Regiments had been closely connected since the 13th Hussars were brigaded with Skinner's at Meerut before the First World War and they went together to fight in France. After the amalgamation of the 13th with the 18th Hussars, they were again brigaded together in Risalpur, from 1936 until both Regiments relinquished their horses on the eve of another World War.

Two years later, in May 1966, the Queen approved another alliance, this time in conjunction with the President of Pakistan, between the Regiment and the 6th Lancers. The 6th had been formed in 1921 from an amalgamation of the 16th Bengal Cavalry and 13th Bengal Lancers. Both regiments served in Mesopotamia during the First World War, where the 13th Lancers took the place of Skinner's in the same Brigade as the 13th Hussars.† After amalgamation the new unit was renumbered and became known as the 6th Duke of Connaught's Own Lancers (Watson's Horse), a title they bore until 1947.‡ In

---

* Skinner's were the first of the irregular corps of cavalry to be raised by the East India Company, when James Skinner was appointed to command them in 1803. Apart from infusing them from the start with a corporate spirit and character, he dressed them in the famous canary-yellow tunic, unique in the Armies of the Commonwealth.

† The 16th Bengal Cavalry and 13th Bengal Lancers were originally raised in 1857 to assist in putting down the Sepoy rebellion. John Watson VC, whose name his regiment bore as a secondary title, commanded the 13th Lancers from 1860 to 1871. He is credited with introducing to the cavalry the practice of rising in the stirrups at the trot, on other than ceremonial occasions.

‡ Lieutenant Colonel JM Howson served with the 6th until Partition, when he transferred to the British Army and joined the Regiment.

1931–32 they too had been comrades-in-arms with the 13th/18th in Sialkot.

Another echo of the past came from South Africa. On behalf of the Regiment, Colonel ACW Noel, British Defence Liaison Staff in Pretoria, made a presentation in Pietermaritzburg to Jeremiah Maphanga. Jeremiah had served as a *voorloper* (ox driver) with the 18th Hussars during the Boer War. Aged eighty-five he had regaled the local doctor with his tales of the past. Doctor Stephenson, a keen historian and an expert on the battlefields of Natal, questioned him closely and there was no doubt that Jeremiah had indeed served with the Regiment.

> The Zulus are great rememberers and the detail of the events which befell Jeremiah proved to be absolutely correct . . . He was immensely proud of his Regiment, and the memories of burning farmsteads and cattle being driven off – though not perhaps the most edifying of the campaign – were amongst his most vivid . . . His only complaint of the British was that he was not allowed to carry a rifle.

Eventually word reached Home Headquarters of an Old Comrade fallen on hard times and, as a result, Colonel Noel met Jeremiah and his wife at Doctor Stephenson's house. He told him that he represented 'the Queen's Army and came to him on behalf of the Colonel and all ranks – the sons and grandsons and probably great grandsons of those he had known – with presents in memory of his loyal service'. Colonel Noel then handed over a parchment bearing greetings from Colonel Dunkerly and all ranks, a selection of Army clothing (which Mrs Noel had extracted from the Lancashire Regiment, then stationed in Swaziland), a Regimental tie – and an envelope containing crisp new bank notes.

> Cameras clicked and flash lights blazed but Jeremiah kept his dignity even though he found it hard to speak his gratitude so overcome was he . . . finally, his proudest moment, he was photographed in his Regimental tie which we explained to him could only be worn by members of the 18th Hussars and by nobody else.

Uncertainties Ahead

In December 1966, the Regiment moved unexpectedly to England.

Chapter Nine

Perham Down 1967

A Dated Barracks and a Dubious Role
In 1966 there was still a substantial garrison at Aden. It included an armoured regiment, the 14th/20th Hussars, less one squadron detached in Hong Kong. From early 1963 there was also a substantial force in Borneo, opposing Indonesia's 'Confrontation' with the newly created state of Malaysia.

The Regiment was meant to exchange with the 14th/20th Hussars in Aden and Hong Kong at the end of 1966, but in early 1966 the evacuation of Aden was announced. Too little time would be left before the evacuation to be worthwhile replacing the 14th/20th and the 13th/18th's move to Aden was therefore cancelled. A Squadron, however, was still to relieve the Hong Kong squadron; it had been too late to cancel their move to Germany. The rest of the 13th/18th was to move to England; no role had been identified for them in England nor had they been found a barracks in which to live.

Then the campaign in Borneo ended. That meant that the squadron of tanks in Hong Kong could be replaced by a squadron of Life Guards, the armoured car regiment then in Malaysia. In October 1966, the move of A Squadron to Hong Kong was cancelled and they too were to go to England.

After a stable and largely predictable period in Germany, during which the Regiment reached a high degree of professional competence in the armoured role, they were now confronted with uncertainty in both the short and longer terms. The withdrawal from Empire was gathering speed and overseas garrisons were being reduced or evacuated. After concentrating on winning the Canadian Army Trophy there was an inevitable sense of anti-climax and little in prospect to raise Regimental morale. All that offered was a station 'somewhere in England' for an indefinite period. Lieutenant Colonel Beresford recorded: 'As the 1966 summer went on, employment plans for the Regiment evolved, as much due to the Regiment's own initiative as to any conscious planning by the Ministry of Defence.'

History of The 13th/18th Royal Hussars (Q.M.O.)

Eventually the Regiment was made the responsibility of the Brigadier Royal Armoured Corps, Southern Command, also BRAC of 3 Division in the Strategic Reserve. They were to be equipped with obsolete Centurions armed with 20-pounders. Accommodation was at Cachy Barracks, Perham Down, near Tidworth. Built before the War for two small tank battalions, they were out of date in most respects and scheduled for rebuilding. However, there were tank hangars and there was direct access on to the tank training area of Salisbury Plain.

The Strategic Reserve in the United Kingdom had only one armoured regiment, the 16th/5th Lancers. All that was left for the 13th/18th was to be part of the Army Reserve, made up of units in transit and those waiting to be amalgamated or disbanded. It was a highly unsatisfactory status; the Army Reserve had the lowest priority for equipment and it provided troops for a variety of chores, often non-military. Fortunately, the 16th/5th Lancers were over-stretched and the Regiment might undertake some of their Strategic Reserve commitments.

'To be prepared to go anywhere and to do anything'

Even if it could be considered part of the Strategic Reserve, the role of that Reserve was anything but clear. It was of the essence that its units should be flexible – the phrase 'go anywhere; do anything' became almost a joke. An armoured regiment in the Reserve was expected to undertake any role – whether or not established or trained for it. In stark contrast with the highly organised and high-paced activity of Rhine Army, there was therefore little planned for the Regiment in England. However, earlier operations pointed to the need for all ranks to be physically fit to a much higher degree than was then expected in BAOR. This was in order both to reduce the time needed for acclimatisation in an overseas theatre and to keep down casualties from extremes of climate. The newly-introduced 'circuit training', short daily periods of exercises at a pace which progressively increased, was therefore *de rigueur* for everybody. The Regiment also planned courses for a higher level of individual training than had been possible in Germany, particularly during the preoccupation with CAT.

Perham Down 1967

It was the first time that the Regiment had been stationed in the United Kingdom in peacetime, other than in transit, since 1939.* They had to adjust to the custom of single soldiers leaving for their homes on Friday evenings, only returning in time for first parade on Monday. That inevitably cut into both sporting and social events at weekends.

Recruiting
A key way in which the Regiment could influence its future was through recruiting. An under-strength regiment could not be given an operational role or a major overseas exercise, a strong one had more chance of an interesting life – and therefore held out greater attraction, not only for experienced soldiers to extend their service, but also for potential recruits. So the first priority was to make the Regiment's presence strongly felt in South Yorkshire and to reduce wastage, in the Regiment itself as well as amongst recruits at the Training Regiment and the Junior Leaders Regiment. More recruiters were put to work in Yorkshire, both officially and unofficially, and increased staff were posted to Catterick and Bovington. One benefit of being in England was that it was much easier to launch recruiting tours in Yorkshire. Reconnaissance Troop, led by Captain DJ Delius, was the nucleus for two tours, fitting them into their annual firing at Warcop ranges. Much reduced wastage and increased recruiting saw Regimental strength grow during 1967 by more than thirty, to the highest figure for many years.

Changes of Plan in all Directions
At the beginning of March 1967, the individual training programme was in full swing and preparation was beginning for the Annual Firing. Major EE Hunt, A Squadron Leader, had already carried out a reconnaissance for an exercise later in the year in the Far East. But on 3 March the Commanding Officer was telephoned with orders for the equivalent of an infantry company to be in Aden by 24 March and to remain there for at least two months. They were to relieve a squadron of the RAF Regiment of the commitment for guarding Khormaksar

---

* Then only for a short spell; after relinquishing horses in India the Regiment returned to England in October 1938. On the outbreak of war in September 1939 they left for France, after the briefest of conversion training,

Airfield. A composite Squadron based on C Squadron, under Major GM Chirnside, was hastily formed and its main party left on 22 March. ('I was recalled from skiing in Switzerland; you would have thought we were about to go to war the following day', Colonel GM Chirnside.) Two of the three large troops (ie 'platoons') were drawn from two sabre troops from each of A and C Squadrons and administrative support from throughout the the Regiment. With the help of 1 Royal Ulster Rifles, they were speedily trained in the use of infantry weapons and practised in anti-insurgent and riot drills.

The Far East exercise, Arbiter, was scheduled for July and August and the Aden squadron might not return until after that had begun. What remained of the Regiment was therefore to be formed into another composite squadron for Arbiter, based on A Squadron, and Annual Firing was to be the means of working it up. No sooner had this decision been taken than another order arrived, on the same day that C Squadron left for Aden. The Regiment was to stand by to help deal with oil on the beaches from the world's first major oil slick; the tanker *Torrey Canyon* had gone aground west of Land's End releasing 30,000 tons of oil. Headquarters Squadron noted that over :

> ... several tense weeks, most of the Squadron resembled human yo-yo's as they drew specialised equipment for the impending oil battle only to be told to hand it in again. Initially, the battle was to have been fought on the beaches of Devon, until eventually we found ourselves poised for service in the Channel Isles ... Finally we went nowhere. Annoying as it may seem the battle was fought and won without our presence ...

despite much reconnaissance and planning, during which Major Hunt was despatched to Guernsey with the resounding title of 'Army Liaison Officer to the Governors and Commanders-in-Chief of the Channel Islands'.

Plans could be picked up again for Annual Firing at Castlemartin. The out-dated equipment and shortage of crews made this a far cry from the hot-house atmosphere of Hohne and CAT – something like cricket on the village green as compared with Lords. Tank gunners were in short supply and many were press-ganged who had not shot for several years, but the shooting 'went very well considering all the problems we had to face ...'.

Perham Down 1967

Operations in Aden

Events had continued to move apace in Arabia since B Squadron left Aden in 1958. The plans for Aden to be a principal British base assumed that it would continue to be acceptable to an independent Southern Arabia Federation. But,

> ... as in most pre-independence struggles for power, Aden spawned a complex tangle of rival political factions, some of which sought power through the ballot box while others were keener on the bomb and bullet.'

(*Withdrawal from Empire*, General William Jackson).

Political attitudes in Britain had also shifted further towards greater involvement in Europe and disentanglement from commitments east of Suez. The announcement in 1966, that the Aden base would be ended in 1968 when the Protectorate would be granted independence, sparked a rapid deterioration in an already difficult internal security situation. Until the beginning of 1967 British troops were able to operate in support of the police. In January, however, civil war was obviously developing between supporters of the 'National Liberation Front' (NLF) and the 'Front for the Liberation of Occupied South Yemen' (FLOSY). It became clear that the police were no longer reliable – they had been penetrated by the NLF – and and the High Commissioner, Sir Richard Turnbull, decided that British troops would take over responsibility for internal security. That inevitably placed much greater demands on the infantry battalions; hence the need for reinforcement and the call for close protection for Khormaksar airfield.

One of C Squadron's tasks was to provide mobile vehicle check points (VCPs); two were set up each day to try stop the movement of arms into Aden. But the main requirement was patrolling, particularly of the Causeway where incoming aircraft, only a few hundred feet overhead, were at their most vulnerable to SAM type missiles. The families' areas and the Khormaksar shopping district were also patrolled, in order to deter grenade attacks, as were the likely areas from which mortar attacks could be targeted on to the airfield and its facilities. 'Probably the most irksome task was Squadron searches of the civil labour lines which defied description, the filth was awful and "sanitation" dreadful'. The day before they arrived there had been a mortar grenade attack on the airfield, but C Squadron obviously discouraged any further nonsense of that sort as 'Not a single incident occurred in their operational area during their whole tour . . .', much as it would have been welcomed by the temporary infantrymen.

There were 'seven weeks sheer routine. Slow Landrover patrols round married quarters, the job only being popular between nine and midnight when the girls went to bed; road blocks twice a day, interminable sweeps of the the Dhobi area, Slave Island and Causeway and occasional sweeps of the Khormaksar shopping area; daily there were punctures to mend, and the fitters worked ceaselessly to keep us on the road.' No sooner had the Squadron got into a set routine than, on 3 April, a United Nations Mission arrived, coinciding with very heavy rains, making the area awash with politicians and water. The immediate effect of the rain was 'to dampen the ardour of the terrorists, but then their activities were soon back to normal with a bit extra thrown in while the UN Mission stayed . . .'.*

During the two month stay the boredom of routine guard duties for C Squadron was varied by patrols into Little Aden with 1st Royal Northumberland Fusiliers and 3rd Royal Anglian, two of the garrison infantry battalions. They were finding more than enough to do as the terrorist attacks increased. The Squadron Second-in-Command, Captain RT Cliff, also set up and ran 'a slightly unconventional shooting range by the seaside'. This involved shooting from the back of a Landrover travelling at 30 mph at targets set up on the beach.

Individual members of the Squadron had to be discouraged from visiting the local shopping area, but an escorted morning-off was arranged before the return home. Fortunately it was after the event that they heard that it did not have military police approval. Some members of the Fitters Troop found it was unwise to go un-escorted when they made a return visit for some last minute shopping. They were on the receiving end of a grenade attack and, when the remainder of the Squadron flew

---

* The Mission's three members, from Venezuela, Afghanistan and Mali, were supposed to find an internationally acceptable political solution in South Arabia, but the visit was a fiasco. It certainly did little to help the efforts of Lord Shackleton, a Minister in the Wilson government, who had been given the task of steering Aden to independence.

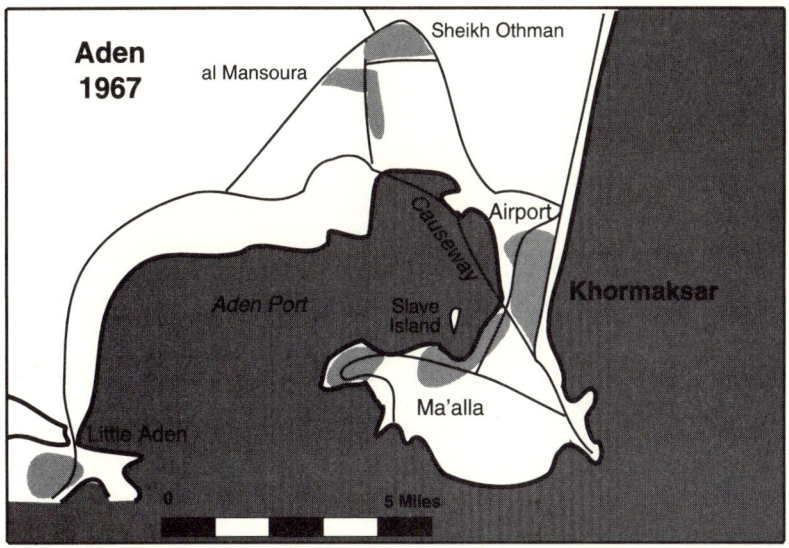

home, they were lying on their stomachs in the local hospital. 'Had the pillar that they all crouched behind been a little wider, their backsides might have avoided being spattered with shrapnel.'

When C Squadron was relieved on 16 May, by a squadron of 5th Royal Tank Regiment, the 13th/18th contingent in the Aden garrison had had their fill of an essential but tedious task. They had hoped for more opportunity to put into practice the hurried training of three months before.*

Far East Exercise

On 6 July the enlarged A Squadron set off for Singapore on Exercise Arbiter. During the earlier run-down of forces in the Far East a regiment less a squadron's worth of armoured vehicles had been 'mothballed' in Singapore, as part of the strategic stockpiling round the world. The task in Exercise Arbiter was for a squadron, at war establishment strength, to practise drawing up their full equipment after flying out from

---

* A fortnight after they left the NLF tried to turn two townships into 'liberated areas', but were worsted in a pitched battle on 1 June with 1st Parachute Regiment.

History of The 13th/18th Royal Hussars (Q.M.O.)

England, in the fourteen days allowed in the operational plan for activating the stockpile. They were then to prove the tanks in live firing and carry out infantry/tank training, at a training area at Marang on the north east coast of Malaya. As the move from Singapore to the training area was by sea, the Squadron also had to waterproof their vehicles for a beach landing from one of the new assault ships, HMS *Fearless*, an LST (landing ship tank) and an LCT (landing craft tank).

The Squadron was 130 strong, including a 'field repair increment' from 3 Infantry Workshops. About half the remainder came from A Squadron with contingents from each of the other Squadrons. As well as Annual Firing and the inevitable inoculations, time had to be found for indoctrination lectures, training in waterproofing, putting vehicles left behind in 'short term preservation' – and plenty of circuit training to make everyone as fit as possible; there would be no time for acclimatisation. Once in Singapore the Squadron had to draw up, prepare and test vehicles and equipment before embarkation. On the blazing hot vehicle park of Nee Soon, familiar to veterans of the previous Malaya tours, the long hours needed to get everything ready in time tested everybody's fitness to the limit, especially the tank crewmen.

With no previous experience of amphibious operations, what was already an awesome project was increased by the unexpected arrival on board *Fearless*, by helicopter, of the Commander-in-Chief Far East. General Sir Michael Carver was a veteran both of Mediterranean landings and tank fighting in North Africa and Normandy during the Second World War. After spending the night on board (and telling the Commodore and the ship's officers over dinner about his putting a naval captain under arrest during the Salerno landing) he came ashore in the first landing craft in order to watch the disembarkation.* Fortunately this landing was unopposed and the principal obstacles were palm trees; the bridgelayer tank in particular was unable to manoeuvre round all of them and the accompanying damage control man was soon busy filling in claim forms.

---

* The full story of the incident at Salerno is in Chapter 8 of *Out of Step*, Field Marshal Lord Carver's memoirs.

Perham Down 1967

A base camp was set up on the jungle edge, near 1st Royal New Zealand Regiment:

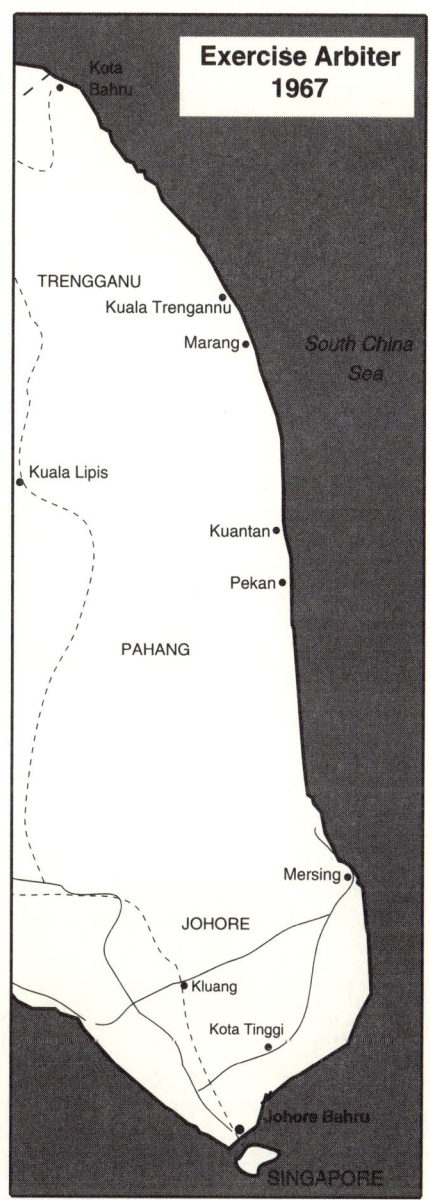

> The weather was extremely hot during the first week (even the Kiwis noticed) and acclimatisation was not really complete for at least another week. However, acclimatised or no, the timetable arranged for us had to be met and the first commitment was live firing. For this the beach was the only possible 'firing point', the 'range' was an area several thousand metres out to sea. A large danger area had to be cleared of any shipping including the local fishing craft... We then engaged with main armament a 'Hong Kong' target and some old buoys. The latter sank in an obligingly satisfying manner after several hits! Balloons released from an assault craft provided targets for the machine guns...
>
> Once firing was complete we plunged into two five-day periods of infantry/tank co-operation, first with 1 RNZIR and then with 1 KSLI.'... to give a taste of what jungle patrols are like, the opportunity was also taken for a large proportion of the Squadron to go out on a twenty-four hour bash 'under instruction' by the Infantry...

The whole exercise attracted plenty of brass-hatted attention and the Commander-in-Chief was followed by his Chief of Staff, Major General Beckett, to watch the firing, and the Army Commander and GOC 17 Division, Lieutenant General Pearson, and Major General Patterson, to observe the training with the infantry.

The original plan was for a return to Singapore in the LST *Sir Lancelot*, but she elected for dry dock instead and most of the Squadron had an extra week before HMS *Fearless* could return. That gave time for getting much of the work done for handing back the vehicles, some football against local teams and sight-seeing tours, but by the time *Fearless* appeared again on the horizon, she was a very welcome sight – the jungle camp had nothing more than basic facilities.

> Back in Singapore, by dint of tremendous exertions, all was got ready for handing back [of vehicles and equipment] . . . Of particular note is the success achieved by our strong REME detachment in having the tanks ready for going back into preservation four weeks earlier than the experts forecast.

Regimental Reunion and Regimental Training

Lieutenant Colonel Beresford was the last man to accept that the absence of much of his Regiment precluded any other activity. Those who remained, plus the Aden Squadron the instant they returned, were urged into feverish activity in preparation for a Reunion Weekend. When first mooted this was to mark the Regiment's first proper tour in the United Kingdom since 1944, but by the time it took place in August the Regiment was already under orders for a return to BAOR. The Reunion was a 'mammoth undertaking, the peak being on Sunday lunch-time when 1,500 guests were fed. Throughout the weekend our guests were entertained by band concerts, a searchlight pageant [organised by Major CJG Delamain] showing the story of the Regiment, receptions in the messes and squadron clubs and an equipment display.' The concerts included performances by an aspiring pop star, Miss Kay Kennedy and her group; Miss Kennedy also augmented local talent at the parties held in squadron Clubs.

The Arbiter Squadron returned at the end of August and the whole Regiment was together again – without outside commitments. That gave the opportunity in October to hold the annual Troop Tests 'in some of the worst weather imaginable'. Then, with the help of several other regiments, both armoured and infantry, almost the whole of the Regiment was exercised across Salisbury Plain in infantry/tank co-operation. Map-reading by day can be difficult, the Plain is almost featureless with few woods, roads, buildings or streams; at night it is doubly so. If cross-country movement at night was to be practised, as in Germany, keeping within permitted bounds was in any case a problem. As the exercise was in weather which varied from 'just about bearable to plain vile' it was hard to keep within the training area. A telephone call from a senior member of the Garrison staff, saying that tanks were coming into his garden, was not greatly exaggerated. His was not the only garden to suffer. (Perhaps the resulting complaints from landowners were the louder because few others in the recent past had practised so realistically on such a large scale.)

Sport from Perham Down
Despite all the other commitments, success was still being achieved on the sporting front. The football team, still under Captain E Henson as Manager and Trooper B Kenyon as Captain, won both the Cavalry Cup and the 3 Division Cup. The final of the 3 Division Cup was particularly satisfying; it was against 1st Parachute Regiment who had previously beaten the Regiment by three goals to one in the Army Cup Fifth Round. At half time the Regiment was losing two goals to nil. 'However, during the second half the Lilywhite fighting spirit was very much to the fore and we ran out winners by four goals to two.'

At cricket the Regimental eleven, led by Lieutenant EL Yorke, won the Southern Command Major Units Knock-out Competition and became 3 Division champions en route. By now there were six players in the team who all possessed 'the natural flair and happy temperament for cricket that is characteristic of West Indians, and it has been great fun to play with them'. Sadly it was to be their last season as they all approached the end of their Army service.

Relying largely on the ponies of the Tidworth Polo Club, Regimental teams competed in the Inter-Regimental and the

Captains and Subalterns – and were knocked out in the first rounds. Better form was achieved at Taunton and Rhinefield tournaments by individual players and useful experience was being acquired for the future. (This was greatly helped by coaching from Lieutenant Colonel RLV ffrench Blake, cousin of the Adjutant, Captain RJW ffrench Blake.) In order to increase pony power a lottery was launched from which enough money was raised over the next three years, from serving and retired officers, for two more ponies to be bought.

A Regimental crew gained third place in the two-day RAC Regimental Regatta at Seaview, Isle of Wight, with winds of force 6/7 throughout.

> There were thirteen regiments competing and considering the crew had no previous knowledge of Mermaids or of sailing at Seaview, local currents and tides could not be used to best advantage . . . the result was very commendable.

Two Officers' Mess guns were taken in the Bulford/Tidworth Garrison Shoot and provided

> . . . very interesting sport at a very reasonable price. On its first two shoots of the 1967/68 season, forty brace of partridge were killed. Salisbury Plain luckily holds many more partridges . . . '

Another Twist of the Kaleidoscope

By mid-1967 a major redistribution of units was needed to cope with the effects of yet more amalgamations and disbandments. The Royal Armoured Corps Depot was now to be manned by an active regiment and the 13th/18th, already in England, were an obvious choice. But they were over strength for the commitment and the 15th/19th Hussars were scheduled to leave Germany. As no other armoured regiment was available, the Regiment was to take their place in January 1968. The change of plan was said to have been influenced by the positive attitude which the Regiment had taken towards the uncertainties of the previous winter and by its eminently satisfactory recruitment state.

Chapter Ten

Münster 1968–72

Rhine Army Again
The Regiment returned to BAOR in January 1968, this time to Münster.* Farther west in Germany than they had previously been stationed, there was easy access both to the Channel ports and to RAF Gütersloh (for the air trooping flights). The Regiment was in Swinton Barracks, one of a group on the outskirts of the university city; near neighbours were the 10th Hussars (soon to be amalgamated with the 11th Hussars to form the Royal Hussars) and two battalions of Foot Guards.

Swinton Barracks had been erected hastily in 1946 to replace a tented camp, in order to get troops into weatherproof accommodation before the onset of another German winter. By 1970 the 'temporary' housing was providing constant problems. The water supply was haphazard and the heating erratic; the cookhouse was rudimentary in the extreme – and the despair of the hygiene experts. For long periods in the winter of 1971–72, in sub-zero temperatures, the only source of a hot shower was a mobile bath unit on the square.

Battle Groups and Combat Teams
The Regiment was again in 4 Guards Brigade, whose Headquarters had also moved to Münster, in early 1968. The Brigade had been reorganised on a 'square' basis, with two armoured regiments and two infantry battalions. This enabled 'battle groups' and 'combat teams' with varied compositions to be formed for training and operations in place of battalion/regiment and company/squadron groups. A 'combat team' was created for a particular task, with the number of troops and platoons required put under the command of a major with his

---

* Like Paderborn the seat of an early German bishopric, Münster was one of sixty-four ecclesiastical principalities not brought under secular control until occupation by Napoleon. After Waterloo it was included in the lands awarded to Prussia. The city centre, badly damaged by Allied bombing in the Second World War, had been rebuilt in the style of the past.

normal headquarters, whether of an armoured squadron or infantry company. An early problem to be overcome was the supply and maintenance of tank troops placed under command of an infantry headquarters for longer than one or two days, or if they were widely separated from the parent squadron.

Until 1971, 4 Guards Armoured Brigade (as it became) was part of 4 Division, in which the Regiment had served longer than any other unit. The Brigade then came under 2 Division which, with 21 Panzer Brigade, formed the 1 (British) Corps Counter Stroke Force. In 1975 an attempt was made to abolish the brigade level of command. 4 Guards Armoured Brigade became 'Task Force Charlie' and the scheme included the removal from regiments and battalions of their reconnaissance capability.*

Operational Role

> Over the years the horizontal arrangement of the NATO troops has been stretched ever more thinly by forces pulling from opposite directions. On the one side the hypothetical fighting front has been drawn east according to the principle of Forward Defence, but meanwhile the military presence in West Germany has been thinned out by the departure of forces for their homelands. . . . The outcome is that significant elements of NATO's order of battle . . . are faced with very long treks from home bases to their assigned stations in Germany.
>
> *Confrontation, the Strategic Geography of NATO and the Warsaw Pact,* Hugh Faringdon 1986)

Colonel Howard recalls: 'We were the right hand regiment of 1 (BR) Corps' first line of defence, covering a wooded hilly area of little armoured attraction. To the south, in rolling open ground which the Soviet forces would surely have chosen was the Belgian contingent's position.' It seemed improbable that the Belgians would be deployed in less than five, possibly seven days. The Regiment therefore made contingency plans for moving to its right. As one Regimental wag had it, heavily

---

* 'The whole plan was ill-conceived, impractical and short lived. 4 Guards Brigade was the first to go and the only brigade not to be restored with its former title.' General Sir Michael Gow in a letter to the author.

Münster 1968–72

influenced by years of living alongside the Foot Guards, 'If the Corps Commander gives the command '1 Corps RIGHT FORM, 13/18H will turn to the right and mark time for 1 million, three thousand and forty three paces'.

The Regiment was always at notice to move to its wartime deployment area, the degree of notice varying with the state of international relations. Frequent exercises tested this rapid exeunt from barracks. Code-named Quick Train they wrought havoc with the garrison social life and meant that the Regiment always had to be at a certain minimum strength. This in turn meant that planning for leave, adventure training and the many garrison administrative duties was a constant problem for squadron leaders.

New Equipment and Organisation

After the step back in England to obsolescent marks of Centurion, there was a good deal of new equipment with which to grapple. Tracked FV432s had arrived for command vehicles and ambulances, and FV434s replaced Saracens and half-tracks for the fitters. Many of the 3-tonners were replaced with the Stalwart six-wheeled, amphibious load carriers. There were new, secure, radios for the links between Regimental and Brigade Headquarters. The Centurion Mark 13 tanks were fitted with infra-red equipment as well as the 0.50 inch ranging gun which had been introduced a few years earlier.

For a period from January 1969 the three Squadron Headquarters Troops gave up their control tanks in favour of the FV 432 command vehicles:

> The control tanks are still available for use should the need arise, but the command elements in sabre squadrons will usually be mounted in FV 432s and Ferret Scout Cars. This arrangement, regarded as normal in many armoured regiments, has as its chief advantage that it makes the crewing in sabre troops more flexible, there being more men available to fill gaps necessarily left by those on courses and leave.

Another new piece of equipment came in February 1971, FV 438 fitted with 'Swingfire' anti-tank guided missiles.

History of The 13th/18th Royal Hussars (Q.M.O.)

Air Troop
Since the early 1960s there had been experimental integration of light aircraft flights with Royal Armoured Corps regiments and a firm scheme was promulgated in October 1963. Armoured reconnaissance regiments were to have a full squadron of helicopters and, with an eye to the Regiment reverting to the reconnaissance role, Lieutenant Colonel Beresford zealously pursued the recruitment of potential pilots wearing the Regimental cap-badge. Some forty officers and bright, junior NCOs were put forward for flying training. (That meant, of course, good people lost from Regimental employment and squadron leaders were not best pleased.) Eventually some dozen 13th/18th pilots were flying helicopters with various Army units around the world.

It also meant that in February 1968 the Regiment briefly acquired its own 'Air Troop' of three Sioux helicopters.* All three pilots in the new troop, Captain NGA Payne, Lieutenant C Blount and Sergeant T Dowdall, were 13th/18th and their knowledge of the Regiment and its working helped greatly in introducing air support into operational training.

However, there had been opposition from the start to the concept of integrating aircraft at regimental level. The advantages were emphasised, of concentrating scarce resources at brigade and divisional level, as compared with the tasking of widely-dispersed sub-units. Duplication of equipment and the heavy calls on REME support were also prayed in aid. The Army Board accepted that the disadvantages of dispersing aircraft outweighed the benefits to Royal Armoured Corps regiments; by 1970 there was a new Army Aviation structure which formed flights and air troops/platoons into Army Aviation Squadrons.

New Squadrons
Until then, however, the Air Troop's arrival prompted the creation of a 'Recce Wing' consisting of Reconnaissance and Air Troops. With Air Troop's excellent communications and ability to move quickly around the battlefield, they used the third dimension as 'eyes' of Recce Wing.

---

* Based on the American Bell 47G3B1, Sioux helicopters were built under licence by Westland at Yeovil.

Münster 1968–72

A Guided Weapons Troop had also been created and in March 1971 Command and Support Squadron was formed. 'Since we were quickly nicknamed "Power Squadron" by the remainder of the Regiment, it was not long before black was adopted as the Squadron colour.' (The colours of the 'traditional' squadrons had long been: A – yellow, B – blue, C – green, HQ – red). As well as the new Troop the Squadron had under its wing the Command and Reconnaissance Troops, and the Regimental bridgelayer tank. (The new Squadron had to be disbanded during the Operation Banner and RAC Centre tours but re-appeared in 1974.)

Crewing of tanks was a major problem and Lieutenant Colonel JRL Howard (who took over from Lieutenant Colonel Beresford in September 1968) devised a 'Basic Organisation Strength Scale' (BOSS). Short-term pressures to deploy as many tanks as possible had to be balanced against longer term career planning and the Scale set out the number of tanks to be manned, relative to squadron strengths.

Headquarters Squadron became Administrative Squadron in June 1971, when 'the long awaited BOSS re-organisation of the Regiment came into effect', but '. . . despite many assurances we seem to have increased rather than decreased in size'.

The new equipment and organisation all called for a great deal of re-training throughout the Regiment. More was on the horizon, with the news that the Regiment was to be re-equipped the following year with the Chieftain tank.

In the Field – Various Fields

Having missed the first part of the 1967–68 winter training season there was a rush to catch up. Within four weeks of arrival, recruit firing was taking place at Hohne, followed quickly by troop training and tests on Soltau. Much of the first part of the 1968 season was spent in the field, first at Soltau for combat team training and then at Hohne for Annual Firing.

Skill in gunnery continued to rate a high priority and the fortnight on the ranges was 'the most intensive, serious and in many ways, most satisfying part of the training year'. In July 1968 Annual Firing was the first opportunity for the whole Regiment to use the ranging gun techniques; there were also many new commanders, gunners and, in some cases, completely new crews. By way of variety, C Squadron under Major CJG Delamain went to Libya for a month in August with 2nd Scots Guards:

> Early on a typically damp Münster morning the main party moved off by bus on the first stage of its journey. The second stage was a flight by VC10, swift, silent and serene like the advertisements say, to RAF El Adem. Then came a journey by truck, which was none of those things and twice as long as the flight, to our home for a month, Curzon Camp. That sounded very grand and imperial. In fact it was more like an outpost of empire than anything else, being a collection of tents in the middle of a howling wilderness, two hours across the desert from our nearest neighbours, the Scots Guards. Here C Squadron learned to live with strange things like sun every day, Ferrets instead of tanks, B vehicles on their last legs, temperatures around 120 degrees in the shade, the 'Curzon Canter' (most inconvenient and no respecter of persons), salt water for everything including tea and getting up at 5 o'clock in the morning.
>
> In next to no time the Squadron had adapted remarkably well to both the climate and its new temporary role . . . sabre troops took part in battle runs with the Scots Guards which were most realistic and gave them a splendid chance to see and join in live firing by infantry, mortars and artillery working together. By the end of our month nearly everyone had covered many miles of mixed desert, and navigation by sun-compass was second nature to many. No-one got lost, which is something of a record, though one sergeant, who shall remain anonymous, had a narrow escape. . . . two rest periods of three days camped on a beach by the Mediterranean provided a very welcome change when they came.
>
> Not all the memories of Libya will be happy ones (Camp Bravo at El Adem was a particularly bad patch), but for all those who went, Libya 1968 was something they could look back on with a sense of achievement.

It was also an event which was not to be repeated; Colonel Gaddafi's coup the following year speedily led to the withdrawal of all facilities for British forces.

B Squadron (Major PC Beaver) also went off in August, but only as far as the Larzac training area in France where they kept company with 1st Grenadier Guards. As previous visits had demonstrated, the area was 'extremely rugged and both by

Münster 1968-72

day and by night there is good chance that a tank can fall, uninterrupted, for some 600 feet. It was a great change, however, to be able to drive across country without worrying about damage to crops . . . '. The Squadron took to their feet in a exercise run by the Grenadiers, climbing the tortuous hills surrounding the plain. 'It was to everybody's credit that we proved to be as fit as the infantry.' The usual trip to the Mediterranean 'was spoilt for Squadron Sergeant Major Anderson, who reported large numbers of idle foreigners sunbathing with no clothes on. He said he was quite sure they had no clothes on, even though they were 300 yards away, because he had a look through his binoculars.' On the way back to Germany, fifteen members of the Squadron paid a successful visit to the 4ème Chasseurs at their barracks near Lyon.*

'Usually brigade, and occasionally divisional, exercises fill the Autumn with expectation, work and excitement.' In 1968 the Brigade concentrated north of Celle, but the planned exercise was abandoned. 'The reason was plain to see; relentless, unseasonable rain had rendered the Lüneberg Heath almost a disaster area . . .' A Squadron, having married up with their infantry, gunners and engineers left for an Assembly Area:

> . . . where, gas masks at the ready, we spent an uneasy night waiting for H Hour. At 0430 hours we were launched against the enemy, 1st Troop led the advance, closely followed by the rest of the Combat Team. Very soon, however, just when the leading tank was about to make contact, the message came: 'Exercise Standfast; no move for 24 hours'. We returned, bewizzled and frustrated, to our Assembly Area . . . All was not lost. Trooper Cassidy kept us amused playing the bagpipes, kindly loaned by our attached platoon of the Scots Guards. His 'Dance of the Two Machets' to the tune of 'A Scottish Soldier' was very entertaining and nearly fatal . . . After a night, by a wonder dry, of troop smokers, when the air was rent with such classics as 'Zulu Warrior' and 'Swing Low, Sweet Chariot', we returned rather sadly to Münster.

---

* In 1963 the 4ème Chasseurs d'Afrique was disbanded 'consecutive à la cessation des hostilités en Algerie', but the following year the Regiment received Balaklava greetings from 'the officers and privates of the 4th Regiment of Chasseurs'. This was the regiment which had succeeded to the traditions of the 4ème Chasseurs à Cheval and the 4ème Chasseurs d'Afrique and which wished to keep up the association created at the Battle of Balaklava.

History of The 13th/18th Royal Hussars (Q.M.O.)

Ominous Reports from Northern Ireland

In August 1969, probably only passing attention was paid in Germany to the news that serious rioting in Belfast had reached a climax on the 14th of that month, when eight people were killed. Troop reinforcements had been sent there the previous day when it had become clear that the RUC had lost control of the situation, but the barrel was being scraped and in October the Regiment was warned to have ready an infantry company equivalent for service in the Province. An ad hoc D Squadron was hastily formed for Operation Matador, and its three 'platoons' began a fortnight's intense training under the guidance of 2nd Grenadier Guards and 2nd Greenjackets.

> Before long the camp was thrown into utter confusion with roadblocks and cordons littering the area. Various members of the Regiment kindly offered their services for car and body-searching. A very successful cordon and search was carried out on Brigade Headquarters where we were lucky enough to capture a real live Roman Catholic padre, much to his disgust.

Memories of anti-riot drills in Singapore doubtless helped the Regimental Sergeant Major, WO1 WF Anderson, to cause 'chaos with his very effective riot. Volunteers armed with a fire hydrant, painful missiles, boots, thunderflashes and smoke bombs were readily available . . .'. By the end of the fortnight D Squadron had reached a high standard of Internal Security drills. Six weeks later, much to *their* disgust, there had been second thoughts and they were stood down.

A new IRA bombing campaign started in January 1970 and that March there was the first Catholic riot directed against troops. The welcome given to the Army by the Catholic community the previous summer had clearly turned sour. By summer 1971 the terrorist campaign rather than communal violence had become the main preoccupation of the Security Forces. Mr Faulkner, the new Northern Ireland prime minister, resorted to internment and in one night 342 people were arrested and detained in a camp at Long Kesh. The camp was to be the Regiment's principal concern during an Operation Banner tour for the first four months of 1972.

Münster 1968–72

Conversion to Chieftain
The principal preoccupation for much of 1969 and 1970 was the conversion from Centurion to Chieftain tanks. Each sabre squadron was to have three troops of four tanks each, with three more in Squadron Headquarters. The first requirement was to re-train all tank crewmen as Chieftain commanders, loaders, gunners or drivers. Next came training in the field and finally, conversion firing on the open ranges. The process was further complicated by the new tanks arriving in 'rather unpredictable dribs and drabs'. First impressions were that the new tank 'seems to be almost a miracle of design and engineering – the best that brains can devise or money buy'.

Miracle of design or no, the Gunnery Wing were less than impressed when: 'At last the long-awaited CIM (Classroom Instructional Model) has come. £100,000 of kit: and when it arrived the electric plug wouldn't fit . . . .' B Squadron also discovered in the autumn, on Exercise Double Drum, that the new tanks bogged down as easily as Centurions; the LAD had to extract five of them in a 'long, wet and extremely hard recovery operation'. As the 'dribs and drabs' went to Squadrons in alphabetical order, C Squadron had to complete their 1969 tactical training in Centurions. By the time that conversion was complete, and the Regiment had had a full training season's experience, they found the Chieftains Mark 1 to be temperamental machines. Engines, air filters and gun control equipment needed an inordinate amount of maintenance if they were to be kept battleworthy.

The calendar from April 1969 to March 1970 was as crowded as ever. Added to hardy annuals was a brief spasm of infantry training for Operation Matador. The Reconnaissance Wing, not involved in conversion problems, took off in May 1969 to stay with 3rd Squadron 14th Cavalry US Army at Bad Hersfeld:

> The Yanks let us 'cabby' the majority of their vehicles from jeeps to their largest vehicle, an ARV, which incidentally was quite fantastic. It has a 1,000 hp engine and can tow seven M60s at a speed of 20 mph. It looks like our CO's Staff Car, Landrover, 432 and the Asst. Adjt's push bike rolled into one . . . The climax of the stay was an exercise that lasted for three days in which Recce Troop ran circles round the Yankee tactics. One of the American soldiers said: 'You see a Ferret Scout Car, look down, pin-point it

on the map and when you look up again the god-darned thing has just plumb disappeared'.

Highest Professional Standards

Lieutenant Colonel JCM Ansell relieved Lieutenant Colonel Howard in December 1970. He was the first Commanding Officer to have graduated from the Royal Academy Sandhurst, after it was created in 1947 from amalgamating the Royal Military College with the Royal Military Academy at Woolwich. On arrival he found the Regiment to be 'on the crest of a wave':

> After ten years as an armoured regiment in BAOR, broken only by the brief UK tour in 1967, it had reached a peak of operational efficiency which would be difficult to better. In all aspects of gunnery, one of the best barometers of an armoured regiment's skills, there was no regiment in Germany, British or Allied, which could match us. In tactical training exercises the Regiment had become a highly skilled professional unit. The ease with which troops, squadrons and even the Regiment itself formed and re-formed with minimum of fuss and preparation, into combat teams or battle groups with infantry, artillery and engineers, became second nature to all the soldiers. This flexibility derived from the confidence that every member of the Regiment had in his own professional skills as well as in those of the Regiment's supporting arms.

But it was not sheer length of service in BAOR alone which had created these high standards. The quality of long service soldiers was 'an enormous bonus'; by the end of 1971 some tank crews had not only been together for three years, but were probably all Class 1 tradesmen. The substantial efforts put into recruitment from South Yorkshire meant that the Regiment was consistently up to and, not infrequently, rather above the authorised limit of its establishment. Recruitment from such a small geographical area meant that a close 'family' spirit prevailed and this gave for great strength of purpose and self confidence throughout the Regiment.

There were, however, drawbacks. One was over-familiarity with the annual BAOR training cycle and another was the ever-increasing number of Rhine Army and Divisional 'housekeeping' chores that had to be undertaken, to the detriment of operational training. The recruitment of high grade soldiers had to be set against the departure of some of the most promis-

Münster 1968–72

ing officers and a chronic shortage of captains placed an extra workload on squadron leaders. Administration inevitably suffered and although some subalterns benefited from early, acting promotion, it was at the expense of young officer training and experience as troop leaders.

Groupings

From 1970 to 1972 the Regiment was brigaded for operational purposes with 2nd Coldstream Guards, many of whose soldiers came from the same part of Yorkshire as the 13th/18th. 'It was not uncommon on training exercises to find a Guardsman in the turret of a Chieftain and a 13th/18th Hussar driving a Guards Armoured Personnel Carrier'. In June 1971 the 13th/18th and 2nd Coldstream Battle Group was demonstrated, complete with all men and equipment to the Chief of Defence Staff, Admiral of the Fleet Sir Peter Hill–Norton. 'He inspected us minutely, drove a Chieftain and sent a very kind signal on the following day saying how much he had enjoyed himself.'

Close links were also established with 194 Panzer Battalion, who lived on the far side of Münster. Joint training with them included a major summer exercise in 1971, lasting ten days. At the end of it 'it was gratifying to note that the Regiment had a far greater percentage of tanks on the road than the Germans, equipped with the much vaunted Leopard'. The previous October, Corporal Ashcroft and Trooper Blakely had spent a fortnight with the Battalion's 4th Company and:

> ... had some long talks about tanks in general and although we admitted the Chieftain had some faults they would not admit that the Leopard had any faults whatsoever. In many ways this was very annoying; they were all sort of brainwashed into thinking it had no faults at all.

A principal drawback of the Leopard was the lack of armour – a curious shift of emphasis from Germany's Second World War tanks. The majority of German soldiers were conscripts completing their 18-month service and the contrast with British training and procedures was revealing:

> ... we attended various lessons on gunnery. Most of these were theoretical and the crews did not get much opportunity of putting the drills into practice... All the tanks had to do gunnery servicing at the same time and an officer sits at a table on the

tank park and reads one item at a time. When the item has been completed a tank commander puts a blue flag on the top of the tank. When all the tanks have a flag flying he goes on to the next item . . .

Corporal Ashcroft found that as a Leopard commander his lack of German was not very important as their only brief was :

> . . . to follow the troop leader's tank and keep within fifty metres of him. We were given no map and if the troop leader is knocked out or my tank breaks down it's just hard luck . . . They didn't seem bothered about firepower, the main thing was to keep up.

(A German crew commander flung briefly into a British tank might well have carried away a similarly simplistic impression?)

Annual Inspections

Unlike religious festivals the great days in the military calendar change their names with confusing frequency. For instance, the annual inspection of vehicles, for long known as CIV, was for a while known as the DIT and is now the UEI. Such changes are no doubt of immense significance and moment to the staff, reflecting changes of deep subtlety and import – within the Regiment the familiar bogey that stalks the tank park in the winter months is easily recognised. The change of name is merely puzzling, annoying or amusing depending how one takes such whimsies. The result of the inspection last December [1968] was most creditable; the inspecting officer said he had never before seen tanks so well prepared.

The other great winter bunfight is, of course, the Brigade Commander's inspection, now known as Fitness for Role (FFR), but indistinguishable from the old Administrative Inspection or 'Admin . . .'

At the FFR in 1969 Commander 4 Guards Brigade, Brigadier JM Gow, late Scots Guards, saw first a foot parade and then a mounted march past. 'It was an act of calculated and unprecedented daring on the part of the Commanding Officer to offer our foot drill to such expert scrutiny, and to command the parade from his polo pony, Rhapsody – both gambles paid off.' The FFR did include an element of surprise which the old 'Admins' lacked; after the pre-arranged programme the inspecting officer would call on squadrons to carry out a task entirely impromptu.

Münster 1968-72

At Brigadier Gow's 1969 inspection he invited B Squadron to march three and three quarter miles in forty five minutes, carrying a wounded man on a stretcher for about one and half miles. 'We did it in 50 minutes – we had not reckoned on the meticulous care which would be lavished on the wounded man by Lance Corporal Hays, the Squadron's only trained First Aid man.' General Sir Michael Gow also recalls, of the same FFR:

> ... at the end of an excellent lunch in the Mess, I suddenly shouted 'Fire', indicating its location. Appropriate action was efficiently taken.

Adventure Training

Adventure training was creating an increasing variety of opportunities for people to get away briefly from the conventional administrative and training treadmill. Each troop was expected, on its own or with one or more other troops, to carry out at least one adventure training exercise during the year, preferably in places as remote from Germany as could be found. They had to include 'a real element of adventure'. (The most irksome requirement for some troop leaders was for a full written report to be completed at the end of each scheme.)

A major enterprise in June 1971 was Exercise Olive Oil in Italy. A hundred members of the Regiment, drawn from each squadron, flew to an American airbase for a fortnight in the Dolomites. They arrived to find that 'Italian Railways had lost the train with all our vehicles, cooking equipment and tentage. Siesta time on a Whit Monday is no time to start borrowing another Army's vehicles and another country's Air Force tentage, but somehow all was achieved and by 2200 hours our camp site near the village of Santa Guistina was completed.' Instructors borrowed from the Italian Alpine Brigade helped in a hastily modified programme for the first week, in which the party's first trek took on a 'formidable' mountain.

When the vehicles eventually arrived, a week late, a two-day Escape and Evasion exercise began, 'during which everyone got soaked' and 'the hunters had their work cut out trying to find the escapees who had been welcomed like the victorious Eighth Army into every little house; it was sad that Corporal Mulloy was caught just after he had persuaded the local Monastery to give him a five course meal and a bed for the night'. The fortnight was finished off with football and a smoker with the Alpini and then two days on the Adriatic. On final departure 'It was a moving sight when the village turned out to say goodbye to us as we left in the Alpini vehicles . . '.

'Bushwhacking'

In 1971 nearly one soldier in five wearing the Regiment's badge was employed elsewhere. Because the Regiment was well-recruited the policy was to rotate as many through posts at extra-regimental employment (ERE) as possible. There were still opportunities for individuals to get to unusual places and members of the Regiment could be found in Singapore, Brunei, the Persian Gulf, and Cyprus. A number were helping to man the young Army Air Corps, both as pilots and ground crew. Meanwhile a strong presence was maintained in Yorkshire with the Queen's Own Yeomanry at York, No 12 Army Youth Team at Sheffield and and the Army Careers offices in Sheffield, Barnsley and Doncaster.

One of those at ERE was Captain PEB Hodgson, who had joined the Regiment in 1967 and was now serving with The Sultan's Armed Forces in Muscat and Oman. He was awarded the Sultan's Bravery Medal with the following citation:

> On 27 April 1972 Captain Hodgson was in command of a troop of armoured cars in support of 3 Company The Desert Regiment who were deployed South of Akoot. Between 1515 hours and 2000 hours both the armoured car troop and 3 Company came under heavy, effective enemy machine gun and mortar fire, causing several casualties including the company commander. Although his armoured car had been damaged by enemy fire Captain Hodgson organised the evacuation of the wounded, supervised the reorganisation of the half company who had lost its commander, controlled accurate air strikes and artillery fire, and at the same time commanding his troop. The gunfire from his troop caused several enemy casualties. After last light, Captain Hodgson cleared the withdrawal of 3 Company, he himself remaining until last to ensure that all were safely back in Akoot.
>
> Throughout the engagement Captain Hodgson showed considerable powers of leadership, disregard for his own safety, and a calm and sensible appreciation of the situation. He undoubtedly remedied what could have been a nasty situation for 3 Company.

17. REME fitters replacing a Centurion engine 'somewhere in Germany'.

18. Exercise Arbiter 1967: Centurions of A Squadron going ashore in north east Malaya.

19. Münster 1969: FFR inspection of A Squadron – L to R Maj Edelsten, Lt Col Howard, Brig Gow, Sgt Newbery, Cpl Bishop.

20. Northern Ireland 1972: A compound at Long Kesh.

Münster 1968–72

Sport at Münster
In spite of almost living in the field during the summer of 1968 the Regiment was 'not without success in sport'. A notable athlete had emerged in the shape of Corporal J Wild who won both the BAOR and the Army long jump individual titles.

'The sailing team has done well': a crew skippered by Lieutenant AJN Collis won the 30 Square Metre Passage Race Trophy in the 4 Division Regatta at Kiel, coming first in all four races. Sailing continued to be a generally popular sport and a number of people took advantage of courses both in Germany and England to qualify at various levels, including two troopers and a REME craftsman who became Offshore Hands in 1969, having never been in a sailing boat before their week's course.

The polo team, commended by *Horse and Hound* for its 'hard riding and close marking', was showing distinct promise. Although knocked out in the first round of the Inter Regimental, it was by the eventual winners, the 17th/21st Lancers. Next came the Captains and Subalterns where the team, led by Captain RJW ffrench Blake, reached the final where they played the favourites, the 14th/20th Hussars. 'It is said that it was a good game to watch, but to the players it felt scrappy and untidy for the most part of it. However we won 4–3 in extra time . . . our first Captains and Subalterns for thirty-two years.' At the end of the season there was a grooms' match against the 10th Hussars, where the Regimental team 'played very well' to win 5–2. The grooms continued to show their prowess in reaching the final of the Grooms' tournament in 1970, by which time there were only five polo ponies in the stables and 'exercise commitments' meant scratching from the Captains and Subalterns. Trooper I Allchurch had several jumping successes, mounted on Mrs Green's horse Hiawatha; he came fourth in the Cross Country at the RAVC show and was well placed in several of the events at the Rhine Army Summer Show, where he was the best other rank rider. More ponies were acquired the following year and with those of the 5th Inniskilling Dragoons Guards and Guards Brigade, the Münster Polo Club was one of the most flourishing in BAOR.

The winter of 1968–69 saw a langlauf team, again with Major PC Beaver, re-enter Rhine Army competition achieving eighth

History of The 13th/18th Royal Hussars (Q.M.O.)

place in the 'Army Combination' after only two weeks' preparation. In 1969–70 two langlauf teams at the Divisional Ski Meeting emerged fourth and eighteenth out of thirty-one. Training in Norway was a principal feature of the 1971–72 langlauf season with skiing 'for miles along great open plateaus' during the day and 'Norwegian girls who came 9 km from the nearest town to see us' at night.

After four years out of Army Alpine skiing a Regimental team came third in the Divisional meeting and reached overall twelfth in the Army Championships. That was followed up with fifth in 1971–72. 2nd Lieutenant RIA Ireland was the leading performer and Major RCJ Dick, the Second-in-Command, won innumerable veterans' prizes.

In 1968–69 the football team failed for the first time for several years to reach the later rounds of either the Army or the Cavalry Cups. By 1970–71 they had clawed their way back, reaching the Divisional final of the Army Cup and winning the Cavalry Cup. During that season the Regimental team won twenty-eight of thirty-two games played and lost three. Trooper Wild was top scorer with forty-two goals, including eight hat tricks. Despite the Regiment's Northern Ireland commitment in early 1972, the Cavalry Cup was won again in 1971–2. The final against the Queen's Royal Irish Hussars was a 'hard match' which went into extra time with the Regiment coming from behind after early setbacks to win 4–2.

Rugger players had an exceptionally successful season in 1968–69, 'not perhaps in terms of matches won, the team was most unlucky to lose the final of the RAC Cup . . . but in terms of the number of people who played, their spirit and obvious enjoyment'. At the start of the 1969–70 season no fewer than forty-two members of the Regiment, including attached, turned out for a trial match and the first XV then won all but two of the fifteen games played. The last game of the season was for the semi-final of the RAC Cup which they lost to 1st Royal Tank Regiment. At seven-a-side a Regimental team was beaten in the final of the Concordia Sevens, a tournament for fourteen selected BAOR and two UK teams.

A good deal of playing at squadron and troop level lay behind the Regimental hockey players' achievements. They won nine of

Münster 1968–72

their fourteen matches in 1968–69 and lost only two. The following year twenty-one games were played with ten wins and six defeats. They too reached the semi-final of the RAC competition, as well as the semi-final of the BAOR Plate. In 1970–71 there were thirteen wins and six defeats out of twenty-three games and two of the leading players, Captain EL Yorke and Lieutenant RStJ Webster played for BAOR. A team could not be produced in 1971–72 because of the preparations for the Northern Ireland tour, but four members of the Regiment turned out for 2 Division.

Other sports mentioned in early reports from Münster were angling, golf, squash, sub-aqua, orienteering and water skiing. By spring 1971 about fifty soldiers had taken to the game of squash and a successful knockout competition was run. From this emerged Trooper Davison who beat all comers and went on to the BAOR Championships, only to be beaten in the first round. At golf a Regimental team won the local league and angling prizes were beginning to be won.

Colonel Dunkerly

Colonel VAB Dunkerly, Colonel of the Regiment from 1959, was forced by ill health to resign in May 1968. He died the following September.

> . . . although a busy and influential man, he devoted his spare time, entirely voluntarily, to the benefit of serving and past members of the Regiment. Many will remember his visits over the last few years and his genuine interest and understanding of our difficulties, yet few know the effort and pain that these cost him. He had since the war suffered considerably, first from a hand damaged in 1945 and amputated a few years ago, and then from a diseased hip for which a further operation was necessary. It was only a week before his death that he learnt that yet another serious operation was necessary. Such was his courage that through all these years he made fun of his disability and little of the pain he suffered.

The new Colonel of the Regiment was Colonel JR Cordy-Simpson, who had commanded the Regiment during its first tour in Malaya; his son, RA Cordy-Simpson, had joined in 1964.

History of The 13th/18th Royal Hussars (Q.M.O.)

In Yorkshire

In 1969 Barnsley Borough Council celebrated the centenary of its charter of incorporation. The Regimental Band played a central part in the proceedings and led the Mayoral procession through the middle of Barnsley. A Regimental team also crossed the North Sea with two Ferrets, a Stalwart and a Landrover, meeting up with a Chieftain earmarked for shipment to Münster en route. The latter was 'carefully sidetracked northwards with the help of a transporter'. During their time in Barnsley they were active:

> . . . chatting up likely lads and lasses, fending off swarms of school children and keeping in with the local police and Borough Surveyors despite having slain a giant lamp post in Barnsley and torn up a brand new stretch of road by Darfield 'Suspension' Bridge.

The centenary celebrations coincided happily with the formal opening on 28 June of the Regimental Museum. Cannon Hall, Cawthorne, is an ex-stately home just outside Barnsley owned by the Corporation. Since 1957 its museum and art gallery had been attracting over 50,000 visitors a year. The ten–year renewable contract was for the Regiment, with Ministry of Defence finance, to convert four rooms and a passage and supply exhibits and show cases; the Corporation supplying heating, lighting, re-decoration and maintenance of the exhibits. Lieutenant Colonel H Wise (18th Hussars 1915-24) was instrumental in arranging the deal, which provided for the first time a place for the proper care and display of the Regiment's links with the past. Apart from items from the Officers' and Sergeants' Messes, a number of individual donations were received and these, together with loans from the Master of the Armouries and the National Army Museum, provided an impressive display to mark the launch of the Museum.

During another recruiting tour in September 1971, at the Sheffield Show, the vehicle team was warned of some expected picketing by pacifist students, but in the event all they received were batches of 'poorly produced' leaflets. 'After nearly four weeks of constant flag-waving we were able to look back on a highly successful tour with considerable interest from a large number of potential recruits, numerous parents and families shown over vehicles, old friends and haunts re-visited, terrific press coverage.' Nine vehicles and a caravan were 'really none the worse for a round of South Yorkshire via Germany, Holland, Belgium and Southern England.'

Life In Münster

The continued strengthening of the links with Yorkshire was helping recruiting to stay well up. Another major factor was the emphasis which the Regiment gave to the 'family spirit'; 70 per cent of new recruits joined because they had been recommended to do so by serving friends and relations. Another Reunion Weekend provided further cementing of the family spirit in August 1970, after which the Commanding Officer, Lieutenant Colonel JRL Howard, said that the compliment he valued most, of the many which poured in, was the frequent: 'This is obviously a happy Regiment'. He was also told by a 'distinguished councillor' from the West Riding: 'You've got a great bunch of lads in your Regiment. Why, even the officers are all right'.

Münster Horse Show

Two weeks before the Münster horse show in 1970 an SOS came from the Show Committee, asking for an arena party. The German Army had been forbidden by their politicians to do the job. Squadron Sergeant Major Laverick and fourteen men (some of whom, as Junior Leaders, had previous experience at the White City Horse Show) stepped smartly into the breach.

> Seldom has the Regiment had such good publicity in Germany. Their smartness, enthusiasm and efficiency were outstanding. They were praised on German television and cheered and clapped more than the competitors themselves. Each soldier received £10 and an electric razor from a grateful committee . . .

The publicity was apparently so good that the Command Secretary saw the soldiers on television and asked 'awkward questions' about a failure to complete beforehand 'some prehistoric DCI' [Defence Council Instruction]. Despite that, the organisers the following year were successful in obtaining the services not only of an arena party, but the Band. Their 'smartness, speed and efficiency' was 'adored by the vast German audiences who showed their appreciation fully'. The Band played topical music and 'judging from the wolf-whistles, the birds thought the Bandmaster [WO1 Titley] "just dishy" '.

'Gazette' in place of 'Journal'

One innovation of the period was not to survive for long. The Regimental *Journal* used to be published several times a year. Gradually it had become an annual, increasingly expensive, event – heavily subsidised from Regimental funds. Partly as an economy, partly to provide more frequent news of the Regiment's doings, the annual *Journal* was dropped in 1968. In its place came a 'newspaper', *The Lilywhite Gazette,* and the first two editions in 1968 were of four pages. At Christmas 1968 the twelve-page edition was an acknowledged attempt to compromise between the two formats. By the eleventh edition, in autumn 1972, there were thirty-eight pages and there was much more of the old *Journal* about it than a newsletter. April 1973 saw the reappearance of an annual *Journal*, which continued to be published until November 1992.

However, the newsletter *cum* newspaper format was employed again with great effect during the tours in Northern Ireland. *LilyWilly* appeared during the first Operation Banner visit. That was followed by *Town and Country* published first in 1975, and then from 1977 to 1979.

An Affluent – and Married – Army

In the 1940s and 1950s there had been only a handful of privately-owned cars. In 1970 the *Gazette* recorded that: 'There are now 225 privately-owned cars in the Regiment, ranging from a Mercedes 230S owned by a bandsman and a Jaguar owned by a corporal, down to several clapped-out Volkswagen "Beetles" owned by officers'.

Rather more than half the soldiers in the Regiment were married and living in excellent quarters close to the Barracks. The contrast between their accommodation and the conditions in Swinton Barracks could not have been more marked, and perhaps accounted in part for the flow of young soldiers to the altar. By 1971 there were 241 families on station, against a total Regimental strength of 439. The additional families inevitably called for greater administrative effort. Frequently a whole squadron would be required for administrative duties in the barracks and the garrison generally.

Münster 1968–72

Amateur Dramatics and Scouting

For a Regiment with such close links with 'B-P' it is perhaps strange that neither scouting nor 'amateur dramatics' often featured in the events recorded each year.* However, in December 1970 what started as 'just a little something to help with the entertainment over Christmas' finished with a cast of over 100, the involvement of the entire Garrison, 'and interrupted all other activities in the Gymnasium. . . . With such a large cast there were doubts as to whether sufficient people were left to form an audience; . . . in fact two performances were given to an audience of over 500'. The show was the Garrison Review *Oh! Münster!*† As usual with such productions it was difficult to say who enjoyed themselves more – the audience or the cast.

A Brownie Pack was also formed, for the first time since Neumünster, and the Commanding Officer wrote to tell Lady Baden-Powell about it. She replied, from her grace and favour apartment at Hampton Court Palace, on 1 January 1971:

```
Dear Colonel Ansell,

I cannot tell you how touched I was and how very pleased
I was, to receive your charming letter of Dec 21st today.

How very good it was of you to write to me like that and
I appreciated hearing of and from you very much indeed.

I am such a VERY back number, in my connection with "THE
REGIMENT"- which is how so naturally my husband and I
used to think of and speak of it in those long ago days,
when he was your 'Honorary Colonel'. Although he had so
many connections with the other regiment‡ he had com-
manded (in 1897!) and had so many other interests as
well, your 13th/18th was, after all his 'first love', &
his years of service with it were really in many ways the
great training ground, preparing him for his ultimate
greatest task as World Chief Scout!
```

---

* Lieutenant General Lord Baden–Powell, was Colonel 13th/18th Hussars from 1922-38. He had a pronounced flair for acting and whilst serving with the 13th Hussars frequently took part in plays and entertainment generally. In South Africa in 1885, wearing old clothes and sporting a red straggling beard, he carried out valuable reconnaissance amongst the Boers. Years later it was argued that, had notice been taken of his reports, there would have been no siege of Ladysmith.

† *Oh! Calcutta!* was the title of a contemporary box-office hit in London

‡ 5th Dragoon Guards.

History of The 13th/18th Royal Hussars (Q.M.O.)

```
And now what delightful news this is that you give me of
the formation of a BROWNIE PACK for the youngsters at
your 'base'; and I hope indeed that this  will start
well, continue to go ON well, and that its members will
WORK HARD and succeed well, adding their own good
strength & influence, alongside their MILLIONS of
'sisters' scattered over the countries of the free world!

I send my cordial good wishes to the 13th/18th BROWNIES -
and congratulations to their LEADERS - and may I also say
- my THANKS TO THEIR COLONEL for the help he will give to
the Pack in their various undertakings!

Thank you again very much indeed for your very kind
letter.                                 Olave Baden-Powell*
```

Departure from Münster

In 1972 the Regiment's turn came for their first Operation Banner tour in Northern Ireland and, after preparatory training, they left for Country Antrim on 10 January. They were back in Germany by 11 May 1972 and, after block leave, preparations began for handing over to 2nd Royal Tank Regiment, with whom places were going to be exchanged in England. On leaving Münster the Regiment parted company with 4 Guards Armoured Brigade, with whom they had been happily associated for nearly nine years.

---

* Lady Baden-Powell was herself World Chief Guide from 1930 until her death in 1977.

Chapter Eleven

RAC Centre Regiment 1972–74

'Three addresses always inspire confidence, even in tradesmen.'
(Lady Bracknell, *The Importance of Being Earnest*, Oscar Wilde)

Three Addresses

On 1 August 1972 the Regiment began its longest tour in England since the War: 'There is a bewildering complexity about explaining life as RAC Centre Regiment which belies its basic simplicity but incessantly hard and sometimes unrewarding work.' The Regiment was split, with the bulk of A Squadron going to Warminster and the other Squadrons being broken up to form composite squadrons at Bovington and Lulworth. Roughly speaking, the 'Vehicle Squadron' at Bovington was found by a mixture of C Squadron and Admin Squadron while B Squadron and Command and Support Squadron formed the Lulworth Squadron. Also at Bovington were Regimental Headquarters and the Administration & Depot Squadron:

> Each establishment presents a different type of soldiering. At Bovington it revolves around providing fit and reliable vehicles for a wide variety of different courses in Driving and Maintenance and Signals; at Lulworth providing fit and reliable tanks and armoured cars for gunnery courses; at Warminster providing a demonstration squadron of Chieftains that spends nearly every week of the year on exercises or demonstrations. Add to this the documentation and administration of everyone in Bovington including the medically disabled, the soldiers awaiting discharge, transitees and prisoners of all RAC regiments . . . plus all students at RAC Centre and the life of the RAC Centre Regiment is starkly, if superficially, depicted.

History of The 13th/18th Royal Hussars (Q.M.O.)

RAC Demonstration Squadron, Warminster

A Squadron, led by Major JAC Blakiston for most of the tour, then Major PC Beaver, found themselves:

> ... under close scrutiny by all ranks and departments of the Army ... Our job is to provide tanks and crews for the demonstrations and exercises organised by the various Schools within the School of Infantry.... Our tanks today may be commanded by a 'junior General' on a course with the Junior Division, Staff College and by a Royal Marine Sergeant tomorrow; a test of Yorkshire patience at the best of times.

Alone amongst the squadrons they kept to a recognisable establishment with four sabre troops, albeit with a substantial administrative element to cope with their detachment some forty miles from Regimental Headquarters. In a typical period covering eleven weeks in 1972, they took part in fifty-six demonstrations or exercises:

> ... the latter normally of one or two days' duration extending into the early morning hours. ... of course there have been disasters ... 2nd Lieutenant Hudson took the order 'to move through 2nd Troop' on Exercise Trout Stream too literally and wrote off two Chieftains ....'

The landmarks of Salisbury Plain, 'The Rings', 'The Firs', 'Strip Wood', 'Picnic Wood', became all too familiar by the time that two seasons had been completed. However, the Squadron did get away for Annual Firing at Castlemartin.

Vehicle Squadron, Bovington

The Vehicle Squadron, under first Major F Harrison then Major CJ Edwards, had nearly 140 assorted vehicles in their care. Most were for the use of students, but there were also samples of the full range of Royal Armoured Corps vehicles then in service, kept 'bulled' to perfection for frequent demonstrations – an average of two a week. Students' vehicles ranged from Centurions and Mark I Ferrets to Mark V Chieftains; from Saladin and Saracen to Scorpion and Stalwart.

> The work starts after these vehicles are returned by courses. The maintenance and cleaning of the vehicles is an endless battle against time and the lack of spares which, due to our low priority here, take a long time to be made available. Many of the vehicles too are venerable in age. There are some in Vehicle Squadron who regard them as pieces of industrial archaeology.

RAC Regiment 1972-74

Lulworth Squadron

Major DJ Delius was the first to be in charge of the Lulworth Squadron, responsible for Gunnery School vehicles and helping with range administration. Major RT Cliff followed him for a few months before handing over to Major RA Cordy-Simpson and moving on to be Second-in-Command. The Lulworth Squadron had to service and maintain the instructional vehicles, particularly the fire control equipment. Their Tank Troop held a large number of Chieftains and a few Centurions and the Saladin Troop also looked after the new Scorpions. Guided Weapons Troop 'are only to be seen on their way to and from the Larkhill ranges (apparently Lulworth isn't good enough for them)'. The MT Troop found themselves driving:

> ... a wide range of vehicles – 10 tonners, ambulances, tractors, bulldozers, the NAAFI truck (apparently one of their highest priorities) as well as the standard line in trucks and Landrovers.
> ... Range Troop apparently man the firing points and do all the physical work on the Ranges. They claim that they work long hours in all weathers and fixing an interview with one of them is tantamount to paralysing the complete firing programme.

The Lulworth Squadron had their full quota of Fire Power demonstrations and other events; the latter included finding a troop to shoot a sequence for a tactical film: 'Apparently they spent more time sweeping rain water off the roads to prevent reflection than anything else.'

The Squadron found that 'the second time round is always easier than the first' and the Firepower demonstrations caused fewer headaches, if no less work. '... we have been able to tell people that the erection of stands for 1,000 spectators cannot coincide with the ammunition fatigues ...'. Balaklava Day in 1973 was meant to go unobserved, as normal work had to continue, but 'with a little juggling, a lot of co-operation from RSMIs and a great deal of secrecy, the Squadron had a most enjoyable day'. Reveille was sounded outside the Officers' Mess at 0630 hours by seventeen trumpeters and the remainder of the camp was then given similar treatment by the whole Band. 'If somewhat unpopular in certain circles, it certainly did our ego a lot of good.'

After the rigours of Swinton Barracks, Münster, it seemed particularly bad luck that the living-in soldiers should have had

History of The 13th/18th Royal Hussars (Q.M.O.)

August and September 1973 with no water, no baths, no showers and no lavatories while new baths were put in, followed by a repeat performance in December and January while the block was repainted and new lavatories installed.

Administration and Depot Squadron

Finally Administration & Depot Squadron, presided over by Major B Harris, juggled with:

> ... a bewildering variety of held strength personnel consisting of anything from 'itinerant buskers', posing as soldiers, in the Guardroom cells, to hobbling medical detainees.... Their task is mainly documentation and administration of transitees, holdees, medical detainees and the occasional 'fuzees' (which are a dissolute form of long absent soldiers).... We have a constant flow through of soldiers from all Regiments in the RAC, a typical month's figures are:
>
> | | |
> |---|---|
> | 19 absentees | 6 re-enlistments |
> | 50 discharges | 4 postings |
>
> 30 transitees for BAOR ex detention, missed flights, courses etc
>
> 30 escorts of absentees from police stations and delivery to Luton en route to BAOR.

Families

An immediate problem of the move from Germany to England was how to fit 180 families into ninety quarters. The overflow was temporarily accommodated at Watchet in Somerset while the families officers at the different locations 'juggled desperately with the deluge of families'. Eventually 169 families were fitted in, with thirty-four at Warminster, forty at Watchet and ninety-five at Bovington and Lulworth. The move was not without dramas. A flight of sixty families bound for Brize Norton was reported to have changed course for Lyneham. Buses and baggage trucks were switched in a headlong dash to Lyneham, only to find that two flights had been mixed up and the Brize Norton party was heading there after all. 'The Families Officer aged a quarter of a century ... as the heavy baggage followed the families at a sober and monolithic pace, ably assisted in its slothful progress by the dockers who were on strike.'

RAC Regiment 1972–74

Detachments and Expeditions

Every opportunity was taken to provide variety through postings, visits and exchanges. There were occasional opportunities for small detachments to get away, such as the secondment for five months in 1973 of a scout car troop to the Parachute Squadron Royal Armoured Corps in Northern Ireland.

Under Lieutenant MH Green, volunteers from each of the squadrons spent a varied time with the Parachute Squadron, rotating in weekly periods between the Lower Falls, Legoniel, Sunnyside and the shore of Lough Neagh. In the Lower Falls:

> . . . some dozens of cars were stopped, scores of people interrogated, several crowds cleared, but our own injuries were happily confined to the odd bruise or cut from a bottle or a brick.

In their first week they directly assisted in the capture of

> . . . a gentleman we were all anxious to meet, being the main exponent and operator of the RPG 7 rocket Launcher; . . . FSC 38 BA 24 immobilised his stolen Morris 1000, probably for good, and trapped him inside . . .

Of other occasions Mr Green will never forget:

> . . . quivering beneath his B47 with his Ferret immobile on top of a massive barricade in Cope Street when a bottle of '68 milk smashed on the turret roof. The smell and hair-setting qualities of this semi-liquid were nothing compared to what had been expected. . . Corporal Bushby and Trooper Dowle once mistook a 3lb blast bomb fizzing a foot in front of their Ferret for one of the Troop Leader's discarded cigarette ends.

Legoniel, just north of Ardoyne, required a 'guard and follow up approach'* with twenty-four hours on duty and twenty-four hours off. On one occasion a youth on a bus pointed a pistol at a trooper, a foolish move since the bus stopped 200 yards up the road and he was 'soon marched in under a hail of abuse from the local population; it later transpired that he had slipped the pistol into his Grannie's shopping bag'.

In Sunnyside the Troop operated under a company of 1st Gordon Highlanders; they patrolled a solidly Protestant area, on their own:

---

* Guarding vital civil and military installations, but being ready to react to incidents as and when they occurred.

History of The 13th/18th Royal Hussars (Q.M.O.)

> . . . which meant we had to develop some pretty sophisticated tactics to avoid being swamped with coffee and cake. . . . Nothing of real note occurred here except that we invariably arrived too late to stop the constant planting of bombs on the Lisburn Road.

They found rural Northern Ireland in the countryside round Lough Neagh 'very unspoilt and beautiful' and it provided welcome relief from the claustrophobic atmosphere in Belfast.

> Our Troop area was militarily interesting and the normal form of OPs, VCPs, searches, foot and vehicle patrols went on round the clock. . . . The chance to get really close to the enemy always just seemed to evade us . . .

But they were able to assist in the capture of four gunmen who had killed two Aghalee policemen. Finally they moved for a short period to Gosford Castle with squadrons of the 9th/12th Lancers and 15th/19th Hussars.

> It was beautiful June weather and the Troop area was half-active and half-friendly so we had sandwiches and tea for NAAFI breaks – once we established which half was which.

In May 1973 a troop of three Centurions, under 2nd Lieutenant PM Davies took part in a NATO combined Exercise, Dawn Patrol, travelling to and from the Mediterranean in HMS *Intrepid*. The Bay of Biscay obviously made a deep impression on several of the troop. Adventure training in Cyprus followed wading training with the Royal Marines, but the exercise proper, in Sicily, lasted only seventy-two hours. Mr Davies went on with 2nd Lieutenant HWF Anderson for six months detachment in Cyprus, to A Squadron 16th/5th Lancers. The latter were Force Reserve for the United Nations Force – UNFICYP.

Two small parties went out to Malaysia for demanding jungle training. In January 1973 2nd Lieutenant RCB Nutting led the first contingent which joined up with members of the Blues and Royals and Royal Hussars for Exercise Jamestown, lasting some five weeks. The following year a composite squadron was formed from Royal Armoured Corps regiments in the United Kingdom, for Exercise Invariant, from the beginning of October to the end of November. The Regiment's party was led by Lieutenant MD Griffith-Jones. Both exercises started at the Training Centre at Kota Tinggi, well known to the Regiment in the 1950s and now run by the Malaysian Army.

RAC Regiment 1972-74

Adventure training took troops from Warminster canoeing in Wales, pony-trekking and fell-walking in Derbyshire and:
> Third Troop left with the assault boats to explore the upper reaches of the Thames, but only got as far as London . . .

Regimental Weekend

With the Regiment in England it was an excellent opportunity to organise another Regimental Weekend. On 4 August 1973 buses left Doncaster, Sheffield and Barnsley in bright sunshine, but: 'from the moment our visitors arrived until the morning they left it rained and the wind blew'. The Band had to work overtime, playing at some of the meals 'in order to help people forget the miserable weather outside'. A cricket match between Officers and Sergeants was abandoned for the Garrison Hall, which became the venue for a mammoth Bingo Session. By the time of the evening entertainments all was going with a swing and both the Junior Ranks Club and the Sergeants Mess were open to the small hours.

Changes in Appointment

Lieutenant Colonel Ansell had handed over to Lieutenant Colonel DAG Edelsten in April 1973 after a varied tour in command which had taken in Rhine Army, Northern Ireland and Bovington.

The following year the Colonel of the Regiment, Colonel JR Cordy-Simpson, handed over to Major General DB Wormald. 'Cordy' (senior) had been one of the best polo players in the Regiment during the pre-war years in India. Serving throughout the Second World War, for much of it in notable command of Headquarters Squadron, he had been awarded the Military Cross for gallantry.

Sport

Although there were generally good facilities for sport at each of the three locations it was obviously difficult for Regimental teams to be fielded during the tour. Despite strenuous efforts from a dedicated squad, the best that could be managed at soccer was to reach the Zone Final of the Cavalry Cup in 1972-3 before being knocked out. However, the Regiment performed with distinction in the local league. Water sports were close at hand; the Sub-Aqua Club flourished and a Regimental water-ski boat was seldom out of use. Major RT Cliff ran the latter from Lulworth Cove and soldiers from throughout the Regiment were inducted into the delights of water skiing. At hockey, 2nd Lieutenant AREdeC Stewart was selected to play for the Army; he also captained the Combined Services Under-23 side.

Teams were entered for both forms of skiing in 1972–73 and the Alpine team finished seventh in the Army finals; the competition was too much for the langlaufers although they 'produced some fairly respectable times in their final championship'. By 1973–74 Lieutenant Ireland had been selected for the Army team and he continued to play a notable part in the Regiment's efforts, which produced a clean sweep of trophies at the 3 Division meeting.

There was a great deal of activity in equitation. Several new ponies were acquired during 1972 and new players recruited in time for the 1973 season from Tidworth, where the ponies were stabled. This was largely a time for individual efforts because of the difficulties of getting together to practise. However, reasonable form was shown in both the Inter Regimental and the Captains and Subalterns and there were high hopes for the following season with 'more ponies than we have had for some years and keen officers who are willing to give it a go'. Those hopes were justified in 1974 with the Regiment winning four Cups at various tournaments and reaching the semi-finals in both the Inter Regimental and the Captains and Subalterns.

The Regimental stables proper was set up at Warminster with A Squadron. There the principal interest was hunting with the South and West Wilts, but 'a small nucleus of interest in racing has recently been re-kindled in the Regiment'. Four racehorses or point-to-pointers were 'all being fed and nurtured with great care by their various owners more, it must be said, in hope than in anticipation of future success'. In fact Cabro, owned by a syndicate of officers, achieved a second, first time out, did nothing of note for the next three races, but came fourth in the 1973 Grand Military Gold Cup at Sandown. After a disappointing start to the following season he showed considerable form towards the end. Ridden by Major Blakiston,

RAC Regiment 1972-74

he ran 'a creditable third after a very exciting race' in the Grand Military. Cabro subsequently won two good handicap 'chases and completed the season with two wins, three seconds and two thirds. Captain JPJ Fairrie and Lance Corporal I Allchurch flew the flag for the Regiment at several point-to-points although the former broke his arm early in the season 'riding a horse that had never jumped before'.

In 1973-74 there was hunting not only from Warminster, but from Bovington, where the Commanding Officer, Lieutenant Colonel Edelsten was on home ground with the South Dorset.

'One of the more pleasant aspects of life during our tour in England were the excellent shooting opportunities given to us in Dorset and Wiltshire.' In particular the Lulworth Syndicate Shoot, over 3,800 acres of the Ranges, provided varied but always enjoyable days out for a number of officers.

Third Summer in Bovington

A major preoccupation for Regimental Headquarters during the first part of 1974 was the re-organisation needed for a return to Germany and the planning of the first year's training in BAOR. The Regiment was to have one further tour with main battle tanks, before altogether quitting the role of armoured regiment.

Meanwhile all the squadrons had a busy summer, but 'probably the most demanding task' was running the RAC Open Day at Bovington. This came immediately before the move was to get under way and, 'as if this was not enough, took place under what seemed to be a very serious threat of terrorist attack'.

> Most of those who helped organise Open Day will remember the feeling of anxiety and helplessness as thousands of Dorset people poured into camp unaware of increasingly menacing and specific intelligence warnings of danger. The day passed without incident, and we shall never know whether we frightened off a genuinely intended attack, or whether it misfired, or was perhaps only an elaborate hoax.

In the Vehicle Squadron: 'it is certain that very few of us knew exactly how many vehicles we owned until we came to count them up for handover. The estimate was 200, including twenty-seven Chieftains and a Massey Ferguson tractor (complete with driver, Mr Randall)'. The Queen's Own Hussars were taking over and their Advance Party, who arrived 'full of enthusiasm', went to work straight away – 'often on vehicles still to be handed over to them'.

Although the tour had had little to commend it from the viewpoint of normal regimental soldiering, it was not without its advantages. Lieutenant Colonel Edelsten thought:

> It was a very good thing for the Regiment to be in England, particularly for the young officers. It was a chance to re-charge their batteries, have a bit of social life and enjoy things a bit away from the grind of soldiering in Germany. It was a relatively happy time for the Regiment, although some of the younger married people had a difficult time for the lack of married quarters. . . . But generally I think the Regiment made the best of that strange interlude while we were spread out all over the place.

RAC Regiment 1972–74

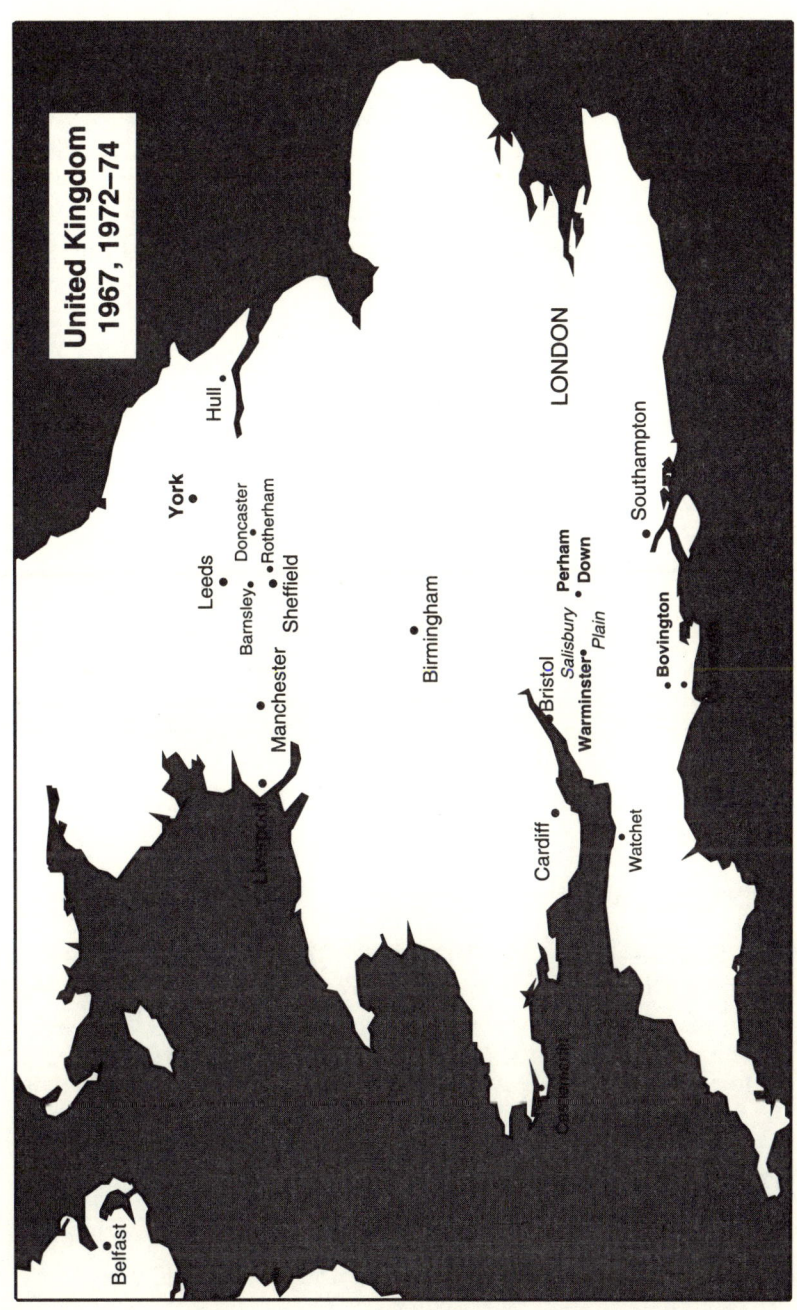

Chapter Twelve

Hohne 1974–77

Back to 7 Armoured Brigade

In August 1974 the Regiment moved from Bovington, Lulworth and Warminster to another new location in Germany: Hohne. Once more, speedy re-organisation was required, back to the establishment for an armoured regiment, equipped with Chieftain tanks. On arrival the Commanding Officer, Lieutenant Colonel Edelsten, outlined the task that lay ahead in transforming the Regiment back from their multifarious duties in England to a fully operational unit:

> He also stressed the renewed importance that sport was going to play in our life in future, a prediction that has since been vindicated in yards of elastic bandage, gallons of plaster-of-paris and dozens of crutches.

The Regiment's predecessors were the Queen's Own Hussars to whom they had handed over in England. After completing the takeover from them by the end of August, September 1974 was a hectic month. The new squadrons and troops had to shake down together: 'many members of the Regiment hardly knew each other, faces were strange, the place was strange and we had a fleet of someone else's tanks and vehicles to get used to'. At the end of the month they moved out for three weeks at Soltau to finish off the process. It culminated in Exercise Richardson's Bluff (named after the 13th Hussars' successful action in Mesopotamia in October 1918). This was the Commanding Officer's test of the squadrons' success in their initial training. 'Surprise was the keynote, night was turned into day, and sleep was a rare experience.'

During the exercise a gunnery training device 'Simfire' was used for the first time. Simfire enabled tanks which 'engaged' their target accurately to disable it. The firing of their gun was marked by a puff of white smoke, their opponent's engine and radio were switched off automatically and red smoke billowed from its canisters. Realistic as Simfire was, it took a long time to set up in readiness for an exercise and was not reliable.

Hohne 1974–77

The winter months of 1974–75 were spent, as ever, on individual training.

> A new feature, however, has been that the Second-in-Command has been given free rein on each Wednesday morning to train the whole Regiment in the various often neglected but vital skills that the modern soldier needs. Major Cliff has brought all his ingenuity and *joie de vivre* into play to couple interest and valuable instruction in these mornings. An inveterate practical joker, he could not resist the temptation to pull four hundred legs, when the Commanding Officer was away in England, by hinting that everyone was in for a long walk, marching them out of Barracks to suitably deceptive tunes – and then conducting helicopter training on the polo ground.

Another Tour in Northern Ireland ...

After barely ten months of finding its feet once more as an armoured regiment, the Regiment had to transform itself into the Operation Banner 'mode' in June 1975. The tour in Northern Ireland dominated 1975, but, from January to May:

> ... the BAOR role as an armoured regiment still had to be trained for and to that end, the Regiment had annual firing, Soltau training, site guards, CPXs and a new event, Exercise Green Pastures, to contend with. Green Pastures was the nearest Hohne ranges could produce to a defensive battle with mortars, artillery, Swingfire and tanks all firing simultaneously. As training it was invaluable, as a control exercise instructive and as a spectacle superior to Blackpool Illuminations.

Training for Operation Banner then began with C Squadron merged into A and B Squadrons. The Regiment returned to Germany from Ireland in January 1976 to find highly 'bulled' tanks and a new Commanding Officer: Lieutenant Colonel DJStJ Loftus had taken over from Colonel Edelsten.

... and another Change in the Offing

Colonel Loftus was told on his arrival that within eighteen months the Regiment was to convert to armoured reconnaissance – and return to Northern Ireland. He feared that it would be difficult to motivate soldiers into putting their hearts and souls into the remaining period of armoured training. 'My fears proved groundless and the Regiment launched itself into a very busy, varied and interesting training programme.' A major feature was to be a month in Canada, in order to make use of the training area at Suffield.

C Squadron, reformed after being disbanded for the tour in Northern Ireland, spent the exercise season pursuing a separate programme, as it was going to Suffield with the 1st Prince of Wales's Own battle group in May 1976, before the 13th/18th group. They had to telescope their preparations into an even shorter period than the rest of the Regiment, going to Hohne in late March and straight on to join up with the 1st Prince of Wales's battle group for a fortnight at Soltau. There they had high pressure 'troop, squadron, combat team and battle group training all rolled into one'.

The rest of the Regiment had to be fully operational by mid-July, when they were due to leave for Suffield. Troop training and annual firing showed a satisfactory standard of armoured skills and an A grading on the ranges. However, a fortnight's preliminary training with the rest of the battle group was not enough, the Commanding Officer considered, to achieve the standard of infantry/tank co-operation to which the Regiment had been accustomed in Münster. One problem was that:

> In common with all other armoured regiments and infantry battalions at this time, we suffered from the excessive turbulence caused by the 1974 Defence Review and the Army's commitment to Northern Ireland. This meant that the composition of our battle group was continually changing.

Suffield Training Area
In order to supplement the over-used training areas in Germany, in 1964 a trial exercise had been held at Fort Wainwright, Alberta. That led in 1972 to the first visit of a complete battle group to Suffield. The Training Area there was 1,000 square miles of undulating Alberta prairie, broken up by several large coulees (ravines) and lakes, some of which dry up in the summer. It is 160 miles south east of Calgary and thirty miles from Medicine Hat. Much of the area has never been cultivated and there are many remnants of old Indian burial and camp sites, the latter recognised by numerous stone circles. These *tipi* rings served to hold down the buffalo skin *tipis* used by the Blackfeet.

Hohne 1974–77

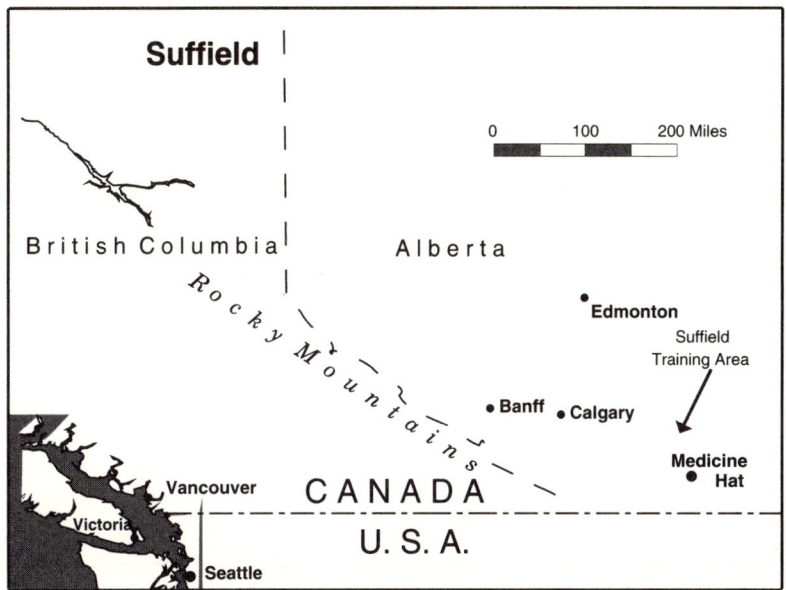

There was a permanent staff for the British Army Training Unit (BATU) Suffield and from 1973 to 1975 Major RJW ffrench Blake was the GSO 2. He found the pioneering task much to his liking, with almost *carte blanche* opportunities for 'free-running' training. Compared with the facilities at Hohne, there was little equipment: no simulator, moving targets or radio-controlled pop-up targets. However, the resident engineer section worked marvels of improvisation and some fifty Centurions were bought from Canada as hard targets.*

When C Squadron arrived in May 1976 they had some teething problems, including the mastering of the Training Area safety requirements, 'the special cries of "automatics unloaded" and "FNAs removed" etc' and:

> . . . those moments of panic and total disorientation when there are no distinguishable features to be seen, the gophers refuse to help and you are convinced that a neighbouring tank at Red will mistake you for a 'pop-up' target.

However, they soon felt ready for anything and:

---

* The British Exchequer was amply repaid when the final drives were sold to the Israelis, who urgently needed them for their Centurions in the Gulf War.

History of The 13th/18th Royal Hussars (Q.M.O.)

> Perhaps the Squadron Semi-Indirect shoot on to Watching Hill at nearly 9,000 metres stands most vividly in everyone's minds. It was very exciting and convinced us all that what the Gunners do, C Squadron can do even better!

Much too exciting for the Squadron Leader, Major ffrench Blake, was the realisation at one stage that the visiting 1 (Br) Corps Commander, Lieutenant General Harman, was being shot over. To Major ffrench Blake's immense relief, not to say surprise, the General took it in excellent part, saying that it was the first time that he had been under fire for years.

When their turn came the Regiment's Battle Group was made up of A and B Squadrons, with 54th Maharajpore Battery RA, B Company 1st Prince of Wales's and a troop from 16th Field Squadron RE: some 575 men. Except for two NCOs:

> ... this was the first visit to Suffield for every member of the battle group. Therefore it took us some time to work out the best way to use the facilities. However, after working-up over four or five days the group made tremendous progress and by the end of the three weeks had reached a high standard of training.

> The Training Area is essentially a battle run which stretches thirty miles from South to North and the same distance from West to East. It consists of open, rolling prairie with no trees and no villages. It is therefore totally unlike any part of North West Europe and accurate map reading poses a considerable problem. It provides a unique opportunity for battle groups to practise all arms tactics together with live firing of armour, infantry and artillery weapons. There is no doubt that the area offers first class opportunities for training, but there is a danger that training for and at Suffield with its unique terrain becomes an end in itself. (Lieutenant Colonel Loftus)

During three weeks of alternately blazing sun and pouring rain at Suffield, visitors included the Colonel and Commanding Officer of an affiliated Regiment, the Royal Canadian Hussars. At the end of the training eighty members of the Battle Group stayed on to canoe and climb in the Rocky Mountains, but the remainder had to get back for major exercises in Germany.

Sport in Hohne

A result of Colonel Edelsten's directive on arrival was that virtually every soldier played sport regularly. As well as the major sports there were clubs for basketball, squash, volleyball, badminton, 0.22 shooting, sub-aqua, canoeing, tennis, motor sports, sailing, gliding and free fall. The wives followed suit and netball, badminton and keep fit classes were all well supported.

A principal aim was to rebuild a Regimental squad for football. There was plenty of scope for the game to be played at troop level and the Football Officer, Lieutenant K O'Sullivan, and his selection committee went talent spotting. They found the makings of a good team which was entered for all the major competitions in 1974–75. Captained by Sergeant B Kenyon, a veteran of the successes of the early 1970s, they defeated some of the more fancied teams and reached the quarter finals in the Army Cup. They were champions of both the Divisional and Soltau Garrison Major Units leagues, but only made the second round of the Cavalry Cup. Disappointing as that was, it had been a good start for a young team. For the following season the team found themselves split up by the Operation Banner tour and had to drop out of the main football events of the season. Halfway through the 1976–77 season they were second in the local league and in the quarter finals of the Divisional Cup, but the next edition of the *Journal* is remarkable in having no entry for soccer. (Nor did the 1979 and 1980 editions).

The 1975 cricket season was more than a little disrupted by training for Northern Ireland, but a Rear Party team reached the third round of the BAOR Minor Units Competition. The polo players managed affairs better with a very active season, playing in 'nearly every tournament in West Germany: Berlin, Hamburg, Münster, Lippspringe, Fallingbostel and, of course, Hohne', as well as the Inter-Regimental and Captains and the Subalterns. They reached the final of both the latter tournaments, but won neither. However there were wins at Fallingbostel and Hohne and close runners-up in Berlin.

Other practitioners of equitation pointed out that 'there is a field of mounted endeavour where no ice clinks in the Pimms glass, no languid feminine clapping marks the touch line and sticks are carried only to encourage the horse . . .'. The Dorfmark Drag Hounds provided 'hell for leather dashes around lines of forty to fifty jumps' all over Lower Saxony. Because of their competitive nature they were 'ideal for teaching both horse and rider to be bold and clever'. During the winter full

History of The 13th/18th Royal Hussars (Q.M.O.)

use was made of the tank gunnery ranges for exercise and 'among the wrecked ironmongery was the great asset of a two-mile sand gallop' which compensated for the lack of a hill on which to get a horse fit. The pressure to improve standards of all riding officers was kept up with early morning schools 'when the most unlikely subalterns could be seen being bumped and ground into wakefulness. The incidence of sprained ankles, wrists, necks – anything to stay in bed – shot up.'

The hard work of the two previous seasons paid off in 1976 when the Regimental Polo Team had its most successful season since 1939. They won both the Captains and Subalterns and the Inter-Regimental and were beaten in the final of the Combined Services. The leading player was Captain RJD Rowe; he and his grey pony Sinbad had almost become an institution and their departure at the end of the season was greatly lamented. Although polo took pride of place in 1976 the Regiment was not unsuccessful in the hunter trial and show jumping world, thanks largely to 'two wonderful little horses', Ambassador and Noya Para. They were placed at a number of events, being ridden by one or other of Corporal Allchurch and the Commanding Officer, Lieutenant Colonel Loftus. As well as the achievements of their charges the grooms of Stables Troop could congratulate themselves on being runners up in the Grooms' own polo tournament.

In 1977 the honours went to the show jumpers and, especially, to Ambassador and Corporal Allchurch. They won or were placed at twenty-two events, missed by only one point the 'leading horse' at the Rhine Army Summer Show, came first equal in the Soldiers' Jumping championship, won the cup for the leading novice hunter trial horse of the year and came second in the season's prize money.

> Corporal Allchurch and Ambassador formed a remarkable team – both small but brim full of guts and ability – and it is difficult to select the high point of their season. Should it be their first and second placings at the 5th Heavy Regiment RA Hunter Trials, their two firsts and second in one day at the Verden Show, their two firsts and two seconds at the Rhine Army Show or their immaculate round over a big 'open' course in the QDG's Hunter Trial? For me it was none of these but the sight of this courageous scrap of a horse flinging himself over fence after fence and almost

Hohne 1974–77

galloping himself into the ground when getting the fastest clear round in the cross-country phase of the Rhine Army One Day Event. (Lieutenant Colonel Loftus, owner of Ambassador.)

The football team failed to come up to expectations and the aim of regaining the Cavalry Cup was not to be achieved.

> The only other remarkable aspect of sport during 1976 and 1977 was the limited amount that the Regiment could play. Brigade athletics were a thing of the past and we were never in barracks long enough to enter any of the major cricket competitions.

Most of the activity in shooting appears to have been on the clay pigeon trap, set up on a semi-permanent basis in front of the Officers' Mess. The practice saw the Sergeants' Mess again beaten at the Balaklava shoot-out by the Officers (and was to stand everybody in good stead in Omagh). There were a few visits to the North Coast and, initially, some fairly large bags of duck. Constant wind changes and extremely cold weather, even for the North German coast, then reduced them considerably and there was more success on the local pond. Amongst the leading shots was Captain MD Griffith-Jones whose wife's recollection is that the visits to the north were 'notable more for the social life than the wildlife – a good number of wives and girlfriends went too, and froze!'

His notable achievement in quite a different sport was marked by the award of Combined Services colours for fencing to Captain Griffith-Jones.

Variety of accommodation

> Undoubtedly the nicest thing about Hohne and very much the gilt on what is not perhaps the freshest piece of gingerbread is the Officers' Mess at Hohne in *Schloss Bredebeck*. Some four or five kilometres out of camp, it is situated on the edge of the ranges and so blissfully unaffected by the noise and hubbub of Caen Barracks. It is surrounded by forest which borders the thirty odd acres of grounds, where there is a swimming pool, an ornamental pond, tennis courts and a substantial fishing lake, not to mention hundreds of jumps for those who ride.

Originally a shooting lodge, the Schloss had been greatly extended to include a ballroom and a number of bedrooms. Common to all the reception rooms were 'magnificent floors and moulded ceilings'. The Officers' Mess silver and other property had recently been restored and showed to great advantage in these palatial surroundings, the envy of all other officers' messes throughout the Army.

Full advantage was taken of the building by the Regiment. For their first Christmas in Hohne, at the prompting of the Second-in-Command, Major RT Cliff, the families took over the Mess instead of entertaining the living-in officers in their quarters. The wives cooked Christmas lunch and there was a large and successful family party for everyone – including a Christmas tree with presents.

But 1977 was also 'the year of "Rattle" ', in which the modernisation of Caen Barracks at Hohne meant that squadron offices and troops' accommodation were 'shoe-horned into several woefully inadequate Rattle transit blocks' nearly a mile from the tank park.

Recruiting Problems

The 1977 issue of the *Journal* had bad news about recruiting which had not been good for the past two or three years:

> By the end of 1975 we had been placed on the priority list* for reasons which were mostly out of the control of the Regiment. The one area in which we can help is physically to support the Army Careers Information Offices (ACIOs) in our recruiting areas of South Yorkshire and North Humberside. This scheme is called Keep the Army in the Public Eye (KAPE) and is normally a biennial affair. The aim of the Tours is not directly to recruit individuals, but to see and be seen in our area. Despite the exposure of Northern Ireland, the image of the Army still suffers from some of the misconceptions of the Colonel Blimp era. The best way to dispel these is to meet and talk to people – in the street preferably – with our equipment on display.

In 1976, with the rest of the Regiment away in Canada, C Squadron had the task of mounting a KAPE tour. Captain CA Le Hardy led a team of twenty-one with a Chieftain tank, two Ferret scout cars, three Landrovers and a Bedford 4-tonner. They set up static sites in places like The Moor in Sheffield, in East Park and the Hull Show, in market places in Doncaster and Goole and outside pubs and leisure centres. Army Cadets

---

* This meant that the Regiment was sent recruits who had not specified a regiment in which they wished to serve.

Hohne 1974–77

and other youth organisations were visited and civic functions like the County Council Open Day in Barnsley (for the new County of South Yorkshire) were supported, while a flying team of a Ferret and a Landrover with a loudspeaker went to outlying villages. The Band appeared at all the KAPE sites and performed at a number of evening concerts: 'The concert for 3,500 children in Sheffield and the enormous crowd at the Arndale Centre in Doncaster proved their value and popularity.' Much of the groundwork for the tour and advice and help during it was provided by local ACIOs, manned by senior NCOs from the Regiment at Barnsley, Doncaster, Hull and Sheffield.

Also playing a significant role was 12 Army Youth Team based on Sheffield, which the Regiment took over from the King's Own Yorkshire Light Infantry in 1969. Lieutenant MJS Wilkins was the first team leader and until 1978 the Team, made up of a subaltern, a sergeant and three junior NCOs, went round those schools who would have them offering extra activities such as trampolining, fencing and rock-climbing. The aim, particularly in more 'anti' areas, was to show that the Army was public-spirited and friendly. As well as school visits they organised firing on ranges and attended cadet camps and Army Displays, including the Aldershot Tattoo. Direct recruiting was not allowed, but their work made a major contribution to the groundwork on which KAPE tours could build.

Despite an improvement in the recruiting figures, manning continued to be a major problem for Commanding Officers. This gave added force to the importance of even stronger links with South Yorkshire and the Chairman of the new County Council visited Hohne in October 1976. With him came the 'Top Two Teenagers', winners of an inter-school competition. Press links too were reinforced, by inviting reporters from the *Barnsley Chronicle* and *Doncaster Gazette* to accompany the Regiment throughout its training period at Suffield.

The following year visits to Hohne were made both the Mayor of Rotherham and the Mayor of Barnsley. In 1976 came news of the granting of the Freedom of Barnsley to the Regiment. The exercising of the Freedom was going to have to wait until after the tour in Omagh, but it was obviously a feather in the Regiment's cap to have established such good relations with municipal leaders – whose politics had not usually embraced much friendliness towards the Armed Forces.

Autumn Training 1976

In a year of 'depressing talk in the newspapers and on television' about Defence cuts and national indebtedness restricting training, the Regiment 'trained harder, travelled further and packed more into a year than anyone can remember'. After a 7 Armoured Brigade Exercise, the season finished with a German Corps exercise Grosse Baer and another British Spearpoint.

Grosse Baer, in which the whole of 7 Armoured Brigade took part, proved both enjoyable and interesting.

> Unlike British exercises in which there is always a detailed 'Pink',* which is strictly adhered to, the German exercise controllers worked only off a large map which contained thrust lines, objectives and timings. This meant that the divisional commanders genuinely had no idea how the battle was going to develop. The result at battle group level was extremely fast running and at times appeared to be chaotic with order, counter-order and disorder.

The Regiment's high state of training by this stage meant that they were able, just, to keep pace with the German units and their 'faster, more reliable equipment'. A Squadron led one wing of 7 Panzer Division for three days in a rapid advance across country and ended up near Walsrode bridging two small streams 'in very quick time'. They enjoyed it enormously.

> It enabled us to work our way as quickly as we could across a wide strip of Northern Germany. Only one tank faltered during the week – Corporal Robinson decided to inspect the underside of a bridge crossing a large stream, but he was quickly pulled out and hurried back to rejoin the Squadron's advance.

That was to be the last exercise in which the Regiment as a whole operated with tanks. For the three weeks of Spearpoint they were split up; A and B Squadrons were reinforced by tanks and crews from C Squadron and joined up with the battle groups of the Irish Guards and the Cheshires respectively, in order to test new establishments. Other tanks and crews 'found themselves becoming casualties and being re-organised in a

---

* Notes for directing staff at Staff College and other training establishments, and for control staff on exercises, are printed on pink paper.

Hohne 1974–77

very realistic if chaotic way', as part of the War Maintenance Reserve. The Regiment also found umpire teams for an exercise which 'seemed to grow and grow in size and demand'. Reconnaissance Troop went to 4th Royal Tank Regiment and Guided Weapons Troop to 1st Royal Tank Regiment. (Earlier in the year Reconnaissance Troop had been issued with Scimitars (CVRT 30) in place of their Ferret scout cars.)

The Rundown

The Regiment was due to start converting to armoured reconnaissance on 1 June 1977, but the Brigade Commander insisted that troop training, annual firing and a brigade test exercise as an armoured regiment were carried out in the spring. A somewhat disgruntled Lieutenant Colonel Loftus:

> We took troop training in our stride, but annual firing was a disappointment. We were one of the three armoured regiments ordered to train for the Canadian Army Trophy. This meant that six weeks in advance of our annual firing a composite squadron had to be formed to train for this competition. The squadron was based on C Squadron, but reinforced with the best crews and commanders from A and B Squadrons. The draw for which regiment was to represent the British Army in the competition took place only one week before the start of our annual firing. We were not selected and this meant that the Regiment had to re-form into its normal organisation and train as squadrons in an unrealistically short space of time. It proved impossible to raise the Regiment to the standard of the previous year and as a result we received a disappointing C grading.

The brigade test exercise in May, Black Jake, was in company with 1 King's Own Royal Border Regiment, It was held south of Hildesheim in an area newly sown with corn and roots.

> In prospect the exercise was a damage controller's nightmare, but the regulations were well obeyed to the extent that some thought we were wasting our time being out at all. The exercise was valuable in some respects, but it did give us a lot of maintenance on our return which we could well have done without.

Thus Regimental Notes; B Squadron remembered it more happily as a time when: 'The weather was wonderful, the villagers very friendly and the exercise really quite enjoyable'. Nevertheless, after reaching a peak in the previous November, the Regiment came to a rather lame halt in its armoured role.

Chapter Thirteen

Two Spells in Northern Ireland

Operation 'Banner' 1972 & 1975

And if their prowess as men of armour often was impaired, their quality as soldiers was enhanced by coming face-to-face with a danger which taxed their discipline to the limit.
History of the Royal Armoured Corps, Kenneth Macksey

Long Kesh 1972
In 1971 the shortage of infantry led to other arms from BAOR being employed in Northern Ireland on Operation Banner – unaccompanied tours of four months. The requirement was for units some 700 strong, which meant that an armoured regiment of about 500 men had to be augmented. When the Regiment's turn came they were reinforced by a detachment from 1st Royal Tank Regiment. (That effectively reduced the Rhine Army order of battle by two armoured regiments bar one squadron, all that was left to 1 RTR at Osnabrück.) The 'Armoured Regimental Group', commanded by Lieutenant Colonel JCM Ansell, left for County Antrim on 10 January 1972, but the unlovely title was soon unofficially changed to 'The LilyWillies', derived from Lilywhites and 'My Boy Willie'.*

Their task was to defend the Internment Centre at Long Kesh, County Antrim, and to help maintain law and order in County Down and parts of County Armagh. Regimental Headquarters was formed from both regiments (including the Adjutant 1 RTR as Operations Officer) and an Administrative Squadron was found largely by the 13th/18th. Reconnaissance and Intelligence Troops came from both regiments and there were four large 'infantry' squadrons. A and B Squadrons, led by Majors JAC Blakiston and RCR Cotterell were 13th/18th, and C and D Squadrons were from 1 RTR. (Amongst others under command of the Guard Squadron at Long Kesh was a 'troop' of some thirty guard dogs.)

---
* Quick March of the Royal Tank Regiment.

Northern Ireland 1972 & 1975

At this stage of the Northern Ireland campaign, for such it had become, it was only the second armoured regimental group to be involved. (The 15th/19th Hussars and 4th Royal Tank Regiment had been the pathfinders.) Pre-tour training was not the well-organised affair that it was later to become and Colonel Ansell was anxious to get the hybrid unit together, away from peacetime barracks, for shaking down and working out 'standard operating procedures'. In November 1971, after a short spell of weapon training in their own barracks, the 'LilyWillies' assembled at the Infantry Training Centre at Sennelager for four weeks' intensive practice in anti-riot drills, fieldcraft, cordon and search.

> It is not easy for a cavalryman to turn himself into an infantryman. So to help us we borrowed a team of really aggressive Brigade of Guards NCOs. The training programme filled almost every minute of our days and nights with hard physical effort. Our instructors induced an air of belligerency over the camp so it was not long before Hussar and Tankie had reached a position of such mutual adversity that the 'giddy harumfrodite'* was perforce welded into a very tight-knit group.

Ulster, and Long Kesh in particular, 'seemed something of an anti-climax after the ferocious and realistic petrol bombing, rock throwing and aggro' that was undergone at Sennelager, wrote Colonel Ansell. Nevertheless, extracts from the operations diary show that it was no picnic and three weeks after their arrival came 'Bloody Sunday' in Londonderry.

A, B and D squadrons rotated amongst the various – and varied – tasks. A Squadron started off with seven weeks of duty at 'The Maze' at Long Kesh, followed by being given 'a very pleasant but very quiet area of East Down to look after. Troops were detached on a weekly basis to camps at Ballykinler and Killyleagh and 'many friendly liaisons were struck with the locals'. They then had a week in the headquarters of the North Irish Militia at Portadown, where they had been sent to restore a degree of harmony after barricades had been erected and the local inhabitants were throwing stones at one another.

---

* ' 'E's a kind of giddy harumfrodite – soldier an' sailor too'. Rudyard Kipling, on The Royal Marines.

History of The 13th/18th Royal Hussars (Q.M.O.)

The situation looked ugly at first, but with the help of a company of the King's Own Scottish Borderers and half a company of Devon and Dorsets we were able to return the situation to near normality in a few days.

3rd Troop A Squadron finished off with an all-night action:

... where the Catholics had taken a dislike to the recently arrived Gordons. The troop, energetically led by Mr Colacicchi with Sergeant Simpson doing the arresting, was lucky to escape with only cuts and bruises.

On their arrival B Squadron (Major Cotterell) was sent for a week to three villages near the border in County Armagh.

'Lily Willy'

Three issues of a newsletter for the Regimental Group were produced during the 1972 tour. The first, dated February, had on its front page:

A MESSAGE FROM THE COLONEL*

The Lilywilly is really a magazine for you our families and friends in Germany. It has been written, somewhat hurriedly and in difficult conditions during the interval between Magic Roundabout and opening time at the Discotheque and we hope it brings with it something of the purpose and steely determination with which we are setting about our task in Ulster. If you find it difficult to understand the rather eccentric jottings that follow, don't be surprised for much of the material for this edition is taken from the Duty Watchkeeper's Official Log, this is written in the early evening during the stress of the fourth instalment of 'Tarzan and the Leopard Woman' on ATV, followed by 'Z Cars' on BBC 1 and the 'News and Fatstock Prices' on the radio. It is therefore only to be expected that the Watchkeeper's imagination spills over onto the log and that gunfighters, stolen cars and mechanical sniffers chase each other across the pages in some lunatic Irish Jig.

Our language too you will find strange and unworldly; is VCP a kind of disinfectant? and what is all this about Rucksack and Kestrel? who told the Signals Sergeant to put the Pye in the Pig and what the hell is a mobile when it isn't? I think I am beginning to discover the answers but if you cannot understand the words I hope that like me you will enjoy the pictures.

* Lieutenant Colonel JCM Ansell

Northern Ireland 1972 & 1975

Two of these were most unfriendly. On the second day Corporal Turton's APC had a Claymore mine explode beneath it. Fortunately the only casualty was the engine.

Sergeant G Nixon and some of 2nd Troop lay in a wet field in ambush for the IRA:

> ... who have a habit of removing HM Customs' caravans. ... As soon as they left the IRA turned up with a car, hitched up the caravan and drove off with it.

The Squadron then had a five-week stint spent primarily on patrolling a large country area on the east coast, just south of Belfast. 'This area was very quiet and the people very friendly.' But the Squadron also helped with searches of Long Kesh, attended Civil Rights marches at Dungannon and Enniskillen, and 'took great interest in digging up graveyards in search of arms and ammunition'. Their spell of guarding the Internment Centre produced no memorable incidents but probably:

> ... proved a profitable time for the two Squadron bookmakers, Corporal Wragg and Lance Corporal Marr, as many had time to spare to take an interest in the racing on the television.

They finished with another quiet country area to patrol, this time to the south-west of Belfast, where they did find however:

> ... some home-made explosive and the Squadron Leader found some rather old weapons which would have been of greater significance to the IRA campaign of the 1920s.

C Squadron spent the whole tour looking after Lurgan, where they shared the dubious comfort of an old factory with Headquarters 3 Infantry Brigade. The need for continuity in Lurgan, particularly for intelligence gathering, meant that it was not possible for the Squadron to have a change of role.

The nature of the job usually required squadrons to operate independently and only rarely were two or three brought together. After one such major search operation, for which Colonel Ansell also had under command 1st Regiment Royal Military Police, he heard from their commanding officer:

> I was particularly impressed with the discipline, sense of purpose and bearing of your men. One seldom sees a cavalry regiment deployed in close formation on foot, particularly in the strength I saw yesterday; it was all most heartening.

History of The 13th/18th Royal Hussars (Q.M.O.)

FOUR MONTHS IN NORTHERN IRELAND Jan–May 1972
Extracts from War Diary

16 Jan	Tp C Sqn attacked with petrol bombs. No casualties.
17 Jan	Lurgan. 4 bomb hoaxes, 8 petrol bombs thrown. Tp C Sqn fired 1 baton round, knocked down youth.
20 Jan	Search Long Kesh compounds. Among finds: 2 poteen stills; model Thompson MG; instructional drawings of weapons; chisels; instrs for making bombs. The start of 2 tunnels also found in huts.
23 Jan	Unrest in Long Kesh, black flags erected in sympathy with 13 civilians killed during rioting in Londonderry. Anti-internment rally Lurgan involving C & D Sqns, Recce Tp. No significant incidents.
31 Jan	Tense day Lurgan - Catholics attempting build barricades.
1 Feb	2 internees found snipping wire fence. Continued tension Lurgan.
2 Feb	Search Long Kesh Compounds 2 & 6. found: 1 pr wire cutters; two plans SMG; IRA Battalion list; £47 in wooden right leg ('I didn't know it was there, honest'); 1 Sam Browne.
6 Feb	Internee McGuigan escaped Long Kesh disguised as priest. Gave press conference in Dublin three days later.
8 Feb	Attempted escape Long Kesh. Internee tried hide laundry basket.
17 Feb	Tarring and feathering Lurgan. Search Long Kesh, after escape bid, found: 1pr wire cutters, 1 bedstead adapted for use as ladder.
21 Feb	Hearse stopped by D Sqn, with tricolour-draped coffin for Dublin, D McCauley 14 yrs shot 20 Feb in exchange with Security Forces.
11 Mar	3 men seen inside Long Kesh. . . Chase with dogs but men escaped. 2 suspicious men later arrested by RUC but escaped. Our ptls searched, apart from shoes, found nothing. Men believed from Eire. Vanguard rally Portadown, 2,500-3,000 people.
22 Mar	Group 50-70 youths attacked veh check point Lurgan with stones. youth reprimanded with baton, no arrests or casualties, crowd dispersed. (Later youth's father complained to RUC.)
25 Mar	Visitors to Long Kesh, woman: 'Please don't let him out, he'll only spend all my money on drink and horses and go back on the dole.'
30 Mar	Situation v. tense Lurgan. RC and Protestant vigilantes out in force.
7 Apr	B Sqn search Grid 291462 revealed: 0.303 Martini Henry rifle; 0.32 revolver; muzzle loading hammer 12 bore shot gun; antique powder horn. (Weapons all dated from turn of century; very rusty)
18 Apr	Minor disturbance Long Kesh. Windows broken and furniture damaged. 6 guard dogs outside compound restored order. Crowd approx 80 attacked tps by Glendennings Factory, Lurgan. 2 baton rounds fired. 5 people knocked out in close quarter fighting . . .
23 Apr	7 shots fired Kitchen Hill factory Lurgan (C Sqn) No casualties.
24 Apr	Search Long Kesh compounds, among finds: 25 poteen stills; 5 typewriters; subversive literature; 2 tricolours; printed hand kerchiefs; model pistols; 4 sewing machines; 2 wire cutters; rope made from mattress cover; homing pigeon. (Next day's request: 'Please sur are youse a giving back urr pigeon?')
1 May	Lift of 79 internees from MacGilligan to Long Kesh. An internee climbed over fence of Compound 9 to collect his football - and climbed back again. (Extra wiring was erected.)

Northern Ireland 1972 & 1975

Sport inevitably took a back seat and even when some was played it was strongly affected by local conditions, as a *Gazette* report noted. Five-a-side games of hockey were played in the old aircraft hangar at Long Kesh and a Regimental Group team was raised to play a Portadown side on two occasions.

> It was expedient that we contrived to win one game and lose the other, since the second fixture took place on the day Direct Rule was announced, which created none too healthy a political climate. This may explain why we were abandoned after the match to entertain ourselves in the clubhouse.

The 'Admin' Squadron under Captain F Harrison had a formidable task during the four months, for which they had:

> ... thirteen Departments, all desperately trying to be independent, drawn from ten different Corps or Regiments.

Amongst them Defence Troop ran the Main Gate and showed great patience in dealing with 'the endless stream of prison warders, contractors, visitors and military who passed through their domain'. Of Recce Troop, 'who nobody really knew anything about' except that they had three officers and two sergeants and the 'quietest of all the Regiment's areas', it was decided that the number of girls they produced for a Squadron dance made them the experts in Community Relations. The combined QM and Tech departments, under Captain PJ Stratton and RQMS(T) K O'Sullivan 'were normally able to get anything for anyone at most hours of the day and night'.

On 2 May C Squadron handed over the operational role in Lurgan to 1st Gordons and on the 7th the remainder of the Regimental Group handed over to 4th Field Regiment RA. At the end of the four-month tour Colonel Ansell wrote:

> Ireland for most of us was dull and frustrating. We came away unscathed, but appalled by the callous brutality of the IRA gangsters and horrified by the bigotry and childlike bloody-mindedness of many of the members of both Protestant and Catholic communities.

As in so many of the 'peacetime' tasks of the British Army the battle in Ireland was fought largely by the junior NCOs and soldiers; the many complimentary messages that were received at the end of the Regiment's short tour signalled their successful adaptation both to the novel role and the demanding environment. Colonel Ansell also paid tribute to the highly

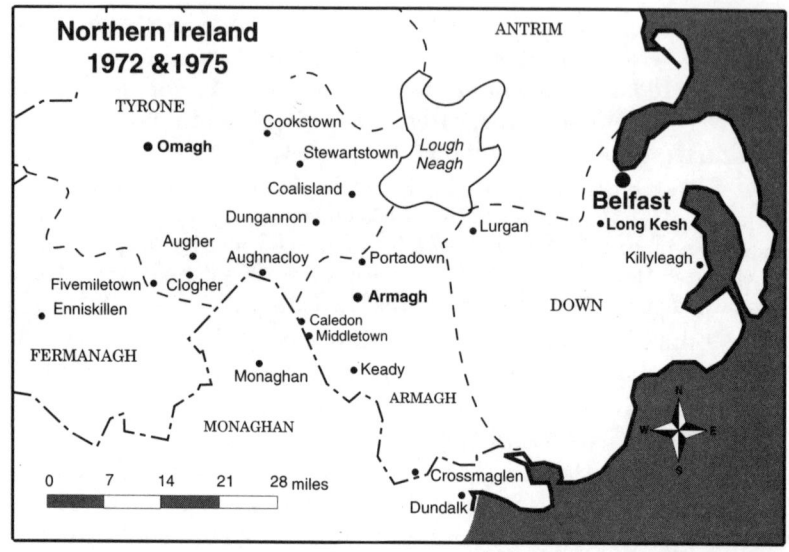

successful temporary amalgamation with '270 LilyWillies from 1st Royal Tank Regiment; we admired their very high professional standards and we enjoyed their company'. At the end of the tour the officers of both Regiments dined together at Osnabrück and the Royal Tank Regiment officers presented the Regiment with two handsome decanters. Each had a silver band round its neck and on one was engraved 'Lily' and on the other 'Willy'. Put to immediate use they form a permanent and fitting reminder to the association.

While in Ireland the Regiment was still responsible for the vehicles, equipment and barracks at Münster - and the families. There were now 225 wives on the station, with a number of children. A substantial Rear Party, under Major DJ Delius, had therefore to be left behind and, in the hangars:

> ... a valiant team is slowly but surely renovating the vehicles. Morale on the vehicle park has been surprisingly high and recently reached its peak when the EME enlisted the support of the Band, who appeared for several days in denims and very successfully carried out a thorough early spring cleaning exercise.

Meetings of a new Families Club were held in what used to be the WRVS quiet room now renamed:

Northern Ireland 1972 & 1975

... the 'Pop Inn' and no longer quiet. Those who believe the streets of Belfast are dangerous should try to establish peace in the children's room when the two- and three-year olds are in full swing with building bricks. In the main room, other weapons are darts, flung with slit-eyed concentration in the general direction of the dart board, and table tennis bats swung with evil intent at a little, inoffensive white ball. Whoever claimed that snooker is a quiet indoor pastime had never seen our wives play.

Perhaps in order to escape the rigours of the vehicle park, the Band visited Northern Ireland and played 'for the more dangerous members of the community (old people's homes and hospitals) and numerous regimental functions.'

Armagh 1975

Warning for the next tour came in 1974, when the Regiment was still in England. After converting back to Chieftains in Germany, in 1975 they were to go to County Armagh in the armoured reconnaissance role, but they would also be expected to act as infantry. A visit in May 1975, to see what the 9th/12th Lancers were doing, made it clear that the task had nothing to do with armoured reconnaissance. However it was to be an 'offensive role' compared with the primary task of the previous tour, and on 1 June the Regiment again set about infantry training in order to transform themselves into a 'General Purpose All Weather, Northern Ireland Unit'.

> The enthusiasm was unbounded and through the extraordinarily hot summer months, until the end of August, we worked long hours, often during weekends, to bring our shooting, patrolling and many other skills peculiar to operations in Northern Ireland up to scratch.

They were helped in training by a small team of senior and junior NCOs from King's Own Royal Border Regiment led by Captain AL Mallinson. (The Regiment was to see him again.)

The Regimental Group this time had an establishment of 350, with Regimental Headquarters, A and B Squadrons (enlarged at the expense of a disbanded C Squadron) and Headquarters Squadron (made up of large parts of Administrative and Command & Support Squadrons). By now training at Sennelager was very realistic. 'Tin City' had been created to simulate a typical Belfast area and was 'inhabited', so far as the

History of The 13th/18th Royal Hussars (Q.M.O.)

Regiment was concerned, by members of the Rear Party before they got down to vehicle maintenance and other Hohne chores. They provided the 'stone and beer can throwing mob' which faced the squadrons for riot drill training. The squadrons found the experience 'almost traumatic. Tin City was a rare experience and everybody said the real thing could never be so hectic'.

A 'cease-fire' in Northern Ireland was forecast to break in early September 1975. After a quiet summer in Armagh, the Regiment's predecessors, 2nd Royal Tank Regiment, were preparing to move when they were suddenly faced with more major incidents than they had seen in the rest of their tour.

> They and our Advance Party rather wondered what had hit them. Although the intensity of that week at the end of August was never quite equalled, it was the foretaste of a tour which has kept every member of the 13th/18th Royal Hussars Regimental Group at full stretch.

During the first week the Group expanded to include most of 1st Light Infantry, which was the Spearhead Battalion (immediate reserve from the United Kingdom), as well as a company of 1st Queen's Lancashire (who remained), and 3rd Royal Fusiliers. Others supporting the Regiment at different times were elements of 2nd Ulster Defence Regiment, 42nd Commando Royal Marines, 39th Medium Regiment RA, 662 Squadron Army Air Corps and 321 EOD Unit.*

Regimental Headquarters and Headquarters Squadron were in Gough Barracks, Armagh with the sabre squadrons deployed to the border with the Irish Republic. A Squadron went to Middletown and B Squadron to Aughnacloy. A specially formed Reserve Troop moved to Cookstown in Police Division M East. The Regimental area extended over forty miles by twenty-two miles and included thirty-five miles of border.

A Squadron
The border was to be a major preoccupation for A Squadron, under Major DJ Delius. They found that they had inherited from Cyclops [C Squadron] 2nd Royal Tank Regiment:

> ... an interesting patch consisting of thirty miles of the border with County Monaghan and some potentially active Republican

---

* EOD = explosive ordnance device.

Northern Ireland 1972 & 1975

areas inland. The day we arrived, the Secretary of State promised the population of Ulster an escalation of military activity; this might have been pure coincidence, but nevertheless we started off at a cracking pace.

Strenuous efforts were made in September to seal all the unapproved crossing points and to funnel traffic along three roads. This met with little resistance, but the Regiment was fired on for the first time west of Keady as it was being closed. In late October concerted attempts were made by local farmers' action groups to remove the 'Braithwaite tanks' and fill in the cratered tracks with hard core and old cars.* Confrontation was forbidden – and avoided – until a re-closure operation in November forced that day's plans to be abandoned. However, the border remained 'relatively watertight' and many hundreds of cars a day went through two permanent Vehicle Check Points (VCPs). 'Early morning arrests, searches and blocking the border, as well as a rather more positive approach to investigating civilian identity and movement, all became second nature to us.' During one scene at the Middletown VCP a farmer pulled up his car, got out and came over to be checked:

> 'Good morning, Mr Murphy' comes the amiable Yorkshire greeting, 'and could we please look in your boot'. 'Oh to be sure' he says as he bends down to pull one off ...

On another occasion a patrol met an old farmer during a border-blocking operation and, after commenting on the standard Irish weather, he said, 'Where do youse boys come from then?' One replied that they had just come from Germany.

> A look of astonishment came over the old man's face, 'Sure but youse all speak pretty fair English then'. A long drawn out conversation then followed until the patrol convinced the old man that we were all citizens of the United Kingdom.

1st Troop. led initially by Lieutenant NR Peyton and then by Sergeant SP Davies, was installed some seven miles away from Middletown at Keady Police Station. The latter boasted a disturbed history; it was now 21 months since it had last been

---

* Braithwaite tanks were metal tanks some 6 ft long, 4ft deep and 3 ft wide, delivered by helicopter to illegal border crossings where they were filled with concrete (also delivered by air) by Royal Engineers and positioned to prevent vehicular access. They had to be guarded by troops on the ground for twenty-four hours after installation, to allow the concrete to set.

'Town and Country'

For the second Operation Banner tour this was the title of the Newsletter. The first of the two issues had a contribution from Sergeant JM Wragg:

Top Sangar or Shooting Incident at Middletown Corral
by HARRY WRAGG

It was about 0035 hrs and I was roused from my nice warm bed (which I hadn't been to in a coon's age) by the sound of a rat-a-tat-tat; yes, the familiar sound of a GPMG. The noise was very loud as the Top Sangar is situated above my bedroom. The next thing I heard was 'Put those . . . lights out!', as the IO (Capt Webster) leapt from the Int Room to the Ops Room to the Top Sangar and back to the Int Room.

While all this was going on I was trying to get dressed in the dark and was having tremendous difficulty in getting my vest over my flak jacket while also trying to wake my room mate. 'Dick', (Sgt Shaw) I shouted, 'Dick, wake up.' No answer. Giving him a dig with my rifle and calling him again. He turned over said, 'What the . . . hell's wrong?' 'They're shooting at us,' I said. A few seconds passed and Dick was asleep again. So I tried once more. 'What's up wi thee', he said. Then he heard the GPMG, ' . . . hell, why dint tha tell me.'

A few seconds later I was clambering up the stairs to the sangar where I saw Mr Colacicchi having the time of his life behind the 'Gimpy'. 'Where are they, sir?' I said. ' . . . knows, I'm only keeping their heads down, I can't see a bloody thing.' 'Where's the IWS.' I said. 'Haven't seen it' came the reply. So I got down on all fours feeling round the sangar for the IWS. Eventually I found it and then exchanged places with Mr C. While all this was going on Mr Brook was popping one or two shots off with his rifle at what he thought was movement. Mr Colacicchi and I thought it was a cow having a human nature phase.

By this time, after repeated calls of 'Are you alright in there,' from the Watchkeeper Mr Nall, RHQ had sparked and Nitesun arrived very quickly. The shooting had stopped by then and Mr Brook had the job of guiding Nitesun over the enemy fire positions; left a bit, right a bit – stop. After about ten minutes Nitesun returned to Armagh and the OC amassed 7 brave men and true in the Ops Room to go out on a foot patrol to see if we could find anything. In the local jargon, FU Neg which, in case you are wondering, means Follow Up Negative.

At 0800 hrs I took out a search team and combed the entire area but again we didn't find anything, which only strengthened our belief that they were firing at us from south of the border. . . .

severely damaged by a bomb, but it still bore the scars and:

> ... the accommodation was somewhat restricted ... The atmosphere in Keady is illustrated by the fact that local shopkeepers curtly declined to serve soldiers, in spite of money being readily proffered and the goods being openly displayed on the shelves. Fortunately by the time we left, this unhappy situation had improved considerably and soldiers now found that they were able to pass the time of day with most of the local population.

The area was mostly rough farming land with barren mountainous ground near the border to the south, rising to 900 feet, with isolated homesteads typical of South Armagh. It is a country where communications are bad and speed of movement limited. Monitoring of activity is therefore difficult, but the troop soon 'got the lie of the land and, aided by a section rotating from the VCP Troop, quickly made their presence felt'.

VCP Troop was one of the multifarious divisions of a squadron; others were small sections responsible for Operations, Intelligence, Vehicle Check Point Intelligence and a Search Team.

3rd Troop (Lieutenant RG Bell, son of Lieutenant Colonel JW Bell) were at Caledon Police Station a few miles north of Middletown. Despite being nearer the border than Keady, 'the immediate surroundings and atmosphere were much more amenable'; they even had space for a ping-pong table. Their area covered rich, rolling farmland and two well-kept country estates, on the one hand, traditionally Nationalist and Republican strongholds on the other.

> Constantly probing for a reaction from the opposition, the troop were called more and more to help patrol in the areas nearer Keady and Middletown. Quietly they maintained their links with local tea shops nearer home which helped balance their views on civilian attitudes.

In Middletown itself the rest of A Squadron took over the abandoned police station, with a permanent VCP on its doorstep for controlling all road movement into County Monaghan between Armagh and Monaghan. The population, halved from ten years before, was only some 250 and a large number of the buildings were derelict having been bombed 'or vandalised by the violent and anti-social element of the local population'. Two shops and a bar remained open, the latter almost twenty-four hours a day catering for 'frustrated through travellers as well as depressed locals. However the bar offers no welcome whatever for British soldiers ...'.

> The ubiquitous Rover Group looked for trouble far and wide. Very early in the tour while they were guarding a fresh border block, some wretched terrorist loosed off twenty-two rounds at them from a safe position in Southern Ireland. The Squadron Leader had to exert considerable pressure to restrain eager men from taking the fight all the way to Dublin. However the Garda and the Irish Army were quickly on the scene and a Scout helicopter droned overhead stabbing the darkness with its powerful light.

The Search Team had one notable success:

> ... the finding of a large culvert bomb near the border – which in part made up for their patient hours of sifting through the countryside and exposing themselves to frightful disease by digging out many disgustingly dirty houses where mother's pride was conspicuously lacking. One discovery was twelve children packed into two beds without either clothes or bedclothes.

And, 'all those apparently fruitless car searches suddenly came worthwhile', when a man was stopped who had narrowly evaded arrest by the RUC (Royal Ulster Constabulary) for causing explosions in Armagh, 'just as he was about to bolt for cover in the South'.

B Squadron

At the end of B Squadron's first five weeks at Aughnacloy:

> ... we might have been forgiven for wondering what the fuss was about. With only two bombs, several arrests and one border closure we were becoming rather bored. However, the politicians came to the rescue and within forty eight hours B Squadron had moved to Dungannon in East Tyrone.

During the five weeks, however, the Squadron, (Major CAGB Robinson) discovered how good their map reading had to be, if they were not to end up in Monaghan while on border patrol. Their camp was on the outskirts of the small, 'rather faded' market town of Aughnacloy about half a mile from the border. Much of the troops' time was on the VCP at the one legal crossing in their area. Market days, the first and third Wednesdays of the month, were the busiest; people 'streamed across from the Free State in cars and on tractors and bicycles – a tide only equalled in the other direction on Sundays, when the pubs

Northern Ireland 1972 & 1975

close over here but stay open down south'. When not on the VCP the Squadron worked in the shallow Clogher valley, about fifteen miles long and seven miles wide. 'On the uplands there are many small sheep farms but in the vale one finds larger and more prosperous holdings.' Augher, Clogher and Fivemiletown lie along the central highway, each with about a thousand inhabitants, divided into equal proportions of Protestant and Catholic.

1st Troop, with Lieutenant ADL Norton and Sergeant AJ Davis, spent the first ten days of the tour:

> ... getting to know the ground. It was easy enough as us Yorkshire experts immediately felt at home on the high ground to the north and south of the valley. Needless to say we have found our fair share of bog ... Getting to know the people can be a problem as it is difficult to decipher a conversation between two people in a mixture of broad Yorkshire and bog Irish. The other difficulty is the size of the families, who are more like clans and our greatest challenge is the McKenna family, which has a current Orbat of about 250 members.*

Staff Sergeant M Baxendale led 3rd Troop, who 'made many friends, including one kind lady giving us tea and buns at half past midnight', but Sergeant D Davies, the Troop sergeant, 'nearly had a heart attack' when he arrived at the scene of an explosion to find a police car had been blown up by a culvert bomb 'where he had been sitting two days before'. Fortunately the two policemen had only minor injuries.

In Dungannon the Squadron took over from the Royal Regiment of Fusiliers and had a spate of culvert bombs in their area during November. Several went off very close to Ulster Defence Regiment patrols and two more exploded under civilian cars. One was thwarted by the RUC who arrested five men near Coalisland, found with 40 lbs of Co-op in an oil can on the back seat of their car.† A suspect was heard to remark of the bomb: 'I don't know anything about that - I was sat in the front.'

---

* Orbat = Order of battle.

† Co-op. Homemade explosive based on agricultural fertiliser, bought from the Co-op in their named bags. Very large amounts were needed for significant explosions – normally 500-1,000 lbs but very occasionally 2,000 lbs. Some mixes failed to detonate. 'All one heard was the click of the detonator and a search would reveal a large device under the bridge or culvert which was the target – to one's enormous relief! Sadly others worked only too well.' Major DJ Delius.

History of The 13th/18th Royal Hussars (Q.M.O.)

Sergeant Davies:
> ... did a three day OP* in the country and having settled his men into a bush, had to wait in terror as the cows ate the succulent leaves which provided his hiding place – we told him not to wear aftershave. ...

And Mr Norton and Lance Corporal Quirke:
> ... were in their OP for the second night when footsteps were heard coming closer and closer. Suddenly they were ambushed by a powerful torch, a stick and two small boys – sons of the local baddy. Each group bolted in opposite directions.

Headquarters Squadron
'The operational re-deployments that have occurred over our time here have been rapid and complex', said HQ Squadron Notes in *Town & Country*, October 1975. This placed considerable demands both on the 'very old and run down' transport and on the cooks in the various locations. The Master Chef, WO2 Dick, reported that at one time over 1,150 were being rationed in the Regimental Group. The vehicles in Transport Troop ranged from Landrovers and 4-tonners to:
> ... a vast water cannon which does its best to imitate something once seen in the Elephant House at London Zoo; in between we have a variety of 'Q' vans which some people believe are covert. Trooper 'Basher' Barton who drives the ration truck, tells us he gets disturbing numbers of cheery waves from the locals as he goes on his rounds.

The Troop had a ratio of about one and half vehicles per driver and, in order to keep up with their various and varied details, all had to become quick change artists – 'one minute in combat kit and the next in scruffy civvies'.

Reserve Troop
Formed with the intention that it should be what its name implies, Reserve Troop's mission changed twice before the tour started. Some thirty strong, including three officers and fourteen NCOs, its eventual task was to co-operate 'in the closest possible manner' with the RUC of Cookstown, in whose station they lived. Their area ranged 'demographically and

---

* Observation Post.

Northern Ireland 1972 & 1975

topographically' from the highly Republican Ard Boe in the east, on the edge of Lough Neagh, through the fertile central Loyalist plain to the Republican uplands of the west. Cookstown itself is in the central plain, but it had an active Republican element 'only too keen to upset this peaceful market town'. The Troop, led by Captain RCB Nutting, had four sections working a fixed four-day rota of Patrol, Patrol, Stand-By, and Guard, but were reinforced from time to time by detachments from the Queen's Lancashire Regiment and the Royal Marines. On those occasions the Troop's normally 'adequate' accommodation became distinctly uncomfortable.

The Troop had a larger area than either of A or B Squadrons, with fewer soldiers, and:

> ... domination of the ground was nigh on impossible, but we like to think that although we may not have neutralised every terrorist in our four months, we gave them something to think about.

Behind Captain Nutting's brief description was 'work of such high order that the Troop Leader was mentioned in despatches.' (*Light Dragoons,* Colonel Mallinson)

ATO's Escort

An ATO (Ammunition Technical Officer) was an officer or NCO of the Royal Army Ordnance Corps who had the task of defusing explosive devices. The Regiment provided 'their' ATO with an escort consisting of Corporal IRE Sheldon and three troopers. They protected the four-man bomb disposal team which was on call twenty-four hours a day and had:

> ... the unenviable task of dealing with suspicious objects ranging from milk churns to civilian cars all round the Armagh area ... Not only were we responsible for protection but also crowd control – a possible explosion appears to have a morbid attraction to an Irishman and he has an unstoppable desire to get as near to the object as possible.

They went to over a hundred tasks during the tour, some were hoaxes but many were genuine. Eleven bombs were defused, including a pressure plate device in Stewartstown, a 200 lb car bomb in Dungannon, three large culvert mines and several duffle bag bombs.

History of The 13th/18th Royal Hussars (Q.M.O.)

The Culdee Search

On one October day the Regiment undertook a 'cordon and search' operation of the Culdee Estate in Armagh. Captain JAMA Selfe, commanding Headquarters Squadron, described the day's events:

> Against a background of ruthless bombing and shooting, our orders were to search selected houses in this pleasant, well laid out, but staunchly Republican estate. After nine months of cease-fire – suggested by the IRA but largely observed by the Army – we ran the risk of triggering off a violent response and thereby furnishing the excuse for a breakdown in the uneasy truce. It was doubly important that nothing went wrong and that above all we found enough to forestall charges of harassment.
>
> The cordon provided by 42nd Commando Royal Marines went in at 0615, well before first light, and the Ulster Defence Regiment regular search teams, mobile screening centres and B Squadron Reserve Force followed in silence, but inevitably engines raced, gears were crashed and oaths were uttered. . . .
>
> Someone down by Navan Terrace heard the sound of a rifle being cocked; 250 troops had surrounded a small, hostile estate, in dense fog, at the crack of dawn without so much as a dustbin lid being rattled in muted resentment; the eerie silence lent credibility to thoughts of an ambush; no lights, no talking, keep under cover. But grudgingly dawn broke and the gunman – if gunman he was – merged into his background. . . . Progressively we relaxed as the sun broke through and our search teams and local people went about their business. The cordon paced watchfully and the reserve sat smoking and joking about how they would tackle the half-hoped for riot which never came. Schoolchildren passed through the checkpoint, the paper van braved the caltrops* and two burst tyres spectacularly halted it outside the cordon – no papers today.
>
> The day dragged on slowly until the radio crackled . . . A hide had been located in the garden of No. 123 – a seedy bungalow with an unrestricted view of the sunlit spires of the Catholic Cathedral. A detonator and length of fuse were unearthed near a forsythia bush. This highly hostile bush was executed by machete. Attention was now turned on the house. Several sapper knocks went unanswered and the ATO prepared to open a booby-

---

* Caltrops: originally spiked balls used to impede cavalry, now a device to puncture car tyres.

Northern Ireland 1972 & 1975

trapped door. Moments before the rubber bullets were released a confused and presumably innocent old man stumbled to the door in his pyjamas. But, we reasoned, where there was one there should be others . . .

A helicopter, grounded by the morning fog, now droned overhead. The Colonel spotted movement in a nearby wood and closer inspection revealed a radio controlled detonator flushed out of its usual hide by the search. Back on the ground the cordon was besieged by children returning from school. . . . we mounted our trucks to leave. As the sun set on a chilly Armagh estate we summed up – a long day, a few useful points and a low profile maintained.

Review

A report in December 1975 summed up the tour and concluded:

From this catalogue of events, which by no means includes all, this is obviously an extremely active area. We have had a number of useful finds of weapons, radio arming devices and explosives, but these have been in little country hides and the result of much hard work. Twenty terrorists have been arrested and charged by the RUC, and the changing attitude of the local people promises an end to the acute shortage of intelligence which we inherited from a summer of cease-fire.

Living in small, widely separated patrol bases, we have found little time for sport and recreation; however, B Squadron have fielded a rugger team, a sponsored run for a local children's hospital has raised £270 and Balaklava did not pass unnoticed. As we came to the end of an interesting tour we can be sure that we are well known in our area. Three small children were seen last week scratching graffiti on the newly varnished door of the Keady cinema. A patrol discovered '13th/18th Rule OK?' – we hope so.

Certainly their work was well thought of; the Regiment was 'regarded as the equal of most infantry battalions which had run that "patch"'. (*Light Dragoons,* Colonel Mallinson)

Rear Party

The main part of the Regiment returned to Hohne on 4 January 1976. As before, those who stayed behind in Germany did not find that they had time on their hands:

History of The 13th/18th Royal Hussars (Q.M.O.)

There are many difficulties in taking a backstage seat to the main production, but curiously those of us who did not go to Northern Ireland found that we had so much to achieve that we wondered sometimes who had the more important job. The capital equipment of the Regiment is worth something over £12 million and the Rear Party either serviced it, counted it, replaced it or threw it away.

A maintenance team of a sergeant and seldom more than eight men a day worked with the LAD from October to December through:

> ... basic maintenance, crew jobs, REME jobs, re-spraying and the 857 REME inspection before the annual PRE* on all vehicles. The Band did sterling work on the turrets. Even some wives discovered how to clean a sprocket and that the tyres on a Chieftain cannot be pumped up. The result in December was perhaps the most outstanding PRE report the Regiment has ever had.

---

* Periodic REME Inspection.

Part 3

ARMOURED RECONNAISSANCE

1977 to 1992

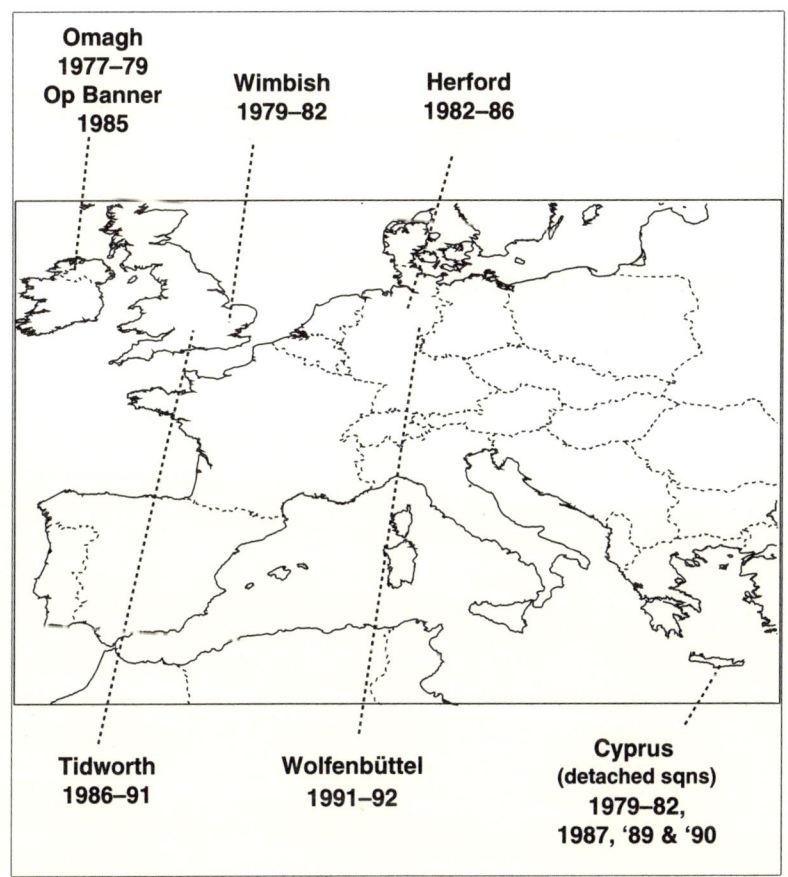

Introduction to Part 3

Light Cavalry Role

The World Community needs, more than it has ever done, skilful and disciplined warriors who are ready to put themselves at the service of its authority. Such warriors must properly be seen as the protectors of civilisation, not its enemies. The style in which they fight for civilisation – against ethnic bigots, regional warlords, ideological intransigents, common pillagers and organised international criminals – cannot derive from the Western model of warmaking alone. Future peacekeepers and peacemakers have much to learn from alternative military cultures, not only that of the Orient but of the primitive world also. There is a wisdom in the denial that politics and war belong within the same continuum. Unless we insist on denying it, our future, like that of the last Easter Islanders, may belong to the men with bloodied hands.
A History of Warfare by John Keegan

An International Change of Scene
When the 13th/18th Hussars relinquished their Chieftain tanks in 1977, there was scant indication on the international scene of the remarkable changes to come during the next decade. The super-powers had come cautiously together for talks on a Strategic Arms Limitation Treaty (SALT) and since 1974 the NATO and Warsaw Pact countries had been discussing the reduction of non-nuclear forces in Europe. But in 1975 the Russo-Cuban intervention in Angola's civil war was followed by a series of menacing Russian moves in Ethiopia, Vietnam and Afghanistan. This hardened America's distrust and sharpened its interest in re-armament, rather than arms control. With the creation of links between the USA and China the USSR's continuing fear of encirclement became more acute. (Ironically, the Soviets' own economy had become increasingly dependent on surplus American grain.)

In May 1979, when the Conservatives returned to power for the first of Mrs Thatcher's administrations:

Introduction to Part 3

... some easing of the Continental bias in British defence policy was to be expected ... This did not happen because equipment-cost escalation accelerated and began to shrink Britain's newly tailored NATO suit. . . . By the time Mr John Nott became Minister of Defence in January 1981 it was clear that Britain's economy was just not growing fast enough to contain the steep rises in equipment prices. The probability that Britain's contribution to NATO would have to be cut rather than improved, as the Government had intended, brought on the 1981 Defence Review.
(*Withdrawal from Empire,* General Sir William Jackson)

Nott saw Britain as having four main defence roles:

... an independent element of strategic and theatre nuclear forces committed to the Alliance; the direct defence of the United Kingdom homeland; a major land and air contribution on the European mainland; and a major maritime effort in the Eastern Atlantic and Channel.

... The ink was barely dry on the draft when the Argentinians invaded the Falkland Islands, convinced that Britain no longer had the political will nor the military resources to defend them. (ibid.)

The debate on the validity of Britain adopting an exclusively Continental strategy was re-opened.

Genuine Disarmament?

The advent of Gorbachev as Russian leader in 1985, matched by a change of heart in Washington, transformed the disarmament scene. One factor was the progress which the Americans were making in the pursuit of 'Star Wars' technology, with which the Russians could not hope to compete. But the USSR:

... was incapable of financing the Cold War and the US too was heading towards insolvency. As both superpowers took account of the depreciation of their super-status in the world, they were forced to acknowledge the need to disarm.'

(*World Politics since 1945,* Sixth Edition, P Calvocoressi)

The disarmament talks made way in 1989 for talks on 'Conventional Forces in Europe', in which all European states were involved. Those talks and the Stockholm conference on 'Confidence and Security Building Measures and Disarmament in Europe' were making good progress in the closing years of the 1980s. Meanwhile in Russia the Gorbachev new broom needed above all to cut costs to save the USSR from catastrophe. The twin banners of *glasnost* and *perestroika** were waved over the decaying empire, but they encouraged dissidence and that was to lead speedily to nationalist separatism and the break-up of the Union.

The dismantling of the Berlin Wall in November 1989 signalled the approaching end of the threat to Western Europe from the Warsaw Pact countries. Western euphoria encouraged belief in a great 'Peace Dividend' and the following year the Minister of Defence, Mr King, announcing his proposals for reductions in the Armed Forces, gave preliminary notice of the 'Options for Change'. But 1990 also brought early notice that Universal Peace was not about to break out. The bellicosity of Iraq and its invasion of Kuwait led to the United Nations mounting Operation Desert Storm in order to free the small state.

The 13th/18th in the 1980s and 1990s

In 1977 the Regiment reverted to the essentially light cavalry role now known as 'armoured reconnaissance'. An eighteen-month tour in Northern Ireland (in a largely infantry role) was followed by three and half years in an English barracks. From there elements would be deployed across several of Britain's remaining commitments: practising the reinforcement of Rhine Army, garrisoning the Sovereign Base Area in Cyprus as well as United Nations peace-keeping, and, in one of the final problems of the vanishing Empire, monitoring the Lancaster House Agreement on Rhodesia.

The 1981 Defence review had included the imposition of a moratorium on much of the Army's training and 'housekeeping' expenditure. This manifested itself in a variety of ways including severe restrictions on track mileage, curtailment of some exercises and outright cancellation of others, restrictions on the replacement of clothing and cuts in the amounts of ammunition and pyrotechnics used for training.

The experiments since the mid-1970s with organisational changes included groupings such as 'task force' and 'field force'

---

* *glasnost* – openness, especially an end to the falsification of economic performance; *perestroika* – restructuring of the economy in the broadest sense.

Introduction to Part 3

in place of brigades. Their own reconnaissance capability was removed from infantry battalions and armoured regiments and the task was given for a time to armoured reconnaissance regiments.

Returning to Germany in 1982 the Regiment found BAOR little different in its training for all-out war with the Eastern bloc. They were able for the first time to concentrate properly on being a medium reconnaissance unit, rather than a general purpose force deployed to a ragbag of commitments – useful as those often were for the development of junior officers and other ranks. However, the 13th/18th were called on in 1985 to provide another Operation Banner contribution to the Security Forces in Northern Ireland. This time an augmented squadron had to serve as Prison Guard Force. When they left Germany in 1986 there was still little which reflected the radical changes on the international horizon.

The Regiment returned to England for four and half years at Tidworth, during which a squadron was permanently under command of NATO's Allied Command Europe Mobile Force (Land) and a troop went to Belize. The great event of the period was the presentation of a new Guidon by the Princess of Wales.

Despite having a squadron at 48 hours readiness at one stage, the 13th/18th as such were not deployed in 1990 on Operation Granby, the British contribution to the United Nations' force in the Gulf War. However, they were represented by the Band and by a number of individuals.

By 1991 the Regiment knew that it would cease to exist as The 13th/18th Royal Hussars and in August came the announcement that The Light Dragoons would be created in December 1992, from the amalgamation with 15th/19th The King's Royal Hussars. In May 1991 the 13th/18th were back where this History began – in Wolfenbüttel – and it was from there that those who were to be Light Dragoons moved to Hohne in 1992.

Chapter Fourteen

Omagh 1977–79

Partial Conversion

At the end of May 1977 the Regiment was still in Germany, about to begin conversion to armoured reconnaissance. During the previous winter some sixty soldiers had been converted to one trade on the new vehicles.* However, the 13th/18th were due in Northern Ireland in October, for an operational tour of eighteen months in which they would have primarily infantry tasks. The two months available before working up for Ulster, was sufficient only to ensure that the remaining men in sabre squadrons had one trade apiece, without any tactical training. Theoretically, all the vehicles on an armoured reconnaissance establishment could have been manned, but crewmen would have to obtain their second trade in Northern Ireland.

> . . . as the Regiment would operate mainly from Land Rovers in Ireland, they would have eighteen months in which to forget their new trades! [However] . . . it was a relief for the Regiment to start the Northern Ireland training; we were left in peace to get on with it and the training objectives were both clear and attainable.
> (Lieutenant Colonel Loftus)

The Queen's Silver Jubilee Celebrations

Being left in peace included missing the Queen's Silver Jubilee Review of the Army at Sennelager. Except that is, for the Guidon Party and the Band. On 7 July there was a 'thin white line down the centre of the huge massed bands and an immacu-

---

* Fully trained soldiers in the Royal Armoured Corps should have each of the three principal trades – in signalling, gunnery, driving and maintenance – for their regiment's principal equipment. Recruits came from the RAC Training Regiment at Catterick as B3 tradesmen with one trade, in gunnery or D&M (driving & maintenance), and half the signalling requirement. Within eighteen months of joining a regiment the other half of signalling was meant to be completed, together with the trade not yet acquired, creating B2 tradesmen. Within three to four years B1 trades were taken at the RAC Centre, as 'gunner mechanics', 'driver mechanics' or 'control signallers'.

Omagh 1977-79

late Guidon Party on parade directly under the Royal Box. What a magnificent spectacle it was . . . It was a once-in-a-lifetime occasion for those taking part.' (It followed many mornings of rehearsal for the Regimental Quartermaster Sergeant, WO2 JL Platt, with the practice blanket on its pike and an escort of Staff Sergeants A Collins and P Holmes, 'marching around the camp area under the direction of the Regimental Sergeant Major [WO1 J Henderson] and occasionally accompanied by the Regimental Band . . . '.)

In England, people came from 'all over the country and all sorts of jobs' in order to represent the Regiment when the Queen made her Jubilee visit on 12 July to Barnsley and Cannon Hall, site of the Regimental Museum. In the party with Lieutenant RG Bell were two warrant officers, four staff sergeants and five sergeants. This array of senior ranks at first led to 'chaos with counter-order and disorder as everyone decided how it should be done and what to say if spoken to. However, in the end it all went very smoothly and we had many appreciative remarks sent our way.'

Training for Northern Ireland

There was still a deal of expertise from the previous tour Northen Ireland, but, while the training arrangements in BAOR were excellent for urban areas, rural training facilities were almost non-existent. Particularly lacking was instruction in the expertise needed by the Close Observation Troop for covert surveillance. 'Nevertheless the training instilled the most important qualities of initiative and alertness and covered the most important skill of personal weapon training.'

During the period on the Sennelager Training Area, the Regiment was still subject to VIP visitations. As well as Divisional and Brigade Commanders, 'we were not even spared a visit by the Commanders-in-Chief of British Army of the Rhine and US Army Europe'. In a different category was the Colonel of the Regiment, Major General DB Wormald. He was written into the exercise as a leading judge who had to be escorted in the border areas: 'He was able to offer many penetrating suggestions about minor tactics which, though drawn from Normandy in 1944, were still highly relevant.'

History of The 13th/18th Royal Hussars (Q.M.O.)

One Man Per Twenty-Six Square Miles
The Regiment moved into Lisanelly Barracks, Omagh in October 1977. Earlier in the year, following a period of relative stability in the Province, the 'Way Ahead' policy had been introduced; in future the RUC was to take the operational lead against the terrorists with the Army in support.

In 1977 the IRA were reorganising into a new cell framework. This was perhaps just as well for the Regiment which, to begin with, had an unrealistic area of operational responsibility. It included the whole of County Fermanagh and most of County Tyrone, stretching sixty-five miles from east to west and thirty-five miles from north to south. 'We were responsible for about 150 miles of a very difficult border area with the Republic of Ireland and for the notorious Ard Boe on the eastern shore of Lough Neagh.' By the time a commitment to guard border police stations had been met, there was only one man per twenty-six square miles left for patrolling the area. However, a 'most encouraging feature is the friendliness of the local population, and we must thank our predecessors the 9th/12th Royal Lancers for this happy state of affairs'.

The 13th/18th came under command of 3 Infantry Brigade with a special establishment. Each of the three squadrons was organised into four troops, with two sections of some eight men apiece, mounted in either two Landrovers or a Landrover and Ferret Scout Car. The numbers of men involved overall meant that reinforcements had to be drafted in and several sabre troops had one or two troopers from other Regiments, including the Scots Dragoon Guards and 15th/19th Hussars. Command and Support Squadron disbanded and its members were distributed amongst the sabre squadrons and a much enlarged Headquarters Squadron.

Initially, one squadron was in County Fermanagh, about forty miles to the south west of Omagh and another was in the eastern part of County Tyrone, forty miles in the other direction. The third sabre squadron was in Omagh on what was 'optimistically called "Off Ops". In other words, except for those on leave, they do guard duties and other dirty jobs around camp.' Once every three weeks the sabre squadrons rotated their locations and jobs. 'This is not a tidy arrangement, but is

Omagh 1977–79

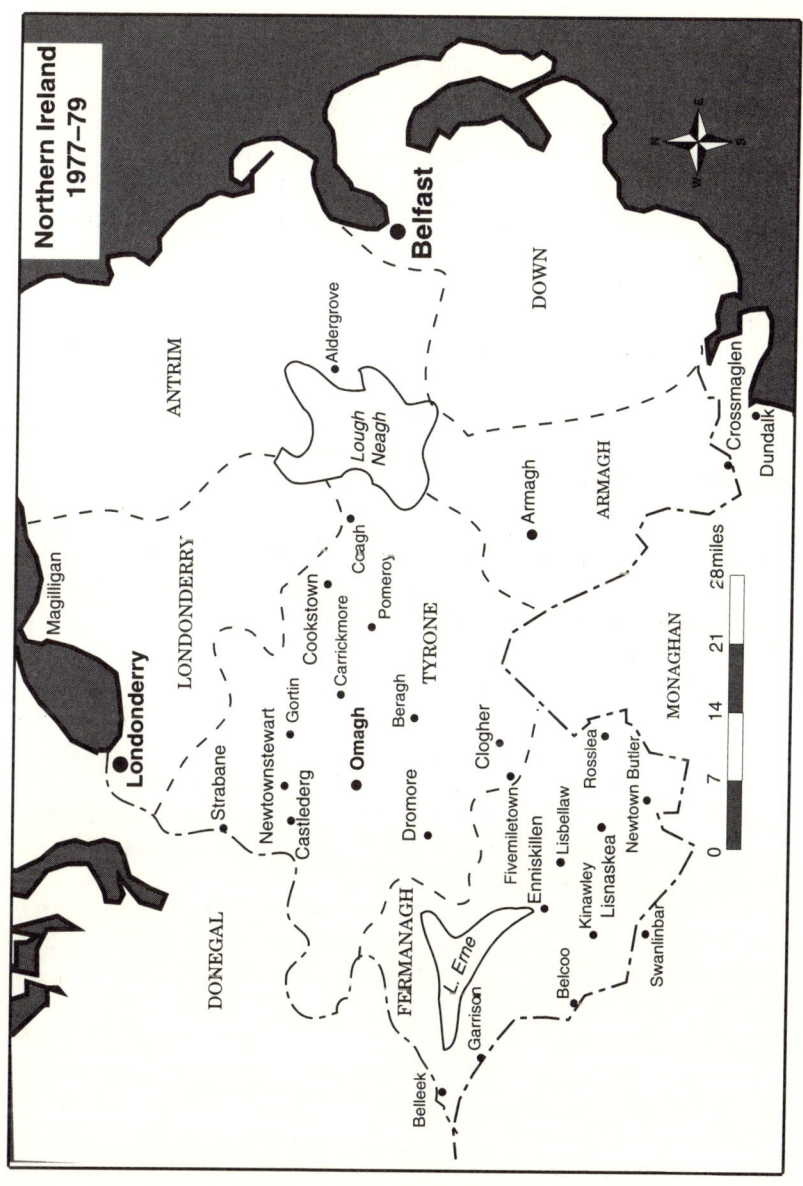

the only way of ensuring that every soldier spends at least three weeks out of nine with his family.' It also had the operational advantage of preventing troops from developing routines which could be observed and taken advantage of by the terrorists.

In April 1978 the operational task was made more realistic when the Tyrone commitment was handed over to the Queen's Own Highlanders. Two squadrons at the Regimental base gave scope, not only for better coverage of County Fermanagh and the immediate area of Omagh, but also for reducing the backlog of soldiers without armoured reconnaissance trades.

> Soldiers were fired off to the RAC Training Regiment, Catterick and to Y Squadron, The Queen's Own Yeomanry for trade training. However, even this has not been enough, so we have managed to persuade the powers that be to give us an extra year to convert to our new trade structure.

Sundry Specialists

Amongst the specialisms for a Northern Ireland tour, Intelligence loomed large. There were two 'cells', one for Omagh under WO2 P Torr and the other for St Angelo (base for the Fermanagh squadron) under Lieutenant AREdeC Stewart. They too were reinforced for a period by members of the outgoing regiment, the 9th/12th Lancers. Reconnaissance Troop disappeared into the Close Observation Troop, which had to be specially organised and trained. MT Troop and the sabre squadrons acquired a variety of civilian vehicles such as vans, used by SQMSs delivering supplies and stores to outstations, and unmarked 'Q' cars, in which journeys – theoretically – could be made without attracting unwonted attention.

Another important task was recognised by the full-time employment of a public relations officer, first Captain MD Griffith-Jones then Captain WG Baker Baker, with Corporal J Morley as photographer.

A Dog Troop was created, under Corporal K Hanson, then Corporal J Gallagher (who had spent two years with dogs at the Royal Military Academy Sandhurst). The task of the six 'sabre toothed Alsatians and their eight intrepid handlers' was to patrol the perimeter fence of Lisanelly Barracks. Headquarters Squadron Leader, Major CJ Edwards wrote:

Omagh 1977–79

They more than earn their daily can of dog meat. I know they scare us, let alone any would-be intruders. When those magic words ring out at night, 'Halt, or I'll release my dog', everything within earshot freezes.

One dog went wild while being exercised and badly marked his handler, Trooper J Horne. There were women and children about and Horne held on to the dog until he could secure it to a fence. His bravery was marked with the award of a QMO – the dog was later destroyed.*

The Regimental Band also helped with camp security and provided most of the extra men needed when Headquarters Squadron was called on for support of the police and UDR, augmented by what could be gathered from the various departments.

Although relegated to humdrum, run-of-the-mill operations such as escorts, cordons and VCPs, there were was never any lack of willing volunteers only too keen to get out from 'behind the wire'.

Headquarters Squadron also provided a home for 3 Section (Omagh Det) 321 Explosive Ordnance Disposal Unit RAOC or ATO Felix for short. A Warrant Officer RAOC was ATO (Ammunition Technical Officer), and his team was found by a nucleus of 13th/18th with others in a variety of other badges.

Air Support

A vital element in many operations in Northern Ireland was support by Army Air Corps helicopters. The Regiment could usually look to three of the six Gazelle aircraft operated by 3 Flight AAC.† The Flight's operational tasks ranged across border reconnaissance, evacuation of casualties from mined vehicles, lifting in search dogs and reaction to bombing and

---

* The practice, begun in the 1960s, of awarding QMOs to Class 1 Tradesmen had been extended to mark something of particular merit achieved by other soldiers.

† The Flight was established in 1943 in 656 Air OP Squadron RAF. They were in Malaya during the Regiment's 1950–53 tour, when another flight shared Paroi Camp with Regimental Headquarters and C Squadron. More recently 3 Flight had been merged into what became for a while the 15th/19th Hussars Air Squadron, commanded by Major AJN Collis. In 1977 it reverted to the 3 Flight title and became part of 7 Regiment AAC, but as luck would have it, Major Collis finished his tour with them as the Regiment arrived.

shooting incidents, including night flying using 'Nightsun' – a powerful, stabilised searchlight. Living in the same camp they also paid a full part in the resident Regiment's sporting and social life and amongst the pilots was a 15th/19th Hussars officer, Lieutenant RI Webb-Bowen. He was to become the second Commanding Officer of The Light Dragoons.

Air support also came from Royal Air Force and Royal Navy helicopters, particularly for operations in Co. Fermanagh. Based on RAF Aldergrove they were invaluable for moving troops speedily to and from cordon and search operations and for special route clearance – a modern version of 'picketing the heights' as in operations on the North West Frontier and in Arabia. Sometimes an airborne reaction force was kept at five to ten minutes readiness at a sabre squadron base.

Nine Week Cycle of Activities

> One result of giving supremacy to the RUC was that they and the Special Branch were very reluctant to give high grade intelligence to the Army, other than the SAS. This meant that we were unable to expect, and in the event did not get, any spectacular successes against the IRA. We were only able to provide a framework of security within which the RUC could gather evidence and make arrests. Although rather dull, this policy worked extremely well. The area was dominated by the Security Forces, IRA incidents remained at a low level and the RUC made a satisfactory number of arrests. (Lieutenant Colonel Loftus)

A Squadron *Journal* Notes described the flavour of life for sabre squadrons. 'To begin with the best bit – three weeks "Off Ops" in the Regiment's barracks in Omagh.' During these 'a fairly even tenor of Regimental life is achieved'; leave could be taken, vehicles maintained and repaired, NCOs' cadres, gunnery and driving courses run. The second three weeks was as Brigade Reserve or 'M Ops' (ie police Division M) which usually meant being sent to 'almost any of the attractive little concrete forts scattered about Co. Tyrone and Co. Fermanagh'.

> It is a topsy-turvy time as troops can be split, vehicles re-allocated and troop leaders left out of a job by the unconventional needs of Counter Insurgency operations. The trick is to have a sleeping bag handy, the vehicles topped up with petrol and a wife with a sense of humour.

Omagh 1977–79

The third week was 'L Ops' (ie police Division L) when the Squadron reassembled in Omagh after M Ops and a long convoy wound its way to Co. Fermanagh, there to split into troops at various 'outstations', which would not appear:

... in any respectable estate agents' brochures unless they were trying to sell to Howard Hughes, and only then if he'd realised all his assets and was carrying the lot in folding stuff.

It is in Fermanagh that the spotlight can be turned on individuals in the Squadron as they go about their daily business of searching cars, culverts, derelict houses and fields – not to mention 'lurks',* 'heli-Ops', foot patrols, mobile patrols, guards, Intelligence tasks and, of course, sending the weekly post-card home to Mum and Dad.

SHQ Troop lives at St Angelo. Life centres on an electronic palace where anything that moves is covered in fablon, plotted on the magnetic map and reported to RHQ. Sergeant Rogers can be seen in one corner biting the heads off drawing pins, the Squadron Leader in another 'bumpering' the floor. The technological heart of the room is a radio cubby hole whose doors are firmly shut to visitors above the rank of major, in case troopers manning the sets should be seen wearing T-shirts or other non-uniform items. The Ops Room really starts to hum if there is an incident. In fact a very tight little team is instantly in action and the whole affair is dealt with in our stride, especially the influx of folk demanding to know what has happened! (Record: two brigadiers, two colonels, two lieutenant colonels and seven majors. Majors had to share coffee cups.)

'Incidents...'

After the first month of almost total quiet following their arrival the Regiment had eight incidents over the next four weeks of 1978. The atmosphere of the time and typical tasks of the tour are best described by accounts from the monthly issues of *Town and Country* – the 'Newspaper of the 13th/18th Royal Hussars' – and extracts from the Regiment's War Diary.

---

* 'Lurk' A short-term OP during a patrol 'either to check on the activity of an "interesting party" at his or her home, or sometimes to show that we, the Security Forces, were interested in them or knew about them.' Lieutenant Colonel RCB Nutting.

History of The 13th/18th Royal Hussars (Q.M.O.)

Not a very Festive Christmas Season

The season opened with an attempted ambush of a UDR mobile patrol near Kinawley, on the night of 14 December. Some forty high velocity rounds were fired by a group of gunmen who had been lurking in a hedge abut fifty yards from the road down which the UDR were driving. Fortunately no one was hit, though there was one confirmed hit on a Landrover. The patrol returned the fire and alerted A Squadron [Major PAJ Gibson] at Angelo. Immediately Staff Sergeant Swift and his section came out to give assistance, whilst the Angelo troop was also called in to provide a cordon. In the morning a full follow up was mounted.

On the night of 21 December the terrorists attacked more easy targets, the Brookland Hotel in Ballinamallard and the Killyhevlin Hotel just outside Enniskillen. A Squadron, still at Angelo, were involved at both of these incidents; part of a series of bombings in the Province . . . In both cases there were no casualties, and little structural damage to the buildings.

In what became a fairly hectic week for A Squadron, on 23 December gunmen placed a device in the Carrybridge Hotel near Lisbellaw.

One shot was fired into the ceiling of the kitchen, successfully scaring a couple of old ladies who were part of the staff. A Squadron provided cover and jointly with the RUC cleared the building, whilst our Felix neutralised the device. Meanwhile, a few miles away, a device was discovered in the Valley Hotel at Fivemiletown. The incendiary was found in the boiler room of the hotel, but a member of the staff moved it into the yard where it was later dealt with by our ATO and the RUC.

Meanwhile in Dromore, on the night of 17 December, two RUC officers had been ambushed as they were turning their car after checking the pubs in the town. One of them was wounded in the arm, and the other had his face cut by flying glass, 'but nonetheless was able to return fire which hastened the gunmen on their way. C Squadron [Major CNP Speers 16th/5th Lancers], based at Omagh, were tasked with the follow up and with 6 UDR spent the following day carrying out a massive area search. Unfortunately, none of the gunmen has been caught.'

C Squadron were soon in business again, when the Milltown Service Station, just north of Newtownstewart, was bombed. Three small devices were planted and the fire following the explosions destroyed the garage and a small cafe which was part

21. 1969: opening of the Regimental Museum – Col Cordy-Simpson with, L to R, Alderman Barton, Lt Col Wise, the Mayor of Barnsley.

Barnsley

22. 1976: the Regiment entertains Yorkshire top brass – L to R. The Mayors of Rotherham and Doncaster, Lt Col Loftus, The Chairman South Yorks County Council, Maj Gen Wormald, The Mayors of Hull and Barnsley.

23. 1970: Adventure training in the Dolomites with the Alpini: L to R, Cpl Leak, Tpr Lawton, Tpr McKenzie, Tpr Kowtuniw, Tpr Chapman, L Cpl Torr, Cpl Flanagan, Tpr Sims.

24. A Squadron leaguered non-tactically on the Canadian prairies.

25. Guided weapon firing.

Omagh 1977–79

of the premises. The only casualty was a dog which was in the building and which the terrorists failed to release. C Squadron provided the back up for the RUC and ATO who moved in during the morning, once the fire was out.

The incident at Fivemiletown completed the 'Christmas Run' and for a week nothing happened. Then, on the night of 2 January 1978, gunmen placed four bombs in the little town of Castlederg, damaging shops and a garage. The getaway car, stolen from a local school teacher, was discovered on the border. B Squadron's troop at Rockwood, which had assisted in Castlederg during the incident also played a major role in the clearance operation which was mounted two days later.

On 29 January, 2nd Troop B Squadron (2nd Lieutenant D Cavenagh, Scots Dragoon Guards) were on mobile patrol on the Border, south of Kinawley, when a Claymore-type device exploded, narrowly missing the patrol. A man seen running away was fired at, but 'No casualties were sustained by the patrol and no hits were claimed.' The device was found to consist of two milk churns full of explosive, but only one had actually exploded. The patrol had had a narrow escape.

Cordon and Search

On 3 February a local Catholic priest telephoned Omagh RUC Station to say that an unknown male caller had just telephoned him with a message that three bombs had been placed in the Courthouse which were due to explode in fifteen minutes.

> Felix and one troop were tasked to give assistance to the RUC, and 6 UDR who cordoned and cleared the area. At approximately 4.30 there was a small explosion just behind the door of the Director of Public Prosecutions Office which caused little damage and no casualties. At 6 o'clock, another device was discovered; this was cleared by 8.30. The building was finally cleared by an RE Search team at about two in the morning. It would appear that the first device only partially functioned, hence its singular lack of effect, and the second device was incomplete. The RUC are now looking for a young man and woman whom they would like to question in connection with these offences.

On the following day another bomb was reported:

> ... in the toilet of O'Neill's bar, just behind the Courthouse. Shortly after 5pm the RUC, 6 UDR, our Ten Minute Troop and Felix were in the area. In the event, the device turned out to be

History of The 13th/18th Royal Hussars (Q.M.O.)

bomb-making equipment and parts of a bomb similar to those used in the previous day's attack on the Courthouse – it was not an explosive device as such – and was later destroyed by Felix.

Sometimes a major part of the Regiment would be called on to take part in cordon and search operations:

> ... on the morning of 7 February Sergeant Eaglesham, a postman and part-time member of the UDR, was callously assassinated by gunmen as he left Rock Primary School near Pomeroy which was part of his daily round. ... the school was in use at the time and was only just out of the line of fire.

A Squadron provided the cordon after that murder, and, following another killing the next day, of Lance Corporal Gordon (UDR) and his daughter, C Squadron joined the RUC and 6 UDR in a massive house-to-house search. It covered the 160 square miles between Omagh, Gortin, Greencastle and Pomeroy. The search failed to locate the killers, but four people were arrested by the RUC following the discovery in a derelict house of equipment 'likely to be of use to terrorists'.

The search continued over the next two days. C Squadron, 29th Field Squadron RE, 6 and 8 UDR and the RUC all took part in more house-to-house questioning and searching. Every house and derelict building was visited and some 320 square miles were covered by a total of 500 men. 'It is a tribute to the determination and co-operation of all three branches of the Security Services that so much was achieved in so short a time.'

On 26 February an SAS patrol operating in the 'Diamond' (Republican area between Lough Neagh and Cookstown) challenged two men in a farmyard with a home-made mortar. The men ran off and the patrol opened fire, killing one instantly. The second got away by car, but later that evening a man with gunshot wounds was admitted to hospital.

> ... he may have driven from the scene of the shooting to the Parochial House in nearby Aughnamullen, where the priest fetched an ambulance. Immediately following the shooting a troop from C Squadron, then in Cookstown, was despatched to the Diamond where they found the body of a man, later identified as that of Paul Duffy (21), and the mortar bomb which he was carrying when he was shot. The area was staked out and thoroughly searched for the next two days. When the area was finally cleared a total of three cassette incendiaries, a pistol and nine mortar bombs had been found.

Omagh 1977–79

Two days afterwards Paul Duffy was buried in the Mullanghoe Cemetery only about half a mile from where he was shot. 'The ceremony was closely observed by B Squadron and no further incidents took place. The IRA has admitted that Duffy was one of their "volunteers".' Of course there were also false alarms:

> Late in the evening of 13 February the RUC received a report that two men had been seen tampering with the school bus at Donaghey Primary School. C Squadron provided a stake out, and the following morning a full clearance operation was mounted, since the bus driver was a part-time member of the UDR. As a result of this report the school was closed and some of the local inhabitants were evacuated to the Village Hall. Nothing was found on the bus, or in the school and at 1230 the area was declared clear. That such a large operation should be mounted on the basis of a comparatively vague report is a measure of the importance that is being attached to the safety of members of the UDR.

Attacks on the 13th / 18th

On 15 April, an A Squadron patrol from Kinawley was about a mile from home, on the Swanlinbar road, when a massive explosion ripped up the road yards in front of the leading Landrover. Debris and boulders were showered for hundreds of yards. The Landrover rolled into the hole, despite which the crew got out, took up fire positions and returned the fire of a sniper who had begun to engage them. Remarkably, injuries to the crew were mainly restricted to cuts and bruises, although the machine gunner, Trooper SPF Moore, fractured his right wrist. Even so, he still managed to get his gun into action.

> . . . as much as 800 pounds of explosives were used in the bomb – quite possibly one of the biggest mines ever. Not only did it cut the Kinawley–Swanlinbar road, thus causing considerable inconvenience to the locals, but it also shattered windows and cracked the walls of a neighbouring farmhouse. A second farm, more in line with the explosion, was showered with debris; craters and skip-marks caused by flying boulders, some as much as three feet in diameter, were found up to 400 yards from the explosion. A Squadron mounted an immediate follow up assisted by the RUC, who questioned the local inhabitants closely, but no sign was found of either bomber or gunman, who, it is believed, may have escaped across the Border which was only a short distance from the firing point. No arrests were made.

History of The 13th/18th Royal Hussars (Q.M.O.)

On the morning of 11 June a patrol was 'blown off' the main Wattlebridge–Newtown Butler road by a command-detonated explosion. Earlier that morning five members of the IRA had held a Mr Fitzpatrick and his family in his home a short distance from Wattlebridge. The men all wore dark green jackets and black berets and four of them were masked. An hour later they took Mr Fitzpatrick's car and had it standing by while they positioned the explosive and lay in wait for a patrol.

> At 0930 as a patrol from B Squadron drove past Wattlebridge the IRA detonated the explosion and ran for their car making a quick getaway. In the explosion Trooper K Thompson received severe head injuries and was casevaced to the The Royal Victoria Hospital, Belfast; two other members of the patrol received slight injuries. A subsequent follow-up was put in by B Squadron who found a shotgun belonging to Mr Fitzpatrick laid across a battery. It showed all the signs of being a booby trap and ATO was called in. It proved to be nothing and was cleared.

On 5 November Rosslea RUC Station, housing a troop of Queen's Dragoon Guards under command of the Regiment, came under fire 'from the area of the Rosslea Arms'. The follow up next morning found rounds from Armalite, Garrand and M1 carbines.

Attacks on the RUC and UDR

On 22 March another attempt had been made on the life of a member of the UDR. The Northern Ireland Housing Executive was asked to send a plumber to repair a boiler at a house near the Diamond.

> The plumber for the area, a UDR part-timer, was tasked and on his arrival was shot at by some armed youths who were hiding in the house. Although twice wounded, he made his escape on foot across some fields. He then commandeered a car and went to Coagh Police Station [northern edge of the Ard Boe] . . . Both B and A Squadrons were involved in the follow-up, but regrettably nothing was found.
>
> . . . The most transparent feature of PIRA attacks during the past three months is that they have been directed against our comrades in the RUC and UDR. Following the callous murder of Reserve Constable Rankin in Castlederg on 4 July, there have been several attacks on the RUC in both Fermanagh and Tyrone. On 7 July, the Rosslea RUC were lured into a border crossing at

Omagh 1977–79

L7A; only their professionalism and PIRA's military incompetence enabled them to escape from a large device, dug into a culvert on the border.

Back in the Castlederg area, a 300 lb culvert bomb was cleared by ATO on 20 July. It was apparently aimed at UDR foot patrols on the border.

At the end of July a Clogher RUC patrol narrowly escaped death from the explosion of a 50 lb device between their two Landrovers, followed by automatic fire as they drove through a well-planned, but poorly executed ambush in the townlands of Durless. In the follow up by the Regiment, the Second-in-Command, Major JAC Blakiston, was first on the scene with a 'brick' of four men who, with a 'brick' from the Queen's Own Highlanders, located the terrorists' firing point.*

It was Beragh RUC's turn on 5 August, when another 300 lb device failed to explode, as they drove over it at Ninemilebridge.

On 17 August, Chief Inspector Murphy narrowly escaped with his life when he was ambushed on the Omagh to Cookstown road.

Four days later, a Fermanagh County Council van was ambushed on the Garrison–Belcoo road, often patrolled by the Regiment. The UDR driver's quick reactions undoubtedly saved many lives. Although wounded, and with a man dying beside him, he drove the rest of his work mates to safety.

Reserve Constable Donaghy met his death while building a bungalow for himself near Loughmacrory. Three gunmen killed him in front of his brother and his fiancée.

This chronicle of terrorist activities during the last three months serves to emphasise the continuing pressures put on members of the RUC and UDR in their gallant fight for peace in Northern Ireland. Constantly under possibility of attack they carry on their work regardless, striving to make Ulster peaceful and happy once again. When we leave here in eight months time, we must not forget our friends in both of these organisations and the advice and co-operation they have given us; nor must we forget that they live here permanently while we are here for four, six or eighteen months.

---

* 'Townlands' – a small group of fields. 'Brick' – originated in urban operations to describe a sub-section of four infantrymen. Used by the Regiment, it usually meant the four to five men who could be carried in a Landrover.

History of The 13th/18th Royal Hussars (Q.M.O.)

Province-wide bombing campaign

On 14 November 1978, there was a province-wide bombing operation by the IRA.

> Shops and other buildings in the heart of Omagh were wrecked last week after a car bomb exploded shortly after 11.30 am on Tuesday. In a barrage of blasts throughout the Province, seven other towns and cities were attacked, including Enniskillen, Castlederg and Cookstown. However, the attack by the Provisional IRA in Omagh was by far the worst, with over eighty buildings damaged in the town centre. The bomb, which exploded at 11.32 am, was outside Kinloch's butcher's shop. A warning had been made to McDermott's chemists twenty-eight minutes earlier. Within minutes of the warning members of the RUC were on the scene, and it was undoubtedly through their swift action in clearing the houses and shops that no lives were lost. Quickly following were members of the UDR and 10-Minute Troop, who had been crashed out immediately after the car, a grey Fiat, had been identified. The car had been hijacked at gunpoint in Carrickmore that morning, and the owner ordered not to report the theft. ATO and his crew were immediately on the scene, but the car exploded shortly after his arrival.
>
> The majority of the buildings on Bridge Street and High Street took the brunt of the blast, although every building in Bridge Street received extensive damage. High Street. however, did not escape as the blast funnelled out from Bridge Street, and windows in the Courthouse were broken. In the opposite direction, Wellworths received damage as well.

Amongst those treated at the Tyrone County Hospital, mostly for shock and cuts, was Mrs Pamela Christian, wife of Corporal AM Christian, Cooks Troop. There was also a half-hour spate of bombings in the centre of Castlederg. After a warning to the RUC shortly before 7 pm:

> ... the town was swiftly cleared by members of the Regiment and 2nd Light Infantry, together with local policemen. A total of four bombs destroyed John Street in the space of twenty-one minutes. Three of these were placed in business premises which already had been broken into and looted by the terrorists. A fourth bomb had been placed in a Land Rover which destroyed McLaughlin's electrical shop. Fires began as a result of the bombs, and these burnt long into the night, burning many buildings, including some which had not been ravaged by IRA bombs. As dawn broke over the town, still sealed due to a suspect device, all that

Omagh 1977–79

remained was a picture of holocaust. Later in the day ATO, already weary from the previous bombs, carried out two controlled explosions on suspect devices. One of the devices caused a fire which burnt for a couple of hours. It was not until Thursday that shop owners were allowed to inspect the damage caused by the bombs. Although estimates have not been received, thousands of pounds worth of damage has been caused . . .

Increased IRA Activity

On 3 February the brother of Mr F Maguire MP received a telephone call warning of two bombs in Lisnaskea. While the RUC were setting up a VCP, a bomb exploded injuring them slightly. ATO later cleared the second bomb, while Corporal S Hawley's cordon annoyed some locals including the MP, who complained of harassment

On 18 March Kinawley RUC Station, 'home' for 2nd Troop C Squadron (2nd Lieutenant PT Roberts), was attacked with a 1,000 lb bomb.

> The drama began late on Sunday evening when a blue Ford Cortina with an attached horse-box drew up to the RUC station; simultaneously dropping the trailer, the car made off at speed towards Derrylin. Immediately this action alerted the attention of Trooper G Scott on sentry duty, who recognised it as a bomb and called the Ops Room who ensured that all soldiers and police were clear of the front. Within thirty seconds of the trailer being dropped off, the bomb exploded, shattering the concrete blast wall, and causing extensive damage to the interior of the police station. Cars parked inside the station were wrecked as was the sangar in which Trooper Scott was on guard. Immediately before the blast Trooper Scott threw himself onto the floor of the sangar, thereby saving his life, as the blast tore the roof off. His next action was to dash through the rubble out on to the road and immediately set up a checkpoint.

The bombers had previously hijacked two cars, the first of which 'was abandoned due to mechanical trouble'. The second car was later found left near Kinawley church. Immediately following the explosion another car was hijacked, in which the bombers fled towards the South, leaving it on a minor road on the border. In all such cases the abandoned cars had to be treated as 'suspected IED'.*

---

* IED = improvised explosive device.

History of The 13th/18th Royal Hussars (Q.M.O.)

> As the night lengthened more troops were flown in to seal the area, and Royal Engineers from Ballykelly were rushed to the scene to help in the clearance. As dawn broke on Monday the full extent of the damage could be seen; a vast crater in the road . . . The troop at Kinawley were without any heating, light, water or gas throughout the night. Their only means of communication was by the radio, their telephone lines having been cut by the blast. . . . One fact stands out above all, the courage and devotion to duty of Trooper Gordon Scott, putting his friends and comrades before himself he alerted them, so they could get to safety.

Later in the evening of the blast the Commanding Officer, Lieutenant Colonel Stephen, paid a visit. He was astonished to see former Officers' Mess waiter, Trooper Scott, all in one piece and saluting him from the side of the road. 'When he was asked what it was like coming so close to death Scott gave his classic reply "Better than serving gin and tonic in the Officers' Mess, Colonel". It was not just for that remark that he is congratulated on his justly earned Mention in Despatches.' Regimental Notes in the same *Journal* recorded:

> The last six months of the Regiment's tour in Northern Ireland passed quickly, speeded by an increased level of PIRA activity throughout the Province. This was directed towards the border areas, and in particular the counties of Armagh, Fermanagh and Tyrone. A glance at our numbers in relation to the geographic area for which we were responsible, which included three-fifths of the border of the Province, is enough to see that we were under considerable pressure. It required a determined effort on the part of the whole Regiment, but particularly the younger soldiers, to keep terrorist activity in check. As we left, an extra Marine company was deployed in to Fermanagh, and it is to be hoped that this increased troop level will dampen the terrorists' ardour.

On 8 May, at Campsie, in Omagh:

> The Provisional IRA had chosen the worst time of day for this latest attack. It happened as many school children were walking away from Omagh's primary school at lunch time. Together with shoppers Campsie was full as the bomb exploded. The bomb blew off the boot of the blue Wolseley revealing three milk churns inside, one of which was partially exploded. As ATO arrived on the scene, the area was quickly cleared and the remaining two milk churns were examined. It was later estimated that the milk churns had contained a total of about 300lbs of home-made explosive. The area remained sealed off until all the evidence had

Omagh 1977–79

been removed and the Fire Brigade had cleared up the area. There was no doubt that many lives would have been lost, including several children, had this bomb exploded. Indeed, as one police spokesman said, 'If the bomb had gone off we would have been picking up pieces of children, instead of pieces of the car'.

It was also one of the last incidents of the Regiment's tour as they handed over to 2nd Royal Tank Regiment by 24 May 1979. Regimental Notes in the *Journal* expressed the sentiment of the time:

> It was impossible to leave without a sense of regret. We had made many friends, but also seen a number murdered. As always the details of incidents have become blurred, and one is left with overall impressions. There are recollections of innumerable patrols, of long periods of boredom, interspersed with frenetic bouts of activity. There were times when it seemed that we were set for success but we had to be content with the vicarious pleasure of prevention rather than positive victory. As always there was the frustration of being prevented from coming to grips with an enemy who had a convenient and permanent bolt hole to hand.

Appointment Changes

Meanwhile the military treadmill had ensured that there was the usual number of changes in appointment throughout the Regiment. In August 1978 Lieutenant Colonel Loftus had handed over command to Lieutenant Colonel GMcL Stephen (late Royal Scots Dragoon Guards) and, in November 1978, Major DJ Delius took over as Second-in-Command from Major JAC Blakiston.

Lieutenant Colonel Stephen was the first Commanding Officer since 1948 who had not previously served in the Regiment. Nor had he served with English soldiers before and he was not a little worried at what lay in store for him. But he was made very welcome and was 'quietly accepted' as the Commanding Officer.

> One thing became apparent to me very early on; the 13th/18th were every bit as much a family Regiment as the Scots Greys. Thirteen of the officers' fathers had been in the Regiment and several more had had a brother or an uncle; it was a very close-knit Regiment, but not a bit 'exclusive'.

History of The 13th/18th Royal Hussars (Q.M.O.)

Trials with 'Fox'

A Squadron was able in 1978 to regain touch with armoured warfare, when they carried out troop trials for rural counter-insurgency duties with the new Fox Combat Vehicles Reconnaissance (Wheeled), CVR(W). Equipped with Rarden cannon, they also had image-intensification night sights which were extremely useful for observation and it was inevitable:

> ... once the Regiment had Fox armoured cars with their 30mm automatic cannon, that some attempt should be made to fire the main armament in Ulster. To Armoured Corps ears the plop of a rifle or pistol is not remotely satisfying. Ulster, however, lacks an armoured car range, has no workshop making suitable targets, has no store of 30mm ammunition ... A Squadron's Recruit Firing at Magilligan in Co Londonderry is therefore a 'Do It Yourself' story. The first stage consisted of acquiring a set of templates from Lulworth, then attempting to squeeze them into the danger area of the rifle ranges dotted about the Province. After some false starts Magilligan looked promising. Stage two involved convincing the rather sceptical Small Arms School Corps experts at Headquarters Northern Ireland of the accuracy of the calculations....

> ... On Sunday 11 February a modest convoy of three Foxes and a 4-tonner led by an SHQ Landrover set out from Omagh. As it was early in the morning the Foxes produced only an odd turned head as they passed through Strabane and Londonderry en route. (It had been anticipated that they would be be represented as the latest tool in the hands of the 'hated Forces of Occupation'.) On arrival at Magilligan two cheery Irishmen handed over the accommodation. Not one signature was required! Perhaps because it consisted of former prison blocks which had been vacated by the inmates in favour of more luxurious apartments in a nearby building. ... Magilligan ranges is a strip of sand dunes about a mile wide sticking out five miles into the North Atlantic. From October to April it is swept by a pitiless wind which never drops below Force Seven. The placid and floppy screen target can become a lethal wind-borne missile if not securely held by a minimum of six men. The great moment of 0830 on Monday morning arrived. Amazingly the eight targets had survived a nights buffeting and they were greedily engaged by the three Foxes. ... each vehicle fired 250 rounds in two days and a night firing session without a single stoppage or misfire.

Omagh 1977–79

Keeping in Touch

Town and Country was a lavishly illustrated paper the content and quality of which, by the time of the ninth issue, apparently needed some justification:

> The Regimental *Journal*, produced yearly, is intended for external consumption . . . and is the means by which other regiments, our old comrades and the public can judge the standard of our Regiment. Thus the standard of material should be high, with well-written articles, and good high quality photographs. *Town and Country,* on the other hand, is intended in the main for internal consumption and members of the regiment serving all over the world. It should, I feel, be a reflection on the day-to-day life in Northern Ireland, viewed perhaps with a humorous approach. In *Town and Country* we should be able to laugh at ours and other people's mishaps (and in that I include spelling and printing errors!).

Much of the photography was of high quality and this was recognised when Corporal Morley, the Regiment's PR photographer, won the title of Best Unit Photographer of 1979. His portfolio for the fifth Army Photographic Competition included his coverage of the bomb damage in Omagh, a controlled explosion at Castlederg, and A Squadron night firing on Magilligan Ranges. The winning photograph was entitled 'The ones who really suffer', showing an injured woman being helped away after a 200 lb car bomb exploded in Omagh.

The Other Side of Military Life in the Province

As in other stations before and since, the Regiment was at pains to make friends with their neighbours and this was of particular value at such a difficult time in the Province. There was a particularly close liaison with the police Chief Superintendent for 'M' Division in Omagh, Mr Ivan Sterritt, whose office was only 400 yards from the barrack gate and with whom Lieutenant Colonel Stephen became great friends. The *Journal* also noted:

> It was not all drama and work however. The Irish are nothing if not hospitable, and we were all looked after. The Officers enjoyed some marvellous hunting, shooting and fishing, and everyone in the Regiment was able to take advantage of the considerable personal hospitality which was extended. We made many friends – some, in fact, even got married!

History of The 13th/18th Royal Hussars (Q.M.O.)

More Football and Cricket than in BAOR

Although squadrons spent only three weeks off operations followed by six weeks in outstations, they managed to play more football and cricket than in BAOR. The operational commitments must have taken their toll, however, as there were few major sporting achievements. An unusual success was coming in second in the Northern Ireland Army swimming finals. After winning the Northern Ireland Doubles Competition at tennis, the Regimental team was beaten in the United Kingdom semi-final.

Reports on football were sparse, but *Town & Country* recorded wins in the first two rounds of the Cavalry Cup.

A lyrical introduction to the *Journal*'s sailing notes said:

> 'Seven tenths of the world is water, six of these are in Ireland, and the remaining tenth passes through daily in the form of rain.'
> A slight exaggeration perhaps, but County Fermanagh does possess an extraordinary amount of water. Amongst the myriad of smaller lakes which lie scattered like a thousand rain drops over the county are several large lakes. The largest of these is Lough Erne, which is over fifty miles long . . . the loughs offer the largest area for cruising in the British Isles, and the surrounding countryside with woods rolling down to the water's edge paints a scenic background.

The Regiment had a glass fibre clinker rowing boat, a speed boat with a number of water skis and, on loan from the Army Sailing Association, two GP 14s and one Enterprise sailing dinghy. These were all put to good use right up to the end of September 'when the last boat was pulled out of the water by a cheerful if somewhat cold looking crew, and laid up for the winter'.

Field Sports

There were also unrivalled opportunities for field sports. There was an apparently unlimited supply of excellent but cheap coarse and game fishing. The fly fishermen found themselves 'an earthly paradise within the boundaries of the Regimental area', most of the better trout waters of Northern Ireland being within one hours drive of Omagh.

Thanks to the hospitality of the Ellis family at Rash House, the 'Omagh regiment' ran its own shoot there as well as getting away to a variety of other places. At Castlederg, in the Regiment's operational area, there was a notable snipe bog – the town's rubbish tip. Leading shots were Captains MD Griffith-Jones and EWJ Nall and Lieutenants NJ Norman and AJ Tillard (Major General PB Tillard's son). Because of the practice at Hohne, all the guns in the Regiment were able to take full advantage of the wonderful opportunities with which they were presented, particularly at Rash House.

At least three hunts meet within striking distance of Omagh and:

> No notes on hunting in Ireland would be complete without a mention of the overwhelming hospitality which goes with it. To begin with, amateur drinkers should arrive very late at the meet if they expect to ride away from it. At the end of the day it is is unusual if you don't find yourself enjoying an enormous alcoholic tea by the fireside of a man you only met for the first time that morning. If the sport does not compare with the Beaufort or the Belvoir it is certain that every man will give you good morning and good night, and more than likely a good hour's yarn at the covert side.

The stables had an unexpected addition to the strength in an 'incident which captures the peculiar "Irishness" of our life'. It concerned a mare called Lily. Major Blakiston had bought her for the Regiment from south of the Border and she was ridden by Colonel Stephen and the Adjutant, Captain RCB Nutting. She was an eight year old, heavily built, half-bred Irish hunter, considered unfortunately to be barren. Horse and riders enjoyed a good season with the Fermanagh Harriers and she was entered in the Harriers Hunter Trial. Colonel Stephen:

> . . . took her round the course twice on a cold blustery Irish day with intermittent moments of hail and sunshine. We did the pairs in the morning and cleared thirty-two jumps of varying complexity and were disqualified before we had completed half the course, but we finished. . . . We had a clear round in the afternoon, but were too slow to get anywhere.

She was subsequently entered in the Fermanagh Point to Point, with Captain Nutting up:

> Starting was the first thing which Lily did not do well; however, things got no better. She ploughed her way through the first fence, jumped the second beautifully, if half a furlong behind,

demolished the third fence and then threw her jockey clear over her head at the fourth.

Four weeks later, she produced a splendid foal:

> ... to the amusement of most of us and the embarrassment of pundits, owners and dealers alike.

The new filly was named Caprice*; she cleared her first jump at four days old when following the lead of her mother, who had escaped from her stable into a paddock.

Christmas Pantomime

The more isolated the station, either through geography or operational circumstance, the more likely that self-entertainment will burgeon. Omagh was no exception and December 1978 saw a Christmas pantomime being mounted, *O'Laddin*. Contributions both in front of and behind the curtain came from across the Regiment. The Band was obviously an essential ingredient and the Bandmaster, Mr I Thompson, wrote an overture based on 'a pastiche of most of the best Middle Eastern musicals'. He also arranged the music for the songs to suit the 'somewhat limited range of the actors'. Mrs Stephen and Mrs Peto both of whom were professional artists of some note, created a 'splendid impression of the city of "Old Angelo" – a metropolis of Fermanagh'. The cast itself was a remarkable cross-section of the Regiment and its families, with 'the high point of the whole performance' being reached by the Regimental Sergeant Major WO1 JL Platt and his six Thieves, led by the Regimental Quartermaster Sergeant, WO2 J Mallows.

Lisanelly Cub Pack

The Regimental links with Scouting were maintained through a Cub Pack formed on arrival in December 1977 from members of the previous pack, run by the 9th/12th Lancers, and the

---

* After the mare ridden by Captain WH Eve, 13th Hussars, when he was killed in the last mounted charge by British Cavalry, at Lajj, in 1917. She galloped off into a sandstorm with seven bullet wounds in her neck. Remarkably she was spotted over a year later, in the lines of an Indian cavalry regiment, by Captain Eve's groom, Private Hogg. Claimed back by the 13th, she was brought back after the war, to retirement with Captain Eve's widow in England. Caprice and her foal were the models for the silver statuette which for many years was the officers' wedding present. (The full story was told by Colonel AL Mallinson in 'Changing Fortunes of a Cavalry Charger' in *Horse and Hound*, 3 May 1990.)

majority of 'boys of the Regiment' aged between eight and eleven. The initiative was largely that of Staff Sergeant KM Local, the Chief Clerk, as Group Scout Leader with Corporal K Bailey as Cub Scout Leader. Both had qualified as leaders in Germany. The various parents played their part, particularly in fund raising to help with camping and other enterprises.

Keeping Touch with Yorkshire
A valuable contact for the Regiment was a visit from the Secretary of State for Northern Ireland in the Labour Government, Mr Roy Mason, who was also MP for Barnsley. Invited by Lieutenant Colonel Loftus to meet his constituents in the Province he came to Omagh, wearing a Regimental tie, on 14 March 1978.

In May, two correspondents from the *Sheffield Morning Telegraph* spent two days with the Regiment and their reports were reproduced in *Town and Country*. The *Telegraph* also provided the Regiment's newspaper with 'Letters from South Yorkshire'.

It was now almost sixteen years since Lieutenant Colonel JR Palmer had set up Home Headquarters. During that time he had been instrumental, 'in assisting the Regiment organise numerous Regimental Weekends, both in the United Kingdom and Germany, the task of getting soldiers, relatives, friends and Association members en route from Yorkshire, being solely his. The many funds held at Home Headquarters have prospered, thus ensuring a sound financial backup to the Regiment'. It was also largely due to his enthusiasm and hard work, with the help of Colonel Harry Wise, that the Regimental Museum was set up in Barnsley's Cannon Hall. He handed over in April 1978, to Major EJS Garbutt, some 46 years after he joined the 13th/18th, on their way from Egypt to India in 1931.

Political Incident
Two months after Colonel Stephen's arrival a junior Defence minister came to the Regiment, in what turned out to be a very different visit from Mr Mason's earlier in the year. The tour brought him to St Angelo while A Squadron Headquarters was dealing with an incident. It is perhaps not surprising that the attention paid to the visitor was not what it might have been in

quieter circumstances, but he subsequently complained that he had been 'brushed off, couldn't get a drink at lunchtime and was offered food in the canteen with the men'. Major General RB Trant carried out a follow-up visit as a result, but his initially hostile attitude, based on the minister's report, was entirely changed by his own full-day tour. 'Everywhere he went everybody was on the ball . . .' (Colonel Stephen).

Overseas expeditions

Liaison was maintained with two of the allied Regiments. Captain WG Baker Baker, Lieutenant SW Ledger and Squadron Sergeant Major Torr spent what was obviously a memorable long weekend with the 4ème Chasseurs. Even more memorable for Captain JAMA Selfe and Lieutenant NJ Norman was their visit to India for the celebrations to mark the 175th Raising Day of Skinner's Horse and the 200th Anniversary of the birth of Colonel James Skinner.

To Cyprus and England

A Squadron was the first to leave Northern Ireland, flying straight to the Sovereign Base Area in Cyprus where they took over from a squadron of the 9th/12th Lancers. The remainder of the Regiment moved to Essex.

Chapter Fifteen

Wimbish 1979–82

Roles Galore

From May 1979 to November 1982 the Regiment was based on Wimbish, in Essex. They were the armoured reconnaissance regiment of 7 Field Force*, whose headquarters was at Colchester and whose operational role was to reinforce BAOR and provide Rear Area Security. Throughout the period at Wimbish the Regiment always had one squadron, sometimes two, away on detachment in Cyprus.

The world-wide threat of terrorist attack increased during the 1970s and security of major airports was of particular concern. One periodic commitment required all or part of a squadron to be on standby for speedy deployment at Heathrow. It was practised in Operation Trustee and in 1981 a troop of B Squadron 'for once was actually crashed out and spent a day frightening passengers while on patrol with the Airport police'.

The industrial disputes of the time also made their claims on the Regiment and temporary crews of ambulances and 'Green Goddess' fire engines had to be found from time to time.

Like its predecessor, the armoured car regiment, the armoured reconnaissance regiment was responsible for 'medium' reconnaissance, ie covering the front or flanks of a formation, but to this had been added 'close' reconnaissance for infantry battalions. In the United Kingdom, one squadron was equipped for close, and two for medium reconnaissance, but one of the medium reconnaissance squadrons was largely notional, because of the permanent detachment to the Sovereign Base Area in Cyprus. The theory was that the squadron in Cyprus would be brought back, in time of crisis, to man the vehicles of the second medium reconnaissance squadron.

---

* 'Field Force' was the name for an independent formation of brigade size in the 1970s, during the attempt to do away with a brigade level of command. In January 1982, 7 Field Force reverted to 19 Infantry Brigade.

History of The 13th/18th Royal Hussars (Q.M.O.)

Medium reconnaissance was now carried out in the 'Combat Vehicles Reconnaissance [CVR], Fully Tracked' range, which appeared in the 1970s. Amongst them was FV101 Scorpion, armed with a 76mm gun, and FV106 Scimitar armed with 30mm cannon. Initially, armoured reconnaissance regiments in BAOR used Scorpion, those in the United Kingdom had a mix of Scorpion and Scimitar. Others in the range were FV103 Spartan (personnel carrier), FV102 Striker (guided weapons), FV104 Samaritan (ambulance), FV105 Sultan (command vehicle) and FV106 Samson (recovery). The medium reconnaissance squadrons had four troops, each with two Scorpions and two Scimitars.

The close reconnaissance squadron was equipped with Fox (CVR (W) [Wheeled]), armed with a 30mm cannon; the five troops had six Fox armoured cars apiece.

No Air Squadron

Those who had been involved in the 1960s with Air Troop's Sioux helicopters knew their potential for armoured reconnaissance. Since then the Sioux had been succeeded by the Scout helicopter, armed with the SS11 wire-guided anti-tank missile. Sadly, however, earlier hopes of an 'Air Squadron' manned wholly with 13th/18th Hussars pilots was not to be.* Although armoured reconnaissance regiments in Rhine Army retained their Air Squadrons until the late 1970s, there was none on the UK establishment.

New Colonel of the Regiment

Major General DB Wormald, the Colonel of the Regiment, handed over in May 1979, to Major General HSR Watson. General Wormald had joined the Regiment in 1936 and, until 1945, served continuously in A Squadron, commanding it for much of the Second World War. His distinguished and gallant conduct earned him the DSO and MC and Bar. Later he

---

* The Regiment's Air Troop in Münster had been absorbed into 4 Guards Brigade Air Squadron, which subsequently became 662 Squadron Army Air Corps. When the Cold War came to an end and with it the prospect of drastic cuts in the number of armoured regiments, there was a belated attempt to promote the concept of 'Air Cavalry' units, which would take over the anti-tank helicopter role. But it was far too late; the Army Air Corps' own regiments were by then too well established.

Wimbish 1979–82

commanded the 3rd Hussars and, on their amalgamation with the 7th, the Queen's Own Hussars. It was almost thirty years after leaving the Regiment that he returned as Colonel, 'a mark of the high esteem in which he was still held' as the *Journal* said.

As GSO2 in the Royal Armoured Corps Directorate in the late 1940s, the then Major Wormald had:

> ... seen the need for reconnaissance vehicles to be tracked rather than wheeled, for the new armoured car to mount a 76 mm gun, and for the commander to be able to lay and fire it himself. General Wormald knew from experience that dug-in tanks could inflict fearful casualties. (Obituary in *The Daily Telegraph* 1994.)

His insistence on the need for tracks, rather than wheels, stemmed from an incident in 1940. While making his way back from Belgium with his troop of light tanks, he was hailed by a squadron of the 12th Lancers. Their Morris CS9 armoured cars were bogged down in a field and needed tracked vehicles to get them out.

Carver Barracks

By 24 May 1979 the Regiment, less A Squadron, had completed its move into Carver Barracks which, as RAF Debden, had opened shortly before the Second World War. Squadrons of Hurricanes stationed there played an active part in the Battle of Britain. Later it housed first a Canadian squadron, then American volunteer 'Eagle Squadrons' until they were taken over by the US Army Air Force. Post-war years saw a gradual decline in flying activity and RAF Debden was the RAF Police Depot from 1960 to 1975. Debden village was actually further away from the barracks than the hamlet of Wimbish, some three miles from Saffron Walden. Wimbish therefore became the preferred address.

> The camp was due to have been converted in time to house our predecessors, on their return from Northern Ireland in 1977. We found that it was still far from ready. One formed the impression that soldiers were the last people that the planners and contractors had envisaged as even arriving. . . .

However, nearly a year later:

> ... It is now possible to view the situation with a slightly more dispassionate eye. There is no doubt that in time Debden will be a

splendid Royal Armoured Corps barracks. It is close to both London and Cambridge. It is in a delightful part of Essex and the people have gone out of their way to make us feel welcome. Thetford and Salisbury Plain are both within reach for training. The airfield has been secured against PSA* attack and will afford an invaluable area for training, recreation, and farming.'

But:

The current debits are still alarming. The 'custom built' vehicle hangars are still unfinished, leaving two squadrons, Tech, and the LAD cheek by jowl in one old pre-war RAF hangar. The gym remains a skeletal structure and the soldiers' quarters are unlikely to be ready before May 1980. ... These problems are however temporary – the only irredeemable damage is to the playing fields. Previously these had been in the middle of the camp, surrounded by the messes and quarters and forming a natural amphitheatre. Planners' madness and customer weakness allowed the builders to shave off a third of the area to accommodate the extra quarters required. The football, rugby, and hockey pitches have been consigned to the outer darkness of the airfield, and the cricketers will never have a full-sized pitch to play on. ... [By 1982, however] ... as the scars of the rebuild have disappeared, we have started to appreciate and enjoy the benefits of the previous two years' inconvenience and hard work. We now have a superb, modern camp with first rate facilities.

The families of NCOs and troopers were faced at first with indifferent accommodation, in quarters at another disused RAF station some fifteen miles away, at Duxford. Apart from the discomfort, this also meant a daily bus ride for husbands before and after work. Some forty wives had to be left behind, for between fifteen and eighteen months' separation, during B Squadron's unaccompanied tours in Cyprus, but 'great pains were taken by a number of people in Wimbish to mitigate the effects of an inevitably difficult time'.

The initial welcome from the local inhabitants was warm, albeit a little cautious, as the Regiment were the first cavalry to be seen in the area since Cromwell. They were made to feel very much at home and, in return, did what they could to be 'good local citizens and an asset rather than a hindrance to the

---

* PSA – Property Services Agency, responsible for military barracks et al; 'farming' refers to hay grown on the old airfield – shades of the use made of the grass between the barrack blocks at Wolfenbüttel in the 1950s.

Wimbish 1979–82

area'. There were some complaints at first about 'tanks tearing up the roads', but these were successfully dealt with at an early Open Day. One exhibit was an 8-ton Scorpion which was lowered on to six beer glasses; such was the low ground pressure that the glasses did not break.

The Band contribution under WO1 GE Locker was particularly valuable; they were in constant demand, playing at over sixty separate engagements during 1981 alone, including three weeks in London parks. By the time the Regiment left they had 'built up a most formidable reputation around much of East Anglia and, indeed, London for their skill, resourcefulness and versatility . . . they were superb ambassadors for the Regiment.' (Lieutenant Colonel ffrench Blake). But regimental bands continued under attack from the remorseless demands for economy and by 1985 were cut to twenty-two members.

Armoured vehicles were also in demand and one or more appeared at over thirty local fêtes and functions in one year.

Training

Training from Wimbish was not easy, but there were compensations. The Thetford training area was reasonably close at hand and the Regiment's new vehicles, unlike the Chieftains, could be taken anywhere. There was space in the camp area for troop level collective training and a training room was set up with a large relief map. For B and C Squadrons the emphasis after arrival was to resume the trade training on armoured reconnaissance vehicles, interrupted by the Omagh tour.

Exercise Crusader

With up to two squadrons away and troops of the close reconnaissance squadron often dispersed to their affiliated infantry battalions, the commanding officers (Lieutenant Colonel GMcL Stephen until March 1981, then Lieutenant Colonel RJW ffrench Blake) seldom had opportunity to exercise their full command in the field. However, in the autumn of 1980, with both A and B Squadrons in Cyprus, the rest of the Regiment 'played a large and important part in Exercise Crusader, the largest exercise since the 1950s' (Exercise Battle Royal). Crusader was the name given to the first part of the exercise, the mobilisation and movement from the United Kingdom to

History of The 13th/18th Royal Hussars (Q.M.O.)

Germany; the actual manoeuvres were another of the many Exercise Spearpoints.

Headquarters Squadron ran the Kit Issuing Centre at Grantham for thousands of reservists going through mobilisation procedures and C Squadron, the close reconnaissance squadron, went through the reinforcement hoop. They:

> ... drove out of camp on 2 September to start Crusader with the long drive to Rheinsehlen camp. After three long days and nights, with a crossing of the Rhine by ferry on Exercise Cargo Canoe, twenty-five out of thirty Foxes drove into Rheinsehlen. Work-up training the following week kept everyone busy. As well as tactical and replenishment training much real practice was made of the Kinetic Energy Tow Ropes, German tractors and even US Chinook helicopters, in aiding the progress of vehicles over our own water sandwich. Then the great climax – Spearpoint. Most troops had four days of action on the ten day exercise. . . . For many it may be the first and last time that enemy on the ground and in the air are seen on such a large scale on an exercise. There were many opportunities for gaining good intelligence and 5th Troop in particular took full advantage using quiet vehicles under cover of darkness and fog.
>
> On occasions during the exercise, the Commanding Officer had a brigade-size group under command. The style with which the battle was played was both fast and stretching. RHQ had very little sleep for the first week, and yet the manner with which all conducted ourselves was admired and commented on later.

Lieutenant Colonel Stephen recorded the frustrating climax:

> ... there was a big set piece which was supposed to be 'free play'; it was anything but. We had a splendid plan for wiping out the Parachute Regiment when they dropped on us, but we weren't allowed to do it. At the last minute it was said that 'it wasn't fair'!

Close Reconnaissance Work

The Fox armoured car gave trouble throughout its service, most finding it not at all 'user-friendly'. During a fortnight in the Sennybridge Training Area in September 1979 the twenty-eight, 'not new', Foxes issued to C Squadron (Major AJN Collis) were all dismantled six hours before their only forty-eight hour squadron exercise. 'Some new cracks never seen before in a Fox' were spotted on the mounting pads holding the steering box onto the vehicle. 8 Field Workshops REME 'who had previously complained of not having enough to do were deployed to C Squadron's camp in the hills to carry out a ten-hour job on each Fox'. Enough serviceable vehicles were ready for two troops to take to Barnsley for the Freedom parade, leaving the remainder of the Squadron to prepare for Eastern District's 'March and Shoot' competition. 'As we were surrounded by an infantry-heavy Field Force, a little training to avoid embarrassment seemed in order. On the day the "platoon" really grafted and put everything they had into it.' After forced marching, an assault course and falling plate competition the C Squadron 'platoon', led by Captain PG Scrope, won the trophy – 'The Golden Boot'.

Exercise Gobi Dust
In May 1982 A Squadron exchanged equipment, barracks and roles with C Company, 3/70 Armor, US Army. A Squadron (Major JAMA Selfe) went to Fort Polk, Louisiana where they had a week's vehicle familiarisation and basic skill training before taking over twenty-one M60 tanks. With these they had a week on the ranges followed by a 'force-on-force' exercise*, Gobi Dust, against the Alabama National Guard. 'The exercise was still being written by our hosts as we were being deployed. As an exercise it was uneventful although we seemed to be playing only to National Guard rules which were apt to change quite suddenly.' They made the most of their weekends, taking in the French quarter of New Orleans, Astraworld ('Houston's answer to Battersea Park') and the NASA Space Centre.

Exercise Gryphons Gambit
Meanwhile C Company 3/70 Armor were grappling with Foxes on a Regimental Exercise 'notable for its lack of incidents, despite having advanced and withdrawn over most of East Anglia'. This was the only opportunity which Regimental Headquarters had during Lieutenant Colonel ffrench Blake's tour for commanding a battle group in England. It finished with a hard-fought battle on Thetford in pouring rain, much to the frustration of the television cameras which were pursuing Captain 'Buster' Thrasher, C Company's commander.

---

* ie 'own troops' and 'enemy' were fully represented rather than having a notional enemy.

History of The 13th/18th Royal Hussars (Q.M.O.)

Exercise Autumn Circuit

Autumn Circuit, the last exercise before the return to Germany was to be on Salisbury Plain. The opportunity was taken for the move there to simulate a screen operation over a corps frontage. This meant moving through the centre of St Albans, upsetting the municipal authorities who had declared it a 'nuclear free zone'. There was also a near crisis from shortage of fuel. Account had not been taken of how much would be consumed by stationary vehicles maintaining radio watch. Fortunately RAF Benson came to the rescue – their stocks were largely drained.

Cyprus Detachments

Between 1979 and 1982 the Regiment had two separate tasks in Cyprus; throughout the period one squadron was detached to the garrison of the Sovereign Base Areas; another had to be provided for two six-month spells with UNFICYP, the United Nations Force which had been on the island since 1964. First A, then C, Squadrons were detached to the Sovereign Base Areas; B Squadron twice donned the blue berets of the United Nations.

Greeks, Phoenicians, Romans, Byzantian Emperors, Venetians and Turks; all had ruled Cyprus over the centuries and in the dying days of the Ottoman Empire it was Britain's turn. As part of the settlement of the Congress of Berlin in 1878 she 'leased' Cyprus as a military base. *Enosis*, or union with Greece, was then already a major issue amongst the Greek half of the population. By the end of the Second World War the Greek inhabitants far out-numbered the Turkish and *Enosis* had the support both of the Greek Orthodox Church and the Communist Party. The EOKA terrorist campaign began in 1955 and led to inter-communal rioting between the Turks and Greeks, as well as attacks on the British. As in Palestine, the latter were caught up in a seemingly intractable conflict between races and religions. A solution of a sort seemed to emerge in 1957, when Britain's modified defence policy called for Cyprus to be simply an air staging post, rather than a major base. But the terrorist campaign continued until 1959, when the Zürich Agreement provided for an independent Cyprus, with a Greek Cypriot President and a Turkish Vice-President. Britain retained two small enclaves: the western sovereign base area, with the air base at Akrotiri and Headquarters at nearby Episkopi; the eastern, covering Army logistic installations around Dhekelia and a communications centre.

Cyprus became a republic within the Commonwealth under the Makarios presidency in August 1960.

> Foolishly the Greeks would not leave well alone. Both sides, Greek and Turk, stockpiled arms and prepared for another round. In December 1963 the Greeks attacked the Turks in Nicosia. Makarios appealed for help. The two British garrison battalions in the sovereign bases were inadequate to part the two sides; most of 3 Division of the Strategic Reserve was flown out by stages to hold the ring until they could be relieved by a United Nations force in March 1964. Ten years later the Greek National Guard staged the coup which ousted Makarios. Turkish patience ran out and the Turkish army invaded the island in September 1974, imposing *de facto* partition.
>
> (*Withdrawal from Empire,* General Jackson)

Elements of the Turkish army were in the northern, Turkish Cypriot, half of the island; both Sovereign Base Areas were in the southern, Greek Cypriot half. Between the two communities a buffer zone was patrolled by UNFICYP.

Sovereign Base Areas

In May 1979, A Squadron, led by Major PAJ Gibson, joined the Episkopi Garrison in Western Sovereign Base Area (WSBA). The main work horse of the six sabre troops was the Ferret scout car, with four to each troop. For normal day-to-day work Saladin armoured cars were kept in a reserve role. Although based in the WSBA, the main operational commitment for the Squadron was in the ESBA, two hours 'rugged driving' away. Two sabre troops were permanently detached there, under command of the resident infantry battalion. The latter's task was to patrol the perimeter of the ESBA 'to maintain quite clearly in Greek and Turkish minds the Sovereign nature of the ESBA'. The troops were rotated, with each spending two weeks out of every six away from the rest of the Squadron.

That operational commitment largely determined what other military training the Squadron could do. A squadron-size exercise was not possible and everything had to be tailored to the troop rotation. Training outside the Sovereign Base Areas

History of The 13th/18th Royal Hussars (Q.M.O.)

was seldom feasible, 'however, quite a lot of useful countryside lies within the SBAs so the Squadron still manages worthwhile training'. Throughout the year a number of units from elsewhere visited Cyprus for a month of training and troops provided armoured reconnaissance for them. The Royal Military Academy Sandhurst was a regular visitor and the Squadron arranged its own troop training, escape and evasion exercises and Squadron CPXs (command post exercises).

Each year during November they visited the Akamas peninsula for Annual Firing. This included practising on the Squadron's two Scorpions – issued to enable trade training to be maintained. The area is a nature reserve (and provides a haven for the green turtle which breeds there), but that meant that the Squadron had to build its own range and remove whatever was left once they had finished.

When in barracks work began early, leaving the afternoons free for the great variety of sport available, particularly in or on the water – the camp was some 800 yards from the sea. 'The sunshine is devastating until the body is acclimatised, this takes from four to six weeks.' Once used to the weather, 'everybody got brown, wore shorts, sunbathed, swam, snorkled, dived, waterskied, played a host of sports and felt well because, quite simply, it is a healthy climate.' The WSBA was:

> . . . as British as Basingstoke. It has its own courts, taxes, county council, sewage department and police Force. The last named have kept us busy and we them. They number some thirty-five, patrol a mere twenty miles of road and keep themselves amused, at our expense, with radar speed traps.

> Living in a rather colonial milieu, the Squadron's social life is largely self-generated, but none the less satisfying for that. At its heart is unquestionably the Squadron Bar which is also the Corporal's Mess . . . It has been the venue of Happy Hours, buffets, birthdays, farewells, games nights, film nights and bingo nights as well as impromptu livers-in parties. . . . The best smoker occurred at Akamas during Annual Firing. Mere words cannot do justice to Lance Corporal Milne's 'Lion Hunt' or the startlingly realistic mime of Lance Corporal Phillips's unique version of 'Old MacDonald's Farm'. All this done to a backdrop of a vast moon rising from the Mediterranean and surrounded by a tract of country devoid of human life for twenty miles in any direction.

Wimbish 1979–82

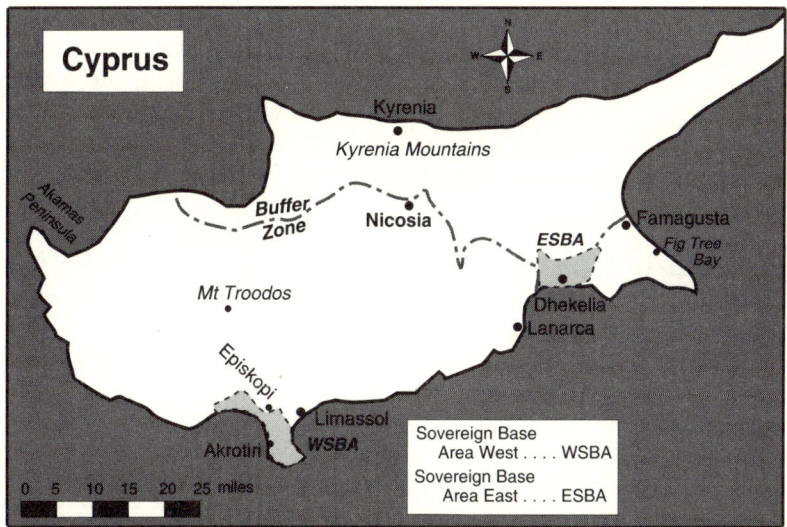

With memories still fresh of the production of *O'Laddin* in Omagh, the Squadron wives put on a self-produced Christmas pantomime.

In February 1981 C Squadron (Major AJN Collis) relieved A Squadron and remained in Cyprus until the Regiment moved to Germany in November 1982. Like A Squadron they found that the greatest problem in Cyprus was that 'there is not enough time in the day to work, play and enjoy all that is offered in a perfect climate'. In their first three months they took part in two Sovereign Base internal security exercises and the Queen's Birthday Parade. Later in the year there were two amphibious exercises, in one of which LSL *Sir Lancelot* again featured.

In March 1982 Major EL Yorke took over from Major Collis 'on the day of a visit by Commander 19 Infantry Brigade who was a touch confused by this and narrowly missed a few buckets of water being thrown over him'.* The well-established

---

* Major Collis stayed on for a further two months preparing his 30 feet boat Aline II for a return journey by sea. Three years before he had found the wreck of a 1913 East Coast cutter washed up on Mersea Island near Colchester. The rebuilding had gone on ever since (with the 'reluctant' help of officers doing 'extras'). The voyage, described in the March 1983 *Journal*, had the distinctly epic quality to be expected of an officer who, in 1973, had returned from ERE in Cyprus overland, via Turkey, with a pregnant wife in a 1959 Alvis.

routine continued until about six months before departure when training began for the return to BAOR. In the final weeks the Squadron concentrated on a local training area for some intensive collective training in armoured reconnaissance, helped by the senior reconnaissance instructor (Major RES Faulkner, 16th/5th Lancers) from the RAC Tactics School.

Force Reserve
In March 1980 B Squadron, under Major RA Cordy-Simpson, arrived for their first six-month, unaccompanied spell on the island with UNFICYP. The United Nations Force operated in the narrow strip of land (the 'Green Line') dividing the two communities – and armies – on the island. Five small infantry battalions, one each from the Danish, British, Canadian, Swedish and Austrian Armies, constituted the principal element of the Force, with B Squadron as 'Force Reserve'. The sabre troops were rotated each month so that each operated at some stage across the island with each of the battalions. (The United Nations Ambassador was Argentinian and the Force Commander was an Irish Major General; despite British differences of opinion with their countries elsewhere in the world, the relationship in Cyprus could not have been better.)

The task each day was to patrol the narrow track of the Green Line that ran between the Turkish and Greek forces. In some places they were separated by several kilometres where there were constant disputes over the ownership of the citrus fruit trees. Much of this no man's land was mined, with only the UN allowed to enter it. In the centre of Nicosia the patrol track was only wide enough for a Ferret scout car to fit between the booby-trapped houses. At the eastern end of the island, the patrol ended at the coast just south of Famagusta. The troops operating with the Danish, Swedish and Austrian contingents lived with their respective battalions in a variety of accommodation; the troop with the Austrians did their best to make a home of an abandoned cardboard box factory. Each troop was rationed by its parent battalion, but some found raw fish not to their liking and a 'milk run' by Squadron Quartermaster Sergeant P Fraser provided cornflakes and British bangers.

Wimbish 1979–82

B Squadron's advance party arrived on 29 February (Major Cordy-Simpson's ninth birthday). It was snowing in Nicosia, almost unheard of, and until mid-April Mount Troodos was covered in snow. Every member of the Squadron had contributed towards buying a new speedboat, which was kept at Fig Tree Bay. This meant that most of them could ski on both snow and water. All were proficient at water-skiing by the end of the tour, 'some, like Lieutenant RM Keane and Sergeant S Hawley, could do almost anything on a mono-ski'.

Like the other members of the Regiment in the Sovereign Base Areas, the Squadron made the best of their time, between the demands of protracted patrolling, including taking leave both on the island and elsewhere. Some ventured to Israel and:

> The prize must go to Lance Corporal Whitelam and Trooper Francis who, having 'done' Israel, then jumped the border on their motor bikes to Egypt, had their photographs taken on a camel at the pyramids and returned back across the Sinai Desert.

Motor bikes were popular as recreation and means of transport for members of both squadrons on the island and at one stage B Squadron owned thirty-six of them – in the 'Force Reserve Chapter'. 'The sight of this lot setting off for Fig Tree Bay was enough to frighten even the Cypriot drivers.' (Before they handed over to C Squadron, A Squadron had seen 'the demise of the Squadron motor-cycle chapter; because of accidents and court bans we are down to our last half dozen stout riders'.)

By mid-September and the return home they had patrolled almost a quarter of a million miles over all forms of terrain and had made many international friends. The officers all came back with new suits and shirts . . . When B Squadron returned for their second tour in September 1981 they were under the command of Major CA Le Hardy.

> Within two days we had two troops on standby for an operation and we had completed our first UN Force Reserve Exercise. [But then we] got stuck into the social life. We lost count after forty parties and sixty-four visitors in our first seven weeks.

Cyprus was also an ideal base from which to launch a variety of adventure training expeditions by individual troops; one of the destinations was Israel, others took to the sea and visited the Greek islands.

History of The 13th/18th Royal Hussars (Q.M.O.)

Rhodesia and Operation Agila

In the colonies of Northern and Southern Rhodesia and Nyasaland, between 1953 and 1962, an unsuccessful attempt was made to solve the problem of white settler minorities through a policy of a gradual multi-racial partnership in the 'Central African Federation'. When the Federation broke up, Britain granted independence to Northern Rhodesia (Zambia), and Nyasaland (Malawi). Residual powers in Southern Rhodesia were retained, however, and that was seen as unfair by the white community. In 1965 the Unilateral Declaration of Independence (UDI) was followed by a long and bitter war against adherents of Joshua Nkomo and Robert Mugabe. Successive British governments unsuccessfully sought political remedies until eventually the Lancaster House Agreement was reached in 1979. The British Army, supported by the RAF:

> ... played a key role in implementing the Agreement. ... it provided the bulk of the Commonwealth Monitoring Force that supervised the ceasefire and the concentration of guerrilla gangs in specified assembly areas. The Force, under command of Major General John Acland, started to arrive in British and US transport aircraft on 20 December. Its total strength was only 1,548 ... a very small force to handle an estimated 13–16,000 heavily armed guerrillas, but it was intentionally so to demonstrate that it was only there to supervise and not to become another faction in the war. There were twenty rendezvous points, from which the guerrillas were to be fed to sixteen assembly point camps. There they were to remain fully armed and so a threat to the Monitoring Force which certainly could not contain them if there was an absence of goodwill. ... They had no way of knowing whether or not they would be murdered in cold blood. It would require only one man to lose his nerve and a whole rendezvous party might be massacred. It is a tribute to members of the Force that its discipline, determination and good sense carried them over the difficult first hurdle of making contact with the guerrillas without any disasters.
>
> (*Withdrawal from Empire,* General Jackson)

The Regiment provided one of the Monitoring Teams – thirteen NCOs led by Major CA Le Hardy. After the first few weeks he wrote:

> ... Our task on the face of it was a very simple one. Travel 200 miles into the bush, stick up a large sign saying 'CEASE FIRE

Wimbish 1979–82

ASSEMBLY PLACE' and wait for the gooks/terrorists/Comrades of the Patriotic Front and then occupy them for two months! In reality it is proving to be an immensely difficult one. The majority of the PF [Patriotic Front] have had little else but the guerrilla life since age fifteen or sixteen or before. We have to maintain an uneasy balance between the relaxed, friendly, open, neutral and the highly alert soldier on operations. . . . *

On 27 December they moved out of the transit camp from 'the sight and sound of the entire World's Press Corps' to a 'wild, savage country in which survival is a major part of daily life'. They spent an uneasy first night with their PF Liaison Officers.

At 2100 hours a massive fire fight started around a village called Hoya which was two kms from us: mortars, heavy and light machine guns and rifles. This went on for twenty minutes by which time the police had deployed to the scene and the firing ceased. At 0500 hrs on 28 December we moved into the bush in a convoy of a Puki (mine-detector), and two Crocodiles (mine proof vehicles), two 4-tonners of stores and six Landrovers. . . . the column had the first contact of the operation. The Puki stopped at a suspect mine and as the police were clearing either side of the track they contacted three/four PF moving towards the track. It is difficult to say who fired first, the police or the PF. However a swift exchange of fire took place. All our group held fire and there were no casualties on either side.

By mid-day we had reached our Assembly place . . . Just before last light at 1845 hrs, we were confronted with our second 'first' for the Regiment on this operation. Fifty PF appeared in line abreast advancing on our position. Fortunately I had persuaded our LO,* who had shown me some PF posters, to put out a selection of these with the words 'PFLO with British Troops' on each one. This proved quite fortuitous as the leader told me that he had decided to attack us. He had seen the white crosses, the Union Jack, and our white skins; presumed we might be British, but decided to attack us in any case because he thought it was a trick. However on his way he had seen the posters and decided to make contact first.

With none of this knowledge we stood-to quietly and quickly when we first spotted them and I went out with the PFLO to

---

* Liaison Officer.

† Copies of Major Le Hardy's regular reports back to the Regiment were passed by Lieutenant Colonel Stephen to a relative of his, Mr Whitelaw the Home Secretary, who used them for briefing the Cabinet.

make contact, not really knowing what was going to happen next. It was with a great sense of relief from all of us that we witnessed a great reunion of the PFLO with his comrades. We doled out cigarettes and food to the 100 or so who appeared before the 'Cease Fire' at midnight and packed them off down the hill.

... I had under command two RV point teams, both from 1 RHA, and between us we coordinated, contacted local leaders, and arranged the transportation and reception of 1,200 PF into this location.... It became apparent early on that the PF had received strict orders about observation of the ceasefire and were determined to obey them. What had been badly under-estimated was the time that it would take for them to contact all their detachments, platoons and sectors ... Each sub-unit operates largely in a vacuum from each other once they have received orders from the sector commanders. They seemed to us to have either not received detailed orders or would not trust them. It was this difficulty that brought a senior commander, called Morgan, here to explain his problem.

I despatched him with Sergeant Lawson and Corporal Drewery on the afternoon of 31 December to make contact with the local leaders to give them instructions.

After a long trek their Landrover hit a land mine, but its mine-proofing probably saved their lives. The mine went up under the front right hand side wheel and Corporal Drewery, the driver, suffered major fractures to his legs.

... Sergeant Lawson remained very cool despite being badly shaken, found the radio equipment – the aerial had been blown off – and having re-tuned, established communications. He then tended to both Corporal Drewery and the injured PF commander before the arrival of the helicopter...

Subsequent stages of the operation:

... were hardly less hazardous and were made much more difficult by the logistic problems of having to provide food, tentage and transport at the assembly point camps. There was little available locally and the Rhodesian security forces were not prepared to provide anything from their own stocks. (*Withdrawal from Empire*)

Major Le Hardy's account continues:

The PF arrived here with nothing but the clothes they stand up in, most which are ragged, their personal weapons, a few magazines of ammo, and two grenades each. The Monitoring

Omagh 1977–79

26. Vehicle check point during the follow up to the murder of Sgt Eaglesham UDR near Rock.

27. After effect of 800 lb landmine exploded in culvert.

28. SSM Cross serves Christmas lunch at St Angelo.

29. Past and present in Wimbish 1979.

30. 1980 Queen's Birthday parade at Episkopi – Lt Alden and Cpl Ackroyd.

Wimbish 1979–82

organisation is now faced with supplying tentage, clothing, food, water storage facilities, cooking utensils etc, etc. This is all in an open area of bush which has nothing except a pumped water supply and a few old concrete latrines. The Commonwealth Monitoring Group is therefore the sole provider for two armies of 20,000 [adherents of Mugabe and Nkomo] and ourselves. All our tentage has been air-dropped or parachuted in and the food largely arrives by road now. . . .

    We seem to live from day to day on a suspected powder keg. The senior PF commander is unpredictable and volatile. I suspect that he is sending men out of the area to continue his contact with 'the masses' and because the Assembly Area is large we cannot monitor movements at night accurately. . . . The ceasefire held quite well for the first seven days, but since then there have been a number of incidents which threaten to destroy it. We had our own forewarning yesterday when one of our groups of PF left our camp 48 hours ago and were killed in a contact with Rhodesian forces 25 kms away. I had the grisly task of identifying them at the police station. . . . (Major Le Hardy)

    In the end 22,100 guerrillas together with some 35,000 refugees arrived in the camps. When the time limit for assembly was reached, after several postponements, the situation became dangerously tense. The Rhodesian security forces started to round up and, if need be, kill those guerrillas who had avoided entering the camps. Those already in the camps had the Monitoring Force at their mercy. Such confidence had been established between the Monitoring teams and the guerrillas in the camps that no attempt was made to use them as hostages. This was primarily due to the British soldiers' ability to strike up friendly relations with most people and to their sense of humour which diffuses most difficult situations. (*Withdrawal from Empire*)

The Monitoring Force was withdrawn after the general election at the end of February 1980, which installed President Mugabe in power in the new country of Zimbabwe. The Regiment's contingent was back in Wimbish by 3 March and Sergeant Lawson was awarded the British Empire Medal. Subsequently a British Military and Advisory Training Team was sent out to help build and train the new Zimbabwean Army, amalgamating elements of the former Rhodesian army with the guerrillas from the two factions of ZIPRA and ZANLU.

    Major PG Scrope joined the Team in early 1981. His task, assisted by an infantry Warrant Officer, was to extract over

History of The 13th/18th Royal Hussars (Q.M.O.)

1,000 ex-guerrillas from the Assembly Areas where the Monitoring Force had left them and form them into a new infantry battalion. Six months later he was able to say that it had been a most satisfying and fulfilling period, but it had obviously had some difficult moments:

> Problems which would be regarded as crises in the British Army had to be accepted as 'routine' occurrences. Unless one had the ability to laugh about these problems one was destined to become a nervous wreck.

13th/18th in the Falklands

A Task Force was sent by Britain to the Falklands in 1982 to recapture the islands after the Argentinian invasion. The small armoured reconnaissance element, two troops, was found by the Blues and Royals, but two representatives of the Regiment were also embroiled in Operation Corporate. Captain Shryane was on board RMS *Queen Elizabeth 2* as she sailed from Southampton on 12 May; he was a watch keeper in Headquarters 5 Infantry Brigade. In South Georgia, the Headquarters transhipped to SS *Canberra*, where Captain Shryane could introduce himself to the skipper, Captain Scott-Masson – father of 2nd Lieutenant PABG Scott-Masson. After initial uncertainty as to whether they were to be deployed, 5 Brigade found themselves very much involved and their battalions took part in the assaults on Mount Tumbledown and Mount William.

Major HJ Tyacke had been in a variety of air liaison appointments, with both the Navy and the Air Force, since his last Regimental job in 1965. Scheduled to be Ground Liaison Officer with the RAF Harriers, once an airstrip had been secured, he should have travelled aboard the container ship *Atlantic Conveyor*. Fortunately for him he was transferred to another ship as *Atlantic Conveyor* was sunk by an Argentinian missile. At 52, he was probably the oldest officer in the Task Force and was relieved to be able eventually to step ashore dry-shod in Port Stanley on the day victory was declared. His services and those of several hundred 'Battle Casualty Replacements' on the same ship had, in the event, not been required.

Wimbish 1979–82

The Freedom of Barnsley
Since the acquisition of South Yorkshire as recruiting area, Barnsley had produced a steady flow of recruits. The town itself embodies the spirit of South Yorkshire and the Regiment felt particularly honoured when the Council proposed in 1977 that the links should be formalised by the grant of the Freedom of the Borough. The Freedom Parade was to take place after the return from Ireland, in September 1979.

> No one could have envisaged how difficult the preparations were to be. It appeared that outside agencies were intent on frustrating our efforts to prepare for the event.

In the weeks beforehand, C Squadron was on troop training in Wales, B Squadron was on security duties and the Band was playing in the London Parks. However, the Household Cavalry Mounted Regiment provided ten troop horses on long loan and the airfield was marked out to look like the centre of Barnsley. Volunteers for a horsed troop came from people who had never ridden before, including Squadron Sergeant Major SP Davies and Staff Sergeant TC Atkinson. To the enjoyment of the inhabitants they 'clattered in and out of Saffron Walden'.

Landrovers and soldiers had to simulate Scimitars and Scorpions, but the Guidon Party and vehicle drivers were able to practise the various manoeuvres on the airfield runways. Three days before the parade the Regiment finally assembled at a barracks outside Sheffield; C Squadron from Wales, B Squadron from Windsor, the Band from London, Headquarters Squadron and RHQ from Essex. They were joined by a troop of the Yorkshire Squadron, Queen's Own Yeomanry. With no opportunity for final rehearsal they drove from Sheffield to Barnsley in the small hours of 28 September ('much to the annoyance of one local councillor who said that the Regiment would never be given the Freedom of Sheffield!'). The vehicles, Fox, Scimitar and Scorpion, lined up facing the Town Hall and 'Barnsley Town Centre began to take on a new shape'.

After the formal granting of the Freedom at a special meeting of the Borough Council, the Mayor, Councillor Harry Fish, made a speech from a dais at the front of the Town Hall. The Colonel of the Regiment, Major General Watson, having accepted the scroll of honorary Freedom, replied on behalf of the Regiment. Then followed a Mayoral inspection of the Parade; the Commanding Officer and Adjutant mounted their horses and led the Guidon Party, 'resplendent in the autumn sunshine' past the saluting base. 'The horses and with them the echoes of the past* having departed from parade, the Regiment took to the vehicles. A single word of command and the engines rumbled into life. The drivers now had to execute a right turn as they moved up the hill and away from the Town Hall.' After manoeuvring into position so that they faced back down the main street, Regimental Headquarters and C Squadron drove past in their wheeled vehicles, followed by B Squadron who:

> ... roared past at high speed as the tracks of their Scimitars and Scorpions reverberated in the narrow confines of the town's Main Street. . . . It was an impressive moment which was enjoyed both by the old soldiers sitting with the official party and the general public who had turned out in considerable numbers to line the streets.

That was followed by a 'superb lunch for the Regiment, laid on by Barnsley Council' at which the deeds of Freedom in a silver casket were presented and the Regiment in return presented a pair of bronze figures, one in 1922 full dress and one in Northern Ireland uniform, mounted on a single plinth.

Distinguished Visitors
The Wimbish tour would have been remarkable, if for nothing else, for the notabilities amongst visitors to the Regiment. The scene was set in the early days, while 'the new barracks inevitably aroused considerable interest, . . . we have had a flood of visitors', including the Permanent Under Secretary and the Quartermaster General from the Ministry of Defence.

6 August 1980 was the thirty-sixth anniversary of a major Second World War Battle Honour, the capture of Mont Pinçon in Normandy by two troops and Squadron Headquarters of A Squadron.

> To commemorate the day and to brief serving members of the Regiment on how one of our more recent battle honours was won, those 'survivors' who could be contacted were invited to spend a day back in the Regiment.

---

* Another 'echo of the past' had been provided by the appearance of the Band in hussar full dress – 'the first time for as long as anyone can remember'.

Wimbish 1979–82

The occasion had been prompted by the gift from Captain DP Hunt (1944-47) of his painting of the action. Amongst the eighteen survivors of the action present were the Squadron Leader in 1944, Major General DB Wormald, and the Squadron Second-in-Command, Major NNM Denny.

Two of the allied regiments, the 4ème Chasseurs d'Afrique and the Royal Canadian Hussars, sent visitors during the three years as did the French 10ème Hussars and 12ème Chasseurs. Other overseas guests came from the Armies of Germany, Singapore, Spain, United States and Zimbabwe, the Malaysian Armoured Corps and the Botswana Defence Force.

Carver Barracks was the venue in May 1981 for a Festival of the Disabled, attended by HRH Princess Alexandra.

> None of us could fail to be deeply moved at the spirit and good humour of so many physically handicapped people of all ages, many of whom had the most appalling disabilities. [Hundreds of letters of appreciation were received afterwards] . . . all of which heaped praise on the quite outstanding way every member of the Regiment responded to the occasion . . . Much of the credit for this successful day must go to the Regimental Sergeant Major, Mr G Smith, who coped admirably with all the problems, not least of which was a turn-out of approximately 2,000 people.

Princess Alexandra was the forerunner of other royal visitors, HM King Hussein of Jordan with Queen Noor, and HM King Constantine, the exiled Greek monarch. (Overheard in the Orderly Room beforehand: 'I have an incoming call for you, Colonel – it's from a firm called "King Constantine" '.)

Appropriately enough, the occasion for the Jordanian visit was a Regimental Families' Weekend in July 1982. In March of that year 2nd Lieutenant Prince Abdullah, the King's eldest son, had come to the Regiment from Sandhurst, to spend four months as a troop leader in A Squadron. King Hussein took the salute at the Parade and 'despite the rather dull weather, it was a most happy and successful day and a real family occasion. His Majesty King Hussein appeared very touched by the warm welcome he received and this was evident in the most

---

* On the fifty-second anniversary of the battle, in 1996, the Regimental Memorial on Mont Pinçon was to be dedicated, to all those who served in the 13th/18th Royal Hussars between 1922 and 1992 see p viii.

moving speech he gave to the Regiment on parade.' His son had made a great impression during his short stay, both for his qualities as a practical soldier ('nowhere more evident than on the ranges at Castlemartin') and his sense of humour.

Accompanying the Prince throughout his time at Wimbish were 'two large detectives and an unruly Alsatian'. One of the bodyguard, Detective Constable Egerton from the Essex police, gave the *Journal* his own impressions of life in the Army:

> . . . The first shock was the haircut, of course. Used to wearing mine a bit longer than my uniformed colleagues, it was a chilly experience to get my hair short enough to fit under a beret. The second was the uniform issue. I always thought that the fictional parodies of the Army Stores were greatly exaggerated . . . There are many images which I recall as I think of my weeks with the 13th/18th Hussars, but the overwhelming impression is one of intense professionalism and an almost family-like relationship between all members of the Regiment.

In April 1982, Field Marshal The Lord Carver attended an Officers' Mess Guest Night and the following day looked round the camp which had been named after him. He also spoke to all the Senior Ranks about his views on the use of reconnaissance: 'We found him to be in great heart, full of anecdotes and practical ideas . . .'.

At this stage, Regimental finances were distinctly straitened. The funds accumulated during the tour in Ireland had been used, albeit to good effect, during the initial settling in at Wimbish, and with much of the Regiment frequently away there was little coming into PRI funds. Lieutenant Colonel ffrench Blake instigated monthly payments into a Guidon Fund, so that the eventual presentation of a new Guidon could be properly marked.

Overseas Expeditions

In June 1980 a close reconnaissance troop from C Squadron flew to Canada for five weeks on one of a series of exercises named Pond Jump West. They were attached to a battle group, based on 3rd Queen's, which trained over the 'huge' exercise area at Fort Wainwright, Alberta. Led by Lieutenant J Scruby and mounted in Landrovers they had ten days troop training and then took part in a five day battle group exercise. 'Not all of

Wimbish 1979–82

this proved to be in idyllic sunshine as there were cold nights and monsoon-like thunderstorms. Other natural phenomena include the 24-hour-a-day mosquitoes that had limitless appetites for good Yorkshire blood.' After the tactical training, interrupted by a visit to the Wainwright Stampede, there followed a great variety of 'superbly organised adventurous training', including walking, climbing, snow climbing, canoeing and pony trekking in the Rockies. In 1981 it was the turn of a troop from A Squadron led by Lieutenant JW Prince-Smith. They went out with 3rd Parachute Regiment and spent much of the time dismounted because of a shortage of Landrovers.

As a prelude to a training advisory team going to Thailand, in 1980 Lieutenant Colonel Stephen and Captain WG Peto visited Saraburi – the Thai Armoured Corps Centre. En route they visited an allied regiment, 2nd Federation Reconnaissance Regiment of Malaysia and also met Lieutenant General Dato Zain Hashim who was in the original Squadron raised by the 13th/18th in 1952. Captain Peto wrote: 'It is difficult to sum up succinctly the four days we had in Malaysia, but perhaps the single word "Hospitality" will do'. In Thailand they were joined by Captain R Lang and a REME officer. The next fortnight 'passed in a blur of visits, discussions and lunches'. The four-man team itself spent ten weeks in 1981 at the Thai Cavalry Centre, introducing the Thais to Scorpions. Writing afterwards in the *Journal*, WO2 J Morgan reported that the course culminated in demonstrations by the students, of their recently acquired D&M and gunnery skills. 'The students made us very pleased by doing everything right and achieving many first and second round hits with the 76mm. It was then presentation and party time . . . .'

In view of the Regiment's Royal link it was not surprising that two of the expeditions were to Jordan. Major Selfe with three other officers were guests of the Jordanian Armed Forces, visiting their three armoured divisions under the guidance of Prince Abdullah, before a holiday in Aqaba. The other trip was classified as 'adventure training', but 5th Troop A Squadron had a remarkable week in the hands of their previous Troop Leader. Starting with two days in a luxury hotel during which their briefing was conducted 'around an enormous banqueting table, eating from silver dishes and being waited on hand and foot by an army of waiters, while a string quartet imported from Europe played Strauss waltzes', there followed visits to the Jordanian Special Forces School and the Prince's own regiment (1st Battalion Mechanised Infantry). Then to the desert for 'some soldiering', as the Prince put it, in Range Rovers and a luxury bus (' . . . 4-tonners will never be quite the same again!'). After a 'hot, dusty and hilly' walk through the hills of the Wadi Ruam desert training area came a desert lunch when three crates of live chickens and sheep appeared. The exercise continued in Ferrets and Landrovers, before two days relaxation on the beach at Aqaba.

> After all that we were ready to return to normal life, but no, four ambulances and two fire engines transported us back to the plane with sirens going and lights flashing. Prince Abdullah gave us a truly 'royal' send off.

Sport from Wimbish

Not surprisingly, a Regiment with often two squadrons away was unable to achieve any major successes on the sporting scene. However, north west Essex provided a number of opportunities which were not lost.

Despite having only one tennis court in the early stages at Carver Barracks, the Regimental team had a successful season in 1979, winning the Eastern District finals of the Army Championships and a semi-final match against the North East District champions, before being beaten in the final. Subsequent years at Wimbish were disappointing from the cup winning point of view, but when four courts were available there was some keen inter-squadron competition.

The cricketers had no pitch at all on which to train before they started competitive games and did well in 1979 to reach the quarter-finals of the Army Cup. There was still no playable wicket for the rest of the tour, and in both 1981 and in 1982 the team's best achievement was runner-up in the Eastern District Cup. However the team Captain, Captain AREdeC Stewart, played forty-three days of cricket for the respective teams of the Royal Armoured Corps, Army and Combined Services.

By 1980–81 the football team was showing more form than in recent years, reaching the fourth round in the Army Cup and

Wimbish 1979–82

performing well in two local leagues, winning the Cadastrian League (mainly Army and RAF units) for two seasons running. The Cavalry Cup, however, remained far out of reach.

One asset already *in situ* at Carver Barracks was a squash court and a lot of use was made of it. The Regimental Team had some successes in 1979–80, doing well in both the Eastern District Inter Unit and Soldier Magazine competitions.

Hunting from Wimbish was in the Puckeridge and Thurlow country, 'not as flat and featureless as people who do not know the area so often imagine', and several officers and wives were able to enjoy good sport. To accommodate the horses the officers' mess garages were converted into 'ten good boxes, by the simple expedient of cutting the doors in half'. Good relations with the Puckeridge were cemented with the Regiment sponsoring their Hunt Ball in 1980-81. There were some 'very good local days, more often noted for speed and distance rather than for leaping much timber . . .'. There was an interesting reaction from Lieutenant Amiot of the French 8ème Hussars when he went out, during a three week attachment to the Regiment. 'He expressed great surprise at what he described as *toujours beaucoup de mouvement*.'

Shooting in East Anglia was of course a great attraction and a gun was kept on Lord Cobbold's estate at Knebworth as well as several half guns on Stanford Training Area. The game book's pages over the period showed the numbers taking part and their success – both well above average for the Regiment.

Also more or less on the doorstep was high quality fly fishing on the River Wissey, 'a little known river of great charm which flows through the Thetford Training Area'.

Skiing expeditions set off each winter and in 1980–81 the Regiment secured third place in the Giant Slalom at the UK Land Forces Championships and second in the Slalom.

Most of the officers who played polo seemed to find their way to Cyprus, but an excellent polo ground was created at Wimbish. It was to be the main ground for the Cambridge University and Silver Leys Clubs as well as any Regimental team that could be got together. By 1982 it was possible for the first time for four years to enter a team for the Captains and Subalterns Cup, albeit one which was knocked out in the first round.

History of The 13th/18th Royal Hussars (Q.M.O.)

Combining three field sports, two Regimental teams took part in a number of Triathlon competitions featuring tests of horsemanship, clay pigeon shooting and fly casting.

Sailing as adventure training was an excellent combination and in 1980 the Regiment secured one of the legs of an eight-leg exercise cruise organised by the Joint Services Sailing Centre, to and from Cyprus. The boat was the 25 ton *Kukri*, a Sail Training Yacht, and the Regiment's crew had the first leg of her return journey, from Cyprus to Sardinia. With a retired officer on board who was the permanent skipper, the Regimental crew was led by Major AJN Collis with two other majors, four captains, one lieutenant, one corporal and three troopers.

The best individual achievement in sport during the period was the remarkable performance over a four year period of Lance Corporal T Haddon in Modern Pentathlon. During that time he progressed from being 'a promising junior' to representing Great Britain at senior level. In 1981 he won the Army Junior Pentathlon Competition; the following year he represented Great Britain in an international competition in Holland and came fourteenth. He was awarded his Army colours and then Combined Services Colours after coming fourth overall in the Inter Services Championship. The 1982 season ended with his representing the Army in the British Open Championships.

Sport in Cyprus
From its 110 all ranks, A Squadron fielded teams in football (two), hockey, cricket, cross country running, squash, rugger, tug of war and pistol shooting. Middle-ranking in most of the leagues, the Squadron A Team at football was much higher in the Major and Minor Units League than a number of major units, with upwards of a 1,000 men. This was largely to the credit of the veteran Regimental player, Staff Sergeant WD Simpson.

Like A Squadron, C Squadron entered teams in every competition on offer, sporting and military. 'Real giant-killing feats' were achieved on the cricket field against major units and the squadron produced five members of the Army Cyprus cricket team which was captained by Major Yorke. The Squadron hosted a tour to the island by the Fantasians, a

Wimbish 1979–82

wandering club made up of ex-Royal Armoured Corps officers which had been founded by Mr AR Wright (served in the Regiment 1966–72, a son of Lt Col ERMcM Wright).

Another Sail Training Yacht, *British Soldier*, provided a seventeen day cruise in September 1981 for a number of the Regiment from Cyprus. The skipper was again Major Collis, with four other members of C Squadron and one from B – the remainder of the crew were from other units on the island.

> The whole trip was an invaluable and exciting experience. The satisfaction for the crew of being able to work the boat and come back severely tanned and fit, having visited thirteen different ports and anchorages on a voyage covering almost 1,000 miles, was a once-in-a-lifetime opportunity.

The highlight for the polo players was a visit to Cyprus in November 1981 by the Royal Jordan Polo Club. After a week of club matches, an international match was attended by 'representatives of the entire island, including the British High Commissioner . . . '.

Farewell to Wimbish

Handing over to the 1st Queen's Dragoon Guards in November 1982 brought the stay at Wimbish to an end.

'We will leave behind us in Essex many happy memories and a lot of friends in Essex, all of whom have contributed to making our tour there such a special one', wrote Lieutenant Colonel ffrench Blake as the Regiment collected itself for the move to Germany. 'Perhaps the final paragraph in the Wimbish Parish Magazine epitomizes the relationship we established':

> We wish the 13th/18th Godspeed and a happy stay in Germany. We shall retain many good memories of their presence and, because several of the men demonstrated their good taste by marrying some of our daughters, there will be many lasting relationships. Carver Barracks has become an important element in our community. The Hussars have made it a pleasure.'

History of The 13th/18th Royal Hussars (Q.M.O.)

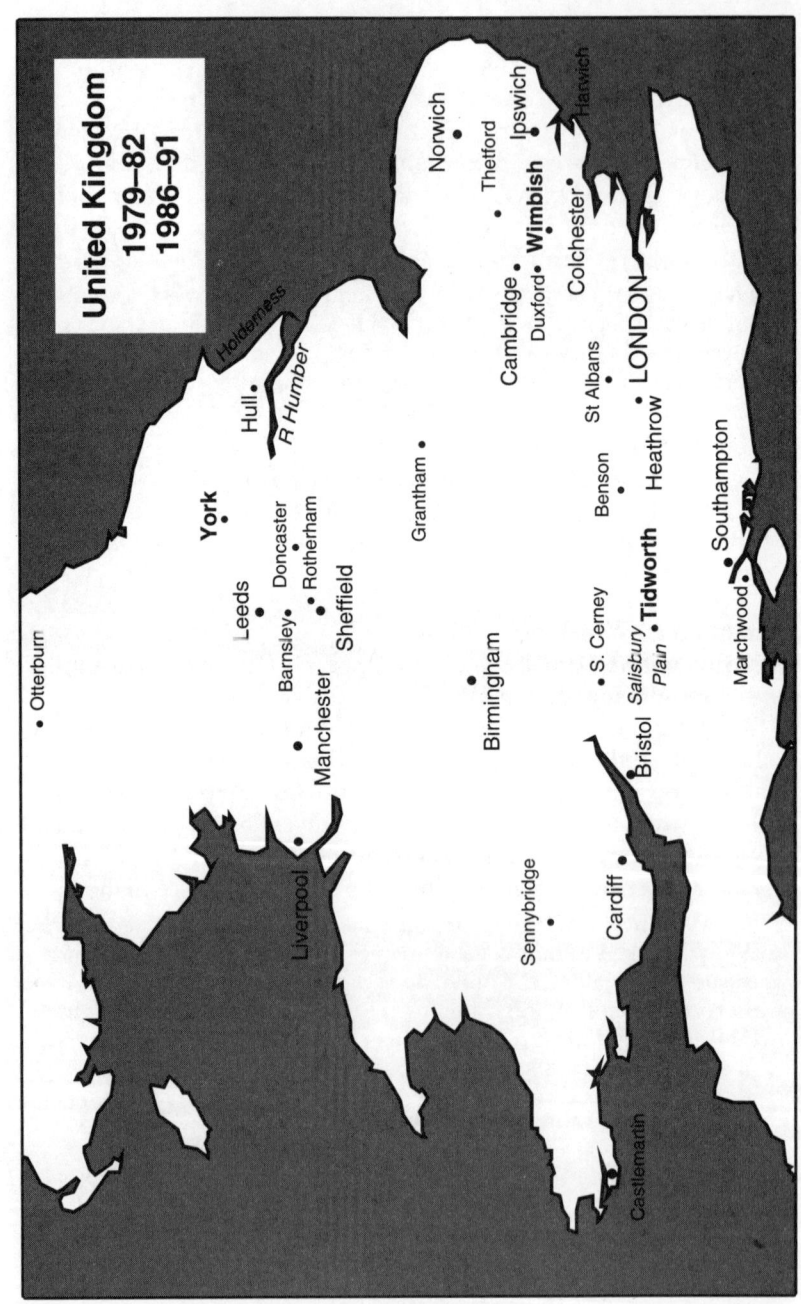

Chapter Sixteen

Herford 1982–86

Back to Germany
Another tour, in another Rhine Army station, began in November 1982. The new station was in the attractive small town of Herford. Harewood Barracks was an ideal home for an armoured reconnaissance regiment. Well-built and compact, the Officers' and Sergeants' Messes were next door to each other, and inside the perimeter, with soldiers' blocks and Regimental Headquarters on the opposite side of the road. The Regiment did not have to share with anyone else and the town centre was within five minutes walk. One drawback was the antiquated feeding arrangements. For the first six months all meals had to be eaten in a disused hangar while modernisation was completed. 'It was a race between the soldiers and the cockroaches to get to the food first.' (Major General Cordy-Simpson)

Since conversion there had been little opportunity fully to practise armoured reconnaissance skills. Only one squadron had been equipped with CVR(T) and there had been little more 'combined' training for the others than providing close reconnaissance for lorry-borne infantry. There had been no support troops on the establishment.

There were no regrets when responsibility for providing close reconnaissance for infantry battalions was relinquished in 1983. The unloved Fox armoured cars went to the infantry and Scorpions to the close reconnaissance troops of armoured regiments. Now there were four similarly manned and equipped sabre squadrons. Each had four medium reconnaissance troops, equipped with Scimitar, a support troop mounted in Spartans and a guided weapons troop in another of the CVR (T) series, Striker. The latter marked the return to the Royal Armoured Corps, from the Royal Artillery, of responsibility for the Swingfire anti-tank missile guided weapon.

History of The 13th/18th Royal Hussars (Q.M.O.)

Operational Role
The two armoured reconnaissance regiments in Germany were initially under operational command of Headquarters Royal Armoured Corps of 1(BR) Corps. (HQ RAC was based with Corps Headquarters at Bielefeld, about fifteen miles from Herford.) Later the Regiment transferred to operational command of Headquarters 4 Armoured Division, also in Herford, under whom they already came for administration.

Operational plans had not changed materially since the Regiment was last in Germany. 1 (BR) Corps still sat astride the most likely axis for an attack by the Soviet Third Shock Army across the Hannover plain. However, a realisation that a battle of attrition could not be won meant that there was now a more aggressive and cohesive Army Group plan, involving the use of powerful armoured reserves. The 13th/18th would have played a key part in providing the Corps Commander with the intelligence on which to determine when to launch the reserves. It called for a high degree of professional competence.

The Regiment's initial deployment would have been close to the Inner German Border, ready to report the first 'hostile act'. Little had changed in nearly forty years, their area in the Harz included places with which the Regiment had been familiar, first in 1945 and then in 1953. A Squadron would have been in Bad Harzburg, B Squadron in Vienenberg, C Squadron just south of Bad Harzburg and D Squadron even deeper into the Harz mountains. Regimental Headquarters was destined for the same building in which RHQ had been housed in 1945 – now a lunatic asylum.

With their special knowledge of the area, a peacetime task from time to time was for a troop from the reconnaissance regiments to patrol the Inner German Border, largely in order to 'fly the flag'. These border patrols could be conducted only by British or American troops; they were always fascinating and those who had not previously seen the Border found it a sobering experience. Each was accompanied by a member of the British Frontier Service, as in many areas the boundary fence could be up to a kilometre from the actual border and there was a risk of straying across it. Both sides viewed the other silently across the fence. No recognition of the other's presence was

Herford 1982–86

permitted; they just watched each other and reported.

Another task was to provide about once a year a guard force at the 'Special Ammunition Site' at Sennelager. 'The US Army is the custodian of the contents, and it provided an interesting insight into the handling of this topical subject; it was, in their jargon, very procedural.' However, to get it wrong was a quick way to end one's career.

Appointments and a new Squadron

In August 1983, shortly after the Regiment's arrival, Lieutenant Colonel RA Cordy-Simpson took over from Lieutenant Colonel ffrench Blake. Like his predecessor, the new commanding officer was the son of a former officer in the Regiment; his father had commanded during the first tour in Malaya. He was to command for much of the tour at Herford, before handing over to Lieutenant Colonel EL Yorke in April 1986.

The early part of 1984 was spent in establishing the new sabre Squadron, D, which was subjected to a miscellany of squadron leaders in its first year. First Major PG Scrope and then Major WA Shuttleworth decided that civilian life beckoned too strongly to resist and by the end of the year Major AD Coker (son of Lt Col DHE Coker) had taken over.

A Squadron had lost Major JAMA Selfe to the staff in 1983 after only eighteen months; Major MB Brook filled the gap before Major RCB Nutting took over for two years. 1983 also saw Major K O'Sullivan hand over Headquarters Squadron to Major JP Gibson. (Of Major O'Sullivan, Lieutenant Colonel Cordy-Simpson said: 'Apart from being a fine Headquarters Squadron Leader, his main claim to fame will be that he was probably the most outstanding Regimental Families Officer that the Regiment had ever had.' He had been commissioned in 1974 after joining the Regiment as a National Service trooper in 1949.)

In 1984 Major AL Mallinson handed over B Squadron to Major NS Southward. (Major Mallinson had transferred to the Regiment in 1982 having helped with Northern Ireland training in 1975 as an infantryman.) Major RNB Quicke took over C Squadron from Major EL Yorke.

History of The 13th/18th Royal Hussars (Q.M.O.)

In 1985, WO1 SP Davies took over as Regimental Sergeant Major from WO1 H Cross. Nearly twenty years before, 2nd Lieutenant Cordy-Simpson and Trooper SP Davies '57 were in 2nd Troop B Squadron and in the same tank. Then they were Squadron Leader and Squadron Sergeant Major together in Cyprus. 'There was not much that they did not know about each other's past.' Otherwise 1985 passed without major change, but that meant of course that there was a bumper crop in 1986. All the sabre squadrons had new leaders: Major WG Peto in A, Major MB Brook in B, Major MP Colacicchi in C and, on arrival in Tidworth, Major AREdeC Stewart in D.

To provide the additional manpower needed to create D Squadron, each of A, B and C Squadrons had to submit their troop nominal rolls to the Commanding Officer. On 1 January 1984 he announced which complete troops would transfer to the new squadron. All squadron accounts were frozen and a quarter transferred to an account for D Squadron.

> Whilst it could not be called a democratic process, it did ensure that the new squadron started on an equal footing and that sabre troops remained intact. D Squadron was able speedily to establish its own identity. (Major General Cordy-Simpson)

Prison Guard Force

Ten weeks of 1985 were to be spent by 135 members of the Regiment as the Prison Guard Force at HM Prison Maze in Northern Ireland. It was thirteen years since the first Operation Banner tour; for most of them it would be their first experience of the role. B Squadron was augmented for the purpose by people from all the other squadrons. The composite squadron came together in July for the rigorous preliminary training at Sennelager, after which the tour which began in September was:

> . . . difficult and frustrating. Our training had left us keyed up and ready for a very active role. The job itself can best be described as monotonous, something indeed of a drudgery. That in turn calls for its own resilience, particularly with regard to maintaining standards. In general people responded well, earning unsolicited praise from those with whom they came in contact; in particular 11 UDR with whom we patrolled (the major relief from the guard routine) . . .

Herford 1982–86

The 'PGF' Squadron Leader, Major NS Southward, summed up:

> A dull but important job properly carried out, and a valuable experience for all of those who went, particularly perhaps in terms of all that was learnt in the pre-tour training.

Exercises and Training

After nearly six years away from Germany many of the individual skills needed had become 'unfamiliar to the older members of the Regiment and new to the younger members'. Indoctrination began with three weeks hard troop and squadron training near Kassel, which coincided with one of the wettest periods of the year. 'Severe and testing troop tests' were won by a B Squadron troop led by Staff Sergeant SD Taylor. (The troop which won troop tests were known as the 'QMO Troop' and the cypher was emblazoned on their vehicles until the next tests.) The 18th Hussar Shield was also introduced, for the troop which achieved the highest score in individual skills such as shooting, NBC warfare, AFV recognition and first aid. Everybody in the Regiment from trooper to captain had to take part. After the troop tests came an ambitious exercise, Kollected Kanter; it was the first time that the Regiment had been able to train together in the field for more than five years.

Exercises normally stopped at weekends, if they were being conducted over open country, and the opportunity was sometimes taken of giving families a taste of alfresco life. On one Sunday during Kollected Kanter, lunch was provided by A Squadron for several wives and children.

> Among the passengers on the coach were three wives from the Royal Regiment of Wales who had unwittingly boarded the wrong coach. Sadly we felt unable to oblige their somewhat naive request to take them up to Soltau where their husbands were awaiting them, two hundred miles to the north.

Not having to practise with any main armament the support troops often went their separate ways during gunnery training and, in March 1984, those from A and B Squadrons took part in an Anglo-French exercise at Trier run by French commandos. On return they tackled the first of what were to be regular demands on their skills in preparing the course for Regimental Hunter Trials. They were also vulnerable to other detached tasks and in 1984 one troop spent ten days guarding Headquarters RAC: 'philosophically they put it all down to training experience, but would rather not do it again next year.'

In January 1985 when the Regiment deployed to the Harz Mountains, Exercise Winter Kanter was particularly testing. 'Both petrol and participants froze; temperatures of minus 22°C were not uncommon.' Much more agreeable was that year's Regimental exercise in the Mosel valley, demonstrating again the opportunities offered to a reconnaissance regiment. Meanwhile the Support Troops went off to what probably sounded more appealing than it turned out to be – training in Northern Italy as guests of the 1st Hussars of Milan in Udine. The journey down, which took 'twenty-seven tiring and hungry hours on goods trains, cattle trucks and milk runs', was still shorter than the thirty-eight hour return trip. A three-day exercise was held in an area round a dry river bed which was transformed the first evening by a monsoon type thunderstorm into a 'well and truly flooded river bed'.

Autumn Exercises

The earlier training and hard work were put to the test in the 1983 exercises: Grand Canyon and, a BAOR hardy annual, Eternal Triangle. In them 'we came of age as an armoured reconnaissance regiment. We learnt that fortune favours the brave and those with dash and initiative invariably make good armoured car soldiers. . . . In less than three weeks every one of our vehicles did something in the region of 800 miles, through all phases of war including long range penetration raids against enemy headquarters.' The raids were enjoyed by the troops selected for them, although they invariably infuriated those that they attacked and tempers often ran high. On Eternal Triangle a series of raids by A Squadron culminated in one on Headquarters 1 Division. An NCO masquerading as REME, 'managed to lift the complete trace for the final attack'. B Squadron were thanked by Commander 4 Armoured Brigade for their 'timely and accurate reporting' which had enabled the Brigade to complete their task three hours ahead of schedule – the compliment was appreciated the more 'when it was later revealed that the Squadron Leader [Major Mallinson] had slept through most of his 'O' Group'.

Herford 1982–86

Exercise Lionheart
In 1984 the whole of 1 (BR) Corps, fully reinforced from England, took part in Exercise Lionheart against an enemy of Dutch, Americans and Germans. (Familiar Regimental faces appeared amongst the reinforcements from the Territorial Army and the War Establishment Reserve.) One of the largest exercises staged by the British in Western Germany, it began with the Regiment deployed along the Inner German Border, watching the main approach routes and covering the deployment of the rest of the Corps; then it almost came abruptly to a halt.

During the overt patrolling phase C Squadron, led by Major RNB Quicke, was in a picturesque stretch just north of the Harz mountains. The sabre troops openly showed themselves in order to demonstrate to the 'invading hordes' that they were ready for them. Meanwhile the enemy, a German division supported by one American and one Dutch brigade, were moving to their initial positions to a plan carefully orchestrated not to conflict with the 13th/18th patrol areas. C Squadron Headquarters was 'tactically' sited in the *gasthof* of a small village well off the main routes. They were there for several days and the local people got to know the Squadron well. Regimental Headquarters warned that careful watch should be kept for covert enemy reconnaissance and, sure enough, early one morning an American patrol was apprehended. They apologised for their unfair play and were released after interrogation at Regimental Headquarters.

The coup inspired redoubling of the Squadron's efforts and their alertness was rewarded the same evening when a German staff car drove through the village, with steel-helmeted driver and an officer reading a map in the back seat. Lieutenant Amos' troop, including Trooper Denby, the largest man in the Regiment, descended on the car, removed the occupants and put to good effect the lessons learned by Mr Amos during a recent prisoner-handling course. When order was restored the German officer, his driver and the contents of his map and briefcases were firmly in Regimental hands. The shock for the officer was intensified by the accusations, from an elderly German woman onlooker, that he was letting down the German officer corps by letting himself be captured. He turned out to be a brigadier general and the Deputy Commander of the German division, who was having a sneak preview of the British position. Loss of face probably contributed to the vigour of his reaction; national pride was seriously dented and dire threats were issued to all and sundry, including Lieutenant Colonel Cordy-Simpson, who happened to be visiting.

The dire threats were followed through with an ultimatum from the German division: they would not participate further unless the whole of the offending unit was removed from the exercise order of battle. That was reduced to those who had taken part in the affair; the troop was put in close arrest, returned to Herford and incarcerated in a hangar. A field board of enquiry with both British and German officers was set up and everyone interrogated. That included, at C Squadron's insistence, the civilians who had been in the village square. They fully backed the Squadron account and, as the exercise drew to a close, the threats of courts martial receded. The troop was allowed to rejoin the exercise, but the Divisional Commander, Major General CJ Waters suggested to the Commanding Officer that they should probably not be deployed opposite the Germans again. 'It was a brave and characteristic decision by the GOC as others were still baying for blood.' (Major General Cordy-Simpson)

No apologies were received by the wretched members of C Squadron for the treatment with which their zeal had been rewarded and one of them sent an account to his father, Mr Wiles. Mr Wiles wrote to the Prime Minister, Mrs Thatcher, who ordered a ministerial enquiry which again exonerated the troop.

The exercise proper was a slow affair, so far as the Regiment was concerned, after a busy first few days in which: 'We were able during the night to establish exactly where and in what strength the enemy were crossing and what his intentions were. We were then able to extract ourselves without severe casualties.' Meanwhile Harewood Barracks was being used as a Field Hospital, with the hangars all converted to wards through which some 3,000 'casualties' were passed.

Herford 1982–86

In 1985 the major exercise was Quarter Final. The Northern Ireland commitment had taken away enough manpower to crew two and half sabre squadrons, but reinforcements from The Queen's Own Yeomanry and The Royal Yeomanry filled a number of gaps. It was an exercise which everybody enjoyed. They manoeuvred over huge distances and found gaps which they were able to exploit in the enemy's defences. Two troops of A Squadron were left hidden behind the enemy's lines and constantly harassed 7 and 11 Armoured Brigades' logistics, while C Squadron turned round all the enemy's tactical road signs prior to his advance, causing total chaos. It was a high point for the tour in Germany and the Regiment earned praise from all quarters.

By the autumn of 1986 the move to England was imminent and for Exercise Bold Guard the 13th/18th were called on only to provide enemy and umpire teams. One *Journal* comment was:

> Some may be forgiven for thinking the exercise was scripted by Walt Disney, but there were occasions when we felt that both our reputation and role were being abused by being asked to do tasks more appropriate to a bad episode from the 'A Team' [television programme]'.

Gunnery

Gunnery Camp in April 1983 led to 'a very creditable "B" grading' and some spectacular pictures of night firing by Scimitars were taken for an article in *Illustrated London News*. 1984 brought another 'B' and in 1985 'B+' was achieved. A similar standard of shooting was not always so evident with guided weapon firing. The Swingfire missile, each of which cost £7,000, often behaved extremely erratically. One even tried to launch itself with the missile bin down in the safe position inside the vehicle.

Two years later, during Regimental firing and a visit by Major General MF Hobbs, the Divisional Commander, a B Squadron Scimitar caught fire whilst 'bombed up'. The Scimitars were parked in line and, but for the 'courage and cool action' by Corporal E Bell and Lance Corporal WJ McKendrick, at least one Scimitar and maybe several others could have been destroyed. 'More importantly, thanks to them and others, notably the Squadron Sergeant Major [WO2 B Farmer], nobody was injured in an accident which could have been lethal.' Corporal Bell and Lance Corporal McKendrick were both awarded GOC's Commendations.

NCOs Cadres

The first Junior NCOs Cadre for a number of years was run in February 1983; those taking part probably remembered the cold as much anything else.

> On one memorable occasion it took the students twenty minutes to break through the ice on the swimming pool before taking the plunge.

Promotion to Lance Corporal could be achieved only by successful completion of the course, which was intended to test young soldiers to the full. The top students earned promotion immediately and were usually being considered for further promotion within eighteen months. The details of the Cadre in December 1983 show what was expected of a Junior NCO in the Regiment:

> The Course lasted three weeks, with only one afternoon and night as stand-down. For the rest of the time the thirty-six students lived in and worked together. Each day started with PT from 0615–0650. Showers and breakfast were squeezed in before the Cadre was inspected by their bed blocks at 0745 and the pressure was kept up until lights out at 2230 hours. The syllabus included:
>
> 23 periods drill
>
> 27 periods skill at arms, including teaching practices
>
> 10 periods fieldcraft and tactics
>
> 10 periods signals

Other activities ranged through milling, casualty handling, NBC and combat survival. The first exercise included a surprise period as a prisoner of war, navigation without map or compass from an uncertain start point to an emergency RV, killing and cooking the only meal of the exercise, swimming the Mittelandkanal during the night of gales and then abseiling from the Weser Aqueduct in Minden. The final exercise was a Corps reconnaissance role test in which the students filled every appointment in the three troops from gunner to Troop Leader. Twenty-four of the original thirty-six finished the Cadre in fine style.

Herford 1982–86

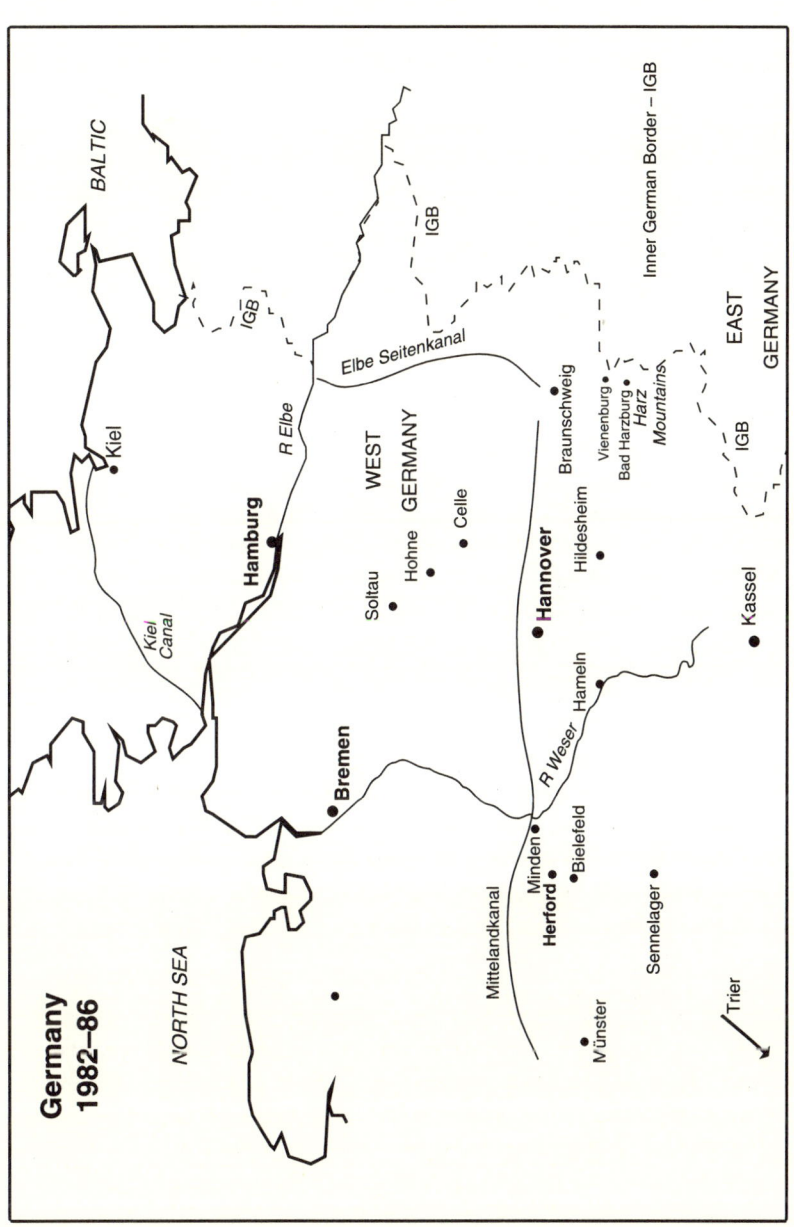

History of The 13th/18th Royal Hussars (Q.M.O.)

The successful formula was largely repeated in subsequent years, although in 1986 a mechanised exercise had to be foregone, partly because of track mileage restrictions, partly because it had proved difficult to monitor the candidates' performance; a disproportionate amount of damage had also been caused to both vehicles and scenery. A dismounted exercise in the Harz Mountains was held instead and the thirty soldiers, who completed every phase without injury, 'knew that they had overcome a considerable challenge'.

Another qualification for promotion was passing the Basic Fitness Test (BFT). Since the early 1970s completion of the Test twice a year had been expected, but the Regiment's performance had not been good; there had been a 14 per cent failure rate on first arrival in Germany. 'Far too many soldiers considered the Basic Fitness Test something to be taken only when all excuses to avoid it had failed' (Lieutenant Colonel Cordy-Simpson). The pass rate was transformed to a 100 per cent – and the Regiment achieved the second fastest time in BAOR in the Tickel Trophy, in which a random selection of a unit was made to complete a BFT. (The 'random' selection had to include a lieutenant colonel; this meant that the Commanding Officer always had to make an appearance!)

Boeselager Competition

In 1984 the Regiment represented Britain in the Boeselager Reconnaissance Competition run by the Germans for all NATO nations and competed for extremely seriously. The first contest had been in 1971, when armoured reconnaissance battalions of the Bundeswehr and guest teams from other nations competed for a cup named after Colonel George Freiherr von Boeselager.* In 1984, as well as the ten Bundeswehr teams, there were ten teams competing from eight other NATO nations. Each consisted of nine men and one reserve who had to complete eight 'stations': an armoured reconnaissance patrol course of about twenty-five kilometres in three hours, a helicopter reconnaissance, small arms firing, a three and half kilometre run (including crossing the Elbe Seiten Kanal, a testing assault

---

* A gifted German cavalry commander of the Second World War who died, aged 29, leading his brigade on the Eastern Front.

course and throwing hand grenades), a tactical swim across the canal with 35 kilo packs and weapons, AFV recognition, a driving skills course and an 'extremely demanding' night orienteering march covering numerous stands over a twenty kilometre course across difficult country.

After weeks of intensive training the Regimental team, led by Staff Sergeant SD Taylor, achieved only seventh place amongst the guest competitors and fifteenth overall in 1984, but a 'massive amount of experience' for the future. That obviously paid off in 1985 when, led by Lieutenant JW Prince-Smith, the team picked from an an original squad of eighteen came third overall in the *Ausländer* competition. 1986 saw that improved to second amongst the *Ausländer* – to the 9th/12th Lancers. They finished first overall with the Regiment fourth. By this time, the team leader was Lieutenant ADC Ibbotson, whose troop had won the troop tests in 1985.

Sport

The price of acquiring the individual and collective skills needed for an armoured reconnaissance regiment in Germany was paid on the sports field:

> Although we have played plenty of sports, there has been little time to put together strong Regimental teams. Troops, and particularly our close recce troops, have been away here, there and everywhere, and have been unable to participate in much of our sporting activity. In addition, as a result of our long period both in Northern Ireland and the split between Cyprus and Wimbish, much of our expertise has disappeared.

Compulsory sports and hobbies were instituted by Lieutenant Colonel Cordy-Simpson on Thursday afternoons. Every soldier had to join a club and remain with it for at least six months.

> Every sport was catered for: rugby, soccer, cricket, hockey, squash, tennis, volley-ball, badminton, basketball, boxing, judo, weight lifting, swimming, ten pin bowling, archery, tug-of-war, riding, small bore shooting, canoeing, clay pigeon shooting, table tennis, climbing, fencing, parachuting, board and dinghy sailing.

Each sport or hobby had an officer or senior NCO who was responsible for organising it and for providing the instruction, or finding the instruction – from outside the Regiment if necessary. Over the next two years the Regiment's success in mastering its military role was matched by a number of sporting achievements.

Football at Regimental level had been in the doldrums for some years, but a determined effort to get back amongst the leaders in 1984–85 saw the Regiment reach the Divisional Final and, for the first time in many years, the BAOR final of the Cavalry Cup. The second round of the Army Cup, also not achieved 'for a very long time' was reached in 1986–87, but in that season no advance was made beyond the first round of the Cavalry Cup.

Equitation in Herford started at a disadvantage, with the stables in 'someone else's barracks'. For the first year not only did most of the work fall on wives, but they 'carried the colours well in both competition and hunting field'. Mrs Selfe won the Combined Training Trophy at the Herford Show and Mrs Mallinson won the Dressage Phase at the Rhine Army Summer Show. The Regimental Hunter Trials, in April 1983, were held on the Bückeburg Training Area near Minden – 'a superb piece of galloping country'. A hundred entries, including some twenty German owned and ridden horses, completed a testing course in five events. The following year there were some 145 entrants, including about thirty Germans and a second event in November 1984 saw a similar entry. The expertise in both course-building and organisation was such that in May 1985 a combined one-day event and hunter trials was mounted.

Drag-hunting was pursued with both the Weser Vale pack of bloodhounds (run by the Household Cavalry from Detmold) and several local packs. A racehorse, Bossy, was presented to the Regiment by Major WG Denney (1944-60) and run by a Regimental syndicate. She started with lots of promise, winning a maiden plate at Hannover, but was then dogged by bad luck and injury until a ruptured intestine finished her in her box at the trainer's yard. 'She had given many officers a taste of ownership and a lot of fun.'

During the four years in Herford the aim was 'to create and maintain a base from which polo in the United Kingdom could progress'. By 1985 Regimental polo teams were able to put up good performances in both the Inter Regimental and the Captains and Subalterns, but in 1986, although the Regiment had a nucleus of up and coming players: 'sadly, we still lack the ability to be able to mount one and all at the same time'.

There were annual migrations to the mountains, named Exercise Snow Queen, in search of snow. In 1983 lack of it and poor facilities did little to encourage newcomers to skiing, but the following year a 'magnificent' hut, better instruction and plenty of snow improved matters considerably. 150 soldiers attended a two week course in 1984 followed in 1985 by another 120 members of the Regiment who, for around £30 each:

> ... spent two weeks in Bavaria receiving tuition in downhill skiing, langlaufing and winter survival. In near perfect conditions groups of eight to ten soldiers grunted, groaned or posed on the slopes at Oberjoch ... The Exercise gave a marvellous opportunity for young soldiers, who have usually regarded snow as something to throw or avoid, to enjoy living in winter conditions experiencing the thrill of downhill and langlauf skiing.

They also provided a pool of winter sportsmen on which to draw for competitive skiing. Other commitments prevented the fielding of a downhill team in 1983–84, but the langlauf team, after training in Norway, won the *Daily Telegraph* Cup at the 4 Division Meeting and qualified for the Army Championships. The downhill team came seventh of twenty in the 1986 Divisional Championships, with three members qualifying for the Army Championships. There they came fifteenth of twenty-two and amongst those beaten was the Austrian Army B Team. After two years of qualifying for the Army Championships, a 'somewhat depleted' team was unsuccessful in 1987, but the langlaufers performed creditably at the RAC, 4 Division and UKLF meetings before finding the standard of the leading teams in the Army Championships to be far beyond the rest.

The Regiment's cricket eleven made a good start to the season in 1984, but then fell off. It was 1985 before they could record the 'most successful season for some years, crowned by the Regiment becoming RAC champions'. That was surpassed in 1986 with wins in three competitions – RAC, 4 Division and League – and runners up in two more – BAOR Major Units and League Cup. Leading players were Trooper MJ Hough and Captain CJR Blunt, not to mention the Commanding Officer, Lieutenant Colonel Yorke.

History of The 13th/18th Royal Hussars (Q.M.O.)

The rugby players had a successful season in 1986–87 reaching the semi-final of the RAC cup. Other matches played included two against the South Yorkshire police, visiting Germany; their 'greater weight and experience told in the end', but they 'proved to be a very sociable team indeed . . .'.

Both offshore and dinghy sailing continued to be popular Regimental activities, both as adventure training and recreation, but 'with the notable exception of one series of invitations, game shooting existed only in the imagination of professed Regimental shots'. A Regimental crew usually achieved respectable results at the annual RAC Regattas at Kiel and in 1985 it was won by a crew skippered by Lieutenant JW Ogden.

Some of the less popular sports were sufficiently encouraged by the Thursday afternoon clubs and hobbies sessions to achieve competition success in 1986, as in archery, water-polo and tennis. With increasing support 'The Lilywhite Company of Archers' was able to meet three times a week and entered the BAOR Open competition. Sergeant LF Noble and Staff Sergeant R Norton achieved 'Golds' in the senior and novices events respectively.

Individual sporting achievements

2nd Lieutenant JAG Oxley obtained a last minute ride, on Indian Eagle, in the 1983 Grand Military Steeplechase and successfully completed the course. This was by way of pipe-opener to 1984 and his first win in the Grand Military, riding HM The Queen Mother's horse Special Cargo. Remarkably this was followed by two more wins in 1985 and 1986. In 1986:

> . . . the pressure and hope was clearly there to make it a hat-trick.
> . . . Special Cargo was facing a determined challenge from Burnt Oak, a previous winner, and things seemed far from certain – not least when the race was slipped a day because of the appalling conditions. The race went well for Gerald on the first lap but a stirrup leather broke some half dozen fences from home and he was extremely lucky not to be unseated. Kicking off the other stirrup he then proceeded to ride long but made ground in a most impressive way. By the last fence it looked as though he had clinched it and he then finished in fine style several lengths clear. It was a fine feat of horsemanship, albeit without doubt an extremely painful one.

Herford 1982–86

Now serving away from the Regiment, Lance Corporal Haddon continued to be very successful in National and International competitions for Modern Pentathlon, Modern Tetrathlon and Fencing.

In 1983 Captain AREdeC Stewart spent three months away captaining the Army Cricket Team, which achieved some notable successes, including winning the Inter Services Competition.

In 1984, Captain SD Burgess played squash for the Royal Armoured Corps and the following year performed for Rhine Army as well; Captain PT Roberts captained the BAOR windsurfing team and had personal victories at a number of competitions. The EME, Captain MD Smith, was captain of the National Free Fall Parachute Team and in the Army Basketball team.

In 1986, Lieutenant JW Ogden was runner-up in the BAOR Dinghy Championships; Corporal Smith was a finalist amongst the BAOR Superstars at the competition held during the Rhine Army Summer Show at Sennelager; Captain PT Roberts came second in the Army Windsurfing Championships. Trooper MJ Hough played cricket for BAOR.

Visits to and from Herford

Brigadier General Wagner, who had commanded B Squadron in the 1960s, and was now Deputy Commander of 3 (US) Infantry Division, enjoyed a 'busy and memorable weekend' with the Regiment in April 1983. His fellow guests were three representatives of the 4ème Chasseurs. Links with the Chasseurs could be particularly close during this period. In 1984 the support troops exercised with them and the Regiment acted as hosts to a party of Chasseurs for a small exercise in 1985. In subsequent years both skiers and others enjoyed Chasseurs' hospitality in the French Alps.

Later in 1983 Lieutenant Colonel Jarymwycz, Commanding Officer of the Royal Canadian Hussars was visiting during the farewell to Lieutenant Colonel ffrench Blake. He recorded his weekend in a series of cartoons, a number of which illustrated that year's *Journal*.

History of The 13th/18th Royal Hussars (Q.M.O.)

Amongst the other 'first for a number of years' events was a major CCF visit in 1983, from Ampleforth College, when thirty boys spent a week covering everything from basic reconnaissance tactics to Chinook helicopter training. They were followed in July 1984 by cadets from Eton;

> For the first few days the cadets were put through an intense programme, which attempted to condense eight weeks basic training into three days and included such essentials as 'Intro to Steam Iron Handling' as well as the more mundane arms training, map reading and fitness – every scholar's nightmare! Thus prepared, fifty cadets were then crewed on the Regiment's complement of Spartans to form a Cadet Company/Squadron and shipped off to Soltau to act as enemy to the Black Watch. . . . After a little goading here and there they became competent at making a 'brew', trench digging and even washing.

They were finally whisked off to the mountains for 'a spot of adventure training. After all this exertion they showed a remarkable capacity for champagne at the final Bar-B-Q.'

In 1985 cadet contingents from Ampleforth and Radley overlapped for a week which included five days of Exercise Kadet Kanter – 'five days of charging around the German countryside yelling and attacking anything that moved, paddling across rivers and learning to wash on exercise'. (The Regimental mentors on each of the visits appear to have had trouble with matching schoolboy notions of cleanliness to Army expectations.)

Yorkshire

In 1983 and 1985 there were combined KAPE and Band tours of South Yorkshire and North Humberside and, in August 1985, a Families Weekend was held at Herford. C Squadron were principally responsible for organising the event, for which 170 members of soldiers' families found out what life in the Regiment in Germany was really like for their sons. Some sixty of the visitors lived in the single soldiers' accommodation and ate in the cookhouse – about which 'many favourable comments were recorded'. The programme included a whistle-stop tour around the Inner German Border, a ringside seat at the Pied Piper ceremony in Hameln and a morning with the Regiment in the field. 'A fair smattering of the citizens of South Yorkshire

Herford 1982–86

can now drive Scimitars; they could probably carry out an OP as well.' An All Ranks Dance was attended by 600 people – 'some were still there at 5 am while others had great difficulty making the 9 am bus to Hameln'. The finale was Beating the Retreat on the square against a backdrop of floodlit Scimitars.

Close contact with Barnsley was maintained and most years saw visits from the incumbent Mayor and Mayoress. As Lieutenant Colonel Cordy-Simpson wrote at the time;

> No town can have done so much for this Regiment and we are honoured that they continue to make the time to foster our close affiliation.

Regimental Band

Throughout the tour the Band continued, as ever, to provide performances of the highest standard and versatility. The Bandmaster, WO1 GE Locker, having successfully built up the Band during his appointment, hung up his baton on being commissioned and became the Assistant Adjutant. He was succeeded by WO1 A Chatburn who continued the good work. Not surprisingly the Band achieved an 'Excellent' grading in the quinquennial Kneller Hall inspection in 1986. By now all its members were equipped with ceremonial full dress and were very much in demand in Germany. They also had a proper wartime role as all had been trained as medical assistants.

More Farewells

In late November 1986 the Regiment left Herford for Tidworth, after handing over to the 16th/5th Lancers. The move was no less complicated than any of its predecessors. D Squadron was to come under NATO command, with the prospect of future deployment to Norway, Turkey and Denmark. In January 1987 A Squadron was scheduled for Cyprus. The farewells included a 'good send-off' organised by 7 Panzeraufklarungs Battalion, a German medium reconnaissance battalion. The Regiment had a close partnership with them throughout the tour and they helped the Regiment's team prepare each year for the Boeselager Competition.

Chapter Seventeen

Tidworth 1986–91

Tangled Chains of Command
From 30 November 1986, the Regiment was based at Assaye Barracks in the military town of Tidworth. Assaye Barracks was one of the late-Victorian complexes created on the edge of Salisbury Plain. The next door barracks (named Aliwal after another Indian battle honour) had been the home of the 18th Hussars from 1910 until they left for France in 1914.* A principal attraction at Tidworth was the polo ground, in a delightful setting, and, later in the tour, a brand new, purpose-built Sports Centre. This was administered and manned by the Regiment and, although a 'garrison facility', in practice became 13th/18th territory.

They took over from the 16th/5th Lancers as the armoured reconnaissance regiment of the United Kingdom Mobile Force (UKMF) in a tangled web of operational and administrative command. The Regiment less D Squadron came under 1 Infantry Brigade. D Squadron lived with the Regiment, but was permanently attached to NATO's Allied Command Europe Mobile Force (Land), coming under the Deputy Commander South West District for operational, training and some administrative matters. Each of A, B and C Squadrons went to Cyprus for six-month unaccompanied tours with UNFICYP.

At first the guided weapon troops from each sabre squadron were concentrated in C Squadron, for ease of training and administration. C Squadron therefore had no reconnaissance or support troops and one of the GW troops had to be seconded to D Squadron for the AMF(L) exercises. This convenience tail wagging the operational dog was changed in November 1988, when all four squadrons reverted to the same, armoured reconnaissance, organisation, although one of the others had to detach a reconnaissance troop to D Squadron from time to time to help with their exercises.

---
* There are a number of plaques commemorating 18th Hussars officers in Tidworth Garrison church.

31. Families' Weekend at Wimbish – HM King Hussein inspects B Squadron, with Maj Gen Watson and Maj Mallinson.

32. Herford 1983: Regimental band (BM Locker) in full dress.

33. HRH The Princess of Wales at Tidworth with Maj Fishwick and SSM Hawley.

34. 3rd Troop D Squadron (Sgt Waites) exercising the Regiment's Freedom of Barnsley.

The variety of commitments brought with it a variety of vehicles, including the tracked, over-snow, vehicle BV 206 Haglund held by D Squadron for Arctic operations.

Cyprus

The tasks for the squadron with the United Nations Force in Cyprus were as they had been for previous tours, as were the opportunities for sport and recreation. Major WG Peto commented:

> The Cypriot communities had needless to say done absolutely nothing to ameliorate the political situation since the last tour in 1982. Some of the nations contributing to the Force had done something, however – they pulled out.

Not surprisingly they were popular assignments, despite the six months of separation for families. A Squadron (Major Peto) led off in January 1987, pulling out of Assaye Barracks as the snow started to fall. Their particular memories were of the inordinate number of visitors.

> It was almost inevitable that all visitors were late, but Major Peto soon adopted the principle that 'we were given forty-five minutes and that's what they'll get', regardless of the programme timings.

They included the Secretary of State for Defence, twelve Swedish journalists and Professor Bebler, 'a Yugoslav know-all'.

B Squadron's visit in June 1989 began with the fifteenth anniversary of the Turkish invasion or 'intervention'. Greek Cypriots staged a series of demonstrations along the entire buffer zone, which ended with 110 women and the Bishop of Larnaca being arrested by Turkish police. They were imprisoned for fourteen days during which the United Nations protected area in Nicosia was picketed by up to 7,500 women. B Squadron, led by Major SN Fishwick, was responsible for manning the entry check points and controlling the crowds until the release of the last detainees. They could then revert to their normal role – and the 'numerous sporting competitions around which UNFICYP appears to revolve'. Football was played against a variety of local teams, both Greek and Turkish Cypriot. On one occasion Squadron Sergeant Major S Hawley presented a Squadron pennant to the Turkish team and 'rather let the side down by accepting kisses on both cheeks in return.'

History of The 13th/18th Royal Hussars (Q.M.O.)

Disaster struck C Squadron twice during their tour in 1990. Soon after their arrival a Ferret overturned on the UN patrol track, killing Lance Corporal A Rimmer, REME. In September, four NCOs of the Squadron died in a traffic accident: Corporals KJ Easter, CH Garrard-Cole and Lance Corporals MD Owen and S Shrubsole. Major EWJ Nall, the Squadron Leader, wrote of the blow to the whole Squadron and the stoicism and resilience which enabled them to get on with their job without letting events defeat them.

Protecting NATO Flanks

AMF(L) had the task of protecting NATO flanks, which stretched from Norway in the north to Greece in the south. As part of the Force, D Squadron spent two months each year in Norway, a month in Turkey and varying periods in other parts of Europe, notably Denmark and north east Italy. 'In getting to these foreign climes we seem to have spent the rest of the year [1987] in either Marchwood military port or South Cerney.' While this 'hectic life of movement round the outer confines of Europe' was 'great fun and professionally stimulating', it did mean protracted periods of separation from wives and girl friends.

Norway

D Squadron under Major AREdeC Stewart first arrived in Norway for Exercise Hardfall in January 1987. After four days on board RFA *Sir Geraint:*

> ... everyone was thankful to have escaped the heaving sea and their heaving stomachs. ... The temperature, taking into account the wind chill factor, was minus 57°C! The locals assured us that they had not experienced such cold conditions for fifteen years, and normally in January it was a mild minus 15°C. One week later it was a very mild 5°C and the rain, which was to follow the Squadron round the world, had melted all the snow that we needed for training.

Soldier Magazine reported on the 1990 expedition:

> Training and exercising in Norway bring to life the excitement, travel and adventure that Army recruiting posters promise, but enjoyable as the visits are to the land of the mythical troll, they are certainly no winter junkets. It is true that you learn to ski in

Tidworth 1986–91

the Army's time . . . and the local overseas allowance is welcome. But during a five-or six-day trek with a 60lb bergen to carry, you are not too interested in the après-ski (if there were any) after a nine-hour night-time skiing stint.

You learn to dig a snowhole for overnight cover. With temperatures that can drop to minus 30 and below, it is not the sort of bed-and-breakfast accommodation holiday brochures drool over – and it is certainly not for the claustrophobic. Force 12 blizzards can blow up without warning, and if you get your feet wet, a change of socks is essential to avoid trench foot, frost nip or frostbite. Self-discipline is vital and you have to work to the rules to survive. Soldiers well used to operating Scimitars and Scorpions in the temperate climate of the United Kingdom find their vehicles suffer too. They freeze! Then there are problems observing the fall of shot on a bright day, and heat and smoke from the barrels can obscure the view.

D Squadron, 13th/18th Royal Hussars, have become regular visitors to Norway . . . Sergeant Stuart Wiles, on his fourth visit, said: 'when a BV 206 got stuck in the snow, a farmer got us out with his tractor. If you break down outside a Norwegian's home they will take you in, feed you and give you a bed for the night.'

Turkey

In June 1987 D Squadron discovered that:

. . . AMF(L) exercises are different and the deployments to AMF(L) exercises are very different; the deployment to an AMF(L) exercise in Turkey is indescribable. Suffice to say that it took five separate air parties which flew into three different airfields. Two train parties were then locked under armed guard into the carriage with no ventilation and no cooking for two days. Two Landrovers disappeared for twenty-four hours, and fifteen of us together with twenty-six weapon bundles, were abandoned on the side of the road at 1 am by an itinerant Turkish coach driver. Maps, all of which were classified Secret or higher, could not be drawn until after a 100 mile road move. Eventually we did all meet up with our vehicles in the same place to find amazingly we were the first complete AMF(L) element to be in location.

Once we had a chance to look at our maps which, as they were thirty years old, made us little the wiser, we assessed that we were . . . eighty miles west of Mount Ararat and seventy miles from the Soviet border. We had also been transported back to the twelfth century where everyone lived in stone and turf huts, vehicles were horse-drawn and the women were in purdah. The SQMS, however, was able to find the only Tuborg retailer within 500 miles. This eased the situation. The weather did not. Because we were 3,000 metres above sea level there was still snow on the slopes and a frost at night. At 4 pm every day there was a monsoon which left us soaked for the night. On the brighter side, from sunrise until the daily monsoon, there were cloudless skies and temperatures of 35°C. . . .

The exercise itself started with one week's deterrence operations* during which we put on parades, equipment displays and cross trained with other AMF(L) contingents.

. . . There were nightly visits from the US battalion who had discovered our supply of Tuborg. The Squadron taught them 'Ilkley Moor' which was considerably better than the ghoulish US song 'Napalm sticks to the kids'. During combat operations we spent most of our time pretending to be tanks and ignoring the US EW† team who made great efforts to jam, intrude and confuse the Squadron net. We ended up as a flank protection force in a beautiful valley among the buttercups and snow drifts, being re-supplied by helicopter. Our return journey to England was on a par with the initial deployment.

However, the D Squadron visit to Turkey in 1988 was rated the high point for that year. Following three days of 'excellent troop training', the combat phase of Exercise Ally Express saw the Squadron permanently in action and:

. . . reacting with great speed to some realistic reconnaissance tasks . . . Most notable was an anti-heliborne operation 40 km to our rear. Within an hour the reconnaissance troops had located and cordoned off the enemy, SHQ had established an ICP for the area and an HLS for the Belgian battalion had been secured.' ‡

In 1989 'political shenanigans between the Turks and the Syrians scuppered D Squadron's planned exercise to Turkey and the carpet trade suffered accordingly'.

Gulf War

The invasion and annexation of Kuwait in August 1990 seemed at one stage likely to involve at least a squadron of the Regiment in actual operations:

---

* Designed to demonstrate NATO's forward presence on its flanks.
† Electronic warfare.
‡ ICP = incident command post; HLS = helicopter landing site.

Tidworth 1986–91

The Gulf crisis saw Headquarters and B Squadrons off to Porton Down for some intensive chemical warfare training. Having completed it and being more ready than most for war, they remained sitting in Tidworth feeling frustrated . . .

although at one stage B Squadron was at forty-eight hours notice to move and the Squadron Leader was despatched to sit at the airport. During B Squadron's abortive preparations the Regiment was visited in September 1990 by SACEUR (Supreme Allied Commander Europe) General J Galvin, accompanied by 'a procession of senior British Army officers'.

However, the Regiment did have a total of seventy-one men involved in Operation Granby, of whom thirty served in the Gulf in 'a variety of jobs, ranging from the Band, who are all trained medics, to the intelligence cell with its chemical warning skills'. The Band was under command of 1 Armoured Field Ambulance, but its members were distributed on attachment to a wide range of units.

Major RNB Quicke was Mentioned in Despatches for his part in Operation Desert Storm. Seconded to the 16th/5th Lancers, he commanded their B Squadron, armed with Scimitar and Striker, which led 1 (UK) Armoured Division into Iraq and subsequently Kuwait.

> The role of the recce was to thread its way between the forward Iraqi positions at night and attack the reserve brigades using artillery, air and *in extremis* direct fire. At times the squadron was 120 kms in front of the main UK brigades, out of contact with Divisional Headquarters, and with a finite amount of MLRS ammunition, the only ground-based weapon system that could support us.* Air support did come in but the weather was so appalling that the A10 crews couldn't see the targets. What confused matters was that some Iraqis were fleeing from the main UK brigades' attacks, some were attempting to reinforce their own brigades, and some were trying to attack us. The net effect was Iraqi armoured vehicles driving in all directions in appalling visibility, disappearing and reappearing in the sand storms. Direct fire was the order of the day and accounted for T55 and T62 tanks, MTLBs and many soft-skinned vehicles. The GW missile Swingfire proved particularly devastating, removing turrets from tanks with surprising ease. . . .

---

* MLRS – multiple launch rocket system.

History of The 13th/18th Royal Hussars (Q.M.O.)

> It had been a wonderful opportunity to put into practice all the lessons learned on the German plains. It had also been an opportunity to learn a new lesson – sleep deprivation. Commanders in recce units with their role and the likely pace of battle do not get any opportunity to sleep. I remained awake for ninety-two hours before having my first chance of a tactical doze. It also proved to me that we must always have the technological edge. We comprehensively defeated the Iraqis because we could fight at night, we could move at night without getting lost, they couldn't – and we had good logistic support and they didn't.

Captain RW Pakenham-Walsh was attached to the 14th/20th Hussars as Intelligence Officer. Returning late one night from a Brigade O Group he found himself in the middle of an Iraqi battalion position of some 300 men.

> If pressed as to what action he took, he will reply: 'I withdrew my service revolver from its holster'. History relates that they then all surrendered to him, which does demonstrate that, having seen his cap badge, the indigenous population have obviously not forgotten the Regiment's last successful foray in their country!*

Others in the Gulf included Lieutenant Colonel NS Southward, awarded the OBE for his services as Military Assistant to the Commander British Forces, General Sir Peter de la Billière, and four warrant officers and NCOs who were the NBC team at Headquarters 1 (UK) Armoured Division. They included Corporal WJ Blake who received a GOC's Commendation, as did Sergeant M Waters of the Band.

The homecoming of the Band was marked in moving manner on the square at Assaye Barracks. Their bus drew up to one end of a human tunnel stretching across the square, at the other end of which were their families.

Presentation of new Guidon

The Guidon presented by the Duke of Gloucester in 1961 was due for replacement and a new one was to be presented in July 1987.

> The Guidon Parade and the celebrations connected with it did, of course dominate 1987 for the Regiment. It all went off exactly as I had hoped: a vividly colourful parade, a happy mix of formality and informality and, above all, a truly memorable Regimental

---

* Arriving in Mesopotamia in 1916, the 13th Hussars played a distinguished part in the campaign against the Turks for the rest of the war.

Tidworth 1986–91

reunion in the presence of the Princess of Wales. We were delighted to entertain so many distinguished guests, including . . . representatives of Allied regiments and to see such a vast turnout of Association members. . . . The pride with which all those at regimental duty took part in the event was clearly reflected in their performance throughout the celebrations, not least on parade and I was tremendously proud of them. (Lieutenant Colonel EL Yorke)

The whole event was preceded by massive, and intricate, preparations, which had to be fitted in to the many other commitments. An Inter-Squadron Drill Competition helped to achieve faultless performance on the day and, as in 1961, a 'Guidon Officer' was appointed; this time it was Major MP Colacicchi:

> My first priority seemed to be to find areas suitable for the various activities. Many pleasant hours were spent bicycling round Tidworth looking at games fields and gyms, regimental squares and paddocks . . . The next task was to book all the varied equipment that is obtainable through the 'system'. . . . It was during this time . . . that I became aware of the 'Royal Visit' syndrome. The moment one mentioned that the particular piece of equipment was required for the visit of a member of the Royal Family, a complete change of attitude became apparent and suddenly nothing was too much trouble. . . . The dais, the VVIP pack (smart glass and crockery for the Princess of Wales's table), miles of white rope, to name a few items, are strictly reserved for Royal visits . . .

Getting together ceremonial uniforms and accoutrements was a major headache, but Mr Peter Wiles, father of three members of the Regiment (and recent correspondent with the Prime Minister), came to the rescue. He 'lovingly overhauled or repaired as necessary just about every item in our meagre ceremonial store . . . Thanks to him we now have a ceremonial pack of substantial proportions'.

On 29 July the Parade itself followed a similar form to the 1961 event, except that it was the Guidon presented by the Duke of Gloucester which was paraded for the last time. There were some notable differences, starting with the arrival of the Princess by helicopter and her transfer to an open carriage, provided by the Royal Mews. Captain SW Ledger commanded an escort in full-dress, made up of Sergeant Allchurch and four

History of The 13th/18th Royal Hussars (Q.M.O.)

other NCOs and troopers. They were mounted on black horses loaned by the Household Cavalry Regiment, whose instructors had coached the escort in their role.

The Band was augmented for the Parade by thirteen members of the band of the South Nottinghamshire Hussars Yeomanry. A vehicle march past featured the range of vehicles manned by the Regiment in its multifarious roles, painted in the camouflage demanded by service in a variety of climates as well as the white of the United Nations. A twenty-one gun salute was fired by eight Scorpions, and a Daimler armoured car and a Sherman tank (named Balaklava), led the old comrades past the saluting base.

> . . . there were, believe it or not, no disasters. There were setbacks, of course, but nothing happened, either on the day or during the preparations that could be termed disastrous. Of course, the weather on the morning of 29 July was appalling, especially at 0630 hours when the Regiment was doing aerobics on the square. However, it did clear up and the second half of the Parade was conducted in sunshine.

The following year, on 8 June, the Old Guidon* was laid up in the Warrant Officers' and Sergeants' Mess after a short service. (It was held in the newly-furbished Mess garden.)

A New Royal Connection

During the Guidon Parade, The Princess of Wales had 'expressed a desire to see the Regiment in the field . . . ' and on 23 June 1988 she arrived for what 'proved to be an extremely light-hearted and successful visit'. It included a journey by Haglund to Salisbury Plain, where A Squadron provided a mock battle depicting a typical reconnaissance action in the withdrawal phase. Two Strikers from C Squadron:

> . . . thundered over the bridge before the order was given to blow the demolition . . . The explosions and noise at such a close range had little effect on HRH who was wearing Amplivox and in a trench, unlike the gathered Press, who were 'unfortunately'

---

* The normal 'life expectancy' of a guidon is twenty five years, but in 1995 the Guidon presented in 1987 was marched off parade as an Old Guidon, together with the Old Guidon of 15th/19th The King's Royal Hussars, when The Princess of Wales presented their first Guidon to The Light Dragoons.

Tidworth 1986–91

unprotected. Still it made the news on TV, and photographs of HRH appeared as far away as Yaramuta, Australia.

The Princess evidently flourished under the personal instruction provided for her in the various armoured reconnaissance skills, including the achievement of 'crew gunner standard with panache and ease' and driving a Striker 'confidently and aggressively to the Regimental leaguer'.

Colonel-in-Chief

The Regiment had been without a Colonel-in-Chief since HM Queen Mary died in 1953. It gave past and present members great satisfaction when the gap was filled by the appointment on 21 April 1989 of HRH The Princess of Wales. (The delight of those at Regimental duty was enhanced by the declaration of a day-off by their new Colonel.) The Princess had already endeared herself to all ranks during her visits for the Guidon Presentation and the follow-up in 1988. Another visit followed in June 1989, after the Princess's appointment. The theme was a *Day in the life of a Lilywhite*, during which each squadron presented different aspects through a series of skits. These included Lance Corporal GA Hickson presenting a posy of flowers while balanced on top of the rest of D Squadron.

What was to be her final visit to the 13th/18th was made by the Colonel-in-Chief on 28 February 1991, by happy coincidence the day that the Gulf War ended. The emphasis was on families, particularly of those serving in the Gulf, and the Princess's visit included the Garrison Wives' club. A Squadron provided a further topical note with an insight into NBC warfare, while C Squadron demonstrated the flavour of life in Cyprus with the UN.

Belize

In 1979/80 the small ex-colony of Belize in Central America was threatened with annexation by Guatemala. An appeal for help to the former governing power brought a British battalion group to defend a country nearly the size of Wales. A detachment of the 13th/18th was sent there for six months from September 1987 – nearly 200 years after the 13th and the 18th Light Dragoons had last been involved in operations in the Caribbean. In the eighteenth century both Regiments had suffered terribly from sickness, principally yellow fever, and between them lost over 800 men. In the twentieth century an augmented troop from B Squadron suffered no fatalities, during the six months they spent in Belize, but it was still essential for them to take careful precautions against tropical disease. The weather was very hot and humid and as a result 'a vast insect population thrives'. Apart from the inevitable preliminary 'jabs', personal hygiene was therefore taken seriously and malaria pills became part of the daily routine.

After post-Guidon block leave, the detachment under Captain JW Ogden had a 'frenetic' three week training programme, before flying out to take over the eight Scorpions of the Force Reconnaissance Troop from the Scots Dragoon Guards. The rest of the Force consisted of 2nd Parachute Regiment, an artillery battery and an engineer squadron.

> Belize is an extraordinary country . . . a fairly typical Third World banana republic with all that that entails, whilst still retaining some vestiges of an ex-British colony . . . The population is a mix of Caribs, Creoles, Hispanics and even a strange European sect

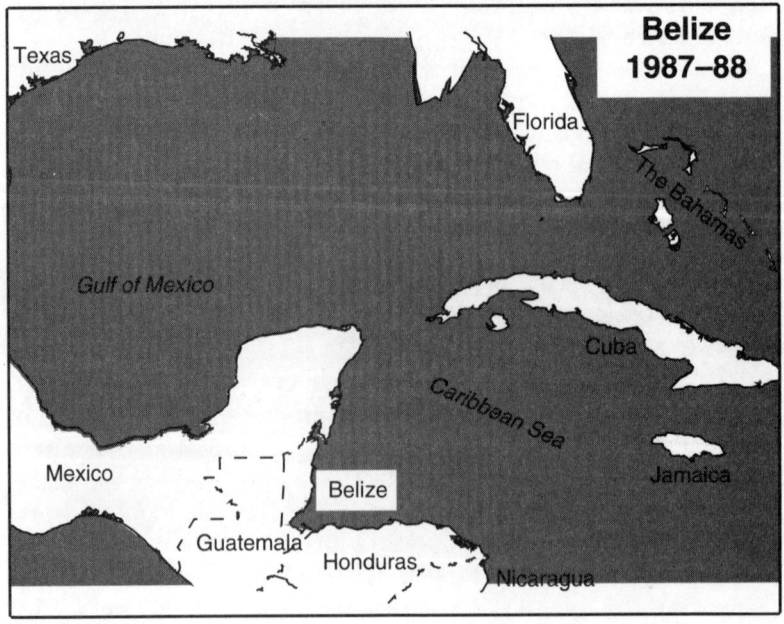

Tidworth 1986-91

called Mennonites. . . . A mixture of mangrove swamps, thick jungle, and appalling road conditions make tracked movement interesting and vehicle maintenance testing.

The Troop was run as three sections which took it in turn to carry out patrols, lasting three to four days, for 'route proving, map updating and a general armoured presence on the ground'. They were also able to get away on adventure training, including an 'eventful' canoe trip on the Belize River. The Force had its own Adventure Training Centre, with courses in diving, wind surfing and sailing, and 'rest and recreation' was provided by trips to the cayes and to Mexico (Belize's other neighbour to the north).

Training

Despite the inherent ability of their vehicles to take them far and wide, much of the Regiment's training when not on detachment had, perforce, to take place on their own doorstep – Salisbury Plain. However, there were some notable exceptions.

Exercise Bold Grouse

For a sizeable proportion of soldiers, their first exercise away from Salisbury Plain came in September 1988 when the Regiment less D Squadron went to Denmark for Exercise Bold Grouse. Based in 'the friendly township' of Naestved, home of the Garde Hussars, they spent the first week in Regimental training on the island of Lolland. In the 'fast moving' exercise proper, the Regiment practised its role as armoured reconnaissance to UKMF and troops covered more miles in a day than they would manage in a week on the Plain. 'Recce regiments do have more fun.' Able to go where they wanted within reason, vehicles averaged over a thousand miles apiece; the tanks of the Scots Dragoon Guards could only notch up a fifty-six track mile average on the training areas to which they were confined.

> We never ceased to wonder at the kindness of the Danes, who would look upon the arrival of vehicles in garages and barns with a total lack of surprise and the offer of coffee, *gammeldansk* and buns.

The Band turned out in combat kit ('a rare sight') in order to practise their medical skills with 16 Field Ambulance. However, they reverted to normal splendour in order to take

History of The 13th/18th Royal Hussars (Q.M.O.)

part in a Massed Bands display for a VIP cocktail party at the *Kastellet* in Copenhagen. The Stables Troop also featured in the display and provided a mounted escort for the Guest of Honour, Crown Prince Frederick, on horses borrowed from the Garde Hussars.

Exercise Highwayman
The first major manoeuvre in many years to make use of public rights of way, roads and small areas of private land was Exercise Highwayman in February 1989. It was preceded by a Press Open Day, aimed at placating local residents in advance and that seemed to have helped considerably. There had also been a successful application for fifty-seven reservists to fill spaces in support troops and the Regimental Signals Officer's job 'was made considerably easier by those reservists who brought their company mobile phones with them'. The exercise ranged for five days over a wide area of South West England 'to places that had never seen the Army out in force'. One Scimitar

> ... had an argument with a cottage, needless to say the Scimitar won and achieved amazing headlines in the tabloid press ... Still the Commanding Officer says that there is no such thing as bad publicity ...

Exercise Viking
Later in 1989, in September, Exercise Viking was a two-sided Regimental FTX, designed to train for 'Out of Area' deployment (ie outside NATO). 'Blue Force' consisted of Regimental Headquarters with two sabre squadrons and 3 Battery 47th Field Regiment RA; 'Orange' was two troops of D Squadron dressed in their Arctic gear. First came amphibious training at Marchwood with 27th Port Regiment RCT, then Blue Force moved to Harwich ('Namimbo' for exercise purposes) by LSL [Landing Ship Logistic]. A cordon and search operation on the North Norfolk coast was followed by raid, and advance to contact on Thetford Training Area. During the Thetford phase, Blue Force was joined by a company 6th/7th Queens, and Orange by 81st Security Squadron US Air Force. After forty-eight hours came a move into Southern Yorkshire on 'convoy escort' and an advance to contact up to the River Humber, culminating with an amphibious crossing of the Humber,

landing under the Humber bridge. During the night A Squadron was 'bumped' and Lieutenant CJS Whitaker was run over by a Samaritan which badly crushed his pelvis – fortunately not causing permanent injury. The exercise finished with clearance of the Holderness peninsula and the establishment of reporting centres for surrendering 'guerrilla' forces. Over the twelve days the Regiment had covered 700 miles .

Exercise Druid's Drake
The Plain did provide the setting in July 1990 for Exercise Druid's Drake. It was 'used throughout its length and breadth' and A Squadron 'seemed to spend most of our time rushing from one end to the other'. It was extremely hot and after a couple of days, 'even our wives would not have been pleased to see us, let alone smell us'. A Regimental and Brigade exercise which made as much use of Salisbury Plain as possible, the highlight was to be live firing. B Squadron found the five hour wait for it in their vehicles, with temperatures 'well into the 30s' very uncomfortable – but good practice for what might have been their lot a few months later. When they were eventually allowed to join in, 'the Plain started burning furiously and nearly caught the Squadron in their fire positions'.

A Squadron had a scientist attached for the duration of the exercise, whose task was:

> . . . to see how we all lived and worked. Unfortunately he could not get used to what we take as normal living and eating in the field and, having had a panic attack when 'the enemy' were reported to be close, he asked to be removed from the exercise.

Troop tests
Troop tests continued to play an important part in the annual training cycle and in 1989 they were held 'over the rugged countryside of Wales', following annual firing at Castlemartin. 'Use of ground was the key to success and many commanders had to suffer the ignominy of being pulled out of the bog by the fitters.' One vehicle overturned, trapping the driver, but Corporal S Cotton ignored pools of petrol and loose batteries to rescue him. He was awarded the C-in-C's Commendation for his bravery.

History of The 13th/18th Royal Hussars (Q.M.O.)

Gunnery
During the time at Tidworth, there was a 'consistent improvement in our gunnery, which included the introduction of 76 mm Scorpion into our armoury. By the end of the period high standards had been achieved in GW and 76/30mm firing.' (Lieutenant Colonel Yorke)

C Squadron's initiation as the Guided Weapon Squadron came at Otterburn in 1987. The first firing day was 'disastrous because of thick fog and only two missiles were fired all day (one failing to leave its launcher). The second day was not much better, with twenty three missiles being fired at various targets which swam in and out of view with every new wave of mist. Fortunately, the third day was totally different and the weather and our shooting were immaculate.'

Swiss Commando Patrol Competition
Major Peto, now the Second-in-Command, 'with little else to do had taken to reading DCIs . . .':

> The announcement of the Swiss Commando Patrol Competition in 1968 seemed to be not only abroad but also good fun. Captain Ibbotson was one of those officers who carry immense weights for immense distances for no apparent reason. Putting the two together, painting a Land Rover blue, sponging free tickets from P&O and assembling a team consisting mainly of Boeselager veterans, they were launched into the unknown.

The Regimental team, led by Captain Ibbotson with another officer and five NCOs, took first position in the foreign section. There were forty-seven other teams competing, from France, Italy, Germany and Belgium as well as Switzerland. It was the first occasion that a British team had taken part and the 'syllabus' was found to be extremely varied, including the use of esoteric weaponry and explosives and 'numerous forays over a number of increasingly high mountains'.

Adventure Training
Adventure training featured prominently throughout the period, with every opportunity being taken, or created, to provide challenges to all ranks outside the normal routine and in a great variety of locations – from the island of Jersey to the Himalayas, as well as on the high seas.

Tidworth 1986-91

Expeditions went to Kenya in 1988 and 1990, during the second of which a successful assault was made on the 17,058 feet high Mount Kenya. In 1988 'heavy packs, bad knees, poor fitness and finally the dreaded pulmonary oedema (altitude sickness) had forced the team down from Mintos Camp at 14,000 feet'. That disappointment aside, the expedition was:

> ... a great success ... in four weeks we covered thousands of miles, only had one serious breakdown, and experienced the varying contrast of climate and terrain that this beautiful country is so famous for.

The 1990 effort encountered as much by way of human as natural obstacles, starting with a journey via Moscow for some of the group in order to take doubtful advantage of the services of Aeroflot, 'cheaper than any other airline'. Later there was literally an encounter with the local constabulary when a police stop sign was driven into, followed shortly by an election riot. However, six of the ten members of the team had reached the summit, 'which claims more lives than any other mountain, usually casualties of altitude sickness'.

In January 1989 the majority of the Regiment found themselves in Scotland, on Exercise Highland Winter. 'Climatic conditions were perfect with howling gales and torrential rain.' Captain SEW Dennis, the woman Medical Officer, 'braved the Scottish mountains with a bergen on her back. Those who found her striding past them should take comfort from the fact that she is a climber of some repute.'

The following year the African and Scottish mountains paled into insignificance when a team from the Regiment, in company with Skinner's Horse, set off in June on Exercise Kulu Conquest. Two years of planning and training culminated in Captains AMG Phillips and ADC Ibbotson reaching the summit of White Sail, over 21,000 feet up in the Kulu Valley of Himachal Pradesh, after they and their team had met and overcome all the problems which the Himalayas can provide.

Three months after returning from India, Captain Phillips led another team in the 1990 Swiss Commando Patrol Competition. After entering at short notice the Regiment was again awarded the prize for the highest placed foreigners, beating entries from French, German, Canadian and Italian Army regular units. This time there had been a strong British entry

History of The 13th/18th Royal Hussars (Q.M.O.)

and it was 'particularly pleasing to defeat teams from 42 Commando RM and the King's Regiment who had trained hard for the event'.

Sport

The Commanding Officer, Lieutenant Colonel EL Yorke, thought that the sporting achievements of 1987-88 were 'unparalleled in recent Regimental history, certainly in the last twenty-two years'. He also pointed to the 'vast range of sports and hobbies now on offer in the Regiment, whatever the degree of competence achieved'. The enthusiasm for, and the achievements in sport, undoubtedly helped attract young sportsmen to the Regiment, to the benefit of future years.

Football

Despite the players' efforts and the enthusiastic support of the Regiment, the Cavalry Cup had not been won since the 1971-72 season. But in 1987-88 they were United Kingdom finalists and the elusive Cup itself was gained in 1988-89. (In almost a traditional appointment for the Quartermaster, the team manager during the period was Captain SP Davies.) The semi-final the following year was against the 9th/12th Lancers at Wimbish; it was lost by a goal 'scored in the dark after twenty-eight minutes of extra time'.* At the final against the Queen's Own Hussars in 1991 the last goal was again in extra time, but on that occasion the 13th/18th were the winners – for what was to be the last time.

Cricket

A good all-round sportsman, Lieutenant Colonel Yorke's particular enthusiasm was for cricket and his time in command was marked by some major achievements. Although it was recorded as less successful than 1986, 'largely because there were not as many competitions to win', thirteen out of fourteen competitive fixtures in 1987 were won by the Regimental eleven. Unfortunately, the match lost (against the Royal School

---

* A shadow cast over the occasion was the recent death in an avalanche of Major Hugh Lindsay, Football Officer of the 9th/12th Lancers, whilst he was skiing with the Prince of Wales. His widow attended the match as her husband would have wished.

Tidworth 1986–91

of Artillery) meant being knocked out of the Army Cup. It was a 'disaster on the scale of Yorkshire losing to Shropshire'. However, 'all opposition was destroyed in the Salisbury Plain cricket league'.

After two years of enthusiastic and determined planning and fund raising by the cricket officer, Captain CJR Blunt, a Regimental cricket team left in April 1988 for Exercise Kalypso Wicket in Barbados. 'The tour was designed as the highlight of seven years' hard work building up an increasingly talented cricket team, that Army life would surely not allow to stay together for long.' Captained by Major AREdeC Stewart and including the Commanding Officer, the team had a fixture list of five matches, not to mention the opportunity to savour Caribbean delights. Despite some very close finishes against formidable opposition, the Lilywhites were unable to achieve a win – 'The tour had been a great success, except of course for the results'. After that amount of working up, back home they were again South West District winners and this time reached the Army final, only to lose to the Light Division Depot.

Hockey
In 1986-87 a highly successful RMA Sandhurst hockey team included four prospective Regimental officers. 'This influx of young blood to add to the solid and experienced Regimental team provided a realistic chance of winning the Army Cup.' However, a good start to the 1987-88 season and winning the SW District competition came to an abrupt halt in the Army Cup Quarter Final. Hockey continued as an important Regimental game, but with no major competition successes.

Rugby
Like hockey, rugger had an enthusiastic following, but an oft-recurring lament in the sports pages of the *Journal* was a failure in successive years to field a regular team. By 1987-88 there was 'a XV growing in talent, strength and morale with every game' and the United Kingdom semi-final of the Cavalry Cup was reached. The following year they managed to get to the final but that was their best in competitive terms.

History of The 13th/18th Royal Hussars (Q.M.O.)

Sailing

The sailors claimed in 1987, with some justice, that theirs was the 'most consistently successful sport'. In that year they were RAC Regatta Gold Cup winners, a success which was repeated in 1988. The following year the competition was held in the middle of troop tests, but reputation was saved with 'an honourable second place'. During 1990:

> There has been varied and wide participation, ranging from hot tropical climates to cool northern Britain, from 55 foot gin palaces to 8 foot windsurfers which sink under a person's weight. The highlight of the year has been Captain Ibbotson's round Britain sail on a 16 ft 'Hoby Cat' catamaran. This six week epic journey was an amazing feat of endurance.
>
> ... C Squadron made the most of their time in Cyprus; Captain Ogden organised various expeditions and the Squadron ran many windsurfing courses.
>
> ... At Seaview [RAC Regatta], the Regiment performed with its customary excellence, this year coming a creditable second, only just failing to win.
>
> .... Major Roberts and Captain Levey competed in the Army Windsurfing Championships in June. The first day saw brilliant sunshine and force 6 winds which proved too strong for many competitors [but] Major Roberts revelled in the conditions, winning all the races. ... The second day dawned to a force 8 gale, the committee boat had sunk overnight and conditions were extremely poor. Racing was abandoned and ... Major Roberts therefore became Army Champion again.

Water polo

From time to time a few enthusiasts lifted Regimental swimming out of its normal limits of the inter-squadron competition, and in 1987 the water-polo team were South West District champions and runners-up in UKLF.

Tennis

In 1987 the Regimental Tennis Team 'surpassed all expectations' and won the United Kingdom Inter-Unit Cup Competition', going on to lose in a close match against the 15th/19th Hussars in the Army finals.

Tidworth 1986–91

Archery
Archery was one of the new sports which had burgeoned at Hohne and the keenness of its followers was rewarded in the 1987-88 season with winning the Army indoor championships.

Skiing
Alpine skiing and langlauf were pursued with great keenness, helped both by the enforced exposure to snow in Norway and rigorous training schemes organised by the Royal Armoured Corps. Gradually the Regiment advanced up the scale of achievement in the alpine events, with a team led by Captain SR Levey qualifying for the Army Championships in 1987-88. Lieutenant JME Cobb was captain the following year, when eighth place was secured in the Army championship, 'by far the best result achieved by the Regiment in recent years'.

Sponsored with financial aid and ski equipment by the firm Lillywhites, the 1989-90 team was again led by Mr Cobb. In the RAC Championships in Switzerland they won the Giant Slalom, slalom and the overall competition. Moving on to Austria 'the team settled down to ten days of intense racing ... Gältur is situated just beyond the edge of the world and there are certainly no distractions'. After winning every alpine event at the UKLF championships the triumphant team moved on to Les Menuiries in France for the Army Championships. Here came anti-climax with the best team result being fourth in the Giant Slalom. But that did not detract from what was overall a most successful season. They returned to Tidworth 'groaning under the weight of silver that they had at last won'.

Although Captain R Peel secured an individual place in the Army competition in 1988-89, the langlauf teams could not match the downhill achievements.

Equitation
With a 'flourishing polo club and miles of open countryside on the doorstep, plus excellent stabling in our own lines' all was set fair for all forms of mounted sport from Tidworth. The Stables Troop under Sergeant Allchurch played a major part in what was accomplished. Opportunities for hunting included the Royal Artillery Hunt on the Plain and the Tedworth for 'more traditional countryside and a less military flavour'.

History of The 13th/18th Royal Hussars (Q.M.O.)

Polo
On arrival the Regiment took on responsibility for running one of the largest polo clubs in England. At one point, twenty-three soldiers were working in the stables and on ground maintenance. 'This was a major commitment of manpower and no doubt politically incorrect, but a Hussar regiment should occasionally behave like one ... (Major Peto).'

The first season was successful, 'not so much in booty won, but in achieving the primary aim of re-introducing polo as a major activity'. However what was probably the nadir of Regimental polo was reached in Cyprus, when an A Squadron team was defeated by an RAF team 'consisting of one officer, one wife and two school children'.

In 1989 the Commanding Officer 'could at last face the Trustees [Serving Officers' Trust], and indeed officers past and present at the annual dinner, and speak convincingly about the success and progress of Regimental polo'. Not since 1976 had a Regimental team competed in the finals of both the Inter-Regimental and the Captains and Subalterns, albeit this year emerging as runners-up on each occasion.*

Shooting
The Game Book began to have entries at an early stage after arrival in Tidworth, with its excellent Garrison shoot. Several soldiers as well as officers took an interest, taking up pottering permits at very much reduced rates. Beating was popular; volunteers received £5, rations, refreshment and 'a day away from the tank park, not to mention the rare chance of possibly being shot at by their Squadron or Troop Leader'.*

Racing
The efforts of a few enthusiasts meant that racing continued to be followed by the Regiment as a whole with great keenness. At

---
* A malign influence on sport followed Exercise Viking: 'Despite even more care ... in East Anglia, the commanding officer received a letter complaining of inconsiderate behaviour, ending: "I shall put a curse on All Queen Mary's Own officers. For this season you will all miss even low partridges and pheasants and all your horses will be unsound and you will kill no fishes. the curse will lift next August." The game book for that season is the emptiest it has ever been and the Regiment lost to the Navy in the finals of the Inter-Regimental Polo at Windsor in front of the Queen.' (*The Light Dragoons*, by Col Mallinson)

the Grand Military Meeting of March 1988 they were represented by two serving and two retired officers. Riding again for HM The Queen Mother, Lieutenant Oxley (now in the Reserve) came second in both 1988 and 1989, before achieving his fourth Gold Cup win in 1990.

Individual Achievements
As well as team successes, the performance of a number of individuals was recognised at Army and Inter Service level. Captain JW Ogden and Lieutenant HP Ogden represented the Army at sailing in 1988 and 1989. Lieutenant NH Shaw represented the Army at tennis in both 1988 and 1989 and was joined by Lieutenant RE Determeyer in 1989. At archery, Squadron Sergeant Major R Norton, Sergeant LF Noble and Corporal E Bell all turned out for the Army as did Lance Corporal PJ Delaney in swimming, Captain PT Roberts at windsurfing, Lieutenants NH Shaw and RE Determeyer at hockey. Lieutenant NH Shaw also played tennis for the Combined Services.

South Yorkshire
'One of the many advantages of this posting is that we will be able to renew our strong links with South Yorkshire.' In December 1986 the Band played for large crowds outside Barnsley Town Hall during a visit by HM The Queen, and the Colonel of the Regiment and the Commanding Officer attended the luncheon given by the Mayor to mark the occasion.

Mayoral visits from Barnsley were easier to arrange than in Germany and the Mayor and Mayoress were of course amongst the guests at the Guidon Presentation. The Mayor's visit in March 1988 coincided with the 18th Hussar Shield individual skills competition, for which he awarded the prize, as well as the Cavalry Cup final on the Tidworth Oval, when the Regiment lost to the 9th/12th Lancers.

KAPE Tour
October 1989 saw the first KAPE tour to be undertaken by the whole Regiment – 'a big effort to help solve a big problem'. A, C and D Squadrons with Headquarters Squadron in support set off for South Yorkshire and Humberside.

History of The 13th/18th Royal Hussars (Q.M.O.)

Armed to the teeth with drill ammunition, bristling with an assortment of weaponry and bursting at the seams with leaflets and glamorous photographs, we threw ourselves at a largely unsuspecting public. As we quickly learned, being parked outside supermarkets was the best way to keep the public unsuspecting. There is something very unruffable about the average housewife doing her shopping.. . .

Other sites were more successful: 'Schools and youth clubs seemed to be most fruitful locations . . . the display at Doncaster FC did not generate much interest except from old timers who wanted to reminisce'. The grand finale was a parade at Barnsley to celebrate the tenth anniversary of the granting of the Freedom, consisting of both a march and drive past and a horse-mounted Guidon party. 'The tour was a success, with numerous young men recruited as well as many ties strengthened in the local community.'

Friendly Relations

In January 1987 a naval affiliation was forged – with HMS *Avenger*, a Type 21 Frigate. That was marked by an exchange of visits later in 1987. In May a group from *Avenger* came to Tidworth and a return match in September provided a party, representative of each squadron, with two days at Devonport during the ship's major refit. They were given the full range of naval hospitality as well as opportunities, at one end of the scale, to tour a nuclear submarine and, at the other, to move whale-boats competitively through the water. After the ship's work-up, three members of the Regiment joined a cruise to Gibraltar in 1988 and in 1990 two more flew out to the Falklands to join *Avenger* for her voyage home to Plymouth.

The cordial relations with the 4ème Chasseurs continued to provide skiers with a combination of extra practice and 'outstanding hospitality'. As their guests at the French Cavalry Championships in March 1988 'it soon became apparent that Lilywhites were coming down the mountain at considerable speed'. The Regimental team found themselves 'in a virtually unassailable position', but potential embarrassment was avoided, a French regiment had to 'win'. Nevertheless a special cup was presented to Captain Ogden's victorious team by the Prefect of the Hautes-Alpes.

Tidworth 1986-91

The link with Skinner's Horse prompted a joint dinner night in the Officers' Mess in May 1990 with twenty-six members of the Indian Cavalry Association. Colonel Douglas Gray played a leading part and also organised a remarkable visit to India for four officers at the end of the year.

Colonels and Commanding Officers

Lieutenant Colonel AL Mallinson had taken over as Commanding Officer in November 1988 from Lieutenant Colonel Yorke and on 13 May 1990 Colonel RJW ffrench Blake was appointed Colonel of the Regiment in succession to Major General HSR Watson. General Watson had been in post for eleven years. 'During his time as Colonel he has, first and foremost, been a constant source of advice to the five commanding officers who have spanned his tenure.' At the Southern Reunion of the Regimental Association he was presented with a silver mare and foal* 'as a token of our enormous respect and gratitude' from past and present members of the Regiment.

Life in and from Tidworth

Tidworth was four to five hours travelling time from South Yorkshire for those wanting to get home. Long weekends were therefore organised on a monthly basis to allow for the northern exodus.

Families living in or near the garrison played a part in most Regimental events and in July 1988 the Wives' Club swapped places for a day, 'leaving the men to mind the children and cook the meals'. Wearing their husbands' boots and overalls they tackled weapon and driver training in the morning, including firing 9mm pistols and an assault course in the afternoon. (The event was obviously popular as it was repeated in Wolfenbüttel in August 1991.)

Garrison and RAAT Duties

One of many 'garrison duties' was that of Tidworth Garrison Duty Unit, which almost wrote off a complete squadron for a week. It required a permanent Quick Reaction Force to be at five minutes' notice to move. However, with no terrorist attacks, the week would pass very slowly.

---

* The statuette of Caprice and her foal. *See* Chapter 14.

History of The 13th/18th Royal Hussars (Q.M.O.)

The resident squadrons also had numerous RAAT (Regular Army Assistance Table) tasks on Salisbury Plain – and elsewhere. They ranged in attraction from the secondment of a major for two weeks in Hong Kong to the provision of ten pristine and working CVRs for Troop Leaders' courses:

> ... to wreck, bog and dirty. Servicing and cleaning vehicles is a dull task at the best of times, but there is the pride of ownership. Cleaning your vehicle after it has been wrecked by others is soul-destroying. (Major Peto)

Aid to Civil Authority

Overcrowding in prisons in England and Wales led to Rollestone Camp being used as a temporary prison for 360 inmates. C Squadron provided the guard for a week in May 1988, coming away with a vivid impression of the difference between

> ... the generally excellent conditions and facilities which the prisoners enjoyed ... and the pretty squalid conditions our soldiers put up with.

From October 1989 to March 1990 a number of people were deployed as medics and ambulance drivers to Dorset, London and the West Midlands during a strike of ambulance men.

Guard Force Duties and new Equipment

Another task was 'Guard Force Duties' and in 1987, C Squadron helped guard some Americans who were deploying some 'sensitive equipment' (ie missiles) onto Salisbury Plain.

> The week proved to be very useful training indeed and was quite enjoyed by all. The Squadron achieved a 100 per cent success rate in apprehending all twenty-six intruders who attempted to interfere with the American equipment, thanks to the Striker's thermal image sight (rather old) and our Spyglass portable thermal image sights (very new).

Spyglass was issued for support troops and was half the size of the OTIS sights in sabre troops. (Although mainly used at night, the thermal image sights are also effective during the day for 'seeing through' foliage etc.) The big drawback to Spyglass was its battery consumption, as C Squadron Quartermaster Sergeant found when he asked the Technical Quartermaster's department for what amounted to the Regiment's annual allocation – for one squadron for one week.

Tidworth 1986–91

Also new was the rifle SA 80. It was issued first to D Squadron in May 1988 and was carried by the Junior NCOs Cadre when passing out in November; its first appearance on a cavalry parade.

Visitors

Contingents from school cadet corps continued to come each year for a period of dreadful warning as to the rigours of military life: Tonbridge and Radley in January 1987, Radley again in July 1988 and Downside in March 1990. Higher education was represented in February 1987 by Cambridge OTC.

Notable amongst military visitors in 1988 was the French 'Director Royal Armoured Corps', General Julien de Zeligcourt, for whom A and C Squadrons provided a vehicle display.

Changing World Scene

Three years after arrival in Tidworth the world scene had changed dramatically. On 9 November 1989 the Berlin Wall came down and the frontiers of Eastern Germany were opened. On 3 October 1990 Germany was unified. An immediate effect for the Regiment was the cancellation of a planned exercise in Schleswig Holstein, but, in characteristically sardonic vein, Regimental Notes in the 1991 *Journal* began:

> In the year that has seen the last stages of the crumbling of the Berlin Wall, the re-unification of Germany and war in the Middle East ... the Regiment has carried on as normal.

Lieutenant Colonel Mallinson sounded a warning note:

> ... the Regiment has seen four different sets of camouflage paint on its vehicles this year ... D Squadron started 1990 north of the Arctic Circle painted white and then repainted sand and green for the arid scrub of Eastern Turkey. One of A Squadron's troops did the same, while the others remained in standard North European green and black for our exercises with the United Kingdom Mobile Force on Salisbury Plain and Schleswig Holstein. C Squadron put their vehicles into preservation and took over UN white Ferrets in Cyprus. B Squadron painted all theirs sand colour when they were put at seventy-two hours' notice to move to the Gulf ... Throughout all this there has been the uncertainty about the future following the Options for Change announcement.
> ... if no more money is available for a big coat then it has to be

cut according to the cloth. This year we have seen too many exercises cancelled, too few training resources and too many cuts in the maintenance budget. We have been promised a smaller but better Army. If 'smaller' is the essential price for 'better' then it should be worth it.

Tour in England ends on high note
The advance party had already left Tidworth for Germany when the Cavalry Cup was won on 11 May. The following day the Colonel-in-Chief took the salute at the Cavalry Memorial Parade in Hyde Park, at which there was a big attendance by Old Comrades and serving members of the Regiment. The Princess of Wales lunched afterwards at Claridges with officers and their guests. It was a splendid occasion to mark the end of the four-year tour in England and the Regiment 'could not have have left for Germany in better spirits'.

Chapter Eighteen

Wolfenbüttel 1991–92

To Germany for the Final Chapter
The Regiment's first tour in Northampton Barracks at Wolfenbüttel began in July 1946. Then came the spell from 1953 to 1956. A third tour began in May 1991 after taking over from the Queen's Dragoon Guards. One enormous difference from the two earlier tours was that there was no potential enemy on the doorstep of Northampton Barracks. It was now possible to drive out of the gates and head east without encountering the watch towers, wire and minefields of the IGB (Inner German Border). For those who, not long before, had warily patrolled the Border and exchanged stares with its guards it was an eerie experience. Since 1945 time seemed to have stood still in much of Eastern Germany, particularly in the neighbourhood of what had been first the inter-zonal boundary and then the IGB.

As in 1953, at the start of the second tour, there were new incumbents for the posts of Commanding Officer, Adjutant, and Regimental Sergeant Major: Lieutenant Colonel AREdeC Stewart, Captain CJS Whitaker, and WO1 S Hawley. Colonel Stewart, like three of his predecessors in recent years, was the son of a 13th/18th Hussar.

The Die is Cast
Three months after taking over, he had to announce that the Regiment was to amalgamate in December 1992 with 15th/19th The King's Royal Hussars.

In the early stages of agonising over the Options for Change the 13th/18th naively thought themselves to be only marginally at risk, while a number of other regiments began nervously to look round for potential partners in the looming amalgamations. (In May 1990, when Colonel ffrench Blake took over from General Watson there was no apparent threat to the Regiment's existence.) When it became clear that the Royal Armoured Corps was to lose eight of the nineteen regiments left from the economies of earlier years, the Regiment found that they were likely to be the 'odd man out' amongst the regiments of hussars. That led to the improbable proposal at one stage that they should amalgamate with the Life Guards – a future which could lead only to disappearance within the Household Division.

The Gulf War put defence economies 'on hold' and provided breathing space for the Regiment to negotiate arrangements more to its liking. After fruitful discussions with 15th/19th The King's Royal Hussars, the joint case was put at what Colonel ffrench Blake remembers as a 'fraught' meeting of the Cavalry Colonels. A decision was deferred for a month, but the final result was favourable, including as it did acceptance of the Regiment's insistence, despite strong opposition, on staying as armoured reconnaissance. The principles followed were the same as those laid down by Field Marshal Sir Richard Hull, for the previous batch of amalgamations. These were that there should be proportional reductions amongst the different categories of regiment (hussars, lancers etc), that like should amalgamate with like (eg hussars with hussars) and that due regard should be had for 'seniority' (ie date of raising).

A Hectic Eighteen Months Begins

> In spite of, and in some ways because of Options for Change, the final eighteen months of Regimental life and events continued at a hectic pace. . . . At first parade on Wednesday 15 May the Regimental flag was hoisted at the main gate of Northampton Barracks, Wolfenbüttel to mark the official change of station.

and the Regiment:

> . . . cracked straight into Troop Training and Troop Tests, thoroughly enjoying exercising in Germany again. Unbound by the limitations of Salisbury Plain, sabre troops bombed around the area honing up their tactics and skills . . . Meanwhile A Squadron conducted their stringent pre-UNFICYP training . . .
>
> (Regimental Notes in the Final *Journal*)

Back to Cyprus

From July 1991 A Squadron spent six months 'vigorously patrolling the Buffer Zone and fending off the sun's harmful rays with little more than a chisel-jawed pose and a pair of

Wolfenbüttel 1991–92

Ray-Bans'. In more charitable vein than the Regimental Notes, *Soldier* Magazine reported:

> This is the second UN tour by A Squadron since 1987 and the sixth since 1980. There is a wealth of experience in the unit with twenty-two troopers on their second tour and several who have been on the island four times. 'You can be more friendly than on the IGB' said Lance Corporal Dave Robson, . . . but you must be diplomatic. If you wave to one side, you must wave to the other too. . . . The UN sectors have operational control of four troops and a fifth has two Ferrets on one hour's notice as the Force Commander's reserve, and another two on four hours' notice. . . . The Ferrets patrol the buffer zone on tracks going through open country or village, making a point of stopping at the UN Observation Posts along the line. It relieves the tedium of the stag*, and maintains good relations with the sectors.
>
> . . . Accommodation for the contingents is not, however, a high priority. Nissen huts and Ferrets from the 1950s add to a sense of time warp as one trundles along the Green Line in Nicosia, deserted but for the occasional guard post. Tablecloths cover tables in the tavernas, with a covering of dust on top. Bottles of wine long evaporated lie where they fell as people fled. Money is still in the tills and the banks where time froze in the summer heat nearly twenty years ago. (*Soldier* Magazine November 1991)

Operational Role

NATO, set up to counter the threat from Soviet Russia, now agonised over what its new role should be. An early move was the establishment of a multi-national Corps under what had been Headquarters 1 (Br) Corps, including 1 (UK) Armoured Division.† The Corps role was reflected in its title: Allied Command Europe Rapid Reaction Corps (ARRC).

From the Regiment's point of view this meant that their last twelve months of training (before being declared 'non-operational') was orientated towards possible deployment, either as part of the ARRC's reconnaissance force or as part of 1 (UK) Armoured Division.

---

* Stag = guard duty.

† Commanded from March 1994 by Major General RA Cordy-Simpson.

History of The 13th/18th Royal Hussars (Q.M.O.)

Training

The accounts in the *Journal* of that twelve months make it appear to the casual reader that little had changed in the familiar BAOR training cycle. Two visits to Hohne for Regimental gunnery were fitted in, during the first of which the guided weapon shoots 'were chiefly notable for the unreliability of missiles'. So also were two periods of troop and squadron training. C Squadron organised the 1991 Junior NCOs Cadre in order 'to select those suitable to be JNCOs within a reconnaissance regiment'. A 'testing and difficult' package was put together which the organisers thought struck 'a good balance between the physical and cerebral'.

Exercise Certain Shield

But another new NATO creation was a Multi-national Airborne Division and in September 1991 Exercise Certain Shield was staged between Kassel and Paderborn to test the new concept. Despite being expected to act as enemy tanks, the Regiment 'acquitted itself with much panache in the field. The sabre squadrons' speed of reaction, flexibility and good use of ground' often foxing the other side. There were amusing moments as in one incident when the Second-in-Command, Major Nutting, narrowly escaped certain death in a Portaloo. 'An inconsiderate gentleman with a large effluent truck and a very powerful suction pump attached the latter to the said portaloo. With a flick of the switch the air turned blue with expletives. . . . rumour has it that it was only the mandatory wearing of '58 pattern webbing at *all* times which prevented the disappearance of a distinguished Regimental officer!'

During a free weekend, the Warrant Officers' and Sergeants' Mess entertained the officers to a dinner night in the field. It was a memorable evening, not least because the Exercise controller, Brigadier RA Cordy-Simpson, was guest of honour.

Boeselager Competition

Particularly pleasing was the demonstration in May 1992, at the biennial Boeselager competition, that the Regiment was still to be counted amongst the leaders in reconnaissance at international level. D Squadron trained and administered the Regimental team from November 1991 and Major Ogden

Wolfenbüttel 1991–92

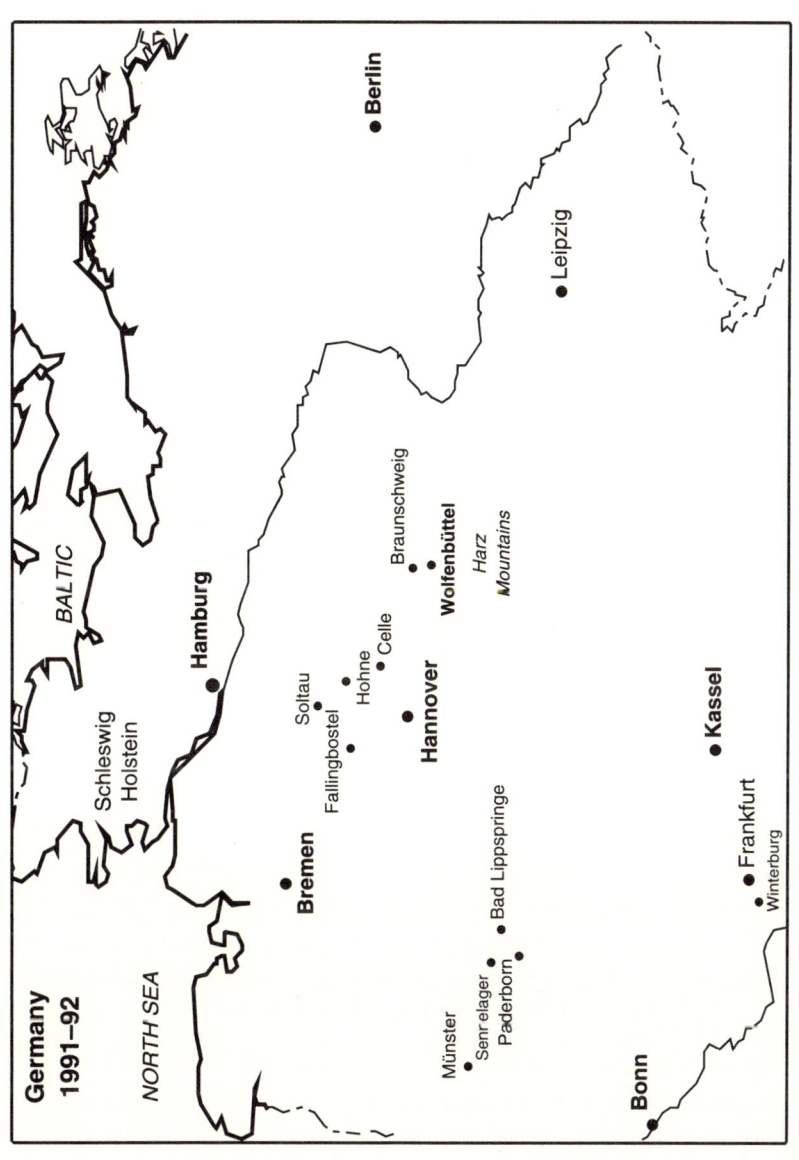

became the Team Captain. Reminiscent of the single-minded approach to CAT in 1966, the programme covered all the skills and fitness demanded in the Competition and the cry from the PT Staff Sergeant of: 'It's for your benefit, not mine, gentlemen' soon became a favoured phrase within the squad.

As part of the working up, members of the squad were entered in two other military competitions. The Hochsauerland March was held near Winterberg; during the first of the two days snow fell heavily and one orienteering course was completed in near blizzard conditions. But the results showed that the Boeselager training was well on course, with Regimental teams getting the first and third fastest times round the course and coming second and third in the *Ausländer* competition.

The reserve squad was entered for the Bellinzona Patrol, held on the Swiss-Italian border. Here a 'little confusion with the translation of the instructions' slowed the times of the Regimental teams and they were not amongst the winners.

Nineteen teams from ten different countries assembled at Augustdorf, near Sennelager, for the four day Boeselager tests themselves. (Amongst them were two teams from former East Germany.) Led by Lieutenant ET Legard and Sergeant ST Thompson, the Regimental team were disappointed by their scoring in the vehicle patrol and driving, but went into first place in the assault course and won the night orienteering outright by over an hour. The remaining events produced good results and overall the Regiment gained second place in the *Ausländer Cup* – 'a fine effort' – beaten only by an experienced Dutch team and well ahead of the Americans.

Final Exercise
After the second visit to Hohne in May 1992, the Regiment moved on to Schleswig Holstein for a final Exercise Kollected Kanter. The close reconnaissance troops of three other cavalry regiments reinforced A Squadron as 'enemy', combating the other three squadrons. With the Regiment practising a long advance across a broad front, it was an exercise which 'certainly had a different flavour, reflecting the changes in Europe'. A major feature was the practice of extended communications – over ninety kilometres from front to rear.

35. Skiing behind a Haglund in Norway 1987.

36. Exercise Viking 1989: vehicles coming ashore from RCL near Hull.

37. Cyprus: L Cpl Robson patrolling the Green Line through Nicosia.

38. Last Parade of The 13th/18th Royal Hussars – The Guidon is trooped through the ranks of past and present members of the Regiment.

Wolfenbüttel 1991–92

Adventure Training
Also fitted into the short spell at Wolfenbüttel was a full programme of adventurous training (as it was now termed). Mountains in Bavaria and the Harz, caves in the pre-Alps and the Ardèche gorge in France, the Atlantic and the Baltic were amongst the targets for groups from the various squadrons.

Sport
Victory in the Cavalry Cup in 1991 had been achieved in the middle of the move to Wolfenbüttel and the 1991-92 football season started well with the first seven matches won. However the team could not beat a strong Queen's Own Hussars team in the BAOR semi-final of the Cavalry Cup.

What passed for a cricket ground at Northampton Barracks was 'something resembling a hay field perched on the top of a hill. The wicket was a strip of concrete over which was an extremely dangerous looking coconut mat.' It was got into sufficiently good shape for play to begin in 1991. However, after winning the first match in the RAC Cup, the next went by default, as operational and exercise commitments prevented the Regiment from meeting the deadline set for it. The following year saw the team reach the semi-final of the RAC Cup, losing by thirteen runs.

For the rugger team there were 'some blinding defeats, miraculous victories and more than one spectacular draw'. Their matches included several against German teams and the final game was in a tournament won outright by the Regiment.

At alpine skiing the 1991-92 season was seen as building up new talent for the future, but the Regimental langlauf team had some success in the RAC Championships, coming fourth, and performing well enough in the divisional competition to go forward to the National and Army Championships. Although not doing as well there as they hoped, 'this was a great experience as we were competing against many of Britain's best langlaufers, past and present'.

The principal complaint about Wolfenbüttel from the sporting point of view was its remoteness, and during the previous tour there had been no hope of playing polo. That had changed dramatically. As well as the ground at Hohne there was now a polo ground at Northampton Barracks newly created by the Queen's Dragoon Guards. Although not playable in the first season its quality by 1992 was rated second only to the Maifeld in Berlin. The Regiment was now strong in both ponies and players and the team was able to play in a 'host of tournaments ranging from Münster, Bad Lippspringe, Hohne and Fallingbostel to Berlin'. Major trophies eluded them but they were never far from the top.

Non-Operational
On its return to Wolfenbüttel from Exercise Kollected Kanter the 13th/18th became 'non-operational' from 1 June and could concentrate on the myriad tasks which had to be completed before handing over the Barracks on 1 December and moving to Hohne for amalgamation.

First priority in 1992 had already been given to assisting those eligible for redundancy by the requirement for 'drawing down' the Regiment by almost 50 per cent. A special office was set up under Captain SD Taylor to help with advice and resettlement and Lieutenant Colonel Stewart emphasised: 'It is at a time like this that the true strength of our family Regiment will be tested. We are all determined not to be found wanting.' Eventually fifty-one soldiers were made redundant, thankfully all volunteers, and some eighty to ninety transferred within the Army.

The run-down of men, but not of responsibility for a full range of vehicles, meant that squadrons were fully stretched. A number of individuals found themselves with responsibilities two or three ranks higher than they thought they had. Their abilities were amply demonstrated during the final visit by the Regimental Association.

Regimental Association Weekend
In 1954, for the Balaklava Centenary, only a handful of unaccompanied Old Comrades had been able to make the trip to Wolfenbüttel. In June 1992, over 170 members of the Association took part in a final Reunion during which 'there was a terrific feeling of comradeship between our veterans and young soldiers'. They were provided with a programme which ranged across all that the Regiment so successfully straddled in

Wolfenbüttel 1991–92

its day-to-day life – military, sporting and social. The principal event, and the most moving, was a Drumhead Service. It began with the marching on of the Guidon, accompanied by the Association standard. At the end of the service itself those who had served in the Gulf were presented with their Gulf medals by the Colonel of the Regiment, Colonel ffrench Blake. The Association members then joined the parade before the Guidon was trooped through the ranks and the parade marched past the Colonel to *Auld Lang Syne*.

The 13th/18th Royal Hussars had marched for the last time.

Message from the Colonel-in-Chief in the final issue of The Lilywhite.

Kensington Palace

This will be the final edition of the Regimental *Journal* and I know many of us will feel sadness that our Regiment is now passing into history. However, I am confident that its spirit, loyalty, unselfishness and dedication will live on as the bedrock on which the new Regiment will be built.

Your achievements are recorded for posterity so that we may all remember the past with justifiable pride laced with nostalgia. Nevertheless, there are new challenges to be faced and, having received the honour of being appointed to be Colonel-in-Chief, The Light Dragoons, I now look forward to watching the next chapter unfurl. In the meantime, I send All Ranks my warmest wishes for the future.

Diana
October 1992

The Link With The Future

. . . the hearty welcome accorded to the Squadron by the corresponding residue of the 13th Hussars was thoroughly appreciated and reciprocated and, in spite of the unforgettable association of the past and the loss of individuality suffered by both Regiments, perfect accord reigned in the new unit, and it would have been hard to have found a more united Regiment.
From the final chapter of *The Memoirs of The 18th (Queen Mary's Own) Royal Hussars, 1906–1922* by Major General Charles Burnett

There were two redeeming features of the 1992 amalgamation – the principal one was that it was to be with 15th/19th The King's Royal Hussars, a Regiment with which the 13th/18th could feel wholly compatible. The second was that their successors, The Light Dragoons, were to be an armoured reconnaissance regiment. Most of the seventy years of the 13th/18th Royal Hussars' existence after the previous amalgamation in 1922 were spent as a reconnaissance unit. They were equipped with tanks for only sixteen years, although those included the magnificent storming of the Normandy beaches in 1944 and the hard-fought battles before Germany was defeated. The return in 1977 to what was now 'armoured reconnaissance' seemed entirely appropriate for Light Cavalry, providing as it does a role which is interesting, fulfilling and challenging.

Obviously there were many difficult decisions to be taken and these were addressed by a joint committee made up of both past and serving members of both Regiments and chaired by Colonel RJW ffrench Blake. He was to be the first Colonel and Lieutenant Colonel AREdeC Stewart the first Commanding Officer of The Light Dragoons. In a special *Newsletter* in April 1992 Lieutenant Colonel Stewart wrote that the key principle:

> . . . has been that each decision should be in the interests of the new Regiment and not the old. History will live on because we are surrounded by it and will incorporate it. This is best exemplified by the new name and cap badge. The Light Dragoons favours neither side, but reflects a title that all four regiments have held in the past. . . . the cap badge is based upon the cross worn by all

The Link with the Future

Light Dragoon officers as a shako plate. Superimposed is a laurel wreath and a royal crest. The wreath was always the dominant feature on 18th Hussars' badges as it was for 13th Hussars until 1900. The royal crest is singular to 15th Hussars. The new is shown by LD in the centre and the fact that the cap badge bears no resemblance to either of our current ones.

It was obviously essential to retain the geographical links of each Regiment, centred respectively on South Yorkshire and Newcastle. However there could be only one Home Headquarters and, to the great regret of the 13th/18th, the choice fell on Newcastle, rather than York, to provide a reasonable spread across Britain of the Royal Armoured Corps. That made it the more important to retain the Regimental Museum at Cannon Hall, outside Barnsley, to demonstrate the continuing ties with the town which had granted its Freedom to the Regiment, and the surrounding area.

The members of the 13th/18th had felt complete affinity with their forebears in the 13th and the 18th Hussars. They were proud to celebrate the achievements of both regiments and cherished the pictures, silver and other mementos which had been handed on to them. Nothing could mark that more graphically than the battle honours inscribed on the Regimental Guidon, bringing together, the services of the 13th and the 18th in former wars, with those of the Second World War.

The Light Dragoons now have their own Guidon and inscribed on it are the principal battle honours of The 13th/18th Royal Hussars and of 15th/19th The King's Royal Hussars. At the presentation by HRH The Princess of Wales in 1995 the music for the march past began with *Balaklava* and *A Life on the Ocean Wave.** Balaklava Day is marked by The Light Dragoons on equal terms with celebration of the 15th Hussars' charge at Sahagun. In years to come, Light Dragoons will doubtless regard as 'their' achievements, the winning by their predecessors of the Cavalry Cup and other sporting trophies.

And so they should.

---

* Played as part of the Regimental Quickmarch by the 13th/18th to commemorate their 1944 landing in Normandy in DD tanks.

Appendix A

Appointments

Colonels-in-Chief

HM QUEEN MARY 1922–53
(Vacant from the death of HM Queen Mary in 1953 to 1989)
HRH THE PRINCESS OF WALES 1989–92 *
* *Appointed Colonel-in-Chief, The Light Dragoons* 1992

Colonels

1942–52	Brig JN Lumley	1952–60	Maj Gen CH Miller
1960–68	Col VAB Dunkerly	1968–74	Col JR Cordy-Simpson
1974–79	Maj Gen DB Wormald	1979–90	Maj Gen HSR Watson

1990–92 Col RJW ffrench Blake *
* *Appointed Colonel, The Light Dragoons 1992*

Officers Commanding

1947–48	RA Hermon	1968–70	JRL Howard
1948–51	EH Tinker	1970–73	JCM Ansell
1951–53	JR Cordy-Simpson	1973–76	DAG Edelsten
1953–56	Sir Delaval Cotter, Bt	1976–78	DJStJ Loftus
1956–59	AAK Rugge-Price	1978–81	GMcL Stephen
1959–62	DHE Coker	1981–83	RJW ffrench Blake
1962–64	HSR Watson	1983–86	RA Cordy-Simpson
1964–66	PB Tillard	1986–88	EL Yorke
1966–68	RS Beresford	1988–91	AL Mallinson

1991–92 AREdeC Stewart *
* *Assumed command of The Light Dragoons 1992*

Seconds in Command

1946–48	JR Cordy-Simpson	1966–67	JRL Howard
1948–51	Sir Delaval Cotter, Bt	1967–68	GM Chirnside
1951–53	MWH Bell	1968	EE Hunt
1953–56	AAK Rugge-Price	1968–70	CJG Delamain
1956–58	JJ Selwyn	1970	JCM Ansell
1958–60	ERMcM Wright	1970–72	RCJ Dick RTR
1960–62	PB Tillard	1972–73	EF Williamson QOH
1962–63	BJW Cobb	1973–75	RT Cliff
1963–64	G Stocker	1975–76	PC Beaver
1964–66	JW Bell	1976–78	JAC Blakiston

Appointments

Seconds in Command (cont)

1978–80	DJ Delius	1984–86	PAJ Gibson
1980–81	RA Cordy-Simpson	1986–88	AL Mallinson
1981–83	PW Hope-Johnstone	1988–89	WG Peto
1983–84	DAH Sievwright	1989–91	RCB Nutting
		1991–92	RM Keane

Squadron Leaders 1947–72

A Squadron

1947–48	NNM Denny	1957–58	RS Beresford
1948	ERMcM Wright	1958–59	HSR Watson
1949–52	J Meares	1960–61	JW Bell
1952	KA Foster	1961–63	CJG Delamain
1952–54	WG Denney	1963–65	EE Hunt
1954–55	DHE Coker	1965–67	JOG Paton
1955–56	WG Denney	1967–68	EE Hunt
1956–57	KA Foster	1968–70	DAG Edelsten
		1970–72	RT Cliff

B Squadron

1947–49	MWH Bell	1962–64	GM Chirnside
1949–54	ERMcM Wright	1964–66	RE Wagner, US Army
1954–56	Sir Charles Dorman, Bt	1966–67	JCM Ansell
1956–58	ER Jolley	1967–68	GVS Goodey
1958–60	G Stocker	1968–70	PC Beaver
1960–62	JS Mangles	1970	RCJ Dick, RTR
		1971–72	RJW ffrench Blake

C Squadron

1947–50	DHE Coker	1959–61	PB Tillard
1950–51	MWH Bell	1961–63	JRL Howard
1951–52	ER Jolley	1963–64	JCM Ansell
1952–54	JJ Selwyn	1964–66	RS Beresford
1954–55	JM Howson	1966–67	GM Chirnside
1955–56	PB Tillard	1967–69	CJG Delamain
1956–57	JW Smith	1969–71	DJStJ Loftus
1957–59	BJ Cobb	1971	EF Williamson QOH

Headquarters Squadron

1947–49	JM Howson	1958–59	ERMcM Wright
1949–50	MWH Bell	1959–60	JW Bell
1950–52	*Disbanded*	1960	WG Denney
1952	AW Gage	1961–62	BJW Cobb
1952–53	G Stocker	1962–64	HJ Tyacke
1953–56	JHW Marr	1964–65	JOG Paton
1956–57	AW Gage	1965–67	BC Douglas-Hamilton
1957–58	DHE Coker	1967–70	AH Blount
		1970–71	DJ Delius

History of The 13th/18th Royal Hussars (Q.M.O.)

1972 (Northern Ireland)

A Squadron	B Squadron	Admin Squadron	Rear Party
JAC Blakiston	RCR Cotterell	F Harrison	DJ Delius

1972–74 (RAC Centre)

A Squadron
1972–74 JAC Blakiston
1974 PC Beaver

Lulworth Squadron
1972–73 DJ Delius
1974 RA Cordy-Simpson

Vehicle Squadron
1972–73 F Harrison
1974 CJ Edwards

Admin & Depot Squadron
1972–73 B Harris
1974 AJN Collis

1974–92

A Squadron
1974–76 PC Beaver
1976–77 DJ Delius
1977–78 DAH Sievwright
1978–81 PAJ Gibson
1981–83 JAMA Selfe
1984 MB Brook
1984–86 RCB Nutting
1986–89 WG Peto
1989 CJR Blunt
1989–91 SW Ledger
1991–92 CP Good

B Squadron
1974–75 RA Cordy-Simpson
1975–76 CAG Robinson
1976–79 PW Hope-Johnstone
1979–81 RA Cordy-Simpson
1981–82 CA Le Hardy
1982–84 AL Mallinson
1984–86 NS Southward
1986–87 MB Brook
1987–90 SN Fishwick
1990–91 PT Roberts
1992 MH Browell 15/19H

C Squadron
1974–76 EL Yorke
1976–77 RJW ffrench Blake
1977–78 MJS Wilkins
1978–79 CNP Speers 16/5L
1979–82 AJN Collis
1982–84 EL Yorke
1984–86 RNB Quicke
1986–89 MP Colacicchi
1989–91 EWJ Nall
1991–92 NA Shryane

D Squadron
1984 PG Scrope
1984 WA Shuttleworth
1984–86 AD Coker
1986–88 AREdeC Stewart
1988–91 RM Keane
1991–92 HP Ogden

Command & Support Squadron
1974–77 DAH Sievwright

Headquarters Squadron
1976–79 CJ Edwards
1979–80 CA Le Hardy
1980–83 K O'Sullivan
1983–85 JP Gibson
1985–87 EWJ Nall
1987–89 MA Cunningham
1989–90 DR Amos
1990–91 CP Good
1991–92 PABG Scott-Masson

Appointments

Adjutants

1947–50	HSR Watson	1971–72	PW Hope-Johnstone
1950–51	DHE Coker	1972–74	JPJ Fairrie
1951–53	RS Beresford	1974–76	MT Ward
1953–56	JRL Howard	1976–78	JAMA Selfe
1956–57	GM Chirnside	1978–79	RCB Nutting
1957–59	SJA Hargrove	1979–80	NS Southward
1959–63	AC Anderson	1980–81	WA Shuttleworth
1963–64	DJStJ Loftus	1981–83	PG Scrope
1964–66	DAG Edelsten	1983–85	WG Baker Baker
1966–68	RJW ffrench Blake	1985–87	NA Shryane
1968–69	GF Burnand	1987–89	DR Amos
1969–71	RA Cordy-Simpson	1989–91	SR Levey

1991–92   CJS Whitaker *

*Appointed Adjutant The Light Dragoons 1992

Quartermasters

1942–54	F Sweeting	1965–68	EJ Henson
1954–59	JJ Reynolds	1968–76	PJ Stratton
1959–62	G Jepson	1976–79	F Harrison
1962	J Wadmore	1979–83	JT Winter
1962–63	PJ Davis	1983–88	R Lang
1963–65	EJS Garbutt	1988–92	SP Davies

Technical Adjutants

1947–48	WG Denney	1949–52	PR Hoad
1948–49	JW Smith	1953–54	JW Bell

1954–56   JS Mangles

Technical Quartermasters

1957–62	PJ Davis	1978–83	R Lang
1962–69	J Wadmore	1983–89	GA Smith
1969–78	EJS Garbutt	1989–91	JM Wragg

1991–92   TC Atkinson

Regimental Sergeant Majors

1947–51	WJ Greenslade	1973–75	JB Hatton
1951–54	HR Parnaby	1975–77	J Henderson
1954–57	G Pateman	1977–80	JL Platt
1957–59	R Chester	1980–83	GA Smith
1959–63	EJS Garbutt	1983–85	H Cross
1963–66	PJ Stratton	1985–87	SP Davies
1966–68	DCK Brant	1987–89	TC Atkinson
1968–71	WF Anderson	1989–91	SD Taylor
1971–73	T Lafferty	1991–92	S Hawley

History of The 13th/18th Royal Hussars (Q.M.O.)

Bandmasters

1947–59	T Geggie	1974–79	I Thompson
1959–67	A Kershaw	1979–85	GE Locker
1967–74	BW Titley	1985–90	AR Chatburn
	1990–92	PM Greener	

Officers Commanding Light Aid Detachment REME

1947–48	J Harris	1968	A Ball
1948–49	WJM Abery	1969–70	ED Lakin
1949–50	GM Williams	1970–71	AJ Hill
1950–52	*No EME appointed*	1971–74	*No EME appointed*
1952–53	E Sewart	1974–75	WG Harrison
1953–54	DP Ballard	1976–77	M Fredericks
1955–57	GWA Pearce	1977–78	PW Jackson
1958–59	H Wright	1978–79	TE Wilkins
1959–60	MP Burton	1979–82	IG King
1961–62	J Allen	1983–84	MD Smith
1962–64	CK ffrench-Nobbs	1984–86	IS Simpson
1965–66	DR Axson	1986–88	PA Shewry
1967–68	JR Eyre	1989–90	SP Fitzgibbon
	1990–92	JA Ellis	

Paymasters

1958–60*	Maj PCA Bridgland	1973–77	Capt WAG Davie
1960–61	Capt LB Jones	1978–80	Maj CT Oakley
1962–63	Maj L Higgens	1980–82	Maj PSD Sheehan
1964–65	Maj JA Flood	1982–84	Capt GW Burton
1966–70	Maj TA Brown	1984–88	Capt T Vidler
1970–73	Capt DJT Dowey	1988–92	Capt PM Barczak

* Until 1958 Regimental Officers were responsible for Pay.

Officers Commanding Home Headquarters

1962–78 Lt Col (Retd) JR Palmer
1978–90 Maj (Retd) EJS Garbutt
1990–92 Capt (Retd) GE Locker*

* To Home Headquarters The Light Dragoons Jan 1993

Appendix B

Honours and Awards

1950–53 (Malaya)

OBE
Lt Col JR Cordy-Simpson

MBE
Maj ER Jolley Capt RS Beresford
Maj ERMcM Wright WO1 HR Parnaby

MM **BEM**
Sgt JC Thomas Sgt RE Weighell R Signals
Sgt F Turner

Mentioned in Despatches

Maj MWH Bell	Lt JRL Howard	Sgt W Anderson
Maj WG Denney	Lt EE Hunt	Sgt A Clegg
Maj KA Foster	Lt JP Paige	Sgt EA Davies
Maj JJ Selwyn	Lt JS Mangles	Sgt WF Smith
Maj G Stocker	Lt ACP Pitcairn	Sgt PJ Stratton
Maj ERMcM Wright	Lt AF Robbins	Sgt JR Teate
Capt BJW Cobb	2nd Lt AA Gregory	Sgt JC Thomas
Capt GM Chirnside	2nd Lt TE Lane	Sgt HN Whiteley
Capt RJ Dodds	2nd Lt GWD Ogg	Sgt J Williams
Capt JW Smith	RQMS G Jepson	Cpl J Tierney
Capt PB Tillard	SSM A Parkin	Sgmn TW Pollard
Lt GVS Goodey	SSM G Pateman	R Signals

C in C's Certificate
AQMS JF Woodfield REME   ORQMS J Wadmore
Sgt J Hipkiss   Sgt D Swaine   Cpl GB Kay
L Cpl W Coulson

1954 1957
MBE **CBE**
Maj HSR Watson Col JR Cordy-Simpson

1957-58 (Arabia)
MC **MM**
2nd Lt MB Barty-King Sgt D Steel

383

History of The 13th/18th Royal Hussars (Q.M.O.)

1958-60 (Malaya)
Mentioned in Despatches
SSM A Palmer Sgt M Dedman
SQMS W Anderson L Cpl W Howson
C in C's Certificate
Sgt J Myson

1962
OBE
Lt Col DHE Coker Lt Col ER Jolley

1967
CBE **OBE** **MBE**
Col AAK Rugge-Price Lt Col PB Tillard Maj EE Hunt

1970
OBE **Queen's Commendation**
Lt Col ERMcM Wright Cpl MA Cunningham

1973
CBE
Brig PB Tillard Brig HSR Watson

1973 (Northern Ireland)
MBE
Maj DJ Delius

1975–6 (Northern Ireland)
Mentioned in Despatches
Maj DJ Delius Capt RCB Nutting Capt (QM) PJ Stratton

1979–1980 (Northern Ireland)
OBE
Lt Col DJStJ Loftus Lt Col GMcL Stephen
MBE
Capt K O'Sullivan
Mentioned in Despatches
Lt NJ Norman Cpl S Hawley Tpr GP Scott
GOC's Commendation
Capt AREdeC Stewart Sgt SR Frudd

Honours and Awards

1980
BEM
Staff Sgt TC Atkinson   Sgt P Lawson

1982
GOC's Commendation
Cpl EL Casterton

1984
OBE	BEM
Lt Col RA Cordy-Simpson	Staff Sgt RJ Todd

1985
BEM
WO2 T Renwick   Staff Sgt S Hawley

1986
BEM
WO2 SD Taylor

1987
GOC's Commendation
Cpl E Bell   L Cpl WJ McKendrick

1989
C-in-C's Commendation
Cpl S Cotton

1990
MBE	BEM	MSM
Maj NA Shryane	Staff Sgt G Nixon	WO 1 LW Wells

1991
MBE
WO 1 LW Wells

1991 (Gulf)
OBE	Mentioned in Despatches
Lt Col NS Southward	Major RNB Quicke
GOC's Commendation	**C-in-C's Commendation**
Sgt M Waters	Cpl WJ Blake

Appendix C

In Memoriam

Officers and Men who died whilst serving
(ERE = while 'extra Regimentally employed')

North Africa
Grandsome J	Tpr	10 Feb 1948	Vehicle accident
Spence PS	Tpr	24 Feb 1949	Road accident
Loader AGD	Sgt	2 Oct 1949	Road accident
Rogers ECH	RQMS	27 Jan 1950	Ammunition accident

Malaya
Carpenter GE	2 Lt	20 Sep 1950	Accident during road patrol
Hudson R	L Cpl	22 Sep 1950	From wounds in road ambush
Burgess J	Tpr	1 Sep 1951	Rifle grenade explosion
Harden JB	2 Lt	6 Sep 1951	Own fire during jungle patrol
Skillen J	Tpr	31 Jan 1952	In hospital
Hammond LW	Tpr	31 Mar 1952	From wounds in road ambush
Hall R	Tpr	26 May 1952	Accident with rifle
Cook DR	Tpr	5 Oct 1952	Natural causes

United Kingdom
White C	Cpl	1 Oct 1953	In hospital - natural causes

Germany
Pears JP	Tpr	14 Nov 1954	Accident
Knight R	Tpr	28 May 1956	Traffic accident injuries
Wells E	Tpr	22 Aug 1957	Accident on exercise

Arabia
Avers F R	Signals Sgmn	18 Mar 1958	Accident
Lloyd R	Cpl	22 Jul 1958	On active service
Poulton H	L Cpl	10 Aug 1958	Heat exhaustion

Malaya
Richardson R	Tpr	28 May 1959	Shooting accident
Whipp R	L Cpl	16 Nov 1959	Natural causes
Warner MJ	Tpr	21 Nov 1959	Natural causes
Guest RJ	L Cpl	22 Aug 1960	Traffic accident

United Kingdom
Breakwell J	Cpl	10 Jan 1961	In hospital

Germany
Jackson TT	Tpr	7 Jan 1962	Whilst on leave
Delaney P	L Cpl	22 Jul 1962	Peritonitis
Watts B	Tpr	10 Jun 1965	Accident on Soltau Trg Area

In Memoriam

United Kingdom

Rylance TM	Cpl	5 Aug 1967	Landing Craft accident (ERE)
Gwilliam HJ	Capt	28 Dec 1967	Traffic accident

Germany

Hobson G	Cpl	16 Mar 1968	Accident in Ferret scout car
Brown M	Tpr	11 May 1971	As result of fire
Wood AR	Tpr	8 Aug 1971	Accidentally drowned
Williams MA	Tpr	1 Sep 1971	Accident, Münster

United Kingdom

Oldham G	Tpr	30 Oct 1971	Car accident, Tidworth (ERE)
Langford A	Bdsm	4 Aug 1972	Traffic accident on leave
Chandler J	L Cpl	30 Sep 1972	Traffic accident
Hinchcliffe S	Tpr	4 Oct 1972	Traffic accident (ERE)

Germany

Jackson D	Tpr	15 Oct 1974	Accident to tank in training

Northern Ireland

Barraclough R	Tpr	28 Sep 1975	Traffic accident

United Kingdom

Dukes R	Sgt	29 Feb 1976	Natural causes (ERE)

Germany

Haley KB	Tpr	17 Jul 1977	Killed by hit and run driver
Henderson J	WO1	1 Dec 1978	Accident (ERE)

Northern Ireland

Shepherdson PR	Tpr	15 Jul 1978	Traffic accident
Smith PJR	Tpr	27 Jul 1978	Accident in Ferret scout car

Cyprus

Randall KWE	Tpr	23 Jan 1982	Accident

Germany

Harding RDS	L Cpl	4 Jun 1984	Natural causes (leave in UK)
Green P, REME	Cpl	14 Sep 1984	Exercise traffic accident

England

Brooke PB, RAChD	Rev	6 Nov 1987	Traffic accident
Fuller S	L Cpl	12 Sep 1987	Traffic accident on leave
Metcalfe C, REME	L Cpl	30 Jun 1990	Traffic accident

Cyprus

Rimmer A, REME	L Cpl	18 Jul 1990	Accident in Ferret scout car
Easter KJ	Cpl	7 Sep 1990	Traffic accident
Garrard-Cole CH	Cpl	7 Sep 1990	Traffic accident
Owen MD	L Cpl	7 Sep 1990	Traffic accident
Shrubsole S	L Cpl	7 Sep 1990	Traffic accident

Index

(numbers in italic are illustrations)

Formations & Headquarters, British
('Brigade' includes 'Brigade Group')
1 (BR) Corps 88, 99, 200, 322, 327, 369
—, HQ RAC 322
1 Division 18, 20, 154
—, (UK) Armoured 326, 345-6, 369
2 Division 200
3 Division 188, 301
4 Division 200, Armoured 322
11 Armoured Division 88-9, 91-2, 106
17 Gurkha Division 138, 196
1 Infantry Brigade 340
3 Infantry Brigade 26, 247, 270
4 Armoured Brigade 326
4 Guards Brigade 147, 161, 163, 199, 210
—, Armoured 200, 220
5 Infantry Brigade 310
7 Armoured Brigade 147, 154-5, 242, 329
7 Field Force 293
11 Armoured Brigade 329
18 Infantry Brigade 35, 47, 85
19 Infantry Brigade 293, 303
20 Armoured Brigade 163
26 Gurkha Infantry Brigade 34, 67, 72
33 Armoured Brigade 91
63 Gurkha Infantry Brigade 34
99 Gurkha Infantry Brigade 72, 84, 138
Aldershot District 11
Berlin Brigade 96, 159
Cyrenaica District 17, 20
Land Forces Hong Kong 59
Land Forces Persian Gulf 120
Northern Army Group 91-2
Singapore District 136
South Malaya District 39, 67
South West District 340
Tripolitania District 20
UK Mobile Force (UKMF) 340, 351
—, NATO & Commonwealth
3 (US) Infantry Division 337
7 Panzer Division 242
21 Panzer Brigade 200
ACE Rapid Reaction Corps 369
ALF Schleswig Holstein 99
AMF(L) 340, 342-4
Danish Brigade 99-100
28 Commonwealth Brigade 128-9
Units, Regular Army
Life Guards 88, 96, 112, 117, 122, 124, 187, 368

Blues and Royals 226, 310
Household Cavalry Regiment 311, 348
Royal Horse Artillery, 1st 308
1st King's Dragoon Guards 13,15, 18-20, 99, 105, 127, 136
1st Queen's Dragoon Guards 127, 280, 367, 374
Royal Scots Dragoon Guards 270, 350-1
5th Inniskilling Dragoon Guards 83
1st Royal Dragoons 88, 100, 102, 142
Royal Scots Greys 161
4th Hussars 29, 31-4, 52, 67
Queen's Own Hussars 229, 232
8th Hussars 83
9th Lancers 148
9th/12th Lancers 226, 251, 270, 272, 291-2, 333
10th Hussars 199
11th Hussars 83, 85, 167, 175-6, 199
Royal Hussars 199, 226
12th Lancers 52, 67, 295
13th Dragoons 1
— 250th Anniversary 182-5
13th Light Dragoons 80, 86, 94, 171, 349
13th Hussars 1-2, 11, 19, 67, 172, 185, 219, 232, 346, 376-7
14th/20th Hussars 166, 175, 187, 346
15th Hussars 377
15th/19th Hussars 3, 111, 118, 127, 198, 226, 245, 267, 270, 274, 348, 367-8, 376-7
16th/5th Lancers 25, 188, 226, 339-40, 345
17th/21st Lancers 162-3
18th Hussars 1-2, 33, 76, 78, 178, 185-6, 340, 377
18th Light Dragoons 1, 76, 171, 349
Light Dragoons 267, 274, 348, 375-7
Royal Tank Regiment
—, 1st 243-4, 250
—, 2nd 220, 252, 285
—, 3rd 55
—, 4th 243, 245
—, 5th 154, 159, 167, 193
—, 8th 154
—, 1st Indep Sqn 97, 159
Royal Armoured Corps
—, Boys' Squadron 8
—, Junior Leaders' Regiment 8,189
—, Parachute Squadron 225

388

Index

(numbers in italic are illustrations)

(RAC) , Training Regiment 189, 268
Royal Artillery
—, 4th Regt 249
—, 21st Regt 154
—, 25th Regt 50
—, 39th Regt 252
—, 47th Regt 352
—, 54th (Maharajpore) Bty 236
—, 93rd (Le Cateau) Bty 158
Royal Engineers
—, 16th Field Squadron 236
—, 29th Field Squadron 278
Foot Guards
—, Grenadier, 1st 161, 164, 204-6, 2nd 206
—, Coldstream, 1st 161, 165-6, 2nd 209
—, Scots, 2nd 47, 205
—, Irish 242
Infantry of Line (alphabetical)
—, Black Watch 338
—, Cameronians, 1st 71-2
—, Cheshire 242
—, Devon and Dorset 246
—, Gordon Highlanders,1st 225, 246, 249
—, 6th Gurkha Rifles, 1st 60, 2nd 69, 72, 128, 131
—, 7th Gurkha Rifles, 2nd, 44, 47
—, King's Own Royal Border, 1st 251
—, King's Own Scottish Borderers 246
—, King's Shropshire Light Infantry, 1st 115-6, 195
—, King's Own Yorks. Light Infantry 241
—, Light Infantry,1st 252, 2nd 282
—, Loyals, 1st 128
—, Prince of Wales's Own, 1st 234, 236
—, Queen's, 3rd 314
—, Queen's Lancashire, 1st 252, 259
—, Queen's Own Highlanders 272, 281
—, Royal Anglian, 3rd 192
—, Royal Green Jackets, 2nd 206
—, Royal Highland Fusiliers, 1st 161
—, Royal Fusiliers, 3rd 252, 257
—, Royal Irish Fusiliers, 1st 158-9, 161, 165
—, Royal Northumbd. Fusiliers, 1st 192
—, Royal Regiment of Wales 325
—, Royal Ulster Rifles, 1st 190
—, Royal West Kent, 1st 47, 68
—, Suffolk, 1st 47, 50-1, 67, 83
—, Wiltshire, 1st 80

Royal Marines 125
—, 42nd Commando 252, 259-60
Parachute Regiment, 1st 193, 3rd 315
Special Air Service 274, 278
Army Air Corps 202, 294, 662 Squadron 252, 3 Flight 273
Royal Corps of Transport
—, 27 Port Regiment 352
Royal Army Medical Corps
—, 1 Armoured Field Ambulance 345
—, 16 Field Ambulance 351
Royal Army Ordnance Corps
—, 321 EOD Unit 252, 273
Royal Electrical & Mechanical Engineers
—, 3 Infantry Workshops 194
—, 7 Armoured Workshops 154
—, 8 Field Workshops 298
(*see also* LAD)
Royal Military Police, 1st Regt 247
Royal Army Pay Corps 17
(*see also* Paymasters)
RAF Regiment 189
Units, Territorial Army (Alphabetical)
North Irish Militia 245
Queen's, 6th/7th 352
Queen's Own War. & Worcs. Yeo. 148
Queen's Own Yeo. 212, 272, 311, 329
Queen's Own Yorkshire Yeo. 148-149
Royal Yeomanry 149, 329
South Notts Hussars Yeo. 348
Ulster Defence Regiment (UDR) 252, 257, 260, 273, 276-8, 324
Warwickshire Yeo. 94, 148
Units, Commonwealth & Foreign
Arabia
—, Aden Protectorate Levies (APL) 113, 115, 117, 124
—, Hadraumi Bedouin Legion 111, 117-8
—, Mukalla Regular Army 118
—, Sultan's Armed Forces (SAF) 111, 118, 119-20, 125, 212
—, Trucial Oman Scouts (TOS) 118, 120-1, 125
Australia
—, Royal Australian Regiment 129, 131, 134, 137
—, 18th/23rd Australian Light Horse 138
Canada
—, Manitoba Mounted Rifles 138-9
—, Royal Can. Hussars 139, 236, 313,337

389

Index

(numbers in italic are illustrations)

Denmark
—, Garde Hussars 351-2
—, Jutland Dragoons 109-10
Fiji
—, 1st Infantry Regt 47, 72, 82
France
—, 4ème Chasseurs 80-81, 94, 205, 292, 313, 337, 362
Germany
—, 7 Panzeraufklarungs Battalion 339
—, 194 Panzer Battalion 209
India
—, Skinner's Horse 185, 292, 355, 363
Italy
—, 1st Hussars of Milan 326
Malaya/Malaysia
—, Federation Armoured Car Squadron 70
—, 2nd Fed. Recce Regt 71, 315
—, Malay Regiment 55, 70, 1st 44, 3rd 62, 79
—, Malay Signals Regiment 70
New Zealand
—, Royal New Zealand Regiment 129, 131, 134, 195
Pakistan
—, 6th Lancers 185
USA
—, 14th Armored Cavalry 97, 207
—, 3rd/70th Armor 299
—, 81st Security Squadron USAF 352
—, Alabama National Guard 299

A

Abayan, Arabia 117
Abbott Mr, Regt Assoc 142
Abdullah, Prince 313-6
Abery WJM, Capt REME 382
Acland JHB, Maj Gen 306
Ackroyd, Cpl *29*
Aden 111-18, 122-3, 144, 146-7, 187, 189-93
Adjutants 381
Adventure Training
—, Bovington/Warminster 226-7
—, Münster 211-2, *23*
—, Paderborn 169-70
—, Tidworth 351, 354-5
—, Wimbish 305, 315, 318
—, Wolfenbüttel 373
AEC (Matador) armd car 7, 33, 96; *3*
Air Troop 202, 294

Akamas peninsula, Cyprus 302-3
Akrotiri, Cyprus 301
Al Kabr, Arabia 117, 124
Alberta 234, 314
Albion HMS 146
Alden JF, 2 Lt 73
Alden WJ, Lt *29*
Aldershot 10-11, 15-16, 53, 78
Alexandra, HRH Princess 313
Allchurch I, Tpr 213, L Cpl 229, Cpl 238, Sgt 347, 359
Allen J, Capt REME 382
'Ambassador' 238
Amery J, War Minister 128
Amos DR, Lt 327, Capt 381, Maj 380
Ampang, Malaya 47
Ampleforth CCF 338
Anderson AC, Capt 381
Anderson HWF, 2 Lt 226
Anderson Jd'A, Maj Gen 106-7
Anderson JH, Tpr 64
Anderson WF, Sgt 44, 383, SQMS 384, SSM 205, RSM 206, 381
Anglo-Malayan Defence Agreement 127
Annual Inspections 106, 138, 210-11
Ansell JCM, 2 Lt 72, 82, Lt 90-1, 97, Maj 378-9, Lt Col 208, 219, 227, 244-7, 249, 378
Antrim Co. 220, 244
Apollonia, Libya 13, 16-17, 22, 166
Aqaba, Jordan 315
Arabia 111-25, 146, 191
Ard Boe, N Ireland 259, 270, 280
Armagh 252, 255-6, 260-1, 284
Armagh Co. 244, 246, 251-62
Army Reserve 188
Ashcroft J, Cpl 209-10
Assaye Barracks, Tidworth 340, 346
Ataq, Arabia 117
Atkinson TC, S Sgt 311, 385, RSM 381, Capt 381
Army Youth Team (No 12) 212, 241
Atlantic Conveyor 310
ATO 259, 273
attap (thatch) 34
Augher, Tyrone 257
Aughnacloy, Armagh 252, 256
Avenger HMS 362
Avers F, Sgmn 386
Avesnes, France 181

Index
(numbers in italic are illustrations)

Axaiba, Arabia 122
Axson DR, Capt REME 382
Ayer Hitam, Malaya 37
Ayer Kuning, Malaya 42, 44, 46

B

Bad Driburg, Germany 89
Bad Harzburg, Germany 322
Bad Hersfeld, Germany 97, 207
Bad Lippspringe, Germany 178-9, 374
Baden-Powell, Lady 219-20
Baden-Powell, Lt Gen Lord 219
Bahau, Malaya 60
Bahrain, Arabia 111, 118, 120
Bailey K, Cpl 291
Baker, Brig 107
Baker Baker WG, Capt 272, 292, 381
Balaklava 1, 80, 205
—, CO's tank 183, 348
—, Celebrations 79-81, 180, 223, 239, 261
—, Centenary 92-3, 374; *12*
—, Regt March 377
—, Sword 93
Ball A, Capt REME 382
Ballard DP, Capt REME 382
Ballinamallard, Fermanagh 276
Ballykinler, Co. Down 245
Band 11, 15, 36, 78, 91, 93, 99, 138, 142, 159, 174, 181-2, 184, 216-7, 223, 227, 241, 250-1, 262, 267, 268, 297, 311-2, 338-9, 345-6, 348, 351-2, 361; *32*
Bandmasters 382
BAOR (British Army of the Rhine) 90, 94 et seq, 99, 147, 157-9, 162, 199, 208, 370
Barbados 175, 357
Barce, Libya 13-17, 19-20, 24, 152
Barce Vale Hunt 18-19
Barczak PM, Capt RAPC 382
Barker Barracks, Paderborn 161
Barnes, Cfn REME 79
Barnett, Correlli *Britain and Her Army* 6
Barnsley 148, 173-4, 212, 227, 241, 269, 291-2, 339, 361-2, 377; *22*
—, Centenary 216,; *21*
—, Freedom of 299, 311-2; *34*
Barnsley Chronicle 241
Barraclough R, Tpr 387
Barrett B, Lt RAAC, 131
Barrett CRB, *History 13th Hussars* 3
Barton E, Tpr 175

Barton G, Tpr 175
Barton P, Tpr 258
Barty-King MB, 2 Lt 113, 115-6, 383
basha 34, 128
Batson F, Tpr 175
Battle groups 199-200
Battle Honours, 2nd World War 108
Bavaria 335, 373
Baxendale M, Sgt 257
Beasley R, Tpr 132
Beaver PC, Capt 179, Maj 204, 213, 222, 378-80
Beckett C, Maj Gen 196
Belcoo, Fermanagh 281
Belfast 206, 247, 251, 280
Belize 267, 349-51
Bell E, Cpl 329-30, 361, 385
Bell JW, Capt 39, 58-9, 381 Maj 135, 171, 378-9, Lt Col 59
Bell MWH, Maj 18, 23, 29, 34, 77, 84, 378-9, 383
Bell RG, Lt 255, 269
Bellinzona Patrol 372
Belsen, Germany 154
Ben Macdhui SS 28-9
Benghazi 13, 15-20, 24, 166
—, Military Hospital 16
Bentong, Malaya 47, 68
Beragh, Tyrone 281
Berescheid, Germany 165-6
Beresford RS, Lt 40, Capt 381, 383, Maj 379, Bt Lt Col 162-3, 379, Lt Col 168, 187, 196, 202-3, 378
Bergen-Hohne *see* Hohne
Berlin 96, 159, 374 —, Wall 155, 266, 365
Bethmann Hollweg A von, 2 Lt, 107
Bielefeld 99, 322
Bishop C, Cpl *19*
Blake WJ, Cpl 346, 385
Blakely Tpr 209
Blakiston JAG, Lt 163, 167, 176, Maj 222, 228, 244, 281, 285, 289, 378, 380
Block, Brig 107
Blount AH, Lt 115, 118, Capt 176, Maj 379
Blount C, Lt 202
Blunt CJR, Capt 335, 357, 380
Boeselager Competition 332-3, 339, 354, 370-2
Bond, Commodore 142

Index

(numbers in italic are illustrations)

Borneo 68, 187
'Bossy' 334
Bourg Leopold, Belgium 158-9
Bovington Camp 8, 189, 221-32
Brackenridge JD, Capt RAMC 17
'Braithwaite tanks' 253
Brant DCK, RSM 381
Breakwell J, Cpl 386
Bredebeck, Schloss 239
Bridgelayer, Centurion *164*
Bridgland PCA, Capt 17, Maj RAPC 382
Briggs, Sir Harold 32, 64
—, Plan 32, 64, 66
Brighton College CCF 173
British Frontier Service 89
British Soldier 319
Brook MB, Lt 254, Maj 323-4, 380
Brooke PB, Rev 387
Brough DWT, 2 Lt 76
Browell MH, Maj 15/19H 380
Brown M, Tpr 387
Brown TA, Maj RAPC 382
Bubu Forest, Malaya 132
Bukit Mandei, Malaya 48
Bulwark HMS 146
Bundeswehr 108-9, 157, 180, 332
Burgess J, Tpr 386
Burgess SD, Capt 337
Burnand GF, Capt 381
Burnett C, Maj Gen *Memoirs 18H* 3, 376
Burton GW, Capt RAPC 382
Burton MP, Capt REME 382
Bushby, Cpl 225

C

'Cabro' 228-9
Cachy Barracks, Perham Down 188
Caen Barracks, Hohne 239-40
Caledon, Tyrone 255
Calgary, Canada 167, 234
Calvocoressi P, *World Politics* 265
Cambridge OTC 365
Cameron Highlands, Malaya 137
Camp 53, Fanara, Egypt 25
Campsie, Omagh 284
Canadian Army Trophy (CAT) 167-9, 187, 243
Canal Zone, Egypt 25
Canberra SS 310
Cannon Hall, (Regimental Museum) 216
'Caprice' 290

Captains and Subalterns Polo
—, 1968, 213
—, 1976, 238
Caribbean 349
Carpenter GE, 2 Lt 386
Carrickmore, Omagh 282
Carver RMP, Gen 194, 295, FM 314
Carver Barracks, Wimbish 295, 313, 316-7, 319
Cassidy, Tpr 205
Casterton EL, Cpl 385
Castlederg, Tyrone 277, 280-282, 287, 289
Castlemartin Ranges, Pembroke 190, 222, 314, 353
Catterick, Yorks 189, 272, 268
Cavalry Colonels 368
Cavalry Cup Football
—, 1965 177
—, 1967 *197*.
—, 1971 214
—, 1972 214
—, 1989 356
—, 1991 356, 366
Cavenagh D, 2 Lt RSDG 277
Celle, Germany 180, 205
Central African Federation 306
Centurion tank 155
Chamberlin NPHR, 2 Lt 170
Chandler DG, ix
Chandler J, L Cpl 387
Chapman, Tpr *23*
Charles McLeod LST 166
Chatburn A, Bandmaster 339, 382
Chester R, RSM 381
Chieftain tank 203, 207
Chirnside GM, Lt 24, Capt 105, 381, 383, Maj 162, 176, 178, 190, 378-9
Christian Mrs P 282
Christian Leadership courses 82
Christophers TE, 2 Lt 65-6
Churchill WSC, Prime Minister 65-6
CIGS 92
Circuit training 188
Clegg A, Sgt 75, 383
Cliff RT, Capt 156, 163, 192, Maj 223, 228, 233, 240, 378-9
Clogg M, Lt Royals 102
Clogher, Tyrone 257, 281

Index

(numbers in italics are illustrations)

Clunie J, Tpr 116
Coagh, Tyrone 280
Coalisland, Tyrone 257
Cobb BJW, Lt 22, 29, 41, 85, Capt 383
　Maj 129, 132, 378-9
Cobb JME, Lt 359
Cockburn RHA, Lt Col17/21L 162-3
Coker AD, Maj 323, 380
Coker DHE, Maj 17, 78, 379, 381, Lt Col
　136, 158, 378, 384
Coker, Mrs DHE 17, 104, 141
Colacicchi MP, 2 Lt 246, Lt 254,
　Maj 324, 347, 380
Colchester, Essex 293
Coldham, L Cpl ACC 173
Collins A, S Sgt 269
Collis AJN, Lt 213, Maj 273, 298, 303,
　318-9, 380
Colonels-in-Chief 78, 349, 366, 378
Colonels 378
Combat teams 199-200
Commanding Officers 378
Commonwealth Monitoring Force 306, 309
Communist Terrorists (CT) 33-83, 65, 129,
　131-4
Conqueror tank 155
Constantine HM King 313
Cook DR, Tpr 386
Cookstown 252, 258-9, 278-9, 281-2
Copenhagen 352
Cordy-Simpson JR, Maj 11, 379,
　Lt Col 53, 81, 87, 378, 383, Col 215,
　227, 378, 383; *21*
Cordy-Simpson RA, 2 Lt 169, 215, Capt
　279, 381, Maj 223, 304-5, 379-80,
　Lt Col 321, 323-4, 328, 332-3, 339, 378,
　385, Brig 370, Maj Gen 369
Coronation Parades 79; *7*
Coronation Park, Kuala Lumpur 47
Cotter Sir D, Bt, Maj 18, 78, 378,
　Lt Col 87, 99-100, 104, 244, 246, 378
Cotterell RCR, Maj 244-5, 380
Cotton S, Cpl 353
Coulson W, L Cpl 383
Cowan M, Lt REME 179
Crimea Centenary, Paris 93-4
Cross H, RSM 324, 381; *28*
Cudworth, Yorks 173
Cunningham MA, Cpl 384, Maj 380
Curzon Camp, Libya 204

Cyprus 212, 226, 266, 292-3, 296-7,
　300-5, 317-19, 333, 339-41, 349, 358,
　360, 365, 368-9
Cyrenaica 12-14, 18, 20-1, 26-8, *1*
Cyrenaica Defence Force (CYDEF) 21
Cyrene 13, 22-23, 166

D

Daimler armoured cars 7, 33, 128
Darfield, Yorks 216
Davie WAG, Capt RAPC 382
Davies D, Sgt 257-8
Davies EA, Sgt 132, 383
Davies PM, 2 Lt 226
Davies SP, Tpr 324, Sgt 253, SSM 311,
　RSM 324, 381, Capt 356, 381
Davis AJ, Sgt 257
Davis PJ, Sgt 23, Lt 102, 141, 381,
　Capt 381
Davison, Tpr 215
DD tanks 2, 377
de Fontblanque, Gen 55
de Zeligcourt J, Gen 365
Debden, Essex 295-6
Dedman M, Sgt 38, 384
Delamain CJG, Capt 105, 181, Maj 196,
　204, 378-9
Delaney P, L Cpl 387
Delaney PJ, L Cpl 361
Delius DJ, Capt 170, 189, Maj 223, 250,
　252, 257, 285, 379-80, 384
Demonstration Squadron, RAC 147
Denby, Tpr 327
Denney WG, Capt 381, Maj 83, 334, 379,
　383
Dennis SEW, Capt RAMC 355
Denny NNM, Maj 313, 379
Derna, Libya 13, 16-17, 19, 24-5, 166
Derrylin, Fermanagh 283
Desert Rescue Patrols 21
Determeyer RE, Lt 361
Devonshire HMT 28
Dewar M, *Brush Fire Wars* 120, 122
Dhala, Arabia 112-6, 124-5
—, Emir of 115
Dhekelia, Cyprus 301
Dick RCJ, Maj RTR 214, 378-9
Dick, WO 2 ACC 258
Dodds RJ, Lt 75, Capt 75, 383
Dogs, Regimental 28
Doncaster, Yorks 148, 173, 212, 227,

Index

(numbers in italic are illustrations)

(Doncaster) 240-1, 362
Doncaster Gazette 241
Dorfmark Drag Hounds 237
Dorman Sir C, Bt, Maj 99, 379
Douglas-Hamilton BC, Maj 379
Dowdall T, Sgt 202
Dowey DJT, Capt RAPC 382
Dowle, Tpr 225
Down Co. 244-5
Downside CCF 365
Drewery, Cpl 308
Drogheda, Earl of 76
Dromore, Tyrone 276
Dublin 248
Dukes R, Sgt 387
Dungannon, Tyrone 247, 256-7, 259
Dunkerly VAB, Col 137-8, 182, 186, 215, 378
Dunlop, Maj Gen 39-41
Durand, Sir Mortimer *13H in Gt. War* 3
Durian Tipus, Malaya 69
Dushera festival 72, 79
Duxford, Cambs 296

E

East Aden Protectorate 111-2, 118
East Johore Bus Company 63
Easter KJ, Cpl 342, 387
Edelsten DAG, Capt 163, 178, 381, Maj 379, Lt Col 227, 229-30, 232-3, 236, 378; *17*
Eden A, Prime Minister 145
Edge SE, Tpr 64
Edwards CJ, Maj 222, 273, 380
Egerton, Det Con 314
Eggegebirge hills 89
Egypt 25, 118
El Adem (airfield), Libya 20, 166, 204
Elbe R., Germany 96
Elbe Seiten Canal, Germany 333
Elizabeth II, HM The Queen 79, 93, 183, 361, Coronation 79, Silver Jubilee 268
Elizabeth, HM The Queen Mother 336, 361; *12*
Elliot HR, Capt 46
Ellis, Pte ACC 79
Ellis JA, Capt REME 382
EMEs *see* LAD, OCs
Emergency, Malayan 31, 47, 65, 83, 127, 131, 135-6
Empire Orwell 111

Empire Pride 28, 126
Empire Test 12, 19
Empire Trooper 86, 126, 142
Endau, Malaya 37, 51, 63
Enniskillen 247, 276, 282
Enosis 300
EOKA 300
Episkopi, Cyprus 301; *29*
Erne, Lough, Fermanagh 288
Esler AR, 2 Lt 179
Eton CCF 338
Etteln, Germany 181
Evan Gibb LST 12
Evans A, Sgt 83
Eve WH, Capt 13H 290
Exercises
—, Ally Express 344
—, Arbiter 190, 193; *18*
—, Autumn Circuit 300
—, Battle Royal 91, 95, 106, 297
—, Black Jake 243
—, Bold Grouse 351
—, Bold Guard 329
—, Bughunt 131
—, Cargo Canoe 298
—, Certain Shield 370
—, Crusader 297-8
—, Dawn Patrol 226
—, Desert Rat 159
—, Double Drum 207
—, Druid's Drake 353
—, Eternal Triangle 326
—, Gialo 24
—, Gobi Dust 299
—, Grand Canyon 326
—, Green Pastures 233
—, Ground Nuts 26; *3*
—, Grosse Baer 242
—, Gryphons Gambit 299
—, Hardfall 342
—, Highland Winter 355
—, Highwayman 352
—, House Warming 109
—, Indian Eagle 336
—, Invariant 226
—, Jamestown 226
—, Kadet Kanter 338
—, Kalypso Wicket 357
—, Kollected Kanter 325, 372, 374
—, Kulu Conquest 355

Index

(numbers in italic are illustrations)

(Exercises) Lionheart 327-8
—, Long John 158
—, Mailed Fist 159
—, Noble Mob 162
—, Olive Oil 211
—, Open Glove 163
(Exercises) Pond Jump 167
—, Pond Jump West 314
—, Quarter Final 329
—, Quick Train 201
—, Richardson's Bluff 232
—, Snow Queen 335
—, Spearpoint 157, 242, 298
—, Viking 352, 360; *36*
—, Winter Kanter 326
Eyre JR, Capt REME 382

F

Facings, uniform 108
Fairrie JPJ, Capt 229, 381
Falkland Islands 265, 310, 362
Fallingbostel, Germany 147, 154, 161, 171, 174, 177, 180, 182-4, 374-5
Famagusta, Cyprus 304
Families 17, 27, 184, 218, 224, 250, 296, 323, 349, 363
Families Weekend 174, 183, 196, 217, 227, 313, 338-9; *31*
Fanara, Egypt 25
FARELF (Far East Land Forces) Cup 82
Faringdon H, *Confrontation* 155, 200
Farmer B, SSM 330
'Farouk' 171, 175-6, 178; *15*
Faulkner B, Ulster Prime Minister 206
Faulkner RS, Maj 16/5L 304
Fayed, Egypt 25
Fearless HMS 146, 194, 196
Fermanagh Co. 270, 272, 274-5, 280-1, 284, 288-90
Fermanagh Harriers 289
Feversham, Earl of 19, 137
ffrench Blake RJW, Capt 198, 213, 381, Maj 235-6, 379-80, Lt Col 297, 299, 314, 319, 323, 337, 378, Col 363, 367-8, 375-6, 378
ffrench Blake RLV, Lt Col 17/21L 198
ffrench-Nobbs CK, Capt REME 176, 178, 382
Fig Tree Bay, Cyprus 305
'Finella' 176, 178
Firq, Arabia 118, 120

Fish H, Councillor 311
Fishwick SN, Maj 341, 380; *33*
Fitzgibbon SP, Capt REME 382
Fivemiletown, Tyrone 257, 276-7
Flanagan, Cpl *23*
Flood JA, Maj RAPC 382
Fort As Sariz, Arabia 115
Foster KA, Maj 83, 379, 383
Fox armoured car 286, 294, 298, 321
Francis, Tpr 305
Fraser D, Cpl 62
Fraser P, SQMS 304
Fraser's Hill, Malaya 47, 64
Fredericks M, Capt REME 382
Freedom of Barnsley 299, 311-2
Frudd FR, Sgt 385
Fulda, R., Germany 155
Fuller S, L Cpl 387

G

Gaddafi, Col 204
Gage AW, Capt 70, Maj 379
Gallagher J, Cpl 272
Galvin J, Gen (SACEUR) 345
Gapis Estate, Malaya 132
Garbutt EJS, SSM 97, RSM 171, 381, Maj 291, 381, 382
Garda (Irish Police) 256
Garrard-Cole CH, Cpl 342, 387
Garrison, Fermanagh 281
Geggie T, Bandmaster 79, 382
Gelbe Kreis 180
Gemas, Malaya 137
Germany, end of Occupied status 95
Ghemines, Libya 24
ghibli 16, 24
Gibraltar 362
Gibson JP, Maj 380
Gibson PAJ, Maj 276, 301, 323, 379-80
Glendale Estate, Malaya 70
Glenorchy SS 28
Gloucester, HRH Duke of 78, 171-2, 346
Gloucester, HRH Duchess of 184
GMC APC 7, 33
Goch, Germany 15
Goldgrund (trg area), Paderborn 168, 183
Good CP, Maj 380
Goodey GVS, 2 Lt 69, Lt 383, Maj 379
Goole, Humber 240
Gorbachev Mikhail 265
Gortin, Tyrone 278

395

Index

(numbers in italic are illustrations)

Gosford Castle, 226
Gough Barracks, Armagh 252
Gow JM, Brig 210-211, Gen 200; *19*
Grand Military Race Meeting 336, 361
Grandsome J, Tpr 386
Grantham. Lincs 298
Gray D, Col 363
Green MH, Lt 225,
Green P, Cpl REME 387
Greencastle, Down 278
Greener PM, Bandmaster 382
Greenslade WJ, RSM 25, 381
Gregory AA, 2 Lt 75, 82, 383
Griffith-Jones MD, Lt 226, Capt 239, 272, 289
Griffith-Jones Mrs 239
Grik, Malaya 132, 134-5
Grimwood SSM 19
Grosses Moor, Germany 157
Gruenther, Gen (SACEUR) 92
Guatemala 349
Guest RJ, L Cpl 386
Guided Weapons 201, 203, 340; *25*
Guidon 108, 175, 182-4, 269, 311-2, 377
—, Presentation 1961 171-172; *15*
—, Presentation 1987 267, 314, 346-8, 361
Gulf, Persian 147, 212, 375
Gulf War 344-5, 365, 368, 375
Gurney, Sir Henry 32, 64-5, 74
Gwilliam HJ, TQMS 172, Lt 153, Capt 387

H

Haddon T, L Cpl 318, 337
Haglund, BV 206, 341; *35*
Haines CJW, 2 Lt 104
Haley KB, Tpr 387
Hall R, Tpr 386
Hamburg 100, 108, 151, 154
Hammond LW, Tpr 386
Hannover 154, 180, 184, 322
Hanson K, Cpl 272
Harden JB, 2 Lt 60, 386
Harewood Barracks, Herford 321, 328
Harding RDS, L Cpl 387
Hargrove SJA, Lt *9*, Capt 381;
Harman J, Lt Gen 236
Harris B, Maj 224, 382
Harris DDA, 2 Lt 46, 60,
Harris, Capt REME 382
Harrison F, Sgt 73, SSM 166, Capt 249, Maj 222, 379, 380-1
Harrison WG, Capt REME 382
Harwich, Essex 10, 87, 352
Harz, Germany 90, 103, 322, 326, 332, 373
Hatton JB, S Sgt 168-9, RSM 381
Hawley S, Cpl 384, Sgt 283, 305,
  S Sgt 385 SSM 341, RSM 367, 381; *33*
Hays L Cpl 211
Healey D, Defence Minister 146
Heathrow, London Airport 293
Helmstedt, Germany 96
Helyar RM, Lt *7*
Henderson J, RSM 269, 381, 387
Henson E, Capt 197, 381
Herford, Germany 321-39
Hermon RA, Lt Col 9, 21, 137, 378
Hertogh, Maria 39, 42, 52, 56
Hickey J, Sgt 156
Hickson GA, L Cpl 349
Higgens L, Maj RAPC 382
Hildesheim, Germany 88, 159, 243
Hill AJ, Capt REME 382
Hill-Norton, Admiral of Fleet 209
Himalayas 355
Hinchcliffe S, Tpr 387
Hind AL, RSM 9
Hipkiss J, Sgt 70, 383
Hird J, Tpr 82
Hoad PR, Capt 381
Hobbs MF, Maj Gen 329
Hobson G, Cpl 387
Hochsauerland March 372
Hodgson PEB, Capt 212
Hodkinson J, L Cpl 40
Hohenstein, Graf Thun 107
Hohne, Germany 147, 154, 184, 232-41, 252, 261, 267-8, 374, Ranges 96, 159, 168, 203, 233-5, 370, 372
Hok JE, Capt 176
Holderness peninsula, Humber 353
Holmes D, Cpl 103
Holmes M, 2 Lt 98, 104, Lt 120,
Holmes P, Sgt 269
Holzminden, Germany 89
Home Headquarters 149, 173, 184, 186, 291, 377, Officers Commanding 382
Hong Kong 31, 52, 55, 58-59, 67, 80, 141, 187, 363
Hong Kong & Shanghai Bank 48
Hope-Johnstone PW, Capt 381,

Index

(numbers in italic are illustrations)

(Hope-Johnstone) Maj 379-80
Horne J, Tpr 273
Horrocks, Lt Gen 106
Hough MJ, Tpr 335, 337
Howard JRL, Lt 15, 22, 55, 61, 70, 383,
    Capt 93, 96, 381, Maj 378-9, Lt Col
    200, 203, 208, 217, 378; *19*
Howard-Allen D, 2 Lt 52
Howarth J, Tpr 181
Howden M, Sgt 104
Howlett M, Cpl 168
Howson JM, Maj 20, 22, 78, 80, 99, 379,
    Lt Col 185
Howson W, L Cpl 384
Hudson CH, 2 Lt 222
Hudson R, L Cpl 37, 386
Hull J, Tpr 73
Hull RA, Gen 128, 141, FM 368
Humber r. 352-3
Humberside 240, 361
Hunt DP, Capt 313
Hunt EE, Lt 73, 77, 83, 90, 383, Capt 99,
    105, Maj 159, 182, 189-90, 313, 378-9,
    384; *5*
Hunt Dr, 159
Hussar Admirals 134
Hussein, HM King 313; *31*
Hutton S, Cpl 179
Höxter, Germany 89

I

Ibans 67-8
Ibbotson ADC, Lt 333, 354-5, 358
Idris, HM King 21, 166
Inter-Regimental Polo 1976, 238
Intrepid HMS 146, 226
Ipoh, Malaya 69, 127-8, 131, 137-8, 140-1
IRA 247, 249, 260, 270, 274, 279-84
Irchin HMS 173
Ireland RIA, 2 Lt 214, 228
Irish Army 255
Isefjaer, Norway 170
Iski, Arabia 120, 125
Isles J, Tpr 140

J

Jackson D, Tpr 387
Jackson P, Capt REME 382
Jackson TT, Tpr 386
Jackson W, Gen *Withdrawal from Empire*
    65-66, 191, 265, 301, 306 et seq
Jacques CB, 2 Lt 69

Jarymwycz, Lt Col Canadian Hussars 337
Jebel Akhdar, Libya 13
—, Oman 118, 120, 123
Jebel Jihaf, Arabia 115
Jemaluang, Malaya 34, 36, 38-9, 42, 52,
    63-4, 72-4, 76-7, 79, 84-5, 137; *8*
Jepson G, SSM 59, RQMS 383, Capt 381
Jeram Padang, Malaya 69
Jerlun, Malaya 134
Johore, Malaya 32, 34, 36-7, 39, 41-2,
    51-2, 62, 64, 67, 70-2, 74, 79, 84, 127-9
Jolley ER, Capt 17, 29, Maj 46-7, 60, 111,
    115, 123, 131, 379, 383, Lt Col 384
Jones LB, Capt RAPC 382
Jordan 313, 315, 319

K

Kajang, Malaya 35, 47
Kalahatri Nautch 72
KAPE 240-1, 338, 361
Karmel NL, 2 Lt 140
Kassel, Germany 163, 325, 370
Kay GB, Cpl 383
Keady, Armagh 253, 255, 261
Keane RM, Lt 305, Maj 379-80
Kedah, Malaya 47
Keegan J, *History of Warfare* 264
Keightley C, Gen 85
Kelantan, Malaya 47
Kennedy, Miss K 196
Kennedy, President 159
Kent, HRH Duchess of 74
Kenyon B, Tpr 178, 197, Sgt 237
Kershaw A, Bandmaster 159, 382
Kharad, Arabia 125
Khormaksar, Aden 191-2
—, Airfield 189
Kiel, Germany 108, 213
—, Canal 100
—, Yacht Club 104
Killyleagh, Down 245
Kinawley, Fermanagh 276-7, 279, 283-4
King IG, Capt REME 382
King T, Defence Minister 266
Klang, Malaya 48, 50, 68
Kluang, Malaya 34, 36-7, 39, 67, 72-3, 79,
    82, 129, 137
Knebworth, Herts 317
Knight R, Tpr 386
Kohl H, German Chancellor 88
Kongkoi (trg area), Malaya 55, 70

Index
(numbers in italic are illustrations)

Korean War 27, 33, 55, 83, 129, 144, 155
'Korsar' 104-5
Kota Bahru, Malaya 75
Kota Tinggi, Malaya 41-2, 52, 63-4, 129
—, Jungle Warfare School 32, 226
Kowloon, Hong Kong 59
Kowtnuniw, Tpr *23*
Kuala Kangsar, Malaya 129, 133
Kuala Klawang, Malaya 70
Kuala Kubu Bahru, Malaya 35, 47, 68
Kuala Lipis, Malaya 48, 75
Kuala Lumpur, Malaya 34-6, 47-8, 67-9, 74-5, 77, 79-80, 82, 85, 135; *7, 14*
Kuwait 144, 266, 344-5

L

Labis, Malaya 72
LAD REME 21, 36, 172, 179, 207, 262, 296, Officers Commanding 382
Ladang Geddes estate, Malaya 43
Lafferty T, RSM 381
Lahej 11, 113, 116
Lajj, Mesopotamia 290
—, Camp, Kuala Lumpur 67
Lakin ED, Capt REME 382
Lancaster House Agreement 266, 306
Lane TE, 2 Lt 383
Lang R, Capt 315, 381
Langford A, Bdsm 387
Larkhill Ranges, Wilts 223
Larzac (trg area), France 164-5, 204
Laverick, SSM 217
Lawson P, Sgt 308-9, 385
Lawton Tpr, *23*
Le Hardy CA, Capt 240, Maj 305-9, 380
Leak, Cpl *23*
Leakey AR, Brig 159
Lech R., Germany 155
Ledger SW, Lt 292, Capt 347, Maj 380
Legard ET, Lt 372
Legoniel, Down 225
Leopard tank 209
Levey SR, Capt 358-9, 381
'Lily' 289
Lilywhite Gazette 218
'Lilywhites' 2, 357
'LilyWillies' 244-5, 250
LilyWilly newsletter 218, 246
Lisanelly Barracks, Omagh 270, 272, 290
Lisbellaw, Fermanagh 276
Lisnaskea, Fermanagh 283

Lloyd MC, Lt 93
Lloyd R, Cpl 386
Loader AGD, Sgt 25, 386
Local KM, Sgt 291
Locker GE, Bandmaster 297, 382, Lt 339, Capt 382; *32*
Loftus DJStJ, 2 Lt 99, Lt 93, Capt 175-6, 180, 381, Maj 379, Lt Col 233, 236, 238-9, 243, 268, 274, 285, 291, 378, 384; *22*
Londonderry 245, 248, 286
Long Kesh (*see also* Maze) 206, 244-51
Louisiana, USA 299
Lulworth, Dorset 221, 223-4, 228-9, 232, 286
Lumley JN, Brig 11, 78, 378
Lurgan, Armagh 247
Lyneham, Wilts 224
Lyon, France 205
Lyttelton O, Colonial Secy 65-6
Lübeck, Germany 100, 108
Lüneberg Heath, Germany 205

M

McGuire, Tpr 181
McKendrick WJ, L Cpl 329-30, 385
McKenzie, Tpr *23*
Macksey K, *History of the RAC* 244
McLeod Barracks, Neumünster 102
Maddelena, Libya 24
Magilligan ranges, Londonderry 286-7
Maguire F, MP 283
Makarios, President 301
Malacca, Malaya 30, 42-3, 74, 77
Malawi 306
Malaya 26-31, 33-55, 58-85, 90, 126-42, 150, 152, 194, 273
Malayan Railways 69, 75
Malaysia 127, 147, 187, 226, 315
Malet H, Col *Memoirs18H* 3
Mallinson AL, Capt 251, 290, Maj 323, 326, 379-80, Lt Col 363, 365, 378; *31*
—, *Light Dragoons* 3, 169, 259, 360
Mallinson Mrs 334
Mallows G, Sgt 167, 290
Mangles JS, Lt 38, 40, 83, 383, Capt 105, 381, Maj 379
Manong, Malaya 134
Maphanga J, (*voorloper*) 186
Marang, Malaya 194
Marchwood (port), Hants 342, 352

Index

(numbers in italic are illustrations)

Margaret, HRH Princess 91
Marr JHW, Capt 79, Maj 379
Marr, L Cpl 247
Mary, HM Queen 2, 78, 349, 378
Mason R, MP 291
Maule KC, Lt 98, 103
Maze Prison (*see also* Long Kesh) 324
Meares J, Maj 22, 35, 47, 50, 379
Medicine Hat, Canada 234
Mee DG, 2 Lt 82
Mersing, Malaya 34, 37-9, 41-2, 51, 62-3, 76-7, 79, 84, 129
Metcalfe C, L Cpl REME 387
Mexborough, Yorks 174
Middletown, Armagh 252-3, 255
Miller CH, Maj Gen 78, 87, 93, 137, 378; *12; History 13th/18th Hussars* 1, 3, 10, 22
Milne, L Cpl 302
Min Yuen 34, 36, 48, 50
—, Definition 54
Minden, Germany 330
Misurata, Libya 11-14
Mittelandkanal, Germany 330
Mogg HJ, Brig 129
Mohne See, Germany 179
Monaghan 255-6
Monaghan Co. 252
Mont Pinçon, Normandy 106
—, Anniversary 312-3
—, Regimental Memorial viii, 313
Moore SPF, Tpr 279
Morgan J, WO2 315
Moritz of Hesse, Prinz 107
Morley J, Cpl 272, 287
Morris N, Singapore Police 56-7
Mosel R., Germany 326
Mount Ararat, Turkey 343
Mount Kenya 355
Mount Troodos, Cyprus 305
Mountbatten, Admiral of Fleet 146
MPAJA 31
MRLA 31-2, 36, 64, 127, 135
Msus, Libya 23
Mugabe R, 306, 309
Mukalla, Arabia 118
Mulloy, Cpl 211
Muscat, Arabia 118, 122
Myson J, Sgt 384
Münster, Germany 147, 176, 199-220, 223, 234, 250, 374

—, Horse Show 217
—, Polo Club 213
Museum, Regt. 216, 269, 291, 377; *21*

N

Naestved, Norway 351
Nall EWJ, Lt 254, 289, Capt 342, 380
Nasser Gamel Abdel 111, 118
National Service(men) 7-8, 11, 22, 27, 34, 127, 137, 148-52, 173
NATO 88, 94-5, 100, 109, 155, 157, 162, 167, 169, 200, 226, 264-5, 267, 332, 339-40, 342, 352, 369
NCOs Cadres 330-2
Neagh, Lough, N Ireland 225-226, 259, 270, 278
Nee Soon, Singapore 32, 126, 129, 194
Negri Sembilan, Malaya 32, 34, 42, 60, 62, 69-70
Neill ID, Ven 171
Neumünster, Germany 99, 102-5, 107-8, 110-11, 126, 139, 141, 151, 154, 219
Neuss, Germany 89
Nevasa HMT 142
Newbery F, Sgt *19*
Newby DA, 2 Lt 73
Newtown Butler, Fermanagh 280
Newtownstewart, Tyrone 276
New Villages, Malaya 32, 55, 66, 77
Nicosia, Cyprus 301, 304-5, 341, 369; *37*
Niedersachsen Meute 175
Nightsun searchlight 274
Nixon G, Sgt 247, S Sgt 385
Nizwa, Arabia 112, 118-20, 122
Nkomo J, 306, 309
Noble LF, Sgt 336, 361
Noel ACW, Col 186
Noor HM Queen 313
Norman NJ, Lt 289, 292, 384
Normandy viii, 48, 106, 137, 312-3, 377
North Atlantic Treaty *see* NATO
North Rhine Westphalia 161
Northampton Barracks, Wolfenbüttel 88, 367-8, 373-4
Northern Ireland 147, 206, 225, 244-62, 268, 324-5
Norton ADL, Lt 257-8
Norton R, S Sgt 336, SSM 361
Norway 342-3; *35*
Nott J, Defence Minister 265
'Noya Para' 238

Index

(numbers in italic are illustrations)

Nutting RCB, 2 Lt 226, Capt 259, 289, 275, 381, 384, Maj 323, 370, 379-80
Nyasaland 306

O

Oakley CT, Maj RAPC 382
Ogden HP, Lt 361, Maj 370, 380
Ogden JW, Lt 336-7, Capt 350, 361, 358
Ogg GWD, 2 Lt 383
Oh! Münster! 219
O'Laddin 290
Oldham G, Tpr, 387
Oliver G, Sgt 165-7
Omagh 241, 270-92; *26, 27*
Oman 111-3, 118-20, 122-3, 212
Operations
—, Agila 306
—, Banner 147, 206, 218, 220, 233, 237, 244-62, 267, 324
—, Corporate 310
—, Desert Storm 266
—, Ginger 131
—, Granby 267, 345
—, Hammer 68
—, Jaya 131-2
—, Matador 206-7
—, Opportunity 48
—, Sickle 68
—, Tiger 129
—, Trustee 293
'Options for Change' 8, 266, 365, 367
Orduna HMT 28
Orr MM, 2 Lt 104; *1*
Orwell HMT 111
Osnabrück, Germany 244, 250
Ostend, Belgium 159
O'Sullivan K, RQMS 249, Lt 237, Capt 384, Maj 323, 380
Otterburn (trg area), Northumberland 354
Overend J, L Cpl 166
Owen MD, L Cpl 342, 387
Oxfordshire HMT 126
Oxley JAG, 2 Lt 336, Lt 361

P

Paderborn, Germany 147, 159, 161-2, 177, 180, 183-5, 370
Pahang, Malaya 42-3, 47-8, 69
Paige JP, Lt 44, 82, 383
Pakenham-Walsh RW, Capt 346
Palestine 10, 20
Palmer A, SSM 384

Palmer JR, Lt Col 149, 184, 291, 382
Paris, Crimea Centenary 93-4
Parkin A, SSM 383
Parnaby HR, RSM 79, 381, 383
Paroi Camp, Seremban 67, 76, 273
Pateman G, SSM 383, RSM 381
Paton JOG, Maj 168, 379
Patterson, Maj Gen 196
Paymasters 382
Payne NGA, Capt 202
Pearce GWA, Capt REME 105, 382
Pears JP, Tpr 386
Pearson, Lt Gen 196
Pearson, Tpr 12
Peel R, Capt 359
Penang, Malaya 30, 82, 142
Perak, Malaya 47, 127, 129, 131, 135, 140
—, Sultan of 141
Perham Down, Wilts 188-98
Persian Gulf *see* Gulf
Pertang Estate, Malaya 42
'Peter' 28, 46
Peto WG, Capt 315, Maj 324, 341, 354, 360, 364, 379-80
Peto Mrs 290
Peyton NR, Lt 253
Phantom umpires 92
Phillips AMG, Capt 355
Phillips, L Cpl 302
Piddlehinton, Dorset 126
Pike DBE, 2 Lt 118
Pitcairn ACP, Lt 69, 383
Platt JL, RQMS 269, RSM 290, 381
Plummer, Col US Army 97
Pollard TW, Sgmn 383
Pomeroy, Tyrone 278
Port Dickson, Malaya 42, 82
Port Said, Egypt 12, 28, 144
Port Stanley, Falkland Islands 310
Port Swettenham, Malaya 48, 50
Portadown, Armagh 245, 249
Porton Down, Wilts 345
Poulton H, L Cpl 386
Prince-Smith JW, Lt 315, 333
Puckeridge and Thurlow Hunt 317
Pyman H, Maj Gen 92-3, 106
—, *Call to Arms* 23-4

Q

'Q' cars 272
Quartermasters 381

Index

(numbers in italic are illustrations)

Qatabah, Arabia 116
Queen Elizabeth 2 RMS 310
QMO award 156, 273
Quicke RNB, Maj 323, 327, 345, 380, 385
Quirke, L Cpl 258
Quorn, Leics 86-7, 126

R

Reg. Army Assistance (RAAT) 364
RAC Centre 147, 221 et seq
RAC Regatta Gold Cup 358
Radley CCF 338, 365
RAF 50
—, Aldergrove 274
(RAF) Benson 300
—, Brize Norton 224
—, Debden 295
—, Gütersloh 199
Ramillies Camp, Ipoh 128
Ramsay AF, 2 Lt 120
Randall KWE, Tpr 387
Rasah Camp, Seremban 42
Rash House 288
Raub, Malaya 48
Razak, Tun Abdul 136
Recruiting 8, 148, 173-4, 189, 216-7, 240-1
Regimental facings 108
Regimental Museum 216, 269, 291, 377
Regimental sergeant majors 381
Rendsburg, Germany 99
Renwick T, WO 385
Reunions 196, 217, 227, 374-5
Reynolds JJ, Maj 89, 381
Rheinsehlen, Germany 298
Rhine R. 88-90, 155, 298
Rhine Army *see* BAOR
Rhodes James R 6
Rhodesia 266, 306, 309-10
Richardson R, Tpr 386
Rimmer A, Cpl REME 342, 387
Riyan, Arabia 112, 118
Robbins A, Tpr 62
Robbins AF, Lt 383
Roberts PT, 2 Lt 283, Capt 337, Maj 358, 361, 380
Robertson JAR, Maj Gen 138
Robinson CAGB, Capt 166, Maj 256, 380
Robinson, Cpl 242
Robson D, L Cpl 369; *37*

Rocky Mountains, Canada 315
Rockwood, Omagh 277
Rogers DS, Sgt 275
Rogers ECH, RQMS 386
Rogge B, Vice Admiral 110
Rollestone Camp (prison), Wilts 364
Rompin, Malaya 42-3, 60, 62, 69-70
Rosslea, Fermanagh 280
Rotherham, Yorks 148, 241
Rowe RJD, Capt 238
Royal Artillery Hunt 359
Royal Air Force *see* RAF
Royal Australian Air Force 51
Royal Navy 274
Royal Ulster Constabulary *see* RUC
Roynon GD, 2 Lt 98, 103-4
RUC 206, 256-8, 261, 270, 274, 276-83
Rugge-Price AAK, Maj 89, 378, Lt Col 100, 114, 378. Col 384
Rutherford P, Tpr 169
Rylance TM, Cpl 387

S

SACEUR 92, 345
St Albans, Herts 300
St Angelo, Omagh 272, 275, 291; *28*
Saffron Walden, Essex 295, 311
Saladin armoured car 7, 223, 301
Salisbury Plain 188, 197-8, 222, 296, 300, 340, 348, 351, 353, 363-5, 368
Sanaa fort, Arabia 114, 116
Sandhurst, RMA 8, 208, 272, 302, 313
Sandown race course 228
Sandys D, Defence Minister 108, 127, 145-6, 149
Santa Guistina, Italy 211
Saracen APC 7, 128
Saudi Arabia 118, 122
Schleswig Holstein, Germany 99-100, 109, 365, 372
Scorpion etc, CVR series 294, 321
Scott GW, 2 Lt 51
Scott G, Tpr 283-4, 384
Scott-Masson, Capt *Canberra* 310
Scott-Masson PABG, 2 Lt 310, Maj 380
Scrope PG, Capt 299, 381, Maj 309, 323, 380
Scruby J, Lt 314
Seconds-in-Command 378-9
Segamat, Malaya 71
Selangor, Malaya 35, 42, 47-8, 52, 67, 75

Index

(numbers in italic are illustrations)

Selarang, Malaya 85
Selfe JAMA, Capt 260, 292, 381, Maj 299, 315, 323, 380
Selfe, Mrs 334
Selwyn JJ, Maj 105, 378-9, 383
Sennelager, Germany 91, 161, 184, 245, 251, 268-9, 323-4, 337, 372
Sennybridge (trg area), Powys 298
Seremban, Malaya 34 et seq, 60 et seq, 82
Seton, Tpr 103
Sewart E, Capt REME 382
Shaw NH, Lt 361
Shaw R, Sgt 254
Sheehan PSD, Maj RAPC 382
Sheffield, Yorks 148, 173-4, 212, 216, 227, 240-1, 311
Sheffield Morning Telegraph 291
Sheldon IRE, Cpl 259
Shepherdson PR, Tpr 387
Shewry PA, Capt REME 382
Shorncliffe, Kent 151
Shrubsole S, L Cpl 342, 387
Shryane NA, Capt 310, 381, Maj 380, 385
Shuttleworth WA, Capt 381, Maj 323, 380
Sialkot, Pakistan 186
Sidi Rezegh, Libya 24
Sievwright DAH, Maj 379-80
Silver Jubilee (HM The Queen) 269
Simfire training device 232
Simpang Rengam, Malaya 129
Simpson IS, Capt REME 382
Simpson WD, Sgt 246, S Sgt 318
Sims Tpr, *23*
'Sinbad' 238
Singapore 27, 29-32, 37 et seq, 69 et seq, 126-9, 131, 136 et seq, 193-6, 206, 212
Sioux helicopter 202, 294
Sir Geraint RFA 342
Sir Lancelot LST 196, 303
Skillen J, Tpr 386
Smith, Tpr 90-1
Smith GA, RSM 313, 381, Capt 381
Smith MD, Capt REME 337, 382
Smith PJR, Tpr 387
Smith JW, Capt 381, 383, Maj 381
Smith WF, Sgt 383
Soltau, Garrison 158-9
—, Training area 161, 203, 232, 234, 338
South and West Wilts Hunt 229
South Cerney, Glos. 342

South Dorset Hunt 229
Southampton 86, 111, 126, 142, 310
Southward NS, Capt 381, Maj 323, 325, 380, Lt Col 346, 385
Sovereign Base Areas, Cyprus 300-1
Spandau Barracks, Berlin 97
Sparkes, L Cpl 90
Special Ammunition Site 323
'Special Cargo' 336
Speers CNP, Maj 16/5 L 276, 380
Spence PS, Tpr 386
Sport
—, Cyprus 318-9
—, Fallingbostel 174-7
—, Herford 333-7
—, Hohne 236-9
—, North Africa 18
—, Malaya 50-3, 81-2, 139-41
—, Münster 213-5
—, Neumünster 103-6
—, Omagh 288-90
—, Paderborn 177-80
—, Perham Down 197-8
—, Tidworth 356-61
—, Wimbish 316-8
—, Wolfenbüttel 98-9, 372-4
Spyglass sight 364
Squadron leaders 379-80
Stalwart load carrier 201
Steel DM, Cpl 37, Sgt 120-1, 383
Steinhuder Meer, Germany 176
Stephen GMcL, Lt Col 284-5, 287, 289-92, 297-8, 307, 315, 378, 384
Stephen Mrs 290
Sterritt I, Chief Supt 287
Stewart AREdeC, 2 Lt 228, 259, Lt 272, Capt 316, 384, Maj 324, 337, 342, 357, 380, Lt Col 367, 374, 376, 378
Stirling WG, Gen 173, 183
Stocker G, Capt 68, Maj 131, 378-9, 383
Stocker MAC, 2 Lt 117
Stockwell HC, Gen 128
Strabane, Tyrone 286
Strategic Reserve 146, 188, 301
Stratton PJ, Sgt 383, RSM 381, Capt 249, 381, 384
Strawson JM, Maj Gen *Gentlemen in Khaki* 144
Suez, Egypt 30, 86, 145-6, 191
—, Canal 126, 146

Index

(numbers in italic are illustrations)

(Suez) 1956 Invasion, 111, 126, 144
Suffield (trg area), Canada 234-6, 241; *24*
Sungei Langat, Malaya 50
Sunnyside, Down 225
Swaine D, Sgt 383
Swanlinbar, Cavan 279
Sweeting F, Capt 9, Maj 89, 381
Swift IN, S Sgt 276
Swingfire missile 201, 321, 329, 345
Swinton Barracks, Münster 199, 218
Swiss Commando Patrol 354-6
Syria 113, 344

T

Tai Lam Camp, Hong Kong 58
Taiping, Malaya 128, 132
'Talbot Green' 176, 179
Tampin, Malaya 34, 74
Tampoi, Malaya 129
Task Force Charlie 200
'Tattoo' 179
Taylor, Bdsmn 175
Taylor SD, S Sgt 325, 333, SSM 385, RSM 381, Capt 374
Teate JR, Sgt 383
Technical Adjutants/Quartermasters 102-3
Tedworth Hunt 359
Teh Hock Kong, JCLO 60
Tel el Kebir, Egypt 28
Telok Forest, Malaya 50
Temengor, Malaya 135
Templer GWR, Gen 66, 74-5, 77, 85
Thailand 132, 134-5
Thark 17
Thatcher M, Prime Minister 264, 328
Thetford (trg area), Norfolk 296-7, 299, 317, 352
Thomas JC, Sgt 52, 63, 383, SSM 70
Thompsett A, Cpl 176
Thompson I, Bandmaster 290, 382
Thompson K, Tpr 280
Thompson ST, S Sgt 372
Thorneycroft P, Defence Minister 173
Thrasher, Capt US Army 299
Tidworth 188, 228, 267, 324, 340, 347 66
—, Polo Club 197, 359-60
Tierney J, Cpl 383
'Tilforce' 134
Tillard AJ, Lt 289
Tillard PB, Capt 29, 37-9, 42, 383, Maj 132-3, 378-9, Lt Col 162-3, 165, 178, 378, 384, Brig 384
Tillard Mrs 141
Tin City, Sennelager 251-2
Tinker EH, Lt Col 21, 36, 53, 378, Brig 120
Titi, Malaya 44
Titley BW, Bandmaster 217, 382
Tmimi, Libya 25
Tobruk, Libya 11-12, 16, 20, 24-5, 166
Todd RJ, S Sgt 385
Tonbridge CCF 365
Torr P, WO2 272, 292; *23*
Torrey Canyon (oil tanker) 190
Town and Country 218, 275, 287
Training
—, Desert 21-5
—, Herford 325-30
—, Hohne 242-3
—, for N Ireland 245, 251-2, 269
—, Malaya 21, 53-4, 137
—, Tidworth 351-4
—, Perham Down 197
—, Wimbish 297
—, Wolfenbüttel 370-3
Trant RB, Maj Gen 292
Travemünde, Germany 108
Trengganu, Malaya 47
Trier, Germany 325
Tripoli, Libya 11, 13-14, 20
Troop Tests 164, 197, 325, 333, 353, 368
Trott, Pte ACC 79
Turkey 342-3
Turle GE, 2 Lt 134
Turnbull, Sir R 191
Turner F, Sgt 383
Turner, Pte ACC 173
Turton, Cpl 247
Tyacke HJ, 2 Lt 71, Maj 310, 379
Tyrone Co. 256, 270, 272, 274, 280-4

U

UDI (Rhodesia) 306
United Arab Republic (UAR) 113, 116
Udine, Italy 326
Ulu Beranang, Malaya 84
UNFICYP 226, 300-1, 304, 340 1, 368

V

Verden, Germany 238
Victory Parade, Kuala Lumpur 135; *14*
Vidler T, Capt RAPC 382
Vienenberg, Germany 322

403

Index
(numbers in italic are illustrations)

VIP Escorts, Malaya 74
Vogelsang (trg area), Germany 165

W

Waddy PL, Lt 24, 40, Capt 105, Maj 182, 184
Waddy Mrs 184
Wadi Mutti, Arabia 120, 125
Wadmore J, ORQMS 383, Maj 380
Wagner RE, Capt US Army 162, 166-7, 379, Brig 337
Wainwright, Canada 167, 234,314
Waites DK, Sgt *34*
Wales, HRH Princess of 267, 347-349, 366, 375, 377-8; *33*
Walker WC, Brig 138
Walsrode, Germany 242
Walter WJD, 2 Lt 176
Warcop (ranges), Cumb. 189
Ward, Pte ACC 173
Ward MT, Capt 381
Warminster, Wilts 147, 221, 224, 228, 232
Warner MJ, Tpr 386
Warsaw Pact 155, 169, 264, 266
Wassung J, Tpr140
Watchet, Somerset 224
Waterloo, Centenary of Battle 182-3
Waters CJ, Maj Gen 328
Waters M, Sgt 346, 385
Watkinson H, Defence Minister 146
Watson HSR, Capt 9, 88, 381, Maj 129, 132, 379, 383, Lt Col 158, 162, 378, Brig 384, Maj Gen 294, 311, 363, 367, 378; *31*
Wattlebridge, Fermanagh 280
Watts B, Tpr 386
Webb-Bowen RI, Lt 15/19H 274
Webster RStJ, Lt 215, Capt 254
Wehrmacht 102, 109, 154
Weighell RE, Sgt R Signals 383
Wellington, L Cpl 183
Wells E, Tpr 102, 386
Wells LW, WO 1 385
Weser R., Germany 89, 155, 163, 179, 330
Weser Vale Hunt 334
Wessex Barracks, Fallingbostel 154
Wessex Drag Hunt 175
West Aden Protectorate 111-3, 117
Wheeler S, Tpr118, 124
Whipp R, L Cpl 386
Whitaker CJS, Lt 353, Capt 367, 381

Whitaker MC, 2 Lt 129
White C, Cpl 386
White Sail mountain, India 355
Whitelam, L Cpl 305
Whitelaw W, Home Secretary 307
Whiteley HN, Sgt 48, 383
Whiteley WJ, 2 Lt 98,
Whitworth, Tpr 173
Wild J, Cpl 213-4
Wiles P, Mr 328, 347
Wiles S, Sgt 343
Wilkins MJS, 2 Lt 179, Lt 241, Maj 380
Wilkins TE, Capt REME 382
Willems Barracks Aldershot 10
Williams GM, Capt REME 382
Williams J, Sgt 383
Williams MA, Tpr 387
Williamson EF, Maj QOH 378-9
Wills R, S Sgt APTC 176
Wilson H, Prime Minister 146, 149
Wimbish 293-319, 333
Winter JT, Capt 381
Winterberg 103, 372
Wintle R, Tpr 104
Wise H, Lt Col 18H 216; *21*
Wolfenbüttel 10, 87-99, 154, 267, 296, 363, 367-9, 373-4
Wolfenbütteler Zeitung 93
Wood AR, Tpr 387
Woodfield JF, AQMS 383, ASM 172
Wormald DB, Maj Gen 227, 269, 294, 313, 378; *22*
Worthington B, 2 Lt 92
Wragg JM, Cpl 247, Sgt 254, Capt 381
Wright AR, Mr 319
Wright ERMcM Maj 34, 67, 75, 83, 140, 378-9, 383, Lt Col 384; *1*
Wright H, Capt REME 382
Wuppertal, Germany 89

Y

Yang Di-Pertuan Agong, HM 135, 141
Yemen 111 et seq
Yong Peng, Malaya 72
Yorke EL, Capt 215, 303, Maj 318, 380, Lt Col 323, 335, 347, 354, 356, 363, 378
Yorkshire 148, 173, 208-9, 216, 240-1, 311, 338, 352, 361-3, 377

Z

Zain Hashim, Lt Gen 315
Zirkler Frl A, 180